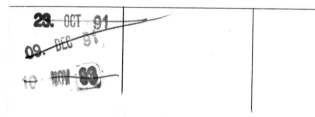

# THE ETHICS
# OF SOCIAL
# INTERVENTION

# THE SERIES IN CLINICAL AND COMMUNITY PSYCHOLOGY

CONSULTING EDITORS:

## CHARLES D. SPIELBERGER and IRWIN G. SARASON

# THE ETHICS OF SOCIAL INTERVENTION

*Edited by*

**GORDON BERMANT**
*The Federal Judicial Center*

**HERBERT C. KELMAN**
*Harvard University*

**DONALD P. WARWICK**
*Harvard University*

HEMISPHERE PUBLISHING
CORPORATION

Washington    London

A HALSTED PRESS BOOK
JOHN WILEY & SONS

New York    London    Sydney    Toronto

In accord with that part of the charge of its founder, Gordon Battelle, to assist in the education of men, it is the commitment of Battelle to encourage the distribution of information. This is done in part by supporting conferences and meetings and by encouraging the publication of reports and proceedings. Toward that objective, Battelle retains a royalty-free right to unrestricted use of all material within the work for use in the performance of its scientific research, for scholarship, and to promote the progress of science and the useful arts.

Hemisphere Publishing Corporation
1025 Vermont Ave., N.W., Washington, D.C. 20005

Distributed solely by Halsted Press, a Division of John Wiley & Sons, Inc.,
New York.

1 2 3 4 5 6 7 8 9 0    D O D O    7 8 3 2 1 0 9 8

**Library of Congress Cataloging in Publication Data**

Main entry under title:

The ethics of social intervention.

(The Series in clinical and community psychology)
Includes indexes.
1. Social change—Addresses, essays, lectures.
2. Social values—Addresses, essays, lectures.
3. Evaluation research (Social action programs)—
Addresses, essays, lectures. 4. Policy science—
Addresses, essays, lectures. I. Bermant, Gordon.
II. Kelman, Herbert C. III. Warwick, Donald P. IV. Title.
HN18.B4595      174'.9'3      78-57507
ISBN 0-470-26362-8

Printed in the United States of America

# CONTENTS

## III    ORGANIZATION DEVELOPMENT

## IV    COMMUNITY-CONTROLLED EDUCATIONAL REFORM

# CONTRIBUTORS

**Kurt W. Back,** *Duke University, Durham, North Carolina*

**Richard A. Berk,** *University of California, Santa Barbara, California*

**Gordon Bermant,** *The Federal Judicial Center, Washington, D.C.*

**Margaret Boeckmann,** *American University, Washington, D.C.*

**R. J. Brouns,** *Battelle-Northwest, Richland, Washington*

**Peter Brown,** *Institute for Philosophy and Public Affairs, University of Maryland, College Park*

**Gerald Cormick,** *University of Washington, Seattle, Washington*

**John Glidewell,** *University of Chicago, Chicago, Illinois*

**Alan E. Guskin,** *University of Wisconsin-Parkside, Kenosha, Wisconsin*

**W. M. Harris,** *School of Architecture, University of Virginia, Charlottesville, Virginia*

**H. Harty,** *Battelle-Northwest, Richland, Washington*

**C. P. Huey,** *General Services, Port of Seattle, Seattle, Washington*

**J. W. Johnston,** *Battelle-Northwest, Richland, Washington*

**Herbert C. Kelman,** *Harvard University, Cambridge, Massachusetts*

**Robert J. Lapham,** *National Academy of Sciences, Washington, D.C.*

**James Laue,** *University of Missouri–St. Louis, St. Louis, Missouri*

**J. C. Little,** *Department of Human Resources, City of Seattle, Seattle, Washington*

**C. Miller,** *School of Law, University of Washington, Seattle, Washington*

**Peter H. Rossi,** *University of Massachusetts, Amherst, Massachusetts*

**Barbara R. Sarason,** *University of Washington, Seattle, Washington*

**Irwin G. Sarason,** *University of Washington, Seattle, Washington*

**P. Smith,** *Smith, Brecker, Winn, and Ehlert, Attorneys at Law, Seattle, Washington*

**Stephanie B. Stolz,** *Alcohol, Drug Abuse, and Mental Health Administration, HEW Regional Office, Kansas City, Missouri*

**Sandra Schwartz Tangri,** *U.S. Commission on Civil Rights, Washington, D.C.*

**Richard E. Walton,** *Harvard University, Cambridge, Massachusetts*

**J. L. Ware,** *Western Washington State University, Bellingham, Washington*

**Donald P. Warwick,** *Harvard University, Cambridge, Massachusetts*

**Carrol W. Waymon,** *The California School of Professional Psychology, San Diego, and Miramar Community College, San Diego, California*

**R. D. Widrig,** *Battelle-Northwest, Richland, Washington*

**Preston N. Williams,** *Harvard University, Cambridge, Massachusetts*

# PREFACE

The origins of this book go back to 1971, when two of the present editors—Herbert Kelman and Donald Warwick—were engaged in collaborative teaching and writing on the ethics and politics of social research and intervention. The first results of this work were published as a chapter on ethical issues in a book about social change.[1] In 1972, the three of us collaborated in developing the themes and format for a national conference on the ethics of social intervention. The conference was held at the Battelle Seattle Research Center, May 10-12, 1973. The participants expressed interest in publishing a book based on the papers presented at the conference.

Between that time and the present, many changes have been made in the original conference presentations. Some of the original contributions were replaced by the work of other authors; others were dropped because the manuscripts never reached final form; most of the papers have gone through several revisions. The relatively complicated format of the book, in which a critique accompanies each of eight major chapters, inevitably resulted in some editorial delay. Also, the editors have prepared comprehensive introductory and concluding chapters that go beyond the conference material to include other relevant experience and literature.

Much credit for the conference and book goes to the Battelle Memorial Institute, in particular to the Battelle Institute program in behavioral and social sciences as it was constituted between 1969 and 1975. As this book is the final publication in the series of conference publications supported by that program, it is fitting to thank those officers of Battelle whose commitment to scholarly work and its dissemination made possible this and all the other work of the program. In particular we thank Ronald S. Paul, Tommy W. Ambrose, and Everett R. Irish for their confidence and support. In this connection, we wish to express our personal appreciation to these officers and to the Battelle organization for their generous support of our work during the periods that we were associated with the Battelle Seattle Research Center: Gordon Bermant as Center Fellow from 1969 to 1976, Herbert Kelman as Visiting Fellow from 1972 to 1973, and Donald Warwick as Visiting Fellow in the summer of 1973.

The staff of the Battelle Seattle Research Center also deserves recognition for their help throughout the conference and preparation for publication. We are particularly grateful to Ellen Brandt, Faith Fogarty, Barbara Hawley, and

[1] Warwick, D. P., & Kelman, H. C. Ethical issues in social intervention. In G. Zaltman (Ed.), *Processes and phenomena of social change.* New York: Wiley, 1973, 377–417.

Lee Porter for their contributions. Finally, we wish to express our appreciation to Gerald Dworkin, John Hogarth, Charles Miller, Laura Nader, and Leonard Ullmann, who participated in the conference and made valuable contributions to the proceedings. The contributions of all other participants are acknowledged in the Contents of this book.

Throughout this project the editors worked as closely together as geography, travel schedules, and other commitments permitted. The order in which the editors are listed reflects only the accidents of alphabet; it is not indicative of priority or seniority.

*Gordon Bermant*
*Herbert C. Kelman*
*Donald P. Warwick*

# INTRODUCTION

# 1
# THE ETHICS OF SOCIAL INTERVENTION: GOALS, MEANS, AND CONSEQUENCES

**HERBERT C. KELMAN**
**DONALD P. WARWICK**

Harvard University

Social intervention is any act, planned or unplanned, that alters the characteristics of another individual or the pattern of relationships between individuals. The range of acts covered in this definition is intentionally broad. It includes such macro phenomena as national planning, military intervention in the affairs of other nations, population policy, and technical assistance. It also applies to psychotherapy, sensitivity training, neighborhood action programs, experiments done with human beings, and other micro changes.

Most of the literature in this area, utilizing the concept of planned change (e.g., Bennis, Benne, Chin, & Corey, 1976; Lippitt, Watson, & Westley, 1958), has confined itself to micro efforts such as organization development or community action programs. An organized attempt by a business corporation to improve communication, morale, and productivity in its U.S. plant is considered planned change, but a decision by the same company to build a new plant in Guatemala is not. In fact, the greater the scale and impact of social intervention, the less likely it is to be called planned change. One reason is that models of planned change place heavy emphasis on the role of the change agent, often a social science consultant. In many cases of macro change, it is extremely difficult to fit the facts of the situation into a paradigm involving change agents and client systems.

We prefer to subsume planned change efforts under a broader definition of social intervention that provides for the ethical evaluation of institutional structures and practices with critical social effects, as well as of situations with more readily identifiable change agents. We can thus explore the ethical implications of government policies or intellectual traditions, for example, even though these are not explicitly geared toward producing social change and are not associated with a single individual or agency. The major focus of this book, however, is on deliberate interventions. In this book, while keeping the broad definition in mind, we use social intervention more narrowly to refer to deliberate attempts by professionals to change the characteristics of individuals or groups, or to influence the pattern of relationships between individuals and/or groups. The last clause in this working definition is designed to cover such interventions as mediation, where the intent is not to change individuals and groups as such, but to shape the course of their relationships and interactions on a short-term or long-term basis.

## VALUE PREFERENCES AND VALUE CONFLICTS

There are four aspects of any social intervention that are likely to raise major ethical issues: (1) the choice of goals to which the change effort is directed, (2) the definition of the target of the change, (3) the choice of means used to implement the intervention, and (4) the assessment of the consequences of the intervention. At each of these steps, the ethical issues that arise may involve conflicting values, that is, questions about what values are to be maximized at the expense of what other values. (We define *values* as individual or shared conceptions of the desirable—"goods" considered worth pursuing.)

Thus, values determine the choice of goals to which a change effort is directed. Clearly, an intervention is designed to maximize a particular set of values. But those setting the goals of the intervention are equally concerned with minimizing the loss of certain other values. These imperiled values thus serve as criteria of tolerable and intolerable costs in a given intervention. Under pressures of rapid demographic growth and limited resources, for example, a government might contemplate a set of coercive population control measures, such as involuntary sterilization. The benefit to be promoted by this program would be the common welfare or, in extreme cases, even the physical survival of the country. At the same time, the policy makers might be concerned about the effects of this program on two other values: freedom and justice. These values would be seen as social goods to be preserved—benefits that should not fall below some minimal threshold. Values may influence the choice of goals not only in such explicit, conscious ways, but also in a covert way. This may happen, as we shall see, when a change program departs from a value-based but unquestioned definition of a problem.

The definition of the target of change is often based on just this kind of implicit, unexamined conception of where the problem lies. For example, a change effort designed to improve the conditions of an economically disadvantaged group—such as the black population in the United States—may be geared primarily toward changing institutional arrangements that have led to the systematic exclusion of this group from the economic life of the country, or toward reducing the educational, environmental, or psychological "deficiencies" of the disadvantaged group itself. The choice between these two primary targets of change may well depend on one's value perspective: A focus on removing systemic barriers is more reflective of the values of the disadvantaged group itself, while a focus on removing deficiencies suggests the values of the more established segments of the society.

Third, values play a central role in an ethical evaluation of the means chosen to implement a given intervention. Questions about the morality of coercion, manipulation, deception, persuasion, and other methods of inducing change typically involve a conflict between the values of individual freedom and self-determination, on the one hand, and the values of social welfare, economic progress, or equal opportunity, on the other. For example, to what extent and under what conditions is a government justified in imposing limits on the freedom to reproduce for the sake of presumed long-run improvements in the quality of life?

Finally, conflicting values enter into assessment of the consequences of a social intervention. One of the consequences of industrialization, for example, may be a weakening of traditional authority structures or family bonds. The extent to which we are willing to risk these consequences depends on whether we are more committed to traditional values or to those values that industrialization is designed to enhance. In other words, our assessment of the consequences of an intervention depends on what values we are willing or unwilling to sacrifice in the interest of social change.

Analysis of the ethical problems that may arise at each of these four points in the change process, and of the value conflicts from which they derive, presupposes consideration of some more general procedural issues that must be faced in any effort at applied ethics. These refer to the procedures to be followed in deriving the values that apply in a social intervention, in determining whose values should be given what weight, and in adjudicating value conflicts.[1]

First, an analysis of the ethics of social intervention presumes some notion of what values should apply and how they are to be derived. The problem is simplified, of course, if the analyst simply accepts the values held by the initiators of the change. Thus, if a government agency says that it undertook a population control program in order to promote the general welfare and that it also considered the costs of the program for individual freedom, an analyst might simply confine his or her attention to the values of freedom and welfare. Few students of ethics, however, would be content to let the individual or group

---

[1] These procedural issues are discussed in greater detail in Warwick and Kelman (1973). Much of the discussion in this chapter is derived from that earlier publication.

initiating a change be the sole judge of the relevant values at stake. The human inclination toward selective perception and self-deception, not to mention the protection of vested political interests, is simply too great to justify this approach. In this example, the concerned observer might also wish to examine the effects of the population program on other values, such as justice, dignity, or the self-esteem of minority groups. To leave the definition of the ethical situation to the sponsor of a program would be to abdicate one's moral judgment.

Thus, before ethical analysis can begin, analysts must lay out the content of the values that, according to their view, must be promoted and protected in a particular intervention effort. In addition to making these values explicit, the analysts must also indicate how these values were derived and why a particular set was adopted. The bases for choosing and applying values are varied and sometimes incompatible (Gustafson, 1970). They may include appeals to revelation, to natural law, to the capacity of human reason as a guide to moral truths, to social science theories of human nature and society, to empirically documented cultural universals, or to the cultural traditions and social institutions prevailing in a particular society. Fortunately, these approaches often yield similar or overlapping sets of values. Nevertheless, explicit attention must be given to the process by which these values are derived. There is no other way to reduce arbitrariness in selecting the ingredients for ethical analysis and to provide a framework for comparing and debating alternative criteria in the ethical evaluation of intervention efforts.

A second fundamental procedural question concerns the weights assigned to the different, and often competing, sets of values held by different groups. Discussions of national population policy within the United States, for example, have revealed the variations in cultural values and perspectives that different ethnic, religious, class, and professional groups bring to the population problem (Population Task Force, 1971). Thus, at the national level, decisions about social intervention must weigh the claims and concerns of diverse groups within the society. The problem of "whose values" becomes even more complex in international programs of development or technical assistance. Such programs are often planned and carried out by individuals and agencies external to the society in which the changes are to be introduced. Therefore, there is a real possibility that the values of the change agents may deviate from those of the local population. The question of whose values determine the goals, targets, and means of change takes on special importance in such cases. The issue is not only whose interests are being served by the program, but whose conceptual framework generates the definition of the problem and the setting of goals. This issue persists even when representatives of the local society are fully involved in the planning and execution of the change program because these representatives, who are often trained abroad, may have adopted the conceptual framework of the external agency. Since the writings of social scientists often provide the conceptual frameworks for development programs, it is particularly important to scrutinize them in terms of whose values they reflect and to balance them by assuring that proper weight is given to competing points of view.

Third, deliberate attention to the content and derivation of values and to the different groups whose values are engaged by a given action often reveals value conflicts. Different values held within the same group and differences in value priorities set by different groups may present incompatible claims. For example, advocates of a noninterventionist population policy typically stress the value of freedom, while those who favor strong measures of population control emphasize the values of welfare and survival of the human species. The critical question is not which of the two sets of values to pick, but what is the optimum balance between them. How much freedom, in other words, ought to be sacrificed in the interests of welfare and survival? Debates on national development often array advocates of cultural diversity, of the right of all peoples to determine their own destinies, and of the importance of traditional values as a matrix for the development of self-identity and self-esteem, against those who feel that traditional values are by definition obstacles to development and must, therefore, be changed as rapidly and efficiently as possible. Again the question concerns the most desirable trade-offs between conflicting values: How much traditional culture ought to be sacrificed for the sake of modernization?

Perhaps the most difficult challenge for ethical analysis is in providing some approximate guidelines for adjudicating such competing claims. Though no neat formulas or mechanistic answers are possible, one can try to establish a rough order of ethical priorities. For example, in the population field, one might start with the proposition that freedom of procreative behavior should be respected unless there are clearly demonstrated threats to human survival or welfare, and that even then the limitations placed on freedom should be proportional to the danger involved. By this rule, it would not be justified to introduce compulsory sterilization or forced abortions because of the mere possibility that human welfare will be endangered by demographic growth within the next century. It might be ethically justified, on the other hand, to remove incentives, such as family allowances, that encourage large families and to provide free family planning assistance. Similarly, modernization efforts might be guided by the proposition that traditional values should be disrupted only if—and only to the extent that—considerations of survival and social welfare necessitate such disruptions.

These analytical steps do not eliminate the need for value judgments, but they do make such judgments more conscious and deliberate. With these procedural issues in mind, we now turn to some of the specific ethical questions raised by the four aspects of social intervention: the choice of goals, the definition of the target, the choice of means, and the assessment of consequences.

## CHOICE OF GOALS

Social scientists and others writing about social change continually make explicit or implicit assumptions about the nature and the end-points of the changes that are necessary and desirable. These assumptions are influenced not only by the values that individual writers bring to their research but also by the interests and orientations that surround the general issue of social change in their societies. The choice of goals for social intervention thus depends on the particular intellectual and political perspectives from which the change agents and their advisors view the situation. Biased views cannot be avoided, but they can be counteracted insofar as they are made explicit and confronted with analyses based on alternative perspectives.

The process of goal setting can be illustrated with a perspective on social change described by Kelman (1968, pp. 62–63). He places social change in the context of a worldwide revolution of human rights, which has set into motion powerful forces toward political independence, economic development, and social reform, both in the developing world and within industrialized countries. Given this perspective, one would start the process of delineating goals for social intervention by asking how the challenge posed by this revolution can best be met. What can be done to facilitate social change and to increase the likelihood that it will move in constructive directions? What kinds of institutional arrangements would improve the living conditions of the masses of the population, would be consistent with their needs for security and dignity, and would broaden the base of participation in social, political, and economic affairs? What conditions are conducive to a population's sense of political legitimacy, its feeling of national identity, and its readiness for involvement in citizenship responsibilities, economic enterprises, and social planning? What techniques of change would minimize the use of violence, the brutalization of the active and passive participants in the change process, and the predisposition to govern by coercion and repression? How can social intervention be introduced without destroying the existing culture patterns that provide meaning and stability to a people, while at the same time helping to build the new patterns and values that a changing society requires if it is to remain human?

This list of questions—and the goals for social intervention that it implies—is clearly based on certain value assumptions. It presupposes not only the desirability of social change, but also a preference for certain kinds of social change. For example, it assumes that social institutions must be judged in terms of their consistency with human needs, and it favors institutional arrangements that encourage participation, legitimacy, nonviolence, and respect for traditional values.

This statement implies a rough ordering of priorities. It suggests that, in choosing goals for intervention, a major criterion should be the concrete needs of individuals rather than some abstract notion of what is good for society. It clearly regards changes that involve violence, coercion, or the destruction of traditional values as unacceptable except under the most compelling circumstances. The application of these criteria to a specific situation, however, requires some difficult judgments. How does one determine which of various alternative policies is most consistent with the concrete needs of individuals, or what circumstances are sufficiently compelling to justify changes that involve varying degrees of violence, coercion, or destruction of traditional values? Different analysts may agree on these priorities, but may nonetheless disagree on how they should be specifically applied.

There are also likely to be disagreements with the implicit goals and priorities as delineated in the statement. We would like to believe that these goals are consistent with basic and universal human needs and that they are widely shared across different population groups and cultures. Yet we are also cognizant of the very real possibility that our ordering of priorities reflects, in some important ways, our own cultural and ideological biases and that—even when it deviates from the governing ideology of our society—it is influenced by our own relatively favored positions within the society and our society's favored position within the international system. Thus, before basing the choice of goals for intervention on such a statement, one must recognize that it represents one perspective, which has to be confronted with those derived from other relevant points of view.

The first and frequently neglected step, then, in an ethical analysis of social intervention is the recognition that the choice of goals for intervention is determined by the value perspective of the chooser, which is not necessarily shared by all interested parties. The goals to be pursued in social change are by no means self-evident. They depend very much on what we consider a desirable outcome and what costs in terms of other values we are prepared to bear for the achievement of this outcome—a complex judgment about which there may be considerable disagreement.

The role of cultural and ideological biases in the choice of goals is often ignored because the change effort may have a hierarchy of values built into its very definition. These values may simply be taken for granted without questioning their source and their possibly controversial nature. A clear example of such covert ideological influence is seen in the definition of national development. The word "development," whether used in botany, psychology, or economics, implies an unfolding toward some terminal state. Typically this state, whether it be adulthood, maturity, or an ideal economic system, is also considered desirable. By implication, a more developed nation is seen as better in some sense than a less developed nation. In the 1950s, the dominant models of national development took as their implicit end-points the economic and political systems of the Western industrial nations. Within this teleological framework, primary emphasis was given to economic values. Works such as *The Stages of Economic Growth* (Rostow, 1960) argued, in effect, that the ultimate measure of political and social institutions was their contribution to economic growth. From an ethical standpoint, the most serious problem with these models was that value judgments were slipped into seemingly value-free definitions of historical processes. Statements about goals for change deemed desirable from a particular value perspective were often presented as empirical statements about the conditions necessary for a universal process of development. Such latent choices of goals are especially troublesome because they are masked by connotations of scientific rigor and historical inevitability.

In recognizing the role of their own value preferences, change agents (or social scientists who conceptualize the process of social change) do not abandon their values or attempt to neutralize them. It is neither possible nor desirable to do so. But being aware of their own value perspectives can allow change agents to bring other perspectives to bear on the choice of goals, which reduces the likelihood that they will impose their own values on the population in whose lives they are intervening. This process of relating our own values to those of others in the choice of goals for intervention—without either abandoning or imposing our own values—can often be aided by a distinction between general goals and specific institutional arrangements designed to give expression to these goals. It may be possible to identify certain broad, basic end-points that are widely shared across different cultures and ideological systems—at least among groups and individuals operating within a broadly humanistic framework. These groups or individuals may at the same time disagree about the specific political, social, and economic institutions that they regard as most conducive to the realization of these ends. Thus, one may be able to define the goals for intervention in more or less universal terms, while recognizing that these goals may be achieved through a variety of specific arrangements and that different cultures and ideologies may differ sharply in their preferences among these arrangements.

Ethical issues in the choice of goals for intervention revolve around the question of what values are to be served by the intervention and whether these are the right values for the target population. Since answers to these questions are likely to differ for different individuals—and to differ systematically for groups with different cultural backgrounds and positions in society—the question of *what* values inevitably brings up the question of *whose* values are to be served by the intervention.

Any society, community, or organization in which a change program is introduced contains different segments, with differing needs and interests that may be affected by the intervention. Thus, a key issue concerns the extent to which the values of these different population segments are reflected in the goals that govern the intervention and the extent to which they participate in the goal-setting process. The question of who decides on the goals often has implications for who ultimately benefits from the outcome of the intervention. Since the interests and values of different groups may, to varying degrees, be incompatible, the change program usually involves some compromise between competing preferences. Representation and participation in goal setting may thus have an important bearing on how the values of a given group are weighted in the final outcome.

The problem of competing interests and values in the goal-setting process is complicated by the fact that the change agents and those to whom the change effort is directed usually represent different segments of the population. In national programs, the government officials and social engineers who initiate and carry out the intervention and the policy makers and social scientists who provide the conceptual frameworks on which it is based usually come from the more established, affluent, and highly educated segments of the society. The target population, on the other hand, usually consists of poorer and less educated segments, minority groups, or groups that are for various reasons (such as age, health, addiction, or criminality) in a dependent status. In international programs, the leadership and conceptual framework (whether Western or Marxist) usually come from the more powerful, industrialized nations, while the change is directed at developing countries. Thus, in both cases, the change agents are in some sense outsiders to the target population in terms of social class, national affiliation, or both. Moreover, they are usually not disinterested outsiders: Social change programs may have important implications for the wealth, power, and status of their own groups. The problem is further exacerbated by the fact that the agents and the targets of change usually represent groups that differ along a power dimension. The change agents come from the more powerful classes and nations, the targets from the less powerful ones.

The change agents are in a strong position to influence the choice of goals for the intervention. Those who formulate and run the program clearly play a direct role in goal setting. Those who provide the conceptual frameworks may have a more subtle, yet highly pervasive, impact in that they establish the perspective from which the goal setting proceeds and thus the way in which the problem is defined and the range of choices seen as available. It is therefore quite possible that the change agents will view the problem from the perspective of their own group and set goals that will, often unintentionally, accrue to the benefit of their group at the expense of the target population. Given the power differential, their intervention may in fact strengthen the status quo and increase the impotence of those who are already disadvantaged. It is not surprising, therefore, that population control or educational programs sponsored by white middle-class agencies in black ghettoes, or by U.S. agencies in developing countries, are sometimes greeted with suspicion by the target populations. Whatever the merits of the specific case may be, there are sound structural bases for fearing that such programs may end up serving the purposes of the advantaged group at the expense of the disadvantaged.

The ethical problems created by the value and power differentials between change agents and target groups are not easily resolved. Clearly, the more the target group participates in the process of goal setting, the greater the likelihood that the change program will indeed reflect its values. But bringing in representatives of the target group or turning the program over to indigenous agents may not go very far in correcting power imbalances. We have already mentioned that representatives of developing societies who are brought in by outside agencies may themselves be Westernized and may therefore operate in terms of the perspectives of these agencies. Similarly, representatives of minority groups, particularly if they have professional training, do not necessarily share the perspective of the lower-class, less educated members of their own group. Turning over a project may create its own ethical ambiguities if, in the process, the outsiders arrogate to themselves the decision of who is the proper spokesperson for the target population. This may be true whether they turn over the project to the established government (which may not be representative) or to an opposition group. In either case, they are deciding which side to strengthen in what may be an internal conflict within the target population and are thus indirectly imposing goals of their own choice.

Despite the ambiguities that often remain when an outside, more powerful change agent involves representatives of the less powerful target population in the change effort, such involvement constitutes the best protection against the imposition of foreign values. Thus, in an ethical evaluation of a social intervention, one would want to consider such criteria as: To what extent do those who are affected by the intervention participate in the choice of goals? What efforts are being made to have their interests represented in the setting of priorities, and to bring their perspectives to bear on the definition of the problem and the range of choices entertained? To what extent does the process enhance the power of the target population and provide them with countervailing mechanisms of protection against arbitrary and self-serving uses of power by the change agents?

## DEFINITION OF THE TARGET

Social intervention usually begins as an effort to solve a problem. A decision to undertake a program of organization development, for example, may spring from a concern about poor communication, intraorganizational conflicts, or underutilization of employee abilities. The adoption of population controls may be an effort to deal with the problem of scarce resources or an attempt to preserve the quality of life. In every case, identification of the problem represents, in large part, a value judgment. What we consider to be problematic— that is, what we see as falling short of some ideal state and requiring action—depends very much on our particular view of the ideal state. Moreover, identification of the problem depends on the perspective from which we make this evaluation. For example, in the face of demonstrations, riots, or other forms of social unrest, different groups are likely to cite different problems as requiring social intervention. Those who identify with the status quo are likely to see the problem as a breakdown of social order, while those who identify with the protesters are more likely to see the problem as a breakdown of social justice.

Identification of the problem has important ethical implications because it determines selection of the target to which change efforts are directed. Where we intervene depends on where we, with our personal value preferences and perspectives, perceive the problem to lie. Thus, those who see social unrest as a breakdown of social order are likely to define the protesters as the proper targets of change. They may use a variety of means, ranging from more stringent social controls, through persuasion and education, to efforts at placating the protesters and giving them a stake in the system. Whatever the means, this is the wrong target from the point of view of those who see the problem as a failure in social justice and who want to direct change efforts to the existing institutions and policies. In their view, interventions designed to reduce the protesters' ability or motivation to protest merely perpetuate injustices and serve the interests of the advantaged segments of the population at the expense of the disadvantaged. In short, who and what is being targeted for change may have important consequences for the competing interests of different groups and for the fate of such core values as justice and freedom.

The issues are well illustrated in debates on the population problem. The specific crises that constitute this problem are variously defined as famine or impediments to economic development, pollution or other ecological damage threatening the possibility and quality of life, exhaustion of physical resources or strains on the carrying capacity of the earth, and revolution or social disorder resulting from population pressures joined with high levels of aspiration. The scientific evidence on the probability of any of these crises is highly ambiguous. Thus, there is ample room for personal values to enter into the definition of the problem.

The definition of the problem, in turn, determines the selection of targets for change. Those who see the problem in terms of the danger of famine and economic stagnation may direct change efforts at increasing economic productivity, including food production. Those who are primarily concerned with pollution and ecological damage may favor interventions directed at reducing the rate of industrialization or at strengthening governmental controls over waste products and other sources of environmental pollution. On the other hand, those concerned with exhaustion of physical resources or with the revolutionary potential of population pressures may prefer interventions aimed at reducing or reversing the rate of population growth. How we define the problem and, thus, whether we then take national economic policy or the child-bearing couple as our target of change, depends on our value preferences and perspectives. For example, groups placing a high value on the preservation of the existing political order are likely to be disturbed by rising population pressures and thus to favor population control. On the other hand, those who advocate revolutionary change may actually favor rapid population growth combined with urbanization as important contributors to political mobilization.

These two views, of course, do not exhaust the possible positions on population control, but they illustrate the point that definition of the target of change has important consequences for the competing interests of different groups within a society.

Social scientists play a major role in identifying, or at least articulating, the problems to which change efforts are to be directed and thus in defining the targets for social intervention. A good example is provided by research on various forms of social deviance. Much of this research has focused on "the deviant behaviour itself and on the characteristics of the individuals and groups that manifest it and the families and neighbourhoods in which it is prevalent, rather than on the systemic processes out of which it emerges" (Kelman, 1970, p. 82). Many reasons for this emphasis can be cited. In part it grows out of the "social problems" tradition, which has fostered among social scientists a commitment to helping troubled individuals and groups. In part it reflects the problem definition of agencies whose mission includes the control of deviant behavior and who sponsor much of the research in this field. Research on the characteristics of deviant populations, though perfectly legitimate in its own right, raises ethical questions insofar as it provides the dominant framework for conceptualizing deviance as a social phenomenon and thus for setting social policy. "By focusing on the carriers of deviant behaviour, social research has reinforced the widespread tendency to explain such behaviour more often in terms of the pathology of the deviant individuals, families, and communities, than in terms of such properties of the larger social system as the distribution of power, resources, and opportunities" (Kelman, 1970, p. 83). Research has thus contributed to a focus on the characteristics of the deviant as the problem to which social policy must address itself. In keeping with this problem definition, the deviant individuals and communities, rather than the institutional arrangements and policies conducive to social deviance, have commonly been singled out as the targets for intervention. This particular way of identifying the problem and defining the target for change tends to reflect the concerns of the more established segments of the population and has potential consequences for the competing interests of different groups within the society.

This example illustrates some of the ethical implications of social science research. Far from being ethically neutral, the models with which social scientists work may play a major role in determining the problems and targets for social intervention. In defining their research problems, choosing their models, and communicating their findings, therefore, social scientists have a responsibility to consider the consequences for the populations affected. More broadly, they have the responsibility to ensure that all segments of the population have the opportunity to participate in the research enterprise, which influences the definition of the problems for intervention, and have access to the research findings, which influence the setting of policy.

## CHOICE OF MEANS

The most difficult ethical choices in deliberate social intervention usually concern the selection of means. Is it ever morally justified, for example, to force individuals to accept a program under the threat of death, physical harm, or other severe deprivation? What ethical problems are posed by manipulating the environment so that people are more likely to choose one alternative over others? Should a change program make full use of group pressures for conformity, or attempt to tamper with basic attitudes and motives? These are real questions in most change programs, and there are no easy answers.

It is possible, however, to clarify some of the issues at stake by relating the various means to the value of freedom. Warwick (1971) has defined freedom as the capacity, the opportunity, and the incentive to make reflective choices and to act on these choices. Individuals are thus free when:

1. The structure of the environment provides them with options for choice.
2. They are not coerced by others or forced by circumstances to elect only certain possibilities among those of which they are aware.
3. They are, in fact, aware of the options in the environment and possess knowledge about the characteristics and consequences of each. Though such knowledge may be less than complete, there must be enough to permit rational deliberation.
4. They are psychologically able to weigh the alternatives and their consequences. In practice this means not only possessing information but being able to use it in coming to a decision.
5. Having weighed the relative merits of the alternatives, they can choose among them. Rollo May (1969) has argued that one of the pathologies of modern existence is an inability to choose—a deficiency of will. A person who cannot pass from deliberation to choice must be considered less than free.
6. Having chosen an alternative, they are able to act on it. Among the conditions that may prevent them from doing so is a lack of knowledge about how to implement the choice, anxiety about acting at all, or a low level of confidence in their abilities, even when they have sufficient knowledge to act.

This discussion of freedom suggests a typology of means used in implementing social interventions. At the "least free" end is coercion, a situation in which people are forced to do something they do not want to do, or are prevented from doing something they do want to do. Next comes manipulation, then persuasion, and finally, at the "most free" end, facilitation.

## Coercion

In simple terms, coercion takes place when one person or group uses the threat of severe deprivation to induce other people or groups either to carry out actions that they desire not to perform or normally would not perform, or to refrain from carrying out actions that they want to perform or, in the normal course of events, would perform. It is difficult to arrive at precise definitions of "threat" or "deprivation," but basically these refer to the loss of highly valued goods, such as one's life, means of livelihood, or the well-being of one's relatives. Coercion should be distinguished from compliance that occurs within the framework of legitimate authority. In a certain sense, tax laws may be coercive because they force people to do things that they would prefer not to do under the threat of penalties. However, insofar as people comply with the law out of a belief that it is right to do so, since they see the law as rooted in consensual processes, their behavior would not be coerced.

Coercion forms an integral part of many programs of social intervention. Some clear examples would be the nationalization of a foreign-owned petroleum refinery or the outright confiscation of land in agrarian reform programs. In both cases, the government's action is immediately backed by the use of physical force—those who do not comply may be evicted or jailed. The population's acceptance of the government's legitimate right to carry out such interventions would usually be minimal. Other examples hover at the borders of coercion, manipulation, and persuasion. It has been proposed, for instance, that governments try to limit population by levying higher taxes against families with more than two or three children, or by depriving such families of social benefits such as free education, welfare, or medical coverage. Such programs could be considerd coercive if the threatened deprivation involved highly valued goods or the threat of great hardship, and if those affected would not accept the legal or moral legitimacy of the interventions. If the rewards and punishments at stake were relatively moderate, on the other hand, the means of intervention could be considered either manipulative or persuasive, according to the circumstances.

Is coercion ever ethically justified in social intervention and, if so, under what conditions? Two broad conditions are commonly invoked to defend coercive methods. The first is a grave threat to basic societal values. Thus, highly coercive population control programs are frequently recommended on the grounds that exce :ve fertility jeopardizes the continued survival of the human race or the material welfare of a nation's citizens. The second justification is the need for prompt and positive action to accomplish the goals of a change program, even when there is no threat to such values as physical survival. This argument is typical of revolutionary governments bent on executing major reforms in a short period of time. The two arguments are related in the sense that a failure to show swift results might create a drastic loss in basic political values such as the legitimacy or credibility of the government.

In the first case, an ethical justification of coercion requires the change agent to demonstrate, rather than assume, the threat to basic values. The population field is punctuated with dire predictions of disaster offered to the public with little supporting evidence. The legal concept of "clear and present danger" would seem to be an appropriate test of any proposal for coercion. Even then, however, coercion may not be justified. In the second case, the defense of coercion usually rests on personal evaluations of the system in question. In gross terms, those who favor a given regime will generally support its use of coercion to promote rapid change, while those who oppose it will reject its coercive methods.

Since the justification of coercive tactics often rests on the legitimacy of those who use them, determinations of legitimacy become an important part of ethical analysis. The legitimacy of a regime, in Western democratic tradition, is evidenced by the fact that its major officials have been duly elected, but there are other ways of establishing that a regime is representative of the population and governs with its consent. Even if the regime is seen as generally legitimate, some of its specific policies and programs may be considered illegitimate by various segments of the population because they exceed the regime's range of legitimate authority, because they are discriminatory, or because they violate certain basic values. Ethical evaluations become even more difficult when coercive interventions are introduced by revolutionary movements, whose claim to legitimacy has not yet been established. In such a case, observers would be more inclined to justify coercive tactics to the extent that they see the movement as representative of wide segments of the population and feel that their tactics are directed at power wielders who themselves are illegitimate and oppressive.

### Environmental Manipulation

Individual freedom has two core components: the availability of options in the environment, and the person's capacity to know, weigh, choose, and act on those options. Manipulation is a deliberate act of changing either the structure of the alternatives in the environment (environmental manipulation) or personal qualities affecting choice without the knowledge of the individuals involved (psychic manipulation). The cardinal feature of this process is that it maintains the semblance of freedom while modifying the framework within which choices are made. No physical compulsion or threats of deprivation are applied, and the individuals may be no more than dimly aware that they or the environment have been changed. Somewhat different ethical considerations are raised by environmental and psychic manipulation.

The term *environmental manipulation*, though it carries sinister overtones, applies to a broad range of activities generally regarded as necessary and desirable. These include city planning; governmental intervention in the economy through means such as taxation and control of interest rates; the construction of roads, dams, or railroads; and the addition of new consumer goods to the market. In each case a deliberate attempt is made to alter the structure of opportunities available, whether through addition, subtraction, or other modifications. Few people challenge the ethics of these changes, though they may question their wisdom. Other forms of environmental control arouse greater moral concern. Limitations on the freedom of the news media are widely attacked as abhorrent to a democracy. Job discrimination, ethnic quotas in universities, and similar restrictions on the equality of opportunity are similarly condemned.

Clearly, people make distinctions between justifiable and unjustifiable control of opportunities. But what are the limits of justifiable manipulation and what ethical calculus should be used to establish these limits? Is it morally justified, for example, to attempt to shape an entire cultural environment in the interest of promoting happiness and survival, as Skinner (1971) has proposed? Perhaps the key question raised by Skinner's proposals is who decides on the shape of the new environment and the controls to be instituted. Other questions concern the priorities in values and the assumptions about human nature by which the controllers operate.

Related ethical issues arise in behavior therapies, which rely on environmental manipulation and use techniques similar to those suggested by Skinner for the design of cultures. Unlike insight therapies, which concentrate on changing motives, perceptions, and other psychic qualities, behavior therapy aims at treating symptoms. Its techniques are based on the principle of selective reinforcement, through which desired behaviors are rewarded and undesired behaviors ignored or punished. Thus, behavior therapies emphasize specific acts rather than global personality characteristics (cf. London, 1969). From an ethical standpoint the principal difference between Skinner's macromanipulation and behavior therapy lies in the degree to which the individuals affected may control the process. Though there are vague murmurings in Skinner's book about "participation by those affected," his basic model is one of total control by an elite of culture designers. By contrast, in behavior therapy, the patients seek help with a problem and are free to terminate the therapeutic relationship at any time. In other words, though the therapy process involves careful manipulation of their behavior, they usually know what is happening and can exercise a fair degree of control over the process.

Other proposals for environmental control fall somewhere between these poles. It has been suggested, for instance, that governments try to limit fertility by manipulating conditions known to have indirect effect on family size, such as education, job opportunities for women, and income. Specifically, Judith Blake (1969) has recommended that women be given more competitive roles, such as improved job opportunities, as a means of reducing fertility. Daniel Callahan (1971) has raised several questions about this form of environmental manipulation, pointing to the ironic possibility that people can be manipulated by increasing their freedom.

Similar questions arise in any strategy for social change that relies on creating new realities that make it more necessary—or at least more possible— for people to change their behavior. In the field of race relations, for example, observers have noted that an effective way of changing individual attitudes and practices is to introduce a fait accompli: If an antidiscrimination law or policy is established without too much ado, people will be confronted with a new social reality that, for both practical and normative reasons, they are more likely to accept than to resist. Such environmental manipulation can be justified more readily if it is part of a larger social policy process that itself has been carried on through legitimate channels and exposed to public debate. It is also more justifiable from an ethical point of view if its effect is to expand rather than restrict the range of opportunities.

In sum, if human freedom and dignity are taken as critical values, there is reason for concern about deliberate attempts to manipulate one person's environment to serve the needs of another. The value of freedom requires not only the availability of options for choice at a given point in time, but an awareness of major changes in the structure of these alternatives. Complete awareness of these changes and their causes, however, is obviously impossible. There is also the danger of a strong conservative bias in defending the environment of choice within which we happen to find ourselves. Most of us, after all, are not aware of the origins of our present options for choice. Why, then, should we have a right to know when they are being changed? In other words, how much awareness of the structure of our present environment and of modifications in this environment is necessary for human freedom and dignity? And, assuming that this awareness will always be less than complete, who should have the right to tamper with the environment without our knowledge and what conditions should govern such intervention? Some thought has been given to criteria for an ethical evaluation of environmental manipulation. For example, manipulation would seem more acceptable to the extent that the people affected participate in the process, are free to enter and leave the program, and find their range of choices broadened rather than narrowed. Manipulation also seems more acceptable if the manipulators are not the primary beneficiaries of the manipulation, are reciprocally vulnerable in the situation, and are accountable to public agencies.

## Psychic Manipulation

Even within a constant environment of choice, freedom can be affected through the manipulation of its psychological components: for example, knowledge of the alternatives and their consequences; motives; and the ability to reason, choose, and implement one's choices. Recent decades have seen dramatic developments in the techniques of psychic manipulation. These include insight therapies; the modification of brain functioning through surgery, chemicals, or electrical stimulation; hypnosis; sensitivity training; and programs of attitude change (cf. London, 1969). The emergence of behavior control technology raises fundamental questions about human nature and the baseline assumptions for ethical analysis.

The ethical questions raised by psychic manipulation are similar to those presented by environmental control, and the same criteria for ethical evaluation are applicable. In many interventions of this type, however, particular attention must be paid to moral problems of deception and incomplete knowledge of effects—conditions on which these programs often rely for their success. The use of deception in such programs is based on considerations similar to those used to justify deceptive methods in psychological experiments and other forms of social research. It is assumed that some of the phenomena that the investigator is trying to create or observe would be destroyed if people were aware of the precise nature of the experimental manipulation or of the behavior under study. The moral problems posed by the use of deception in social research have received increasing attention in recent years (cf. Kelman, 1968, 1972; Warwick, 1973, 1975). For example, with reference to social-psychological experiments, Kelman (1972) has written:

> Deception presents special problems when it is used in an experiment that is stressful, unpleasant, or potentially harmful to the subject, in the sense that it may create self-doubts, lower his self-esteem, reveal some of his weaknesses, or create temporary conflicts, frustration, or anxiety. By deceiving the subject about the nature of the experiment, the experimenter deprives him of the freedom to decide whether or not he wants to be exposed to these potentially disturbing experiences. ... The use of deception presents ethical problems even when the experiment does not entail potential harm or discomfort for the subject. Deception violates the respect to which all fellow humans are entitled and the trust that is basic to all interpersonal relationships. Such violations are doubly disturbing since they contribute, in this age of mass society, to the already powerful tendencies to manufacture realities and manipulate populations. Furthermore, by undermining the basis of trust in the relationship between investigator and subject, deception makes it increasingly difficult for social scientists to carry out their work in the future. (p. 997)

Similar issues arise in all efforts at psychic manipulation.

In some situations, the ethical problem is not outright deception, but the participant's incomplete or distorted knowledge of the effects of an intervention. For example, many individuals enter sensitivity training sessions (T-groups) to learn about group processes and about their impact on others in a group. Though such learning may well take place, some critics have argued that there may also be potentially harmful side-effects to which participants are not alerted. For example, participants may find that the group process releases violent impulses or even pathological reactions in themselves and others. They may be subjected to harsh personal attacks for their feelings and idiosyncrasies or may engage in such attacks on others. Or, according to Gottschalk and Pattison (1969), by fostering "a concept that anything goes regardless of consequences," T-groups "may preclude effective communication. . . . Communication may not be seen as an interpersonal event but merely as the opportunity to express oneself" (p. 835). Of course, properly structured and well-supervised sensitivity training may also bring unexpected benefits. The basic ethical question, however, concerns the right of the participant to be informed, not only of probable benefits, but also of potential dangers resulting from psychic manipulation. This question applies to other forms of psychic manipulation, such as brain stimulation or drug experimentation, as much as it does to group experiences.

Often change agents are unaware that they are engaged in manipulative efforts or that these efforts have ethical implications. They may be convinced that all they are doing is conveying information or providing a setting in which self-generated change processes are allowed to emerge. They may thus fail to recognize the situational and structural factors that enhance their power over their clients and the subtle ways in which they communicate their expectations of them. Even if they are aware of their manipulative efforts, they may be so convinced that what they are doing is good for the clients that they fail to recognize the ethical ambiguity of the control they exercise (cf. Kelman, 1968, Chapter 1). Such dangerous blindspots on the part of change agents, which preclude their even raising the ethical questions, are particularly likely to arise in the more subtle forms of psychic manipulation.

## Persuasion

The technique of persuasion is a form of interpersonal influence in which one person tries to change the attitudes or behavior of another by means of argument, reasoning, or, in certain cases, structured listening. In the laboratory, as well as in the mass media, persuasion is usually a one-way process. In interpersonal relations in natural settings, it is generally a mutual process, in which the various participants try to persuade one another. Persuasion is frequently used as a means of social intervention in the mass media and, at the one-to-one level, in insight therapies.

At first blush, persuasion seems highly consistent with the value of freedom—almost its exemplification, in fact. The communication process appears to be carried out in the open, all parties appear to be free to consider the arguments, apparently have free choice whether to reject or accept them, and no coercion is consciously practiced. Quite clearly, when compared with outright coercion or the more gross forms of manipulation, persuasion emerges as a relatively free method of intervention. But at the same time, its seeming openness may sometimes mask covert and far-reaching efforts at personality change.

Insight therapies such as psychoanalysis would generally be regarded as persuasive means of attitude and behavior change. Through such therapy, individuals are led to a better understanding of the sources of their complaints—why they think, act, and feel as they do. The guiding assumption is that self-knowledge will take them a long way toward dealing with the problems. The techniques used to promote understanding are generally non-directive, and the client is urged to assume major responsibility for talking during the therapy sessions.

In principle, at least, insight therapy shows a high degree of respect for people's freedom. The patients do most of the talking, the therapist does not impose his or her personal values, and the process can be ended by the patient at any time. However, closer analysis reveals numerous opportunities for covert influence. Many patients, for example, report feelings of guilt over violations of sexual standards. Following the moral traditions of psycho-analysis, most forms of insight therapy view the guilt feelings, rather than the sexual behavior, as the problem to be solved. Under the guise of moral neutrality, the therapist encourages patients to understand why they feel guilty and to see that such feelings are irrational and therefore unjustified. Similarly, by deftly steering the conversation in certain directions through probes and nods of assent, the therapist can lead the patient toward desirable attitudes on moral questions or other matters. And, as Perry London (1964) has observed, even the attitude of moral neutrality in psychotherapy is an ethical stance: "It is, from the therapists's side, a libertarian position, regard-less of how the client sees it (indeed, in some ways he may justly see it as insidious)" (p. 13). It is hard to escape the conclusion that the therapist, like the confessor, is an active agent of moral suasion. The ethical problem posed by psychotheraphy, however, is that the values guiding the influence process are hidden behind global notions such as mental health, self-actualization, and normality. The problem is mitigated to the extent that therapists recognize that they are bringing their own values into the relationship and label those values properly for their patients. "Among other things, such a recognition would allow the patient, to a limited extent, to 'talk back' to the therapist, to argue about the appropriateness of the values that the therapist is intro-ducing" (Kelman, 1968, pp. 25–26).

When we move from persuasion in the one-to-one context to efforts at mass persuasion, the question of who has the opportunity and the capacity to mount a persuasion campaign takes on central importance. Since such opportunities and capacities are not equally distributed in any society, this question is fraught with ethical implications. It arises, for example, in the debate over the impact of modernization on traditional values, to which we alluded earlier. In this connection, after defending the need for cultural diversity, Denis Goulet (1971) has written:

> Development economists often ask what they should do about local customs which get in development's way. No sensitive change agent is blind to the traumatic effects of the "bull-in-the-china-closet" approach to local customs. Nevertheless, persuasive campaigns are sometimes necessary, even if they are unpopular. (p. 270)

The question is, who should be responsible for deciding when and where persuasive campaigns are necessary? Should the interested parties from a community be involved in the decision about whether a campaign should be launched, as well as in the later stages of the intervention? Furthermore, how can illiterate villagers argue on an equal plane with sophisticated national planners armed with charts, statistics, debating skills, and prestige? Those in power are usually in a much better position to launch a persuasion campaign and to carry it out effectively. Thus, even though persuasion itself may be more consistent than other means of intervention with the principles of democratic dialogue and popular participation, it often occurs in a context where some are more equal than others.

## Facilitation

Some strategies of intervention may simply be designed to make it easier for individuals to implement their own choices or satisfy their own desires. An underlying assumption in these strategies is that people have some sense of what they want to do and lack only the means to do it. Though facilitation, like persuasion, seems highly consistent with freedom, it too can move close to the borders of manipulation.

An example from the field of family planning can illustrate the different degrees of manipulativeness that a facilitation effort might involve. At the least manipulative extreme, a program providing a regular supply of contraceptive pills to a woman who is highly informed about the possibilities of contraception and strongly motivated to limit her family size, and who knows that she wants to use the pill but simply lacks the means to obtain it, would be a case of almost pure facilitation. At the other extreme would be the case of a woman who vaguely feels that she has too many children, but is not strongly motivated to limit her family size, and who possesses no information on contraception. The clinic arranges for visits to her home with the purpose of increasing her level of motivation and, once the vague concern is translated into a concrete intention to practice contraception, provides her free transportation to a local family planning center. Though facilitation is clearly involved in the latter stages of this program, in its origins it is basically a form of either manipulation or persuasion. That is, it requires that motivation be channeled before actual facilitation can take place. Falling somewhere between these two extremes would be a program designed to assist a woman, already motivated to limit her family size and aware of the possibilities of contraception, in choosing the means most appropriate in her case and in implementing that choice; or a program designed to promote a particular method (such as the IUD) for women who are motivated to limit their family size but uninformed about the possibilities of contraception.

The ethical problems of intervention increase as one moves from more or less pure facilitation to cases in which facilitation occurs as the last stage of a manipulative or persuasive strategy. But ethical questions can be raised even about seemingly pure facilitation. The most vexing problem is that the selective reinforcement of an individual's desires, even when these are sharply focused and based on adequate information, can be carried out for someone else's purposes. Here we face a critical question about the ethics of planned change: It is right for party A to assist party B in attaining B's own desires· when the reason for this assistance is that B's actions will serve A's interests? In other words, does any kind of facilitation also involve elements of environmental manipulation through the principle of selective reinforcement? For example, survey data suggest that many poor blacks and Mexican-Americans in the United States are desirous of family planning services. But racist groups would also like to see these minorities reduce their fertility. If the government decides to provide voluntary family planning services to these and other poor families, is it serving the interests of racism or the freedom of the families in question? While it is sometimes possible to determine that a given intervention leans more one way than the other, it is often impossible to say whose interests are served most by a change program.

Some have tried to handle the charge of manipulation through facilitation by being completely honest and open. Consider the case of a church-related action group that approaches a neighborhood organization with an offer of assistance. In such a relationship, open dialogue about why each party might be interested in the other, joint setting of goals, and complete liberty on both sides to terminate the relationship would certainly represent ethically laudable policies, but they would not remove the possibility of manipulation. The fact remains that the church group is making its resources available to one organization rather than another. It thereby facilitates the attainment of the goals associated with that organization and may weaken the influence and bargaining position of competing groups. In cases where there are numerous organizations claiming to represent essentially the same constituency, as among Puerto Ricans in the United States, the receipt of outside aid may give one contender for leadership considerable advantage over the others. Moreover, since the church group retains ultimate control of the resources provided, it can exercise great leverage in setting goals by the implicit threat of withdrawing its support. It is therefore essential to distinguish between honesty in the process by which an intervention is carried out and the underlying power relationships operating in the situation.

## ASSESSMENT OF CONSEQUENCES

A final set of ethical concerns arises from the consequences of a change program—its products as well as its by-products. Questions that might be raised about a specific case include: Who benefits from the change, in both the short and the long run? Who suffers? How does the change affect the distribution of power in the society, for example, between elites and masses, or between competing social groups? What is its impact on the physical environment? Which social values does it enhance and which does it weaken? Does the program create a lasting dependency on the change agent or on some other sponsor? What will its short-term and long-term effects be on the personalities of those involved? Many of these questions can be grouped under the heading of *direct* and *indirect consequences.*

An ethical analysis of the direct consequences, which flow immediately from the substance or contents of the intervention, would relate them to the set of basic values used as criteria for assessing the intervention. This general procedure was followed by the Population Task Force of the Institute for Society, Ethics, and the Life Sciences (1971) in its examination of specific proposals for population policy. The core values used in its report were freedom, justice, security/survival, and welfare. Among the specific proposals examined in the light of these values were voluntarist policies, such as providing free birth control information and materials, and penalty programs, including those that would withhold certain social benefits (education, welfare, maternity care) from families with more than a certain number of children.

In brief, the task force concluded that voluntarist policies had the great advantage of either enhancing or at least maintaining freedom and, in certain cases, of promoting the general welfare. At the same time, there was some concern that, under conditions of rapid population growth and preferences for large families, relying only on voluntarist policies might jeopardize the general welfare and possibly survival. Also, questions of justice could be raised if one group in the society was growing at a much faster rate than others. The major ethical drawback of penalty programs, on the other hand, was their possible injustice to those affected. The primary impact of measures such as the withdrawal of educational benefits would be precisely on those who needed them most—the poor. Considerations of justice would also arise if, as is likely, society or the family turned its wrath on the poor creature whose birth order happened to be one more than the stipulated number.

In addition to its direct consequences, almost any change program creates by-products or side effects in areas of society and personality beyond its immediate intentions or scope of influence. These indirect effects must form part of any serious ethical evaluation. Such an evaluation requires a guiding theory of change, of how one part of a system affects another. Unfortunately, many efforts at social intervention completely ignore these systems effects, or discover them too late. Among the most common unanticipated effects are the destruction or weakening of integrative values in the society, change in the balance between aspirations and achievement, and strengthening the power of one group at the expense of another.

One of the latent consequences of many programs of modernization is to undercut or challenge existing values and norms, particularly in rural areas. The introduction of a new road, building of an industrial plant, teaching literacy, or even selling transistor radios may expose isolated villagers to a variety of new stimuli that challenge their traditional world view. Though the direct effects of such programs often serve the values of welfare, justice, and freedom, the indirect effects may generate abundant confusion and a search for new alternatives. Similarly, quasi-coercive population policies, such as penalty programs, can affect societal values in subtle ways. Warwick (1971) points out that they might increase political corruption since some people "may find it more palatable to bribe local enforcement officials than to limit their procreative behavior"; or cynicism about government in general, "in cases where the moral or even political legitimacy of a program was seriously questioned by large segments of the population." Incentive programs that, in effect, bribe people not to have children, may also have undesirable long-term effects, such as "encouragement of the same commercial mentality in other spheres of life. . . . Before experimenting with financial incentive programs, therefore, it would be prudent to ask if there are certain goods which we would rather not have bought and sold on the open market, such as one's body, one's vote, and one's personal liberty" (Warwick, 1971, pp. 20–21).

Another common side-effect of change involves a shift in the balance between individual aspirations and the opportunities for achieving them. The delicate ethical question in this case concerns the degree to which a change agent is justified in tampering with aspirations. The dilemma is often severe. On the one hand, to do nothing implies an endorsement of the status quo. On the other hand, in raising aspirations to stir up motivation for change, a program may overshoot its mark. The unintended result may be a rise in frustration. Questions of this type could be raised about the innovative method of literacy instruction developed by Paulo Freire (1971), which attempts to develop not only an ability to read, but also a heightened consciousness of one's position in society and the forces shaping one's destiny. One can certainly argue that this experience enhances the person's freedom. But a change in critical consciousness and political aspirations without a corresponding modification of the social environment may also be a source of profound frustration. Where collective action to change the system is impossible, either because of strong political repression or other barriers to organization, the net effect may be short-term enthusiasm followed by long-term depression. In fact, the experience of having been stimulated and then frustrated may lead to a lower probability of future action than existed before the intervention. One must then ask if it is morally justifiable to raise political aspirations without ensuring that there are opportunities for implementing those aspirations.

A program of social intervention may also have the unintended effect of strengthening the bargaining position of one group *vis-à-vis* another. This problem was well illustrated in a debate at Harvard University in 1969. The focus of the debate was the Cambridge Project, an interuniversity program aimed at developing and testing computer systems for use in the behavioral sciences. The major point of contention was the project's sponsorship by the U.S. Department of Defense. Though the project was not designed to carry out military research or provide other direct services to the sponsor, its connection with the Defense Department aroused considerable concern in the Harvard community. The strongest objection was that acceptance of funds from the Defense Department might increase its involvement in university affairs and broaden its constituency among social scientists. In this way, some felt, the project would reinforce the dominant role of the military in U.S. society and simultaneously weaken the university's capacity for critical analysis of that role. In other words, by accepting a major grant from the Defense Department, Harvard would be lending its institutional prestige to the sponsor, legitimizing the Defense Department's involvement in nonmilitary activities, and perhaps creating pressures within the university to refrain from political dissent. The opponents also argued that a heavy infusion of funds into the area of computer applications would change the ecological balance of social science research within the university. According to this line of reasoning, students and faculty would be drawn to computer-oriented research and away from areas lacking comparable support.

## FOCUS OF THE BOOK

We have reviewed some of the general ethical issues that may arise as social intervention activates conflicting values or interests—whether through the ends served by the change effort, the targets at which it is directed, the means chosen to implement it, or its direct and indirect consequences. To deal with these issues responsibly in a specific instance requires clarification of the values that are implicated by the particular type of intervention and assessment of the impact of the intervention on these values. Assessment of the impact, in turn, calls for empirical knowledge, not only of the general processes of social influence and social change, but also of the specific variety of intervention involved. This book is devoted to such an empirically based analysis of ethical issues in several domains of social intervention.

A total of eight varieties of intervention were selected for analysis: behavior modification, encounter groups, organization development, community-controlled educational reform, intervention in community disputes, income maintenance experiments, public housing programs, and family planning programs. These eight instances of intervention can roughly be ordered on a continuum ranging from microlevel to macrolevel. At one extreme is behavior modification, in which the target of intervention is the individual. At the other extreme is family planning, in which the target is typically a whole society. Between these extremes are programs whose target may be a group, an organization, a community, or a large segment of the population. These distinctions are, of course, somewhat arbitrary, since the target of any given type of intervention depends on the perspective from which it is viewed. Thus, behavior modification—when carried out in institutional settings—may be part of a macrolevel intervention program, directed at particular social groups. At the other extreme, family planning programs often come down to microlevel interventions aimed at specific individuals.

Essentially, the first three types of intervention—behavior modification, encounter groups, and organization development—are directed to client problems. The intervenors are typically professional change agents, addressing themselves to the problems of a specific client system—whether it be an individual, a group, or an organization. This does not mean that the initiative for the intervention necessarily comes from the target person or group. Behavior therapy or T-groups may be imposed on some of the participants, and organization development programs directed primarily to the lower echelons may be initiated by the top management of an organization. Indeed, many of the ethical problems in these types of intervention stem precisely from such possibilities of imposition.

The second two types of intervention—community-controlled educational reform and intervention in community disputes—are largely directed at community conflicts. The intervention introduces, at the community level, a mechanism designed to resolve conflict, whether it be a chronic system conflict or a conflict generated or exacerbated by a community crisis. The initiative for the intervention may come from the community or from the outside. The intervenors may be a community-based organization, an outside agency, or some combination of the two.

The final three types of intervention covered in this book—income maintenance experiments, public housing programs, and family planning programs—are largely designed to contribute to the execution of national policies. The programs discussed in this category typically have specific communities as their targets of change. These programs are, however, local or regional expressions of larger, macrolevel programs designed to deal with national problems such as poverty, urban decay, or population growth. The funding of these programs comes from national sources—the federal government or large foundations—and so does at least a major part of the initiative and leadership. Programs vary in the degree and nature of community participation.

Though differing in the level and target of intervention, the eight types of programs selected for analysis in this volume share, to a greater or lesser extent, four common features:

1. They are *deliberate interventions*. In keeping with the narrower working definition of social intervention presented at the beginning of this chapter, they are explicitly designed to change the characteristics of individuals or groups, or to influence the pattern of relationships between individuals and/or groups.

2. They are *carried out by professional change agents*. The eight instances of intervention differ in the degree to which the role of intervenor has become professionalized. For example, the practitioners of behavior modification, sensitivity training (with some exceptions), and organization development clearly see themselves as professional change agents. Intervenors in community conflicts are just beginning, with some degree of reluctance, to define themselves as professional change agents. Intervenors in national programs are more likely to see themselves as professional consultants or evaluators than as change agents per se. Nevertheless, it is fair to say that, in all eight cases, we are dealing with professionals engaged or participating in the deliberate production of individual and social change.

3. Their theoretical and/or methodological approach has a *social-science base*. Most of the eight instances of intervention are directly linked to a particular psychological or sociological model of change, deriving from such diverse theoretical sources as operant conditioning, group dynamics, organizational behavior, systems analysis, conflict theory, or population dynamics. Alternatively or in addition, they are linked to a particular systematic analysis of the application of social science, deriving from various theories of practice or models of evaluation or consultation.

4. They are *benign interventions*, in the sense that they are intended to serve the needs and interests and enhance the personal welfare of the target individuals and groups. There is often considerable ambiguity about the benign character of the intervention and differences of opinion about whose interests it actually serves. For example, programs of behavior modification in institutional settings, or certain kinds of intervention in community conflicts, or some approaches to family planning may be more oriented toward achieving social control than toward enhancing the welfare of the target population. Similarly, sensitivity training or organization development programs within a business or bureaucratic agency may serve the interests of those who commission the program at the expense of those who participate

in it. Indeed, these possibilities represent some of the most pervasive ethical issues that arise in these various forms of social intervention. In principle, however, they are designed to contribute to the welfare of the target population, and their rationale and justification rest on their adherence to that principle.

These four features make the cases of social intervention selected for analysis in this book particularly suitable for an initial exploration of ethical issues in social intervention. Since the intervention in each case is deliberate, the change agents generally acknowledge some responsibility for its form and consequences. Since the change agents are professionals, they are concerned with the development of and adherence to guidelines for ethical practice. Since the procedures are anchored in social science, there is a systematic basis for predicting and assessing their impact—an essential step, as we have pointed out earlier, in any ethical analysis. And, since the intervention is designed to serve the interests of the target population, there is at least some agreement about the criteria on which ethical evaluation must be based. For all of these reasons, then, there is a greater degree of readiness for a responsible, empirically based exploration of the ethical implications of social intervention in the particular cases that we have selected for analysis. It must be remembered, however, that these cases represent only a subset—and, in some respects, the least troublesome subset—of social intervention as it is broadly defined.

Two chapters are devoted to each of the eight types of intervention. The first chapters in all cases (i.e., Chapters 2, 4, 6, 8, 10, 12, 14, and 16) are written by practitioners of the particular type of intervention under discussion. Although these authors are committed to the approach they describe, they were specifically invited to contribute because of their demonstrated strength in social-scientific analysis and sensitivity to ethical issues. All of these chapters begin with a description of the type of intervention under consideration, although they differ in their choice of objects for description. Chapters 2, 4, 6, 10, and 16 describe an entire category of social intervention (such as behavior modification or family planning), distinguishing various subtypes and introducing concrete illustrations as they go along. Chapters 8, 12, and 14 describe a specific intervention program, illustrative of a more general category, in considerable depth. The authors then proceed to raise some of the ethical issues involved in the particular type of intervention (in their own view or in the view of certain critics) and to discuss them from their own perspective.

The purpose of the second chapters in all of the pairs (i.e., Chapters 3, 5, 7, 9, 11, 13, 15, and 17) is to discuss or respond to the presentations of the first authors. The discussants are, as a minimum, less committed to the particular type of intervention under consideration than are the original presenters. Some are social scientists who have in fact been quite critical on ethical and theoretical grounds of the procedures they are discussing. Others have been engaged in similar forms of practice, but react to the intervention they are discussing with some degree of skepticism. Still others are moral philosophers who approach the task with the analytical tools characteristic of their profession. The discussants vary in the way they have defined their roles: Some respond directly to the presentation of the preceding chapter, reacting to the issues raised and the solutions proposed by the original presenter; others use the preceding chapter primarily as a starting point for developing their own point of view on the issues. All the discussion chapters are designed to examine the ethical implications of the particular type of social intervention from a different analytical perspective.

To maximize continuity, the contributors were asked to center their analysis, insofar as feasible, on three key questions that arise, respectively, in setting the goals, selecting the means, and assessing the consequences of social intervention. The significance and the precise content of these questions vary, of necessity, from one type of intervention to another. In their general forms, however, they can be stated as follows.

1. *In setting the goals for any social intervention, who speaks for the person, group, or community that is the target of the change effort?* What is the source of an intervenor's authority to decide what changes would be desirable in the lives of others? Are there any circumstances under which intervention would be justified without consultation of those intervened upon? What happens when the target persons or groups are considered incompetent to speak for themselves (e.g., because of mental, physical, or intellectual disabilities, minor or criminal status, or lack of information)? Who can properly represent the target's interests under these circumstances, and how are these representatives selected? When the target is a large group or a community, who serves as its spokesperson in setting the goals of the intervention? How are competing interests within the target population weighed and adjusted and who decides what interests are to be represented and how? In deciding whom they will recognize as spokespersons for the target group, how can the intervenors avoid conferring power upon some segments of that group at the expense of others and taking upon themselves the role of kingmakers?

2. *In selecting the means of intervention, how does one assure genuine participation in the change process to the people who are its targets?* Assuming that it is generally desirable to involve people in the decisions that affect their lives, when does a mechanism of participation become a form of manipulation? Can one identify means of intervention that provide the appearance of participation or self-determination without its substance? Under what circumstances does participation have the effect of coopting members of the target group to serve the interests of the intervenor or of the sponsor of the intervention? For example, when the sponsors of a welfare, housing, or other official program provide direct financial support to representatives of the target population in order to facilitate their participation in the

decision-making process, does this have the effect of committing these representatives to the views and intentions of the sponsors? How can those with power and influence help those lacking such resources to participate in planning and deciding without inevitably biasing the outcome? How can they do so without being placed in the paradoxical position of bestowing on the target group the right to determine their own fate?

3. *In assessing the consequences of social intervention, how does one take account of higher-order or unintended effects?* Who ought to take responsibility for such effects and how can this be accomplished? This question has come to have increasing importance in ecologically oriented discussions of economics, wherein industries are charged with the obligation to internalize the costs of their products (e.g., to include pollution and resource depletion costs in their prices). The relevance of higher-order consequences for social interventions is obvious at a number of levels. For example, when urban renewal has the effect of displacing individuals and existing neighborhoods, what are the obligations of those who planned for the renewal and how should these be discharged? Similarly, within therapeutic or encounter experiences, what are the intervenor's obligations, if any, to deal with changes in the lives of members of the client's family? How does one predict and deal with the possibility that positive changes in one part of a system may be accompanied by negative changes in other parts? For example, increased insight may be accompanied by greater anxiety, increased feelings of efficacy by greater frustration, increased mobility by greater alienation, and increased power for some segments of a population by a decline in power for others. How does one predict and deal with the possibility that an intervention may backfire—that a therapeutic or encounter experience may induce a breakdown, or that an educational enrichment program may increase the gap between social classes that it was intended to close, or that a national poverty program may produce new mechanisms for exploiting the poor?

The chapters that follow examine, for each type of intervention, how the problems cited in this list of questions arise, what specific forms they take, how they have been dealt with in the past (if at all), what have been some of the shortcomings in dealing with them, and how they might be approached in the future. The questions, of course, take on different shades and nuances for the different types of social intervention, and the authors were not expected to restrict their analysis to them. Rather, the authors were encouraged to develop their arguments in ways most suited to their particular topics and most congenial to their own perspectives. The framework provided by this set of questions, however, will make it easier to compare different types of intervention along dimensions critical to an ethical evaluation. The concluding chapter attempts to integrate the analyses of specific cases by extracting recurrent themes and identifying some of the broad ethical issues that cut across social interventions in various contexts and at various levels.

# REFERENCES

Bennis, W. G., Benne, K. D., Chin, R., & Corey, K. E. (Eds.). *The planning of change* (3rd ed.). New York: Holt, Rinehart and Winston, 1976.

Blake, J. Population policy for Americans: Is the government being misled? *Science,* 1969, *164,* 522–529.

Callahan, D. Population limitation and manipulation of familial roles. Unpublished manuscript. Hastings-on-Hudson, N.Y.: Institute of Society, Ethics, and the Life Sciences, 1971.

Freire, P. *Pedagogy of the oppressed.* New York: Herder and Herder, 1971.

Gottschalk, L. A., & Pattison, E. M. Psychiatric perspectives on T-groups and the laboratory movement: An overview. *American Journal of Psychiatry,* 1969, *126,* 823–840.

Goulet, D. *The cruel choice.* New York: Atheneum, 1971.

Gustafson, J. M. Basic ethical issues in the bio-medical fields. *Soundings,* 1970, *53*(2), 151–180.

Kelman, H. C. *A time to speak: On human values and social research.* San Francisco: Jossey-Bass, 1968.

Kelman, H. C. The relevance of social research to social issues: Promises and pitfalls. In P. Halmos (Ed.), *The sociology of sociology* (The Sociological Review: Monograph No. 16). Keele: University of Keele, 1970.

Kelman, H. C. The rights of the subject in social research: An analysis in terms of relative power and legitimacy. *American Psychologist,* 1972, *27,* 989–1016.

Lippitt, R., Watson, J., & Westley, B. *The dynamics of planned change.* New York: Harcourt Brace Jovanovich, 1958.

London, P. *The modes and morals of psychotherapy.* New York: Holt, Rinehart and Winston, 1964.

London, P. *Behavior control.* New York: Harper & Row, 1969.

May, R. *Love and will.* New York: Norton, 1969.

Population Task Force of the Institute of Society, Ethics, and the Life Sciences. *Ethics, population, and the American tradition.* A study prepared for the Commission on Population Growth and the American Future. Hastings-on-Hudson, N.Y.: Institute of Society, Ethics, and the Life Sciences, 1971.

Rostow, W. W. *The stages of economic growth.* New York: Cambridge University Press, 1960.

Skinner, B. F. *Beyond freedom and dignity.* New York: Knopf, 1971.

Warwick, D. P. Freedom and population policy. In Population Task Force, *Ethics, population, and the American tradition.* Hastings-on-Hudson, N.Y.: Institute of Society, Ethics, and the Life Sciences, 1971.

Warwick, D. P. Tearoom trade: Means and ends in social research. *Hastings Center Studies,* 1973, *1*(1), 27–38.

Warwick, D. P. Social scientists ought to stop lying. *Psychology Today,* 1975, *8*(9), 38–40, 105–106.

Warwick, D. P., & Kelman, H. C. Ethical issues in social intervention. In G. Zaltman (Ed.), *Processes and phenomena of social change.* New York: Wiley, 1973.

# I

# BEHAVIOR MODIFICATION

# 2
# ETHICAL ISSUES IN BEHAVIOR MODIFICATION

## STEPHANIE B. STOLZ
HEW Regional Office, Kansas City

In the history of civilization, people have continually tried to control their environment and find ways of teaching themselves and their children better means of acquiring new skills and capabilities. Common-sense notions of the ways that reward and punishment can change behavior have existed since time immemorial. Thus, elements of what is now referred to as behavior modification were used long before psychologists and other behavioral scientists developed systematic principles of learning and a technology related to them.

In recent years, the developing technologies of behavior control have been the focus of many different concerns. First psychosurgery and now behavior therapy and behavior modification have acted as conceptual lightning rods in the midst of stormy controversies over ethical problems associated with attempts at social influence. These behavior control methods have drawn to them such highly charged issues as fears of mind control or concerns about the treatment of persons institutionalized against their will. Apparent or actual infringements of rights, as well as some abuses of behavior control methods, have led to litigation,

Portions of the material in this chapter appeared in slightly different form in Stolz, Wienckowski, and Brown (1975). I thank Dr. J. G. Holland for introducing me to stimulating and thought-provoking ideas on both formal and informal occasions, and Drs. D. M. Baer, G. Bermant, B. H. Pickett, R. K. Schwitzgebel, and Ms. L. Scallet for helpful comments on earlier versions of this chapter.

congressional hearings, and calls for curbs on the use of behavior control techniques (e.g., U.S. Congress, 1974).

## DEFINITION OF BEHAVIOR MODIFICATION

This chapter focuses on behavior modification. To clarify what procedures are and are not considered relevant, let me first indicate the relationship of behavior modification to a broader concept—behavior influence.

*Behavior influence* occurs whenever one person exerts some degree of control over another. This happens constantly in such diverse situations as formal school education, advertising, child rearing, political campaigning, and other normal interpersonal interactions.

*Behavior modification* is a special form of behavior influence that primarily involves the application of principles derived from research in experimental psychology to alleviate human suffering and enhance human functioning. Behavior modification emphasizes systematic monitoring and evaluation of the effectiveness of these applications. The techniques of behavior modification are generally intended to facilitate improved self-control by expanding individuals' skills, abilities, and independence.

Most behavior modification procedures are based on the general principle that people are influenced by the consequences of their behavior. The current environment is believed to be the most relevant factor affecting the individual's behavior. Insofar as possible, the behaviorally oriented mental health worker limits the conceptualization of the problem to observable behavior and its environmental context.

*Behavior therapy* is a term that is sometimes used synonymously with behavior modification. In general, behavior modification is considered to be the broader term; behavior therapy refers mainly to clinical interventions, usually applied in a one-to-one, therapist-patient relationship. Behavior therapy may be seen as a special form of behavior modification.

In behavior modification, attempts to influence behavior are typically made by changing the environment and the way people interact, rather than by intervening directly through medical procedures (such as drugs) or surgical procedures (such as psychosurgery). The effects of behavior modification, unlike the results of most surgical procedures, are relatively changeable and impermanent.

As more publicity has been given to behavior modification, the term has come to be used loosely and imprecisely in the public media and often carries a negative connotation. In that vein, behavior modification has sometimes been said to include psychosurgery, electroconvulsive shock therapy, and the noncontingent administration of drugs, that is, the administration of drugs independent of any specific behavior of the person receiving the medication.

However, even though procedures like these do modify behavior, that does not make them "behavior modification techniques" in the sense in which most professionals in the field use the term. In this chapter, the use of the term "behavior modification" will be consistent with its professional use: behavior modification will be used to refer to procedures that are based on the explicit and systematic application of principles and technology derived from research in experimental psychology, procedures that involve some change in the social or environmental context of a person's behavior. This use of the term specifically excludes psychosurgery, electroconvulsive therapy, and the administration of drugs independent of any specific behavior of the person receiving the medication.

Behavior modification is a family of techniques, including a variety of methods based on positive reinforcement, such as token economies, contingency contracting, and modeling; aversive techniques, such as punishment, the removal of positive reinforcement or "time-out," and fines; overcorrection; systematic desensitization; and assertiveness training. Behavior modification methods can be used in a broad range of situations, including the child-rearing efforts of parents and the instructional activities of teachers, as well as the therapeutic efforts of mental health workers in treating more serious psychological and behavioral problems.

## ETHICAL ISSUES IN SETTING THE GOALS AND MEANS OF THERAPY

This chapter addresses some of the ethical issues that are involved in the application of behavior modification methods to the therapeutic process. Although these issues are discussed here as they apply to behavior modification, they have relevance for all types of mental health interventions. Even though this chapter does not attempt to address the issues in this broader context, the full range of concerns mentioned here applies in all mental health settings.

In an ideal situation, mental health workers using behavioral procedures would plan the goals and methods of the therapy together with their clients. Those using behavioral approaches would follow the same generally accepted ethical principles guiding other therapists and so would strive to maintain a suitable balance between the rights of individuals and of society. Although, on the whole, researchers and therapists using behavior modification methods have exercised normal caution, some aspects of the relevant ethical issues have not always received the attention they deserve. Further, apparently simple issues turn out on closer scrutiny to be very complex.

In the last few years, a number of different authors have discussed the ethical issues involved in psychological interventions and in behavior therapy specifically and have suggested broad principles of ethical conduct for the delivery of behavioral services. These principles include the involvement of the client in decision making, informed consent, the balance of risk and benefit, review by outside persons, and monitoring of the effectiveness of the intervention (Bandura, 1969; Franks & Wilson, 1973; Krasner, 1969; Stolz,

Wienckowski, & Brown, 1975; Wilson & Davison, 1974; Yates, 1970). This chapter explores the ramifications of some of these proposed principles of ethical practice. These topics are complex, and there are no easy answers.

## Who Sets the Goals and Means of Therapy?

The decision that a client's behavior should be modified, as well as decisions about in what direction it should be modified and how it should be modified, can be made by society's representatives, such as teachers or policemen, by the therapist, or by the clients or their agents. This general issue is treated first here to emphasize that the most basic decisions made by the behavioral mental health worker—whether to modify, which response to modify, and how to modify— involve value judgments (Begelman, 1973; Halleck, 1971; Krasner, 1962; Spece, 1972; Stolz, 1975) and thus raise ethical issues.

In the past, mental health workers of all types often made those decisions on their own, using simply their clinical judgment, their experience, and their assessment of current social values as the basis for determining treatment goals and methods (Hawkins, 1975). Many therapists have only recently begun to affirm the propriety of involving their clients' representatives more realistically in the planning of treatment programs, including the selection of the goals and the methods that will be used to achieve those goals.

## Who Is the Client?

In each setting where treatment is delivered, for each type of population found in those settings, the mental health professionals must decide who their client is; that is, who the person or group is with whom they should negotiate regarding the choice of goals and means for a behavior modification program.

Typically, the client is the source of the professionals' salary or fee; ideally, the client will be the person whose behavior is being modified. It is often both obvious and correct that the ostensible client is the actual one. For example, a neurotic patient comes to a clinic to be relieved of a fear of flying in planes; the patient has chosen the goal of the therapy and is also paying the professional, and hence the patient is the true client. Or, when a husband and wife are referred to a mental health worker to learn contingency contracting as a method of improving their marriage, it is generally clear that both partners have chosen the goal of improvement of their interpersonal relations. The mental health worker's responsibility, then, is to assist them both in achieving this goal.

Responsible practice calls for the professional to obtain agreement from the true client—the person whose behavior is to be modified—about both the goals and the means of treatment programs, before programs are introduced to change behavior. Even in apparently clear-cut cases where the person paying the mental health worker is the person whose behavior is to be modified, issues arise when the process of obtaining agreement is analyzed. (Some of these issues are especially thorny, however, when the person paying the mental health worker is clearly someone different from the person whose behavior will be modified.)

The ethical situation is somewhat clouded, for example, when a behavioral consultant is asked to help a teacher keep pupils in their seats, working quietly at all times. Are these the optimum classroom conditions for learning, and are the children's best interests served by teaching them to be still, quiet, and docile (O'Leary, 1972; Winett & Winkler, 1972)? The mental health professional may be able to suggest alternative goals, or may work together with the class and the teacher in developing appropriate goals.

Similarly, when an administrator of an institution for the retarded asks behavioral professionals to establish a token economy to motivate the inmates to work on jobs for the hospital, the professionals may want to work together with an advisory committee to determine the relative value of that work activity for the hospital and for the retarded person. When they are asked to have the hospital as their client, they need also to consider the rights of the patients, the potential benefits to them of the activity, and any risks that may be involved. The professionals may decide, for example, that such hospital jobs have minimal benefit for the patients and thus may feel that the institution's goal is an inappropriate one.

Identifying the true client is a critical problem when behavior modification programs are used in prisons. Persons using behavior modification procedures in prisons have been frequently criticized for their attempts to deal with the inmates' rebellious and nonconformist behavior (e.g., Dirks, 1974; Halleck, 1971; Opton, 1974). Because behavioral professionals are often in the position of assisting in the management of prisoners whose rebelliousness and antagonism to authority are catalysts for conflict within the institution, the distinctions among the professionals' multiple functions as therapists, managers, and rehabilitators can become blurred and their allegiance confused. Although the professionals may quite accurately perceive their role as benefiting the individual, they may at the same time appear to have the institution, rather than the prisoner, as their primary client.

When the client is not the same as the person whose behavior is to be modified, special precautions are required. The less directly the participants in the program are involved in the initial determination of the goals and means of the program, the more protections for them should be built into the system. Thus, when the client is an institution rather than the target individual, an advisory committee should be established to cooperate with the mental health professional in choosing the goals and methods of the behavior modification program. This committee should include representatives of those whose behavior is to be modified, their guardians, or advocates.

The establishment of a suitably constituted review committee does not automatically guarantee that approved programs will include appropriate protections. The official guardians of the participants may, for example, have a vested interest in controlling them in a way more convenient for the guardians than beneficial for their wards. Mental health professionals, too, cannot be viewed as entirely disinterested parties, especially when they are employed by the institution charged with the care of those in the program. Further, conflicting philosophies and differing loyalties may make it difficult for the panel members to agree unanimously on decisions.

Such a panel does, however, provide a regularized opportunity for conflicting points of view to be expressed, an opportunity generally not otherwise available. The more public these discussions are, the more protection they will offer for the less powerful participants. The group's discussions can, at a minimum, sensitize program administrators to the critical issues and help them become aware of the conflicting interests involved. Hopefully, the members of a panel would be sensitive to the factors influencing their own and each others' behavior, so that subtle coercions are not used to manipulate the decisions.

Therapists, especially those working in institutions, should be sensitive to the implications of their obligations to the institution hiring them (Bandura, 1975; Halleck, 1971; Holland, in press-b). Because they are paid by the institution, therapists owe allegiance to the institution; because of the traditional therapist-patient relationship, they also owe allegiance to the patient. The greater power held by the institution makes the mental health worker's true client the person or institution who is paying the bills, the one who has hired the professional (Holland, in press-b). Behavioral professionals working for a school system, mental hospital, or prison cannot avoid having that institution as their client, regardless of the extent to which the pupil, prisoner, or inmate is involved in decisions about the goals and means of therapy. Both Holland and Halleck recommend that clinicians redirect their energies from individual treatment to institutional change; Holland (in press-b) even suggests that therapists only modify the behavior of whoever is paying them.

### Informed Consent

Professionals planning intervention programs need to evaluate the extent to which those who will participate in the programs can give truly informed consent to their participation. Informed consent has been characterized as the "central issue on which hang most of the ethical problems of human experimentation" (Beecher, 1970, p. 18). Reflecting the importance of this issue in therapy as well as research, the bulk of this chapter is devoted to a discussion of various aspects of informed consent.

In its broadest sense, informed consent refers to clients' right to decide whether they want to participate in a proposed program, after they have been told what is going to be involved. More specifically, informed consent has three components: knowledge, voluntariness, and competency (Friedman, 1975). "Knowledge" is the "informed" part of informed consent. This refers to information that describes the program and its goals, explains that clients may refuse to participate before the program begins or at any time during the treatment, describes the risks and benefits associated with the program, and offers alternative treatments. "Voluntariness" refers to the absence of coercion when the decision to consent is made. "Competency" reflects an assessment that the clients can understand the information that has been given to them and make an appropriate judgment about it (cf. Friedman, 1975; Martin, 1975).

### Broad Issues Involving Informed Consent

As with other issues discussed in this chapter, the extent to which truly informed consent can be obtained varies across populations and settings. Ascertaining knowledge, voluntariness, and competency is simplest in an outpatient setting with adult patients, yet even there, subtle issues arise, as will be described in what follows. With other client groups, in other settings, determination of the adequacy of informed consent becomes increasingly complex.

The types of people that tend to be involved in behavior modification programs are children; institutionalized persons such as the senile, retarded, and mentally ill; and prisoners. With children and institutionalized persons, uncertainties about whether their consent is truly informed revolve chiefly around their knowledge and competency (Lasagna, 1969); with prisoners, the primary issue relates to voluntariness (Kassirer, 1974a; Spece, 1972).

When the competence of clients to understand the explanations given them and to make a suitable decision is questioned, the alternative generally recommended is to have an advisory committee act as a surrogate for the clients and give consent for them (e.g., Brown, Wienckowski, & Stolz, 1975). Some of the difficulties associated with relying on advisory committees have already been discussed.

A prior problem is involved, however, in the very determination that the clients are incompetent. No objective, generally accepted procedures have yet been developed for doing this, and no operational rules exist specifying how the description of the goals and methods of a proposed program should be modified so that otherwise incompetent populations might be able to understand the explanations.

As a result, client populations can potentially be abused in the determination of their competency, for those in power in schools and institutions, or those with legal responsibility for the clients, can decide arbitrarily that treatment is required and then determine the methods of treatment without consultation with the clients, even though the clients may actually have been able to participate in at least portions of the decision-making process. Parents of retarded persons, for example, are heavily dependent on the staff of the institutions where their children are being cared for and are unlikely to contradict staff requests; the retarded children, on the other hand, might be able to understand the proposed program. Similarly, the guardians of psychotic patients tend to have a strong investment in their remaining institutionalized, so that the guardians are likely to be unwilling to disagree with recommendations from the institution's staff (Spece, 1972); the patients might, in many circumstances, be able to participate actively in treatment decision.

Ensuring voluntariness is especially difficult when those participating in a program are prison inmates (Shapiro, 1974), but it is a problem with any institutionalized group (Martin, 1975; Spece, 1972). Prisoners may not ever be able to be true volunteers, because prison inmates generally believe that they will improve their chances for early parole if they cooperate with prison officials' requests to participate in a special program. There are other pressures as well; for example, participation in a novel program may be a welcome relief from the monotony of prison life.

A recent court decision[1] held that involuntarily confined patients cannot give legally adequate voluntary consent because their environment is "inherently coercive": the patients' privileges and even their eventual discharge may depend on their cooperation. Although this decision, concerning one patient and one experimental psychosurgery, seems to have obvious and important implications for those in other institutions and for other treatments, one analysis (Wexler, 1974) suggests that contradictions between this decision and many others will prevent its extension.

### Alternatives to Informed Consent

The preceding section contended that obtaining truly informed consent from those who participate in behavior modification programs is more complex than it might appear at first. The elements of knowledge, voluntariness, and competency are all critical for consent to be valid; with most of the populations that commonly participate in behavior modification, some aspect of at least one of these elements can be questioned. As a result, some alternative method seems to be necessary to protect the rights of participants in treatment programs and to ensure that they are decently treated.

One possibility is to treat informed consent as a continuous dimension, rather than as a unitary concept that either is or is not fully achieved (Wolfensberger, 1967). In that vein, Davison and Stuart (1975) have proposed a hierarchy of constraints on the giving of consent. In their schema, four sets of factors must be considered in the determination of the level of protection that clients must be afforded in consenting to participate in a program:

1. The extent of freedom or constraint in the setting
2. The extent to which the procedure to be used is an experimental or an established one
3. The degree of risk to which the client will be exposed
4. The degree to which the client can reasonably be expected to gain personally from participation in the program

[1] *Kaimowitz v. Department of Mental Health for the State of Michigan*, 42 U.S.L.W. 2063 (1973).

Davison and Stuart recommend that different levels of protection be offered, depending on the decision about each of these factors.

Ellis (1975) has recommended that the dimensions of knowledge, competency, and voluntariness should be increasingly important and more strictly defined as proposed treatments are more intrusive and irreversible, less important and more casually waived as treatments are less intrusive and more reversible. Both this recommendation and Davison and Stuart's suffer from a weakness discussed earlier in connection with competency—the absence of an objective method of measuring critical concepts. Were Ellis's recommendations adopted, who would determine the extent to which a proposed recommendation was reversible and nonintrusive? Were Davison and Stuart's hierarchy of constraints adopted, who would decide about the four factors? In both cases, the individual who makes this key determination is the one who is actually making the decisions about the treatment, regardless of the use of other ostensible protections, such as consent forms and advisory committees.

A third alternative conceptualizes treatment as a contractual activity (Schwitzgebel, 1975), in which the outcomes are specified in advance, with explicit contingencies for success or failure. Schwitzgebel criticizes the reliance on informed consent on the ground of the relationship of consent procedures to tort law. Under this type of law, a person who touches another without consent is guilty of a tort. Schwitzgebel (1975) argues against the current practice of broadening consent for otherwise "unwanted touching" to include consent to therapy. He contends that using consent procedures in therapy implies that the therapist would be performing a tort if consent were not granted, that the therapist may be doing something presumed to be harmful or wrong, or consent would not be necessary. As an alternative to consent, he recommends contracts; contract law, he says, already prohibits fraud, misrepresentation, and duress in the treatment situation.

Schwitzgebel's recommendations hinge on his legal analysis of tort law and contract law. He points out (Schwitzgebel, 1975) that consent will continue to be necessary for the legally permissible conduct of treatment. It is nonlawyers, however, who for the most part are involved in the practice of therapy and the development of procedures for the ethical conduct of therapy. Thus, although an overexpansion of the legal concept of consent may have been made, consent procedures, rather than contracts, are the current focus of attention. Contracts may well be a useful reminder to therapists of their responsibilities to their clients (Stuart, 1975). Contracting does not, however, resolve the problems involved in obtaining informed consent, because the same coercions potentially involved in obtaining informed consent would be equally present in negotiating a contract.

Wexler (1975) has suggested that at least in cases where the goals of a program are legally adequate and the reinforcers involved are above the legally required minimum, informed consent might not even be necessary. Instead, he suggests, clients could simply be offered a program that involves "nonbasic" reinforcers; they then could cooperate or not cooperate with such a program. Although this is an intriguing, if limited, solution, it may not be generally acceptable, at least in the present climate of strong concern for patients' rights and adherence to traditional methods of obtaining consent.

An important step in clarifying these issues would be made by research addressed to key issues, such as developing an objective method for assessing competency, and determining how procedures should be explained and alternatives described to various client populations (Lasagna, 1969).

### Another Look at Informed Consent

These alternative approaches to obtaining consent have been described in the literature, but have not, to my knowledge, been implemented. Usually, if client populations are thought to be incapable of giving informed consent, an advisory committee is used to pass on the goals and methods of proposed treatment programs. If clients are capable of consenting, then they are presented with a description of the proposed treatment goals and some alternative treatments, and their choice is taken to reflect consent to both goals and means (Brown et al., 1975).

However, these solutions do not reflect some of the more subtle problems with the consent issues than have been discussed here. Offering a client a choice of treatments or establishing an advisory committee may be an illusory solution to the thorny problems of informed consent, merely a shift in the locus of the ethical dilemma. This section discusses additional issues that arise when treatment decisions are being made.

#### Selection of Program Goals

When the client or advisory committee is participating with the therapist in the selection of the goals of the treatment program, what array of goals do they choose from? Often, no "array" of goals may be offered, but rather only a single one, either the goal the client requests or a goal decided on by the therapist after hearing the client's complaints. Behavioral professionals, however, cannot view their role simply as "supertechnicians who [help] people learn to behave in the ways that they prefer" (Halleck, 1971, p. 19). This seemingly uncomplicated and desirable way to deal with the ethical issues does not reflect the realities of the situation (Halleck, 1971). Although the client may seem to be selecting the goal of treatment, in actuality, the process is more complex. Initially, clients typically request nonbehavioral goals, and they must be taught to specify behavioral objectives. Once they have learned to do this, the behavioral professional may permit them to identify the therapeutic goals, but by this point, the clients have already been influenced by the therapist's values (cf. Frank, 1971).

Whatever goal is requested by the client, it becomes the target of therapy only if the therapist consents. When the values involved are widely agreed on, it matters little whether the therapist or the patient decides (London, 1964). Few would protest the goal of increasing academic achievement in school children, or of eliminating severe phobias or life-threatening, self-destructive behavior. Some patients' goals are so inappropriate that the therapist clearly must make the decision. Few would endorse a goal of helping harsh parents become even more oppressive or of eliminating the anxieties of a chronic rapist or pedophile. Many possible therapeutic goals are more controversial than these, however, and customs and values are continually changing.

A problem arises with the process of selection of goals because typically the therapist is from the more powerful classes or has a higher status, while the client is from a less powerful class or has a lower status. In all mental health fields, therapists have tended to view problems from their own perspective, so that treatment goals chosen were those that they would want for themselves or that would benefit those to whom they owed allegiance (Frank, 1961; Halleck, 1971). Thus, the goals of therapy have tended to be in accord with the values of the therapists and their social class. Miller (1969), for example, has criticized behavior therapists for their "unquestioning acceptance of value systems—and implicitly of the social systems which support the definitions of the deviant person or the persons who presents a 'social problem'" (p. 75).

In many instances, the inclusion of clients or their representatives in the decision-making process is beginning to redress the power imbalance, and often this is an effective way of dealing with this aspect of the problem. In prisons and mental hospitals, however, this may not be an adequate solution. Although some prison behavior modification programs are designed to educate the prisoners and benefit them in other ways, other programs are directed toward making the prisoners less troublesome and easier to handle, thus adjusting the inmates to the needs of the institution.

Advisory committees, while helpful in dealing with this problem, cannot resolve all the issues, for the reasons discussed earlier. Special ombudsmen to handle complaints from patients or prisoners are not adequate solutions either, especially because they are likely to be employees of the institution involved (Gray, 1975).

Advisory committees, therapists, and patients alike are all bound by societal conditioning, so that however much discussion is engaged in and however much information exchanged, the behavior finally selected to be modified is likely to be a behavior that society defines as deviant. The behavioral professional then proceeds as though the deviance resides in the environment, or in the clients' learning histories as a product of their environment, and sets up a therapy program that will either alter the environmental contingencies to shape different behavior, or give the individuals new learning experiences, again to shape different behavior.

Implicit in this approach are the assumptions that it is appropriate for society at large to define deviance, and that those who conform to that definition should change (Bandura, 1975; Beit-Hallahmi, 1974; Miller, 1969;

Stolz, 1975). For example, Krasner and Ullmann (1965), discussing the circumstances under which behavior modification is appropriate, suggest that the factors to be considered should include the behavior to be modified, the method of influence used, and the impact on society of the individual's changed behavior:

> If a person is being supported by society (as in a psychiatric hospital), then it is appropriate for an authorized agent of society to alter his behavior. On the other hand, behavior modification is inappropriate if the person is a self-supporting, contributing member of society. The ultimate source of values is neither the patient's nor the therapist's wishes, but the requirements of the society in which both live (p. 363).

This statement implies that therapists, paid by the institutions of society, have a primary ethical obligation to uphold society's values. Krasner and Ullmann appear not to have considered whether the patient might have a right to refuse treatment or the therapist the option to attempt to alter society's values. Yates (1970) similarly suggests that decisions about treatment should be made by society, although he doesn't present any specific indication of how this might be implemented.

This apparently authoritarian atmosphere has been characteristic of most persons writing about psychological interventions until very recently, probably because these issues have been widely discussed for a relatively short time. This approach within behavior modification may also be in part a function of the history of the field. Behavior modification developed on a base of research in the animal laboratory, and, at least in its early applications, was administered primarily to psychotics, retarded persons, and young children, persons for whom instructions seemed inappropriate and with whom discussions about goals and means seemed impossible, or at least very difficult.

For whatever reason, the approach of behavior modification typically defines the problem as existing within individuals, and the goal of treatment as achieving a change in their behavior. An alternative approach, seldom mentioned, sees individuals' behavior as a result of larger societal forces, ones that may need to be changed (Halleck, 1971; Holland, in press-a; Winett & Winkler, 1972). Even though behaviorists commonly reject the medical model (e.g., Krasner and Ullmann, 1965), they still generally accept the values of society as given and define the individuals' behavior, resulting from their reinforcement histories, as the problem. This seems little different from saying that they have a disease. Begelman (1975) makes a similar point in calling attention to the medical model's "tacit canons of moral assessment governing which events are to be declared 'desirable' or not" (pp. 181–182).

In the practice of behavior modification, then, as with other psychological therapies, society has controlled the definition of deviance, located the problem within the individual, and directed treatment toward changing the individual. Rebellious school children are taught to follow rules; questions are seldom raised about whether the classroom activities are boring or aversive (Winett & Winkler, 1972). Alcoholic persons are punished for drinking or trained to make social responses considered more adaptive; questions are seldom raised about the many pressures for the consumption of alcohol, such as cocktail parties, attractive advertising, and interpersonal activities for which drinking alcohol is an essential entrance behavior (Holland, in press-a). Homosexuals are shocked in the presence of photographs of males or given orgasmic retraining; questions are only recently being raised about the societal pressures forcing homosexuals to request a redirection of their sexual interests (Begelman, 1975; Davison, 1976; Serber & Keith, 1974).

What can behavioral professionals, aware of this issue, do that is different from what is now being done? Currently, therapists, probably working together with their clients, decide on the goals of treatment after a consideration of the clients' report of their problems. One suggestion that follows from this analysis is that therapists should be especially sensitive to the source of the definition of deviance and should, as part of the decision-making process, spell out their criteria for determining what is appropriate and inappropriate. When clinicians are negotiating with an institution or advisory committee, they should identify the institution's goals, as well as recommending goals for their client.

Some have suggested that practice should include not only a balancing of the interests of society and the client, but also an expectation that it may well be society, rather than the client, that should be changed (Davison, 1974; Halleck, 1971; Holland, in press-a). Begelman has put it this way: "Behaviorists should make strides in the resolution of the real 'problem': the public derogation of diverse life styles" (1975, p. 182). The least radical expression of this view still suggests that it is the therapist's responsibility to decide "whether the behavior he is being asked to help change should really be changed" (O'Leary, 1972, p. 509) and to alter the client's environment in order to maintain improvements achieved during therapy (e.g., Atthowe, 1975).

To summarize, when therapists present clients with information about possible goals for therapy, the goals offered by the therapists and selected by the clients may reflect a compromise among a variety of pressures—the clients' wishes, as determined by their histories of reinforcement; the therapists' values, as determined by their histories of reinforcement; and society's values, as expressed in the interests and preferences of those in decision-making positions.

### Presentation of Alternative Treatments

Further issues arise if the offer of a choice of treatments is scrutinized. Here, too, therapists are not disinterested decision makers (Gray, 1975), and here, too, neither they nor their patients are free of pressures from society. Simply by their interest in one type of treatment over another, therapists subtly influence their clients to choose the alternative preferred by the therapists. After all, when therapists recommend a treatment, they confer a great deal of legitimacy on it.

Although the current discussions of ethics and informed consent have led mental health professionals to realize the importance of offering patients a fair choice between alternative treatments (Wolfensberger, 1967), whether that is actually possible is seriously questionable. A behavioral professional will undoubtedly prefer a behavioral intervention and will find it difficult to argue persuasively for an alternative treatment. Further, the mere fact that clients have come for treatment to this particular therapist generally means that they have some trust in that individual's judgment and will tend to agree to whatever is suggested.

When, in addition, the therapy is part of a research program, pressures on the therapist-researcher to obtain enough subjects for the study (Barber, Lally, Makarushka, & Sullivan, 1973; Beecher, 1966; Gray, 1975) further compound the problem. In programs combining therapy with research, the hopes of the therapist and "the inborn optimism of youthful science" (Moore, 1969) combine to design the choice so that the client will consent.

Behavioral professionals, whose approach to treatment is based on the notion that behavior is sensitive to its consequences, should be aware that this generalization applies to all their interactions with their clients, not only those designed to produce therapeutic change. The very choice of treatments offered to the client is going to be a consequence of pressures on the therapist; the therapist will design the alternatives so that the client makes the decision most reinforcing for the therapist. Unfortunately, most clients are generally not aware of these pressures on therapists (Gray, 1975) and, hence, are likely to be insensitive to these problems.

The many pressures on therapists, leading them intentionally or unintentionally to coerce the client into cooperating, have led Slovenko (1975) to suggest redefining informed consent to include a consideration of the source of the information given to the patient. To expand on his suggestion, it might be possible, at least when seriously intrusive and potentially irreversible treatments are being considered, to have one treatment described by an advocate of that approach, and alternatives described by other persons, advocates of those approaches.

What other solutions can be offered? It may help to increase public awareness of behavioral principles, so that clients will have a better understanding of how environmental events can control their behavior. As public awarness increases, the likelihood of clients' behavior being manipulated by more knowledgeable individuals lessens. Although professionals in behavior modification may use their understanding of behavioral principles in an attempt to alter other persons' behavior, those other persons can make use of their own understanding and control of themselves and their environment to resist, or indeed to counterinfluence, the behavior of the professionals.

### Selection of the Behavioral Treatment

What are the influences on the therapists' behavior that determine which behavioral treatment they select from among the array available? In general, no specific behavioral technique is mandated for any particular behavioral problem. Rather, when determining treatment for clients, behavioral professionals use their judgment and select from among the family of behavior modification methods.

Of the aversive consequences used in behavior modification, many, such as time-out, fines, overcorrection, and covert sensitization, are not physically painful (Kazdin, 1975). In covert sensitization, for example, the unpleasant stimuli are imaginal. Only a few punishers used in behavior modification are actually painful or physically unpleasant: electric (faradic) shock, emetic (nausea-inducing) drugs such as apomorphine, and paralytic drugs, chiefly succinylcholine chloride (Anectine). This last produces a brief but total paralysis, including paralysis of the respiratory muscles, and thus a temporary but terrifying sensation of death by drowning.

An important distinction between the pain associated with these particular aversive stimuli and the pain associated with common medical procedures such as inoculations and dental operations is that for these behavior modification methods, the stimulus must be unpleasant in order to be effective; for the medical methods, any unpleasantness is an incidental and unnecessary concomitant of the technique. Painless dentistry and inoculations would still be effective; painless electric shock or discomfort-free nausea would not function as an aversive stimulus and hence would not be an effective therapeutic agent.

For what behaviors are unpleasant or painful stimuli and drugs used as aversive treatment? Shock is widely acknowledged to be the most effective, if not the only effective, treatment for severe life-threatening behaviors such as the self-injurious behavior of autistic children (Bucher & Lovaas, 1968; Risley, 1968) and violent attacks on self and others by psychotic adults (Ludwig, Marx, Hill, & Browning, 1969). Shock is also used as a treatment for homosexuality (e.g., Callahan & Leitenberg, 1973; Feldman & MacCulloch, 1971; McConaghy, 1969; Rachman & Teasdale, 1969; Serber & Keith, 1974), pedophilia (Callahan & Leitenberg, 1973; Wolfe & Marino, 1975), alcoholism (e.g., Sobell & Sobell, 1973; Wallerstein, 1956), voyeurism (Gaupp, Stern, & Ratliff, 1971), fire setting (Royer, Flynn, & Osadca, 1971), shoplifting (Kellam, 1969), exhibitionism (Callahan & Leitenberg, 1973; Fookes, 1960; Kushner & Sandler, 1966), transvestism, fetishism (Callahan & Leitenberg, 1973; Feldman, 1966; McGuire & Vallance, 1964; Marks & Gelder, 1967; Rachman & Teasdale, 1969), compulsive gambling, and infidelity (Barker & Miller, 1968).

Emetic drugs are a common treatment for alcoholism (Miller & Barlow, 1973; Rachman & Teasdale, 1969). Also, for over 60 years, emetic drugs have been given to patients for homosexuality. Recent cases have been reported by Feldman (1966) and McConaghy (1969). Emetic drugs have also been used to treat drug addiction (Liberman, 1968; Raymond, 1964) and transvestism and fetishism (see review by Feldman, 1966; Lavin, Thorpe, Barker, Blakemore, & Conway, 1961; Raymond, 1956).

Succinylcholine chloride is used chiefly as a clinical treatment for substance abuse, including heroin addiction (Thomson & Rathod, 1968), glue sniffing

(Blanchard, Libet, & Young, 1973), and alcoholism (Clancy, Vanderhoof, & Campbell, 1967; Farrar, Powell, & Martin, 1968; Laverty, 1966). Anectine was also used in a prison as a punishment for "deviant sexual behavior," evidently fellatio (Reimringer, Morgan, & Bramwell, 1970).

Behavioral practitioners have been accused of emphasizing punishment techniques (e.g., Opton, 1974). When this charge is responded to, it is denied (e.g., Birk et al., 1973). Yet the aversive techniques are part of the armamentarium of the behavior therapist; even those who deny their widespread use acknowledge that they are used occasionally (Birk et al., 1973).

This brief and certainly not exhaustive summary of the literature on aversive treatments was included to emphasize that it is not only an occasional, isolated British clinician who uses these treatments for these particular behaviors. Rather, shock and emetic drugs have been described as "the most accepted behavioral methods for changing sexual variant behavior" (Fensterheim, 1974, p. 21).

Aversive techniques are said to be necessary for the treatment of substance abuse and certain sexual behaviors because the immediate consequences of these behaviors are naturally reinforcing, even though the long-term consequences may be quite detrimental to the individual (Stolz et al., 1975). Note, however, that these strong aversive techniques are generally used for alcoholism, sexual deviance, substance abuse—in short, for behavior that society considers repugnant (Holland, 1975a).

Holland (1975a) has insightfully pointed out that although aversive treatments are used for behavior that is the object of severe sanction and retaliation, scorn and retribution, they are seldom if ever used for behavior that does not draw society's censure. For example, shock and Anectine are not treatments for impotence or nonassertive behavior. When homosexuals are treated, shock is used to punish arousal elicited by one set of stimuli, so that the behavior will be directed to different stimulus objects. Compare this to a treatment that might be suggested for a comparable but socially acceptable case, changing a preschool child's behavior from staying near the teachers to playing primarily with peers: extinction (inattention) would be the strongest treatment used. Alcoholics and pedophiles are administered shocks to decrease the future probability of behaviors that society defines as inappropriate. Compare this to a parallel example, treatment for nonassertive adults, where the therapist generally ignores nonassertive behavior while modeling and reinforcing assertive responses. Here again, extinction seems to be the strongest treatment used to remove the undesired responses.

This view of the use of aversive techniques gives a new meaning to Johnston's (1972) recommendation regarding the use of punishment. Johnston suggested that decisions on whether aversive control would be valuable and effective for a particular behavior be made on the basis of scientific and empirical evidence, rather than on the basis of a personal moral philosophy. In saying this, he was arguing against those who would oppose all uses of punishment on humanitarian grounds. This discussion of aversive control, however, suggests that the moral philosophy of the behavioral professionals may well have been part of the basis for their use of aversive control techniques.

Johnston (1972) makes a good point when he says that "applied researchers and therapists must not fall into the trap (which they insist is already full of others) of investigating and using only those therapeutic tools which suit their personal theories and philosophies" (p. 1051). On the other hand, even if scientific and empirical evidence has shown that a technique is efficacious, it should not be used if it is unacceptable to consumers or their peers (Brown et al., 1975), or if its use is a disguised reaction to the therapist's repugnance with the patient's behavior.

Behavioral professionals have been selecting and recommending treatments not only on the grounds of effectiveness, but also because of unrecognized elements of social retaliation (Holland, in press-a), in at least some cases. Increased sensitivity by mental health workers to the contingencies operating on their own behavior would help to rectify this situation. London (1964) has made a similar recommendation, although in different terminology, in urging that more attention be paid to both clients' and therapists' ideologies, philosophies, and moral codes.

## Conclusions about Issues Related to Consent

Issues involved in obtaining consent to the goals and means of treatment go far beyond the questions of whether a given population is competent to arrive at an informed judgment and is free to do so. Consideration of the problems of obtaining informed consent from prisoners has led some persons to recommend the elimination of experimental therapy programs in prisons, on the grounds that participation must be coerced since consent cannot be truly voluntary ("Experiments," 1976; Footnote 1). Robinson (1974), also, has made the strong recommendation that when consent is compromised for any reason, as when the individuals to receive the treatment are institutionalized, "practitioners must exercise informed restraint" (p. 238), refusing to administer therapy unless the individuals have physically harmed others or themselves.

However, not only in prisons is it questionable that truly informed and voluntary consent can be obtained; rather obtaining truly informed consent in outpatient settings or even in private practice (Halleck, 1971) is questionable because of the wide array of pressures on the therapist and the client. It is, of course, abhorrent to consider abandoning all attempts to help others simply because of defects inherent in the concept of informed consent. Rather, persons engaged in therapeutic endeavors should be sensitive to these complex issues and should strive to behave as decently as possible for the benefit of the client and of society. It seems better to educate therapists about these issues so that they can be aware of the pressures on them, and to build in what safeguards are possible, than to discard all attempts at rehabilitation, whether behavior modification or any other therapeutic method is involved.

# ETHICAL ISSUES RELATED TO
# THERAPEUTIC METHODS

The preceding discussion has been concerned with ethical issues pertinent to both the determination of the goals of therapy and the planning of the methods of therapy. Some additional issues are relevant only to the practice of therapy, once the goals have been decided on, however that might be done.

## Accountability

Integral to the planning of the methods of therapy should be a plan for monitoring the progress of the therapeutic program and for giving information resulting from that monitoring to the clients. In behavior modification, as in all other therapeutic interventions, the results of the therapeutic program must be carefully monitored to ensure that the goals agreed on at the start of therapy are being achieved. If they are not, sound practice requires a reevaluation and revision of the methods being used.

In addition, those conducting behavior modification programs must be accountable to those whose behavior is being changed or to their representatives. Information on the effectiveness of the program should be made available to the consumers on a regular basis.

In short, effectiveness and accountability are key elements of ethical responsibility in behavior modification, and, indeed, in all psychological interventions.

## Aversive Techniques

Behavior modification has drawn much criticism because of its inclusion of aversive procedures. These methods can be and have been seriously misused, becoming means by which those in power can exercise control or retribution over those in their charge. The abusive treatment may then be justified by calling it therapeutic and labeling it "behavior modification."

While many aversive techniques that are used in behavior modification, such as shock and time-out, are effective, it is unfortunately true that they are also cheap and easy to apply, requiring little if any specialized knowledge on the part of the person using—or misusing—them (Baer, 1970). Further, aversive techniques are widely known to be included in the family of behavior modification methods. Thus legitimized, these simple aversive methods are subject to indiscriminate use and other abuses, without regard for individual rights. For example, time-out, which when appropriately used should be for only short periods of time, has, in some settings, involved extraordinarily long periods of isolation in small quarters (Opton, 1974).

Although aversive techniques have great potential for misuse and are unquestionably unpleasant to consider, the gain from their use can be potentially great. In the case of individuals whose self-destructive behavior is life-threatening, the alternative to aversive treatment may be long-term confinement in an institution or prolonged periods in total restraint (Baer, 1970). Thus, a recent policy paper on behavior modification from the National Institute of Mental Health (Brown et al., 1975) concluded:

> Aversive techniques are appropriately used when the risk to the patient of continuing the self-injurious behavior is serious, alternative treatments appear to be ineffective, and potential benefits to the patient from the treatment are great. On the other hand, aversive methods should not be used to enforce compliance with institutional rules (p.16).

Such restrictions would prevent the use of aversive methods for nonlife-threatening behaviors that interfere with the "good" functioning of institutions, such as prisoners swearing at guards. Confining the use of aversive methods to the instances described in the quotation would also, by implication, prevent their use for nonlife-threatening, socially despicable behavior such as pedophilia. For problems like these, more positive remedies would have to be devised.

## SUMMARY AND CONCLUSIONS

The technology of behavior modification, says Skinner (1971), is "ethically neutral. It can be used by villain or saint. There is nothing in a methodology which determines the values governing its use" (p. 150). The mere existence of a technology of behavior change may pose challenging ethical problems (Miller, 1969), but it does not do so because it introduces opportunities for control that were not there before. In the view of persons working in the field of behavior modification, it is the nature of social interaction for people to influence each other. Ethical issues arise because of the way the technology may be applied; the issues are the same as they would be in any attempt to manipulate, change, or control the behavior of others. Bandura (1969) formulates the issue in this way: "The basic moral question is not whether man's behavior will be controlled, but rather by whom, by what means, and for what ends" (p. 85). Behavior modification, then, involves altering the nature of the controlling conditions, rather than imposing control where none existed before.

Any approach to the alteration of human behavior raises these questions, especially if the approach is relatively successful. The ethical problems discussed in this chapter apply to all types of interventions; these issues do not have any unique relevance for behavior modification.

This chapter has analyzed issues related to setting the goals and methods of therapy. In calling attention to problems such as the determination of who the true client of the therapist is, where possible defects are likely to occur in obtaining informed consent, how goals to be offered to a client are selected, and how therapeutic methods are chosen as alternatives, I have attempted to reflect the complexities of these issues.

However, this kind of detailed scrutiny raises more issues than it settles. At this time, no definitive solution has been found for these ethical problems.

Safeguards must be developed that will prevent abuses of the therapeutic setting and yet permit appropriate, ethical practice.

In recent years, an accelerating series of court cases is gradually setting limits within which therapy can be delivered. One with wide-reaching implications was the *Wyatt*[2] decision that, among other rulings, defined as basic rights many items and activities that had been used as reinforcers in token economy programs (Wexler, 1973). The *Kaimowitz* decision (see footnote 1) related to whether prisoners could give informed consent; the decision in *Knecht v. Gillman*[3] listed specific guidelines under which certain kinds of treatment must be administered. These and other cases (cf. Begelman, 1975; Kassirer, 1974a, 1974b; Stolz et al., 1975; Wexler, 1975) are gradually building a body of rulings and case law that is defining more clearly the rights of patients, prisoners, and other participants in therapy.

Concern has been expressed that these decisions will eventually prevent the use of some effective therapeutic techniques (Mabe, 1975). However, the rulings are an important step forward. Even though clinicians may be inconvenienced by having to adjust their practice so that it is in accord with the decisions, this inconvenience is far outweighed by the gain in human rights for patients. No therapeutic program should have to depend for its existence on the continuation of a dehumanizing environment.

Judicial rulings are not necessary to emphasize that aversive techniques are neither legally or ethically acceptable when used solely for oppressive purposes, as an expression of retaliation by society, or without the consent of the persons on whom they are used or their guardians.

In general, the ethical issues in behavior modification, and in the delivery of any type of mental health service, serve to focus a variety of conflicts in values within our society—conflicts between those with more and with less power; conflicts between the view of scientists and therapists as persons always "conscientious, compassionate, responsible" (Beecher, 1966, p. 1360), wise, and restrained (DeBakey, 1968) and the view of professionals as behaving individuals subject to the control of environmental consequences; and conflicts between individuals rights and societal rights. As Gray (1975) points out, although these conflicts make this topic fascinating, they also make the search for clear and simple solutions a frustrating one.

London (1969) sums it up this way: "The fundamental moral issues in behavior control do not change, of course, no matter what technology develops around them. They are now, as ever, only these: Who shall be controlled? By whom? How?" (pp. 180–181). In this chapter, I have tried to show some of the subtle and complex issues that are involved in trying to answer these questions.

---

[2] *Wyatt v. Stickney,* 325 F. Supp. 781 (M.D. Ala. 1971), 334 F. Supp. 1341 (M.D. Ala. 1971), 334 F. Supp. 373 (M.D. Ala. 1972), 344 F. Supp. 387 (M.D. Ala. 1972), and 368 F. Supp. 1383 (M.D. Ala. 1974), affirmed in part, modified in part sub nom. *Wyatt v. Aderholt,* 503 F. 2d 1305 (5th Cir., 1974).

[3] *Knecht v. Gillman,* 488 F. 2d 1136 (8th Cir., 1973).

# REFERENCES

Atthowe, J. M., Jr. Behavior modification, behavior therapy, and environmental design. *American Behavioral Scientist*, 1975, *18*, 637–654.

Baer, D. M. A case for the selective reinforcement of punishment. In C. Neuringer & J. L. Michael (Eds.), *Behavior modification in clinical psychology.* New York: Appleton-Century-Crofts, 1970.

Bandura, A. *Principles of behavior modification.* New York: Holt, Rinehart and Winston, 1969.

Bandura, A. *Value orientations in behavior modification.* Paper presented at the conference on Moral and Ethical Implications of Behavior Modification, University of Wisconsin, Madison, 1975.

Barber, B., Lally, J. J., Makarushka, J. L., & Sullivan, D. *Research on human subjects.* New York: Russell Sage, 1973.

Barker, J. C., & Miller, M. Aversion therapy for compulsive gambling. *Journal of Nervous and Mental Disease*, 1968, *146*, 285–302.

Beecher, H. K. Ethics and clinical research. *New England Journal of Medicine*, 1966, *274*, 1354–1360.

Beecher, H. K. *Research and the individual.* Boston: Little, Brown, 1970.

Begelman, D. A. Ethical issues in behavior control. *Journal of Nervous and Mental Disease*, 1973, *156*, 412–419.

Begelman, D. A. Ethical and legal issues of behavior modification. In M. Hersen, R. M. Eisler, & P. M. Miller (Eds.), *Progress in behavior modification* (Vol. 1). New York: Academic Press, 1975.

Beit-Hallahmi, B. Salvation and its vicissitudes: Clinical psychology and political values. *American Psychologist*, 1974, *29*, 124–129.

Birk, L., Stolz, S. B., Brady, J. P., Brady, J. V., Lazarus, A. A., Lynch, J. J., Rosenthal, A. J., Skelton, W. D., Stevens, J. B., & Thomas, E. J. *Behavior therapy in psychiatry.* Washington, D.C.: American Psychiatric Association, 1973.

Blanchard, E. B., Libet, J. M., & Young, L. D. Apneic aversion and covert sensitization in the treatment of a hydrocarbon inhalation addiction: A case study. *Journal of Behavior Therapy and Experimental Psychiatry*, 1973, *4*, 383–387.

Brown, B. S., Wienckowski, L. A., & Stolz, S. B. *Behavior modification: Perspective on a current issue* (DHEW Publication No. (ADM)75-202). Washington, D.C.: U.S. Government Printing Office, 1975.

Bucher, B., & Lovaas, O. I. Use of aversive stimulation in behavior modification. In M. R. Jones (Ed.), *Miami symposium on the prediction of behavior, 1967.* Coral Gables: University of Miami Press, 1968.

Callahan, E. J., & Leitenberg, H. Aversion therapy for sexual deviation: Contingent shock and covert sensitization. *Journal of Abnormal Psychology*, 1973, *81*, 60–73.

Clancy, J., Vanderhoof, E., & Campbell, P. Evaluation of an aversive technique as a treatment for alcoholism: Controlled trial with succinylcholine-induced apnea. *Quarterly Journal of Studies of Alcohol*, 1967, *28*, 476–485.

Davison, G. C. Homosexuality: The ethical challenge. *Journal of Consulting and Clinical Psychology*, 1976, *44*, 157–162.

Davison, G. C., & Stuart, R. B. Behavior therapy and civil liberties. *American Psychologist*, 1975, *30*, 755–763.

DeBakey, M. E. Medical research and the Golden Rule. *Journal of the American Medical Association*, 1968, *203*, 574–576.

Dirks, S. J. Aversion therapy: Its limited potential for use in the correctional setting. *Stanford Law Review*, 1974, *26*, 1327–1341.

Ellis, J. W. Personal communication, March 22, 1975.

Experiments on people. *New York Times*, January 23, 1976, p. 30.

Farrar, C. H., Powell, B. J., & Martin, L. K. Punishment of alcohol consumption by apneic paralysis. *Behaviour Research and Therapy*, 1968, *6*, 13–16.

Feldman, M. P. Aversion therapy for sexual deviations: A critical review. *Psychological Bulletin*, 1966, *65*, 65–79.

Feldman, M. P., & MacCulloch, M. J. *Homosexual behaviour: Therapy and assessment*. Oxford, Eng.: Pergamon, 1971.

Fensterheim, H. Behavior therapy of the sexual variations. *Journal of Sex & Marital Therapy*, 1974, *1*, 16–28.

Fookes, B. H. Some experiences in the use of aversion therapy in male homosexuality, exhibitionism and fetishism-transvestism. *British Journal of Psychiatry*, 1960, *115*, 339–341.

Frank, J. D. *Persuasion and healing*. Baltimore: Johns Hopkins University Press, 1961.

Franks, C. M., & Wilson, G. T. (Eds.). *Annual review of behavior therapy: Theory and practice*. New York: Brunner/Mazel, 1973.

Friedman, P. R. Legal regulation of applied behavior analysis in mental institutions and prisons. *Arizona Law Review*, 1975, *17*, 39–104.

Gaupp, L. A., Stern, R. M., & Ratliff, R. G. The use of aversion-relief procedures in the treatment of a case of voyeurism. *Behavior Therapy*, 1971, *2*, 585–588.

Gray, B. H. *Human subjects in medical experimentation*. New York: Wiley, 1975.

Halleck, S. L. *The politics of therapy*. New York: Science House, 1971.

Hawkins, R. P. Who decided *that* was the problem? Two stages of responsibility for applied behavior analysts. In W. S. Wood (Ed.), *Issues in evaluating behavior modification*. Champaign, Ill.: Research Press, 1975.

Holland, J. G. Behaviorism: Part of the problem or part of the solution? *Journal of Applied Behavior Analysis*, in press. (a)

Holland, J. G. Is institutional change necessary? In J. E. Krapfl & E. A. Vargas (Eds.), *Behaviorism and ethics*. Kalamazoo, Mich.: Behaviordelia, in press. (b)

Johnston, J. M. Punishment of human behavior. *American Psychologist*, 1972, *27*, 1033–1054.

Kassirer, L. B. Behavior modification for patients and prisoners: Constitutional ramifications of enforced therapy. *Journal of Psychiatry and Law*, 1974, *2*, 245–302. (a)

Kassirer, L. B. The right to treatment and the right to refuse treatment—Recent case law. *Journal of Psychiatry and Law*, 1974, *2*, 455–470. (b)

Kazdin, A. E. *Behavior modification in applied settings*. Homewood, Ill.: Dorsey Press, 1975.

Kellam, A. M. P. Shop lifting treated by aversion to a film. *Behaviour Research and Therapy*, 1969, 7, 125–127.

Krasner, L. Behavior control and social responsibility. *American Psychologist*, 1962, *17*, 199–204.

Krasner, L. Behavior modification—Values and training: The perspective of a psychologist. In C. M. Franks (Ed.), *Behavior therapy: Appraisal and status*. New York: McGraw-Hill, 1969.

Krasner, L., & Ullmann, L. P. *Research in behavior modification*. New York: Holt, Rinehart and Winston, 1965.

Kushner, M., & Sandler, J. Aversion therapy and the concept of punishment. *Behaviour Research and Therapy*, 1966, *4*, 179–186.

Lasagna, L. Special subjects in human experimentation. In P. A. Freund (Ed.), *Experimentation with human subjects*. New York: Braziller, 1969.

Laverty, S. G. Aversion therapies in the treatment of alcoholism. *Psychosomatic Medicine*, 1966, *28*, 651–666.

Lavin, N. I., Thorpe, J. G., Barker, J. C., Blakemore, C. B., & Conway, C. G. Behavior therapy in a case of transvestism. *Journal of Nervous and Mental Disease*, 1961, *133*, 346–353.

Liberman, R. Aversive conditioning of drug addicts: A pilot study. *Behaviour Research and Therapy*, 1968, *6*, 229-231.

London, P. *The modes and morals of psychotherapy.* New York: Holt, Rinehart and Winston, 1964.

London, P. *Behavior control.* New York: Harper & Row, 1969.

Ludwig, A. M., Marx, A. J., Hill, P. A., & Browning, R. M. The control of violent behavior through faradic shock. *Journal of Nervous and Mental Disease*, 1969, *148*, 624-637.

Mabe, A. R. Coerced therapy, social protection, and moral autonomy. *American Behavioral Scientist*, 1975, *18*, 599-616.

McConaghy, N. Subjective and penile plethysmograph responses following aversion-relief and apomorphine aversion therapy for homosexual impulses. *British Journal of Psychiatry*, 1969, *115*, 723-730.

McGuire, R. J., & Vallance, M. Aversion therapy by electric shock: A simple technique. *British Medical Journal*, 1964, *1*, 151-153.

Marks, I. M., & Gelder, M. G. Transvestism and fetishism: Clinical and psychological changes during faradic aversion. *British Journal of Psychiatry*, 1967, *113*, 711-729.

Martin, R. *Legal challenges to behavior modification.* Champaign, Ill.: Research Press, 1975.

Miller, J. S. Social work and therapies of control. *British Journal of Psychiatric Social Work (London)*, 1969, *10*, 74-79.

Miller, P. M., & Barlow, D. H. Behavioral approaches to the treatment of alcoholism. *Journal of Nervous and Mental Disease*, 1973, *157*, 10-20.

Moore, F. D. Therapeutic innovation: Ethical boundaries in the initial clinical trials of new drugs and surgical procedures. In P. A. Freund (Ed.), *Experimentation with human subjects.* New York: Braziller, 1969.

O'Leary, K. D. Behavior modification in the classroom: A rejoinder to Winett and Winkler. *Journal of Applied Behavior Analysis*, 1972, *5*, 505-511.

Opton, E. M., Jr. Psychiatric violence against prisoners: When therapy is punishment. *Mississippi Law Journal*, 1974, *45*, 605-644.

Rachman, S., & Teasdale, J. *Aversion therapy and behaviour disorders.* London: Routledge & Kegan Paul, 1969.

Raymond, M. J. Case of fetishism treated by aversion therapy. *British Medical Journal*, 1956, *2*, 854-857.

Raymond, M. J. The treatment of addiction by aversion conditioning with apomorphine. *Behaviour Research and Therapy*, 1964, *1*, 287-291.

Reimringer, M. J., Morgan, S. W., & Bramwell, P. F. Succinylcholine as a modifier of acting-out behavior. *Clinical Medicine*, 1970, *77*(7), 28-29.

Risley, T. R. The effects and side effects of punishing the autistic behaviors of a deviant child. *Journal of Applied Behavior Analysis*, 1968, *1*, 21-34.

Robinson, D. N. Harm, offense, and nuisance: Some first steps in the establishment of an ethics of treatment. *American Psychologist*, 1974, *29*, 233-238.

Royer, F. L., Flynn, W. F., & Osadca, B. S. Case history: Aversion therapy for fire setting by a deteriorated schizophrenic. *Behavior Therapy*, 1971, *2*, 299-232.

Schwitzgebel, R. K. A contractual model for the protection of the rights of institutionalized mental patients. *American Psychologist*, 1975, *30*, 815-820.

Serber, M., & Keith, C. G. The Atascadero project: Model of a sexual retraining program for incarcerated homosexual pedophiles. *Journal of Homosexuality*, 1974, *1*, 87-97.

Shapiro, M. H. Legislating the control of behavior control: Autonomy and the coercive use of organic therapies. *Southern California Law Review*, 1974, *47*, 237-56.

Skinner, B. F. *Beyond freedom and dignity.* New York: Knopf, 1971.

Slovenko, R. On psychosurgery. *Hastings Center Report*, 1975, *5*(5), 19-22.

Sobell, M. B., & Sobell, L. C. Individualized behavior therapy for alcoholics. *Behavior Therapy*, 1973, *4*, 49-72.

Spece, R. G., Jr. Note: Conditioning and other technologies used to "treat?" "rehabilitate?" "demolish?" prisoners and mental patients. *Southern California Law Review*, 1972, *45*, 616–684.

Stolz, S. B. Ethical issues in research on behavior therapy. In W. S. Wood (Ed.), *Issues in evaluating behavior modification.* Champaign, Ill.: Research Press, 1975.

Stolz, S. B., Wienckowski, L. A., & Brown, B. S. Behavior modification: A perspective on critical issues. *American Psychologist*, 1975, *30*, 1027–1048.

Stuart, R. B. Challenges for behavior therapy: 1975. *Canadian Psychological Review*, 1975, *16*, 164–172.

Thomson, I. G., & Rathod, N. H. Aversion therapy for heroin dependence. *Lancet*, 1968, *ii*, 382–384.

U.S. Congress, Senate, Committee on the Judiciary, Subcommittee on Constitutional Rights. *Individual rights and the federal role in behavior modification*, 93rd Cong., 2nd sess., November 1974. Washington, D.C.: U.S. Government Printing Office, 1974.

Wallerstein, R. S. Comparative study of treatment methods for chronic alcoholism: The alcoholism research project at Winter VA Hospital. *American Journal of Psychiatry*, 1956, *113*, 228–233.

Wexler, D. B. Token and taboo: Behavior modification, token economies, and the law. *California Law Review*, 1973, *61*, 81–109.

Wexler, D. B. Mental health law and the movement toward voluntary treatment. *California Law Review*, 1974, *62*, 671–692.

Wexler, D. B. Behavior modification and legal developments. *American Behavioral Scientist*, 1975, *18*, 679–684.

Wilson, G. T., & Davison, G. C. Behavior therapy and honosexuality: A critical perspective. *Behavior Therapy*, 1974, *5*, 16–28.

Winett, R. A., & Winkler, R. C. Current behavior modification in the classroom: Be still, be quiet, be docile. *Journal of Applied Behavior Analysis*, 1972, *5*, 499–504.

Wolfe, R. W., & Marino, D. R. A program of behavior treatment for incarcerated pedophiles. *American Criminal Law Review*, 1975, *13*, 69–84.

Wolfensberger, W. Ethical issues in research with human subjects. *Science*, 1967, *155*, 47–51.

Yates, A. J. *Behavior therapy.* New York: Wiley, 1970.

# 3
# COMMENTS ON "ETHICAL ISSUES IN BEHAVIOR MODIFICATION"

IRWIN G. SARASON
BARBARA R. SARASON

University of Washington

The emphasis given by Stolz to the careful definition of behavior modification is perhaps one of the most salient points in her chapter (Chapter 2). In the public mind the term still carries the mystique of the all-powerful process that can compel an individual, whether or not he is conscious of the process, into the adoption of whatever behaviors or models of thought are willed by the controller of the process. The definition in her chapter makes clear the limits placed on techniques and on the kinds of behaviors controlled.

Once an explicit definition is in hand it is easier to clarify what behavior modification is and is not and how the process is simply a special application of principles that are operating constantly (both randomly and by intent) in daily life. Bandura's (1969) often-quoted statement to the effect that the question is not whether behavior is controlled but how, by whom, and for what ends should be kept in mind. A careful consideration of these questions together with a recognition of the conflicts to be encountered ethically and legally and the difficulties in resolving them have been particularly well handled by Stolz.

Many attempts have been made to set up guidelines for the behavior modification process. Some of these are logically appealing. None, however, seems to be more than partially helpful when it is implemented. While emphasis on needed safeguards for the patient should improve the standards of practice, it also carries an inherent danger. Many of the suggested criteria have a rational appeal and imply that the ethical problems may be solved in a manner as simple as the checklist used before takeoff by aircraft crews to assure that all systems are functioning. As Stolz points out, these suggested safeguards are useful to heighten awareness of problem areas. They should not be considered as criteria that can be met with ease or perhaps ever be met to perfection because of the conflicts built into the system.

The most difficult problem is related to the dependency of the clients for whom behavior modification is often judged appropriate. Many of the individuals are judged by society to be incapable of major decision making by virtue of mental incompetence or disturbance of thought and for that reason have been institutionalized. Thus it may appear illogical to expect decisions on treatment or goals from these patients. Perhaps it is this situation that makes the courts and the public regard the professional-client relationship in this case with greater concern than the ordinary relationship between physician and patient, lawyer and client, or accountant and client. In each of these latter cases action may be taken, whatever its merits and possible consequences, without a real understanding by the client of the alternatives and hazards or benefits. Yet because the client is assumed to be capable of accepting or rejecting such action, in general the spirit of *caveat emptor* prevails. The rise in malpractice litigation seems to indicate that some individuals, at least, are beginning to doubt the role of the professional as an unquestioned authority figure.

The situation of the prisoner client has some of the same implications. Perhaps the question of ability to make judgments is less important, but nevertheless the question of ability to judge on the basis of accepted social norms may be raised. Since it may be assumed that a difference in behavior from that accepted as normative caused the institutionalization of such prisoners, how should this circumstance affect their role as a decision maker as to therapeutic goals?

In the case of institutionalized patients, the dual role of the therapist as an advocate of what is best for the patient and what is best for the institution causes serious problems. If the patient is not considered competent to make decisions, as in the case of a retarded or psychotic patient, the family may be considered as the ultimate client. Yet the family may have a vested interest because of the need for continued institutionalization of the patient and thus may become a mere adjunct of the institutional bureaucracy.

A familiar example of the extreme to which institutional power may reach is the use by repressive governments of mental institutions as repositories for influential dissidents. However, even in more usual circumstances, repressive influences such as staff convenience, workload, and the avoidance of "problems" that might reflect unfavorably upon the administration can be powerful and sometimes effective forces that may divert clinical workers from adherence to the ethical standards that they endorse in the abstract. There is something very reinforcing to the clinician about working in an orderly, smoothly functioning institution. It is in this regard that some behavioral techniques are subject to misuse. The clinician must resist the pressure or temptation to rationalize punitive or overly controlling procedures as treatment.

Institutional efficiency and stability are important considerations both for staff and patients. However, one might argue that, except for purely custodial settings, the job of the institution is to help patients acquire more adaptive ways of responding so that they can lead productive, satisfying lives. Is a token economy the most effective means of helping individuals acquire new adaptive social responses such as the ability to trust and share with others? While the technology of the token economy is a valuable one, it is subject to simplistic applications and to abuse. Most of the behaviors of hospitalized patients for which tokens are given are not "new" responses; for example, most patients know how to make beds, mop floors, and speak when spoken to. Often the major contribution of a token economy is to provide the motivation for use of responses already in the individual's behavior repertory.

Braginsky and Braginsky (1973) have compellingly described the mental hospital as a haven for certain individuals who elect to live the type of institutional life it provides. The Braginskys point out the individual who wants to maintain his adaptation to life by residing in an institution will learn the rules, mores, and conventions of the mental hospital. If the Braginskys are correct in believing that the mental hospital is a resort or haven of a sort for a large number of patients, then it would not be especially noteworthy if the patients adhered to the rules of the game as laid down by the token economy. Furthermore, if the Braginskys' research has generality (as it seems to have in the case of mental retardation), it would be desirable to explore therapeutic environments other than the mental hospital that show promise of going beyond institutional stability to providing individuals who have a maladaptive behavioral repertory with opportunities to do more than conform, to help them achieve higher degrees of happiness and independence. Fairweather's (1964) efforts to create personally meaningful work and social settings appears especially promising in this regard as does the Braginskys' suggestion concerning the establishment of cooperative retreats.

Common to the approaches of Fairweather and the Braginskys is the emphasis on giving patients, clients, or residents as much responsibility for themselves as they can bear. Clearly, there will be many instances in which an individual is not in a position to assume much responsibility. Yet in any given case the clinician or intervenor should, to the greatest extent possible, plan a therapeutic approach in concert with the patient. Yet another problem recognized by Stolz and others lies in the possible divergence between the value system of the therapist and the patient. This divergence would be likely simply from the class differences often found between therapist and the patient in a public institution. How much consideration should be given to differences in these subsocietal norms? Here the adaptation value of the norms for the patient must be scrutinized.

The guidelines suggested by Davison and Stuart (1975) have a rational appeal and represent a coherent approach to the many questions raised in work with institutionalized persons. The contractual model described by Schwitzgebel (1975) also has considerable rational appeal. The danger in such approaches is the seductive effect of using these guidelines as criteria in their narrow sense and not recognizing, as Stolz has so succinctly pointed out, that to fully meet them is impossible. On the other hand, if they are used as reminders and consciousness raisers, they can serve a useful function.

Perhaps the most useful guideline is that suggested by Morris (1966)—the "principle of least severity." Under this precept clients should be exposed to the least possible risk and discomfort to obtain the greatest possible expected benefit. This would require that patients or inmates not enter programs with a level of comfort less than the institutional practice it is intended to replace. This principle together with the principles of the Wyatt decision[1] which began enumerating the rights of hospitalized mental patients should prevent many of the abuses that have been cited.

Wexler (1973) has pointed out the need for some comparative data on the effectiveness of the token economy as compared with other approaches. He and others suggest that the previously mentioned work of Fairweather must be taken into account as an alternative approach. Wexler believes that, in addition to reliance on behavior modification techniques, the development of problem-solving and decision-making skills is necessary. Some information is already available to indicate that token economies are not effective in altering the behavior of a significant number of individuals. If recent legal decisions in the field of patient rights and the trend to increased legislation in this area are not to drive out the use of this tool, it must be made clear that the procedures are at least as effective and humane as available alternatives.

As Wexler (1973), Davison and Stuart (1975), and Begelman (1975) have pointed out, in spite of the narrowing of options for the therapist because of decisions regarding patient rights, the rights of the patient to secure treatment and to refuse treatment are unclear areas as is the possible conflict between these and the right of society to enforce certain behavioral standards. An additional unresolved problem concerns the rights of society in relation to the behavior of individuals. What should be the decision when these rights conflict? What rights does society have to establish homogeneous behavior?

Stolz's summation of the variables and difficulties involved should help clarify the problem areas and direct attention to standards, areas of conflict, and areas proper for intervention. If court decisions in the area of patient rights are to be helpful to as well as protective of those involved, an effort to provide better comparative data on the efficacy of various methods will be as important as legal precedents.

---

[1] *Wyatt v. Stickney,* 344 F. Supp. 373, 379–382 (M.D. Ala, 1972) (Bryce and Searcy Hospitals).

# REFERENCES

Bandura, A. *Principles of behavior modification.* New York: Holt, Rinehart and Winston, 1969.

Begelman, D. A. Ethical and legal issues of behavior modification. In M. Hersen, R. M. Eisler, & P. M. Miller (Eds.), *Progress in behavior modification* (Vol. 1). New York: Academic Press, 1975.

Braginsky, B. M., & Braginsky, D. D. Stimulus/response: Mental hospitals as resorts. *Psychology Today*, 1973, *6,* 26–32.

Davidson, G. C., & Stuart, R. B. Behavior therapy and civil liberties. *American Psychologist*, 1975, *30,* 755–763.

Fairweather, G. W. (Ed.). *Social psychology in treating mental illness: An experimental approach.* New York: Wiley, 1964.

Morris, N. Impediments to penal reform. *University of Chicago Law Review*, 1966, *33,* 627–656.

Schwitzgebel, R. K. A contractual model for the protection of the rights of institutionalized mental patients. *American Psychologist*, 1975, *30,* 815–820.

Wexler, D. B. Token and taboo: Behavior modification, token economies, and the law. *California Law Review,* 1973, *61,* 81–109.

# II

# ENCOUNTER GROUPS

# 4
# ETHICAL ISSUES IN AND AROUND ENCOUNTER GROUPS

JOHN C. GLIDEWELL

The University of Chicago

The purposeful use of the forces generated in small groups to induce a self-sustaining development of human resources in individuals is a controversial and sharply challenging activity. In spite of this, the use of such forces is widely prevalent today. The conflicts of values and ethical issues that surround such groups deserve careful analysis. This chapter is an attempt at such an analysis by a social scientist who is experienced in the study of small groups and inexperienced in the study of ethics.

It is important to understand that it is not my purpose to evaluate encounter groups. I have conducted such groups for over 25 years, and I believe that on balance they have been valuable to the participants and to the society. I also believe some terrible things have happened in the name of encounter groups, largely as a result of conflicts in values held within the groups as well as between the groups and their environment. Some agents have publicized most unlikely goals, some employers have forced employees to attend training groups under threat of economic punishment, and some agents have exploited the emotional confusion of participants to satisfy their own sexual desires. Such things have occasionally happened. My purpose is to make explicit some of the value conflicts involved and to propose possible management or, where feasible, resolution of the conflicts.

In addition, I shall not undertake to settle questions of fact with

69

empirical data, as important as I believe that task to be. My question is not "What is happening?" My question is "What ought to be happening?"

## THE PHENOMENON

The term *encounter group* will be used to include a variety of social interventions in group contexts: T-groups, sensitivity training groups, personal growth groups, human potential groups, marathon groups, Tavistock workshops, and so forth. I shall specify some characteristics or dimensions along which these groups may be differentiated among themselves and from other groups.

The general goals of encounter groups are to induce self-sustaining changes in the usual behavior of the participants, first inside the group, then in a larger environment. Specific goals are quite varied, but a few are common enough to justify using them as a basis for analysis. These common goals are the development of self-awareness, empathy for others, authenticity, emotional expressiveness, joy, self-esteem, and knowledge of—as well as skill in—controlling such group dynamics as conformity pressures, interpersonal conflict, attraction and repulsion, or allocation of social power.

The prime movers in attaining these goals are the social forces developed in a small group, which is usually composed of 6 to 15 people, in face-to-face interaction, with or without a leader. One such force is often described as a structure vacuum and is evident when the participant is deprived of the usual social cues specifying acceptable and relevant behavior. The lack of such social cues forces individuals to rely on personal predispositions as determinants of their behavior. Through this process, it is reasoned, the true personality or true interpersonal style of the individual can be quickly exposed.

In spite of this strongly felt sense of structure vacuum, the usual basic components of social structure are in fact clearly established. For example, when there are institutionally designated agents, they announce their position. They often explain that, because the method is cooperative, they will not be conventional leaders, will not set agenda, will not give instructions, and indeed will take less responsibility for the success of the group than the participants might usually expect of a group leader. It is, however, clear that these people have been appointed by the sponsoring organization to take some especially important role, and, within some limits, they are prepared to take responsibility for the welfare of the individual participants.

There is at least one role complementary to that of the agent: the participant. The participants are less experienced in this sort of activity, they are seeking some goal and expect the group to be a means of attaining it, and, if they are to remain, they are willing to negotiate a division of collaborative responsibilities between them, their fellow participants, and the agent for the success in attaining their goals.

High value is placed, explicitly and implicitly, on open expressions of feelings, opinions, and ideas. Participants are usually encouraged to say what they think and how they feel about what is happening in the group.

Attention is focused on the here and now. Participants are discouraged from discussing actions, opinions, or feelings experienced elsewhere unless these are clearly connected as antecedents to or consequences of their current group behavior.

The groups tend to move, usually rapidly in repeated cycles, through some characteristic social-emotional climates: a climate of prudent exploration in search for accommodation to unexpected or disconfirming experiences, a climate of conflict and confrontation in search for norms controlling the kind and intensity of hostility to be expressed, a climate of solidarity and mutual affection in search for norms controlling the kind and intensity of intimacy to be established, and a climate of dependency and counterdependency in search of an acceptable division of social power and responsibility between agents and participants.

Often nonverbal methods of communication are emphasized as a part of any climate. Such nonverbal activity is especially provocative because it is difficult to interpret and because it symbolizes many taboo behaviors, for example, hostile striking, infantile clinging, and erotic touching.

Originally (1947–1957), self-analytic groups devoted much time and attention to review, analysis, and consensual control of group climate, group pressure, individual influence (especially the agent's), or nonverbal activity. Indeed, it was often felt to be a bit absurd that quite short events could lead to quite long analyses. Currently, however, some hold that it is the experience, or the process of expression, which is the goal and the essence of the learning. Analysis, especially consensual analysis, it is held, would add nothing and perhaps even destroy the essence of the learning.

In addition, some groups simply provide a context—almost a theater—for the dyadic interaction between the agent and one participant. The use of the group as audience for a sequence of agent-participant exchanges entails little attention to the understanding or control of the social processes or social forces generated in the group.

In this broad and rough sketch, then, I consider a wide range of small, face-to-face, self-improvement groups differing in specific goals and extent of prescribed structure, emphasizing open verbal and nonverbal expression of ideas and feelings, usually about what is currently taking place in the group, but varying widely in attempts at analysis and control of group forces.

For several reasons I use the word "agent" to refer to individuals who conduct encounter groups. An obvious and easier alternative is "leader," but in spite of the widespread public tendency to think of the agent as a leader, individuals who conduct encounter groups often (although not always) intentionally refuse to act in a way typical of leaders in other groups, as I have already indicated. Encounter group agents are in fact authorized to act on behalf of others (participants and sponsoring agency), employed to obtain specified results, however personal or subjective, and trained to induce reactions by their actions. Thus, the usual dictionary definitions of agent are satisfied. In addition, the term is consistent with the term *change agent* used in this book. The most pertinent reason for using agent is that it serves to emphasize that the duties and values of the agent are often in conflict with the duties and values of conventional group leaders. Ethical issues may thus be made clearer.

## VALUE SYSTEM AND SOCIAL SYSTEM

At this point I shall set out a conceptual structure to be used for the analysis of the ethical issues.

The concept of value is not very precise, but for the present purposes, I conceive of a value as any quality or conditon held by the members of a culture (or many cultures) to be good either as an end in itself or as a means to other ends. The values at issue when encounter groups are used as a means of social intervention are life, welfare, justice, freedom, truth, and development.

The value of *life* includes not only the sustenance of life but also physical safety and precedence of humanity over property. *Welfare* is used in its broadest sense to mean an extension of life by the availability of food, health, space, time, privacy, beauty, or money to exchange for them. *Justice* is the fair distribution of goods and harms based, by some standard of comparison, either on equality, or on contribution to the collectivity, or on need for welfare or development. *Freedom* is defined following Warwick and Kelman (1973) and the Population Task Force (1971) as opportunity, capacity, and incentive to make reflective choices and to act on them. *Truth* is valid knowledge and valid representation of the world and the self, based on extrapersonal criteria of validity. *Development* means an increase in the refinement, utility, or time-space availability of resources.

A theme running through the arguments to be presented locates the values involved in a reflexive cycle of values. I assume that individual development depends on individual life. Life depends on the availability of food, safety, health, space, time, or the money to secure them. Life, therefore, depends on welfare. In turn, the general welfare of all those affected by any act depends on justice in the allocation of food, safety, health, space, and time or money. In its turn, justice—the fair allocation of goods and harms—depends on freedom. Fair allocation requires that people act fairly and thus requires the opportunity, capacity, and incentive for individuals or governing bodies to make reflective choices about what is fair and to act accordingly. (A common justification of unjust acts is that of social constraint: "That's the way the system works.") Reflective choice requires foresight, the capacity to anticipate the consequences of one's choices, which in turn depends on valid knowledge of one's self and the world. Thus freedom depends on the availability of truth. Recognition of the truth depends on increasing refinements of cognitive, emotional, and social differentiation, integration, and adaptability to new information. The recognition of truth thus depends on development. Development depends on life, and the cycle is complete. In summary, development depends on life, life depends on welfare, welfare depends on justice, justice depends on freedom, freedom depends on truth, and the recognition of truth depends on development.

Shifting now from the assumed value system to the assumed social system, consider that three principal actors are involved in the encounter group phenomenon: the agent, the participant, and the society. While agents vary widely in their roles, each is readily identifiable. The same clear identity applies to participants. The society, however, has a much vaguer identity. One might specify "interested society" as a geographically scattered collection of people who (1) are in some way explicitly affected by encounter group activities, (2) are in some form of intermittent communication with each other by some media, (3) have an interest in achieving some degree of consensual validation of the claims of encounter group proponents and opponents, and (4) have the social power, separately or jointly, to appoint social agents and warrant their use of coercive power over those who conduct encounter groups. To the extent that the conduct of encounter groups is a professional practice, members of the society are likely, based on past efficacy, to appoint some small board of trusted professional practitioners to certify and maintain surveillance over encounter group activities in the society's general interest. In addition, the practitioners themselves are likely to form a professional association with the aim of prescribing training, limiting entry, and maintaining surveillance over encounter group activities in the interest of the profession.

Because the society is an inescapably vague entity, one has a tendency to overlook its role and to focus on the dyad of agent and participant. As I have argued before (Glidewell, 1972, 1975), society is critically important. It has rights and duties to move the conduct of encounter groups toward core values—those qualities and conditions widely held to be good by the members of the society. The members of the society may take action through informal means (such as withdrawal of patronage) or through some authorized social agent.

Each of the principal actors involved has some duties to each of the other actors to supply some valued resources. Moreover, if one actor has a duty to supply resources to the other, then the other has a right to expect to be supplied with those resources. This complementarity (not reciprocity) of rights and duties is a basic assumption of this analysis. It means that for each duty of one actor to another, there is, by definition, a right of the other to expect that duty to be performed. Gouldner (1960) has shown the clarity and utility of this definition of complementarity in sociological theory and its distinction from the definition of "reciprocity" as used in the following paragraph. Table 1 illustrates the minimal duties and rights of the agent, the participant, and the society as they are involved in encounter groups.

The values involved in evaluating the resources interchanged determine the reciprocity of the interchange. If one receives from the system resources valued equitably to those one has supplied to the system, reciprocity is implied. I assume (with Gouldner) that reciprocity is a strong social force, indeed, a universal social norm. At the same time, I also assume that inequity, a violation of the norm of reciprocity, is quite acceptable under conditions when equality is valued more than equity or when some actors are believed to have more strongly urgent or vital needs than others. The seriously injured person is not expected to reciprocate for help offered; the small child is not expected to reciprocate for nurturance.

I also assume that value priorities depend on time. Some values are sacrified in the short term with the goal of recovery in an enhanced form in the long term. This time factor is critical in most efforts to learn, because learning often involves the disruption of some valued present condition, belief, or skill in order to develop, after a time, a more valued one. Accordingly, time must often be included in the conceptual structure of the analyses to follow.

The agent-participant-society interchange contains inherent value conflicts. Between the agent and the participant there is an issue of justice. The participant exchanges short-term welfare (money, privacy, anxiety) and freedom for both the truth about and the development of his or her capacities. Because of the personal nature of the development, the possibility exists that the participant will acquire a false but enjoyable sense of having struggled and developed, and in return quite willingly pay the agent for that acquisition. Several subtle aspects of such an exchange will be analyzed.

The society loses values in such a shared developmental myth. Justice is

**TABLE 1.** Some Minimal Rights and Duties of Actors Involved in Encounter Groups

|  |  | Right to expect | | |
|---|---|---|---|---|
|  |  | Agent | Participant | Society |
| Duty to supply | Agent |  | Enriched opportunity to develop human resources | Enhanced, socially valued human resources |
|  | Participant | Participation Money |  | Utilization of enhanced resources |
|  | Society | Social power Esteem | Protection from exploitation |  |

lost, and welfare, freedom, and truth may also be sacrificed. The interested society, however, may accept the risk of an unexamined myth. A society will often maintain a myth to protect an ideal of enablement and to relieve an anxiety about the abuse of such an enablement. The role and the several interests of the society will be analyzed.

In the following sections I employ this conceptual structure to consider the value conflicts entailed in goals and goal setting, entry and exit (the process of target selection), the actions of agents and participants (the means chosen), and the assessment of the consequences, anticipated and unanticipated.

## ON GOALS AND GOAL SETTING

Three categories of the goals previously specified can be used as valid representatives of the range of goals currently articulated. The first category includes emotional expression as an end in itself. Closely related is joy, an emotion of great delight, keen pleasure, and personal fulfillment. Such goals are emphasized by growth centers such as those stimulated by Esalen and described by Schutz (e.g., 1968). The second category includes two goals: self-awareness, a valid and accurate recognition of one's actions, thoughts, motives, and feelings; and self-respect, the positive valuing of one's self. Such goals are emphasized by the encounter groups conducted by Carl Rogers (1961) and his associates. The third category includes two goals: interpersonal competence, the capacity to influence one's social environment with efficacy, specifically to influence the social forces generated by interaction in small groups; and sensitivity, a capacity to sense and empathize with the feelings and ideas of others. The goals of sensitivity and interpersonal competence are emphasized by the regular T-groups of the National Training Laboratories (Benne, Bradford, Gibb, & Lippitt, 1975; Bradford, Gibb, & Benne, 1964). All the goals are shared to some extent by most forms of encounter groups, but this differentiation in emphasis aids in specifying the ethical issues surrounding the conduct of the groups.

### The Agent's Duties and the Participant's Rights

The role of the agent is the point of focus in the ethical questions of goal setting in encounter group activities. Should the agent set the goals for the participants or should the agent simply provide the freedom necessary for each participant to pursue personal goals? Should agents provide opportunity, incentive, and ability for negotiation between themselves and the participants, and among participants, concerning what the group and individual goals should be? Should the agents ensure that the goals, however set, are attainable at fair costs, significant for individual development, and extrapersonally verifiable? The question of the attainability of goals at a fair cost is critical in many of the aspects of these controversies.

Some agents maintain that (1) it is not possible for any agent to judge what goals are attainable by any individual, and (2) all participants should be free to choose their own goals. Two values are thus invoked: (1) the value of truth about the limits of the agent's ability and the extent of the person's individuality, and (2) the value of the freedom to set one's own goals. One issue concerns the truth about the agent's ability. If the agent's experience with encounter groups does not make the agent more able than the participant to know what goals are attainable at what costs, then the agent's influence on goal setting will not enhance attainability. Experience in encounter groups does increase ability to judge what goals are attainable at fair costs, and by offering their services publicly, agents are claiming their greater experience. They thereby claim their ability to judge the attainability of goals. Accordingly, the value of the agent's knowledge (the recognition of truth) is in conflict with the value of the participants' freedom to choose their own goals. Freedom to select an unattainable or extravagant goal is indeed freedom. Further, some development may accrue from the experiental disconfirmation of the idea that a particular goal can be attained in an encounter group. But I maintain that such development is less likely and more costly than the development accruing from attaining a realistic goal.

Other agents maintain that, because of their experience in encounter groups and their knowledge of psychosocial development, they are competent to judge not only the attainability of goals but also whether attaining such goals will contribute to the development of most individuals. Accordingly, they make public announcements or advertise specific goals that may be attained at fair costs by participation in encounter groups.

The agent's interest in attracting participants (the value of the agent's welfare) may lead the agent to advertise unobtainable goals, or goals not readily attainable by most participants. The participants' interest in their own development may lead them to be attracted by the opportunity to attain a desired, but difficult goal. In this joint attraction there is a conflict of interest between agent and participant: the agent's value on personal welfare is in conflict with the participant's value on personal development.

To cope with this conflict, agents rarely guarantee the attainment of any goal. Agents often value collaborative goal setting and initiate and maintain negotiations between themselves and participants and among participants. The negotiations concern what goals are to be set and for whom. Inherent in the negotiations is a joint responsibility for the attainability, the cost estimate, and the developmental significance of the goals negotiated. Accompanying the negotiations is a gradually increasing specification of the commitment to agreed-upon goals. Prior to entry, the agents specify some very general goals. After entry, as the group develops and negotiations continue, the goals become more specific and limited by conditions in the group as well as more differentiated and particular to an individual participant. Each of the stages of the negotiations depends on the outcomes of the prior stages, so that the goal may change to become more realistic and more significant for the development of the participant.

The conflict between the development and freedom of the participant must be confronted at all those times (during the continuing negotiations) when the agent is judged to know better than the participant what goals are attainable and significant for the development of the participant. As the agent's influence increases, the freedom of the participant is reduced. The opportunity for the participant's development is enhanced up to the limit of the agent's true ability. As the agent's influence decreases, the freedom of the participant increases. The opportunity for the participant's development is reduced to the extent of the loss of the use of the agent's true ability. As the agent and the participants become preoccupied with extending freedom, they find themselves, often in retrospect, missing opportunities for realistic development. Similarly, as the agent and participants become preoccupied with quite specific and realistic goal accomplishment, they find themselves, often in retrospect, missing opportunities for freedom of choice and action. In the extreme, either condition is likely to cause alarm in both the participants and the interested society.

Agents may claim no special knowledge of what goals are attainable or developmental. They may thus accept no duty to recommend goals and no right to deference to their recommendations. They may still have a duty to negotiate. Such a duty is implied by a joint interest in the value of the truth of attainability or by a joint interest in the value of development, even highly individualized development.

I maintain that the agent has a duty to provide, and the participant has a right to expect, freedom in two domains. The first is the freedom for the participants to pursue their own goals. Because individual goals often conflict, a second freedom is vital—the opportunity, capacity, and incentive to negotiate concerning goal selection. Negotiation does not preclude extreme positions that sacrifice the values of development or of freedom, but, in groups with participants from diverse backgrounds, it provides some checks and balances against extreme sacrifices of one of the conflicting values. When both agent and participants are consensually invested in one of the values, the group may sacrifice the conflicting value so extremely that the interested society becomes alarmed.

The position taken is summarized in Table 2. The agent has a duty to provide and the participant a right to expect:

1. The truth in the specification of goals, including attainability, developmental benefits, and welfare costs.
2. The freedom to pursue the participant's own goals.
3. The freedom to negotiate with the agent and other participants about goal selection.

**TABLE 2.** Rights and Duties with Respect to Goal Setting in Encounter Groups

| | | Right to expect | |
|---|---|---|---|
| Duty to supply | Agent | Participant | Society |
| Agent | | Truth in goal specification, including attainability developmental benefits welfare costs<br>Freedom to pursue own goals<br>Freedom to negotiate goal setting | Truth in goal specification, including attainability developmental benefits welfare costs<br>Position on basis of verification of goal attainment |
| Participant | Truth in goal specification<br>Freedom to pursue own goals<br>Freedom to negotiate goal setting<br>Acceptance of short-term welfare risk | | Truth in own goal specification<br>Position on basis of verification of goal attainment |
| Society | Freedom to pursue goals<br>Freedom to negotiate goal setting | Freedom to pursue goals<br>Freedom to negotiate goal setting | |

Such conditions allow for but do not guarantee the emergence of attainable goals at fair costs and the emergence of developmental goals for all involved. The conditions neither preclude conflicting goals nor ensure the resolution of such conflict. The conflicts occur between agent's values and participant's value. They also occur between the several values of each.

## The Participants' Duties and the Agent's Rights

Implied in the agent's duty to provide negotiation is a joint responsibility. The participants also have a duty to provide the freedom for the agents to pursue their own goals as long as these are not in conflict with those of the participants. When goals do conflict, the participants also have a duty to provide the freedom to negotiate. This requires some competence in negotiation by participants and some knowledge of their particular broader interests in other domains of development—for example, health, economics, religion, politics, aesthetics—domains with goals potentially in conflict with those to be pursued in an encounter group.

Further, the participants' duty to supply the opportunity, capacity, and incentive to negotiate implies that they, too, have some share of the responsibility for setting attainable and developmental goals. The amount of responsibility taken by agents and participants is determined by their relative levels of experience and psychosocial knowledge. The agents' greater experience and knowledge make their duties primary and the participants' secondary. As specified earlier, the conflict is between freedom and development of the participant. The sharing of duties in accord with capacities does not resolve the conflict.

A related ethical issue arises from the position taken by some agents that they must not set any goals for the group or the individual participants. These agents feel that setting goals would ascribe to them greater knowledge than they have and unethically curtail the freedom of the participants. Back (1972), however, has maintained that such disclaimers made by agents of encounter groups are fraudulent because they in fact do pursue a goal—spontaneous expression of feelings as an end in itself. Thus, Back claims, the ethical issue involved is not a conflict between values but a simple fraud, a violation of the value of truth. Clearly both the agents and the participants have the duty to tell the truth, as well as they know the truth, about their own goals and their willingness to negotiate with others about their goals. There can be no foresight to judge the attainability, costs, and developmental significance of any concealed goal. This duty is also a duty to the society, because the society has an interest in knowing the truth about the goals of any activity promising the enhancement of human resources.

The second category of goals—self-awareness and self-respect—presents inherent conflicts between the value of development and the value of freedom. Development can also be a short-term threat to welfare. One participant said this during a T-group:

I began to realize I was being attacked, mostly unfair, accused me wrongly. Everybody. And then I caught one thing. I had, before, when I would see a weakness in somebody, I'd, I'd, uh, bore in, stab. I did alright, I did. . . . And I suddenly knew it, and I died. I hurt. It was like a pain deep in me. I was miserable, hurt, guilty, ashamed, dumb, awful. I had never seen it before. I paid a lot for that, that moment, that truth. I paid a lot.

The goal of self-awareness assumes a prime value of truth, in this case, truth about one's self. Granting for the moment that the truth about one's self is available, should one be compelled to know it? May one choose to be ignorant of one's self? What sacrifice of the value of freedom (for self-deception or self-ignorance) is justified in a search for the value of truth? Encounter group members may be subject to pressures and attacks by the agent and other members. Some of these attacks may be invalid; others may carry some truth. How much freedom from abuse must one forfeit in the quest for self-awareness? Even when validly represented, some truths about one's self can be ignored with little loss, while others may be worth a sacrifice of freedom, especially if it is a limited freedom to choose an uneasy peace in ignorance of one's self.

Further, is self-awareness to be sought at the sacrifice of welfare, that is, health, space, time, or privacy? A new awareness of some true fault in one's self can injure one's health. Shame is not a natural enemy of welfare, but it is hazardous to it. The acquisition of self-awareness in the course of group interaction involves some degree of public disclosure of strengths and weaknesses, a violation of the value of privacy. What intrusions on privacy are justified in the interests of self-awareness?

This conflict between truth and welfare is a source of continuing negotiation between the agent and the participants. It also involves informal communication between prospective participants and others in the society. Casey (1972) has given an expressive example of this in her account of her decision to join a group:

> In the days before going to the first meeting of the group I talked with friends and acquaintances of mine about my forthcoming activity. Invariably comments and questions were couched in risk language. The stake seemed to be my mental health or some part of it. Comments like, "I've heard (or I think) those groups can really be dangerous without a really qualified leader," seemed to speak to the stake. . . . Sometimes the people I discussed this with felt the need to place themselves along the risk continuum with comments like: "I'd like to do something like that but I'd have to be very sure of the leader." (p. 5)

Generally, the risk of welfare and freedom in the quest for truth about one's self is seen as a short-term risk. Any temporary loss of welfare is expected to be more than regained in the long term. In my schema, freedom and welfare require foresight, and truth contributes to long-term foresight. Thus, the short-term loss may be more than regained in the long run. The conflict is generated each time personal welfare is put at risk in the quest for self-awareness.

The third category of goals—sensitivity and interpersonal competence—involves behavior contingent on the behavior of others. Thus, these goals are more nearly amenable to extrapersonal verification. But they, too, may generate a conflict between truth and welfare. If self-awareness places one's welfare at risk, so does sensitivity. The sensing and empathizing with the feelings and ideas of others include especially feelings and ideas of others about one's self. In this respect the ethical issues are similar to those surrounding the self-awareness and self-respect goals. What sacrifice of welfare is justified in the quest for sensitivity? The agent has a duty to protect the participants from long-term losses of welfare due to goals that demand a sacrifice of welfare. The participants have a duty to risk their short-term welfare in the pursuit of personal development.

My position is summarized in Table 2. Participants have a duty to supply and agents have a right to expect:

1.  The truth in the participants' specification of their goals with secondary responsibility for estimating the attainability, welfare costs, and developmental benefits.
2.  Freedom for agents to pursue their goals.
3.  Freedom for agents to negotiate about goal setting.
4.  Acceptance of a short-term risk of welfare.

## The Rights and Duties of the Interested Society

As specified earlier, the interested society has an investment in the possible human resource development or deterioration in encounter groups. Relatives, friends, employers, employees, customers, clients, or sponsors have a right to expect both the agent and the participants to tell the truth about their goals for enhancing the participants' resources, which are of value to these interested parties. They also have a right to expect that these truthfully represented goals are developmental, attainable at fair cost, and verifiable.

A difficult ethical issue is generated by the fact that some of the goals of encounter groups (expression, joy, affection), however well chosen, are inherently personal and idiosyncratic. It is difficult for one to deny or confirm another individual's belief that he or she has attained a capacity to express great delight or deep grief. If validity, that is, truth, requires that progress toward such goals must be extrapersonally verifiable, then a conflict is generated between such personal goals and the value of truth, as extrapersonally established. Encounter group proponents often value the truth of autonomous expression above the truth of extrapersonal verification. The society, however, which requires some shared standard of value in the interest of distributive justice in exchange of resources, even human resources, demands extrapersonal verification. This conflict, among others, often places groups emphasizing expression and joy at odds with their environments. The agent in such cases has a duty to the society to take a position about whether verification is personal or extrapersonal and to provide goals that are verifiable according to the chosen standard.

Agents of encounter groups often maintain that society's insistence on extrapersonal verification undermines the potential usefulness of their work, because the society sets criteria quite incompatible with the true goals of their efforts. The interested members of society maintain that, on the other hand, denial of extrapersonal verification places the agents and their work outside the general duty of accountability. The participants are often in the middle of this conflict. Sometimes they share the agent's commitment to personal verification—they feel they are the only holder of the truth about their own feelings. Sometimes, however, participants share the society's concern about their vulnerability to emotional contagion and to fraud if they are infected by such contagion. The conflict is between two (or more) ways of seeking truth. Extrapersonal verification is the most acceptable verification, but personal verification may be as much as can be expected if the specified goals are entirely personal. Along with the right to expect the truth about goals, therefore, goes the right to expect a clear statement on how goal attainment is to be verified, personally or extrapersonally.

An additional right has already been mentioned: the right of an interested society to be accurately informed about the likely developmental benefits and welfare costs of the goals available. This right may limit the learning opportunities that arise from highly desirable goals that demand great risks of welfare.

In return, the society has a duty to provide both participant and agent with the freedom to pursue their own goals and negotiate with others concerning group and individual goals.

The rights and duties of the interested society generate conflicts between the values of individual welfare and individual development. The acceptance of duties and rights of all the parties varies in cycles. As welfare is sacrified more extensively and intensively, the parties become alarmed, and a shift is made toward greater conservation of welfare. Subsequently, as developmental opportunities are constricted or frequently allowed to pass by, there is another alarm, and a shift is made toward greater risk taking. The continuing value conflict means that legitimate ethical alarms can be expected at regular intervals.

To the extent that encounter groups develop new interpersonal competencies of social worth, the values of development and justice come into play. Competence represents a new refinement of a human resource. How should the new resources be distributed? Insofar as competence is a basis for social power, the choice of participants constitutes a long-term allocation of social power. Because this conflict takes its form primarily at the point of entry into and exit from encounter groups, its analysis will be postponed until the following section.

### Summary

Each of the rights and duties of the parties involved generates some conflict of values: between development and freedom, between development and welfare, and between different bases of verification of truth. My position concerning the duties of the three parties with respect to goal setting is summarized in Table 2. However, even if all parties performed their duties with dedication, wisdom, and expertness, the value conflicts would remain. As the conditions of life and the conditions in an encounter group give high priorities to one value, the conflicting value will be sacrificed. As long as the value priorities of the agent and the participant are consistent, they will generate mutual development. When their values are in conflict, they will generate mutual interference, and all parties will become more vigilant monitors of the others.

As long as the value priorities in the group are consistent with those of the interested society, the group will be approved. Once the priorities conflict, the group activities will conflict with those the society believes are right, and, eventually, some form of social action will be taken to limit the goals and the process of setting them.

This discussion of goal setting necessarily overlaps the next section on entry and exit, because much goal setting must be renegotiated as the participant enters the group and afterward. In fact, as will be pointed out repeatedly, participation in encounter groups requires a gradual and cumulative process of commitment to both goals and means of attaining them, as well as an incremental management of the value conflicts entailed. The process proceeds in stages, and commitment to each stage is dependent on the outcomes of the prior stages. It is necessary, then, to turn next to the ethical problems involved in entry and exit.

## ON ENTRY AND EXIT

Because goal setting can be renegotiated after an encounter group has begun its activities, participants may find that advance knowledge of goals may not be an adequate basis for judging, prior to entry, whether participation will be in their best interest. It therefore becomes particularly

important that participants should have full and informed freedom of choice
to leave as well as to enter an encounter group. Each of the actors in the
encounter groups process—agents, participants, and society—has specific duties
toward the other two actors. In addition, value conflicts among these actors
are likely to surround the points of entry and eixt.

## Agent to Participant

Agents have the duty to supply all available valid information—the truth
as they know it—concerning the possible benefits and costs of entry and exit,
stage by stage in the development of the group. The agents are obligated to
specify what values may have to be sacrificed in favor of others.

The truth of any public statement by an agent or an association of agents
may be questionable. There is no escaping the fact that agents or an association of them may—even unknowingly—enhance their welfare by exaggerating
the value of their services and by limiting the communication of information
about any particular exploitation of participants. Reputation is often cited as
the best check on the statements of agents and is indeed the only recourse for
the participant in choosing to enter an encounter group.

It would appear that agents implicitly accept a duty to provide a basis
for a reputation, as well as a right to issue announcements that enhance that
reputation. Such announcements may take such forms as advertisements,
brochures, articles, books, research reports, and public addresses. Reputation,
however, must entail a conflict for the agent between the truth and a
jeopardized income (welfare). The conflict for the participant is between the
truth and the freedom to choose an attractive agent with a reputation for
questionable practices.

Warwick and Kelman (1973) and the Population Task Force (1971) have
defined freedom as the capacity, opportunity, and incentive to make and act
on reflective choices. The issue of capacity presents knotty problems. Can the
agent be assigned the duty to assess whether a participant has the capacity to
make a reflective choice? Must the agent screen prospective participants and
deny entry to those judged as unlikely to benefit?

One of the great ethical controversies centers around the claim that
professional practitioners—physicians, lawyers, architects, teachers—know
better what is good for the client than the client does. Such an appropriation
of clients' right to determine their own best interests is usually based on some
arcane knowledge (access to truth) that allows the practitioner to see consequences not apparent to the client. Current controversies about the rights of
clients include the positions that—as difficult as it may be—the base of arcane
knowledge must be communicable in common language, and that the appropriation of the clients' rights to determine their own self-interest should
require extensive negotiation, agreement, and regular reconsideration. As a
practical example of this controversy, should people undergoing
psychotherapy be required to provide their therapists' permission or recom-

mendation before being allowed to join an encounter group? The National Training Laboratories has decided that they must. Others would claim that each person should be allowed to make the decision for him or herself—after being supplied with all available valid information about the possible costs and benefits. The critical question is, under what conditions can a person be said to lack the capacity to grasp the significance of the possible costs and benefits?

The agent of an encounter group may forego any claim to the arcane knowledge necessary to anticipate consequences not apparent to the participant. Under such conditions the agent must either assume the participant's capacity to choose or refer the participant to some professional practitioner who does claim such arcane knowledge. If the agent assumes the participant's capacity to choose, the agent must also point out the risk that this assumption may be incorrect.

The key duty of the agent to the participants is to supply them with a clear and truthful statement of all available information about the costs and benefits of entry into and exit from an encounter group (see Table 3). Such truth depends on the agent's competence. Thus, the statement may vary in its

**TABLE 3.** Rights and Duties Involved in Entry into and Exit from Encounter Groups

| | | Right to expect | | |
| --- | --- | --- | --- | --- |
| | | Agent | Participant | Society |
| Duty to supply | Agent | | Truthful basis for reputation (demystification) All available valid information on benefits and costs of entry and exit | Truthful and clear explanation of benefits and costs of entry and exit Usual terms of entry and exit |
| | Participant | Careful consideration of the information available about the benefits and costs of entry and exit | | Acceptance of risk entailed in entry and exit |
| | Society | Review of agent's explanation of benefits and costs of entry and exit | Information, opportunity, and incentive for reflective choice of entry and exit Reputation of agent Appeal from coercive entry or exit | |

truth value directly with the agent's competence. Accordingly, a part of the agent's duty is to specify personal competence, and, with respect and tact, to invite the participants to examine their own competence to use the information the agent provides. Agents have no duty to deny entry or exit—once they have provided full information about the benefits and costs of entry or exit.

Even given the most conscientious performance, some values are sacrificed. If the agent's true information unduly frightens the participants, their capacity for choice and thus their freedom are sacrificed. If the agent's true information stimulates unrealistic hopes for personal development, the participants' capacity for choice and freedom are again sacrificed. If the agent minimizes the risks of welfare, and this sacrifice of the truth goes undetected, even if due to the participants' wishful exaggeration of the value of the prospects, the agent may thereby gain in esteem and in fees. Such situations tend to develop in the short run and may continue in the long run, if the cost of the sacrifice of truth is lower than the gain in experienced welfare to both agent and participants.

### Agent to Society

The agent has a duty to supply society with a truthful and clear explanation of the possible costs, benefits, and the usual terms of entry and exit. One may argue that the issue of freedom of entry and exit should be left strictly to the agent and the participant, but only the society has influence over both agent and participant. Thus, only the society has the power to protect both parties' rights and ensure that both fulfill their duties. In spite of the social isolation of some encounter groups, all groups are open systems and are greatly influenced by their environments. If agents do not supply an explanation of their work, journalists and competing agents will fill the gap—clearly a recent response to the popularity of encounter groups.

If an agent's conceptualization is quite technical, that agent's duty may be to a specified group of technically competent peers to whom society delegates the power to demand truthful and clear explanations. The International Association of Applied Social Scientists has adopted such a position. The association requires its members to periodically submit a theory explaining why they employ specific means for specific ends, including the means of entry and exit. These theories are reviewed for adequacy as one part of a peer evaluation process.

It is important that the agent's duty to society be limited to truth and clarity. It would be counterproductive to force agents to conform to knowledge acceptable to scientists, or to "good practice" acceptable to practitioners. If the agent's activities are unusual or deviant from more popular ones, that fact may enter into the participants' choice. If the society is clearly informed, the participants' freedom of choice is extended.

Perhaps, with respect to each of the three categories of goals of groups (expression-joy, self-awareness–respect, and sensitivity-competence), some consensus of good practice is now developing. It is still the case, nevertheless, that encounter groups, like most new purposive human-development practices, challenge some strong values (e.g., welfare as expressed in privacy) and some well-established ideas (e.g., extrapersonal verification) in the society. Back (1972) has proposed that this challenge of values and ideas, along with the affluence that gives people time to pursue their own development, accounts for the popularity of encounter groups. Whether or not his interpretation fits the data, such a value challenge is enhanced by a diversity of approaches, experimentation, and emphasis on creativity. In time, a consensus of good practice and consistency with accepted knowledge (scientific or otherwise) is likely to become established, and also, farther in time, challenged anew. Encounter groups and their agents will eventually be required to meet some standards of good practice in their public explanations and will eventually find those standards challenged. But the value of development is served by allowing an explicit, carefully reasoned, and publicly observed deviation from some old values and ideas. The fact that the practice is a deviation, however, does not relieve agents of the duty to be truthful, clear, and specific in their explanations of the costs and benefits of entry and exit.

## Participant to Agent

Participants have a duty to carefully consider the explanation given by agents of their goals and procedures and their costs and benefits. This duty of the participant to think is indeed limited by the time believed to be available and by the significance assigned to entering or leaving an encounter group. Assuming that any planned modification of the course of human development entails some dangers, to fail to consider the information available is caprice.

## Participant to Society

The participant has the duty to accept the risk involved in choosing whether or not to enter or exit. As in most cases of rights and duties, reciprocity is involved. Once participants have claimed the right to all available valid information about possible costs and benefits and the freedom to choose, they accept the reciprocal duty to accept the risks that accompany their choice. Once the society ensures the opportunity, capacity, and incentive to choose and act, it accepts no responsibility for protecting participants from a risk they have reflectively and voluntarily accepted.

## Society to Agent

The society places the prime value on truth and thus on an increasingly precise explanation of goals and methods of achieving them. The society has the duty to periodically review agents' explanations of their work. This review is usually delegated to some special group, often the agents' peers or competitiors, composed of people trusted by the society to be competent and interested. Often this periodic review is followed by some form of public legitimation such as licensing or certification, a sacrifice of freedom by both agent and participant. At least some encounter group agents reject licensing or certification, but most of them seek some form of legitimation, whether local, regional, or national. The International Association of Applied Social Scientists is making a strong bid to become the special group to whom the society delegates its power to review the explanations of agents of encounter groups.

One can argue that the society has a duty to the agent to supply opportunities for supervised training toward acquiring and maintaining competence. Where only truth and clarity of explanation are required, such a duty . would be difficult to specify. Where consistency with science and consensual good practice is required, the duty to train is generated.

### Society to Participant

The society has the duty to supply to the participant freedom to choose entry and exit. The society's power over both agent and participant is required to supply such freedom. Agents may enhance the participant's capacity to make a choice and they may advocate the opportunity and incentive for that choice, but only the society may grant the opportunity and control the incentives available. Consider the following illustration.

One of the most irksome tasks of the encounter group agent is to establish a developmental interchange with a participant who has been forced to enter the group by some social organization or agency that has coercive power over that individual. Such participants can, of course, be rejected by the agent, but if their welfare is at stake, as is often the case, a value conflict arises.

Once the coerced participant has been exposed to the activity and goal negotiation in the early stages of the group, full entry, that is, participation rather than mere attendance, may be based on informed choice—a kind of salvaging of freedom of choice with little sacrifice of welfare. This sort of graduated entry may resolve the conflict, but, more often, these participants feel constrained to participate actively, not out of their choice but out of loyalty to—or fear of punishment by—the sponsoring organization. Under such coercion, participants may experience painful conflicts in risking their privacy and welfare in return for a kind of development they do not want. The agent has little influence over such conflicts. Indeed, these participants are under the control of a power that is external to both the agent and the participant.

In such situations, the agent has a duty to inform the society, and the sponsoring agency in particular, that coerced participation is not likely to result in the development of the individual or the organization. Such a duty is a part of the agent's obligation to provide information about the benefits and costs of all forms of entry and exit. The social power, however, to punish the participant for refusing to enter or for insisting upon exit, is out of the hands of both the agent and the participant.

To what extent can society ensure that participants have the opportunity, capacity, and incentive to make a reflective choice of entry or exit? The society, as defined here, is only a scattered collection of people who are in communication, have vested interests, and have the authority to invest social agencies with coercive power. Accordingly, the society can provide some agency to which either agent or participant can appeal against a coercive demand for participation. The traditional agency is the court, but until legal precedents are established or codes enacted, some form of professional or trade association offers the best hope. Currently, in the interest of the agents and the society, the International Association of Applied Social Scientists is trying to develop a program of public education as a means of preventing both ill-advised and coercive referrals to applied social scientists, including encounter group agents.

The fact that the society has not yet acted to establish an agency ensuring freedom of entry and exit does not mean that it cannot act. Indeed several professional associations have taken action to inform their members and the public of the ethical issues involved, especially those surrounding entry into and exit from encounter groups. Information only explicates the conflict between the value of freedom of choice and the value of legitimate guidance (truth). By the definition of freedom and justice proposed here, the society must provide opportunity and incentive to make a reflective choice, and it must either assume the individual's capacity or provide some assessment of that capacity. As long as the society has doubts about the capacity of people in psychotherapy to make considered choice of entry or exit, questions about who is to assess capacity will abound. Should it be the therapist, the agent, the legal guardian, or the participants themselves?

Agents, like other practitioners, do develop reputations among the members of the interested society. The communicated judgment (the contribution to reputation) is often a retrospective one, based on an evaluation of the outcomes actually experienced and their costs in time, money, and risks to welfare. There may be a tendency, as I have reported before (Glidewell, 1972, p. 232), for participants to retrospectively perceive the outcomes to be more valuable than they really were. Encounter groups may increase this tendency. Back (1972) has asserted that, in sensitivity training, "the deep emotional experience may sometimes be threatening and frightening, but generally it is intense enough to leave a feeling of strong achievement, accomplishment, and frequently enjoyment in its wake" (p. 128). If, as seems likely, the emotional intensity of encounter groups does induce overevaluation, reputation is less valuable as a guide to entry.

Encounter groups also have a tendency to induce semimystical evaluations. In describing their experiences to others, participants are often
ambiguous and may make such comments as, "You have to experience it to
understand what it is." This tendency was the stimulus to the title of Back's
book, *Beyond Words*. The peculiarity of encounter groups leads to an
ambiguous or even mystical reputation for the method or for an agent. Such a
mystical reputation may attract participants, but it doesn't inform them in
deciding to enter or leave. Even with these limitations, however, reputation
may aid in making an informed decision about entry. The society usually
accepts a duty to convey the reputation of an agent.

## Summary

Table 3 presents a brief review of the exchange of duties among agent, participant, and society concerning entry into and exit from encounter groups. It is
important to note that the duty of each actor is also the right of the other
toward whom that duty is directed. That is the meaning of social complementarity as Gouldner (1960) has defined it. If any party—agent, participant, or
society—regularly performs a duty, the other party will come to believe it has
a right to have that duty performed. If any party comes to believe it has a
right, the other party is pressed to take on the duty or discontinue interaction. Clearly, much ambiguous negotiation is involved in the development of
complementary rights and duties, and that is what is currently taking place, at
least in the U.S. and Europe.

Must all possible risks be specified? Is that the "whole truth?" Or is the
whole truth less frightening? Should coerced participants be accepted? Many
coerced participants find the training valuable. What is competent peer review
of agents' practices? These controversies focus on whether or not each of the
actors will accept as duties the supplying of those resources that the others
maintain they have a right to expect.

The fundamental rationale of this position about rights and duties begins
with the argument that competence (development) is necessary, but not
sufficient, to recognize and communicate the truth, and, therefore, the agent's
own competence must be specified along with the truthful and clear information and explanation the agent must supply to the participant and the
society. The freedom of choice of entry and exit depends not only on
opportunity and incentive, but also on true information. If opportunity and
incentive, as well as capacity, for reflective choice are to be available, the
society must find some means of preventing coercive demands from social
institutions on prospective participants or enabling these participants to appeal
such demands. The society, however, having provided opportunity, capacity,
and incentive for a considered and voluntary choice, may in turn require that
the participant accept the risk of entry into and exit from an encounter group.

## ON CHOICE OF MEANS

A major concern about the choice of means in encounter groups is focused on the acts of the agent. Most agents claim that the learning experiences in the group can be temporarily stressful and disconcerting, but that the significance of the learning is worth the short-term cost of the stress. What, then, are the agent's duties to limit the losses? What are the duties of the participant and of the society? The agent's duties are the most salient in this regard.

### Agent to Participant

Both the agent and the participant find themselves committed to the valid (truthful) development of the human resources of the participant. To that end, each is prepared to invest some time, energy, and short-term sacrifice of freedom and welfare.

In the commitment to develop there is a duty to provide information, to provide an opportunity to act and respond to others, and to provide an incentive to observe, review, and analyze one's actions and responses. Within all these provisions, there is a duty to represent reality, especially those aspects of reality that disconfirm the participant's current ideas, beliefs, and expectations. Incident to the duties specified may be a number of skills: in the creation of settings, in the design of exercises, in the observation of behavior, in the articulation of interpretations of behavior, in the expression of a group mood, in the explication of a latent consensus, and in the reflection and clarification of the expression of others. Because there is so little current consensus on what constitutes good practice, ethical issues rarely involve the duty to provide a particular skill, except for the skill in representing reality. Incompetence or caprice in the confrontation of participants with disconfirmations of current beliefs dramatizes the inherent conflict between development and welfare.

In the willingness to sacrifice some freedom and welfare, there is a real and pervasive danger. Particular to each individual—agent as well as participant—there is a different and undiscovered limit past which the loss of welfare or freedom is not only overly painful but also deeply harmful in the long term. How can that limit be set? If the limit is too protective, development is reduced to insignificance. If too mush risk is allowed participants not only fail to develop their resources, but may destroy other important resources, for example, their health.

Many agents establish some prohibitions at the outset. For example, physical violence or drugs that reduce inhibitions may be prohibited. At various times, various agents have set limits on the time of meetings, on the discussion of certain problems involving people not in the group, and on the exploration of childhood experiences. Agents have a duty to explicitly set some specified limits on actions that endanger the welfare of participants. Such limit setting is not uniformly enabling or reassuring. Further, explicit limit setting in advance introduces the idea that some not-even-thought-of actions (e.g., violent attack) might have been considered and thereby arouses fears of other unknown dangerous actions one had not even thought of.

Perhaps the most common and most nearly innocuous limit is the explicit understanding that all participants have complete freedom to join or to remain apart from any discussion or activity that they believe would not, on balance, contribute to their learning. Such an option may seem too easy an escape from discomfort, but generally it is a mild counteraction to the strong social pressure to subscribe to a value on risk that often is brought to or generated in encounter groups.

A limit on scapegoating is relevant in groups where emotional contagion is likely. Prohibition is not relevant or effective. The agent is often constrained to support a person being scapegoated and to point out the fact of the scapegoating, along with the conditions giving rise to it. Such an intervention often generates considerations of both the issue of fact (Was it scapegoating?) and the issue of explanation (What brought it on?). From such considerations, group norms develop, and those norms establish limits on scapegoating. As always, the norms require a sacrifice of some freedom and some possibilities for development, both of which are in the interest of the participant's welfare.

How is it possible to know what limit is optimal? It is not possible to know. Both agent and participant must estimate, conduct low-risk experiments, reestimate, and reexperiment, in their attempts to increase the possibilities for learning and reduce the danger of destruction of long-term welfare.

There are ethical advantages to the means chosen by groups whose goal is the understanding and controlling of group pressures on individuals and vice versa. In such groups, any event is subject to analysis, and actions to control the psychosocial forces of groups on individuals are legitimate parts of learning experiences. One powerful limit on danger to individual welfare is the right to interrupt any activity in order to analyze its nature, its antecedents, and its consequences. Under such conditions, the perpetual conflicts between development and welfare are regularly reconsidered, and values are regularly reviewed for priority.

In summary, in order to make explicit the conflicts among development, freedom, truth, and welfare, the agent has a duty to make explicit in advance some limits on the sacrifice of short-term welfare, for example, the freedom to opt out of an activity and the prohibition of physical attack. In addition, the agent has a duty to intervene in some form to protect participants from their own vulnerability to some group pressures, for example, emotional contagion, conformity pressures, and scapegoating.

Many competent observers feel that the agent in encounter groups, by encouraging uninhibited expression of feelings, creates a pervasive and intensive emotional state of affairs that leads participants to believe that they have freely chosen to perform some act. But, in fact, the agent-created situation demands the act, and thus there is no freedom at all. These observers assert that the agent has deceptively induced the participants to act according to the agent's wishes.

Now that is saying quite a lot. I have often been in the agent's role, and there may have been times when I would have enjoyed having such knowledge and power. But the limit on my power has been just the expressive norm: that participants may choose to express any feelings they have about what is going on in the group. As long as that norm holds, any totalitarian suppression of opposing feelings is impossible.

In contrast to totalitarianism, some critics have attributed anarchy to encounter groups. It has been argued that expressions become autistic so that one hears only one's own expressions. I have never seen such a thing, but if it appears, then there is no longer a group, and one may not refer to or decry the power of the group or of a shared emotional state of affairs, or indeed the sharing of anything. Further, under such autistic conditions, agents have no influence; they are neither seen nor heard. In my opinion, the agent's primary duty to prevent such autistic conditions is a simple one. The agent must maintain as close a communication with participants as possible to avoid this situation.

Attributions of totalitarianism and anarchy probably have their basis in the fact that participants sometimes feel as if such conditions exist. Where analysis is a part of the work, once the group has reviewed and analyzed these conditions, fuller understanding and safeguards against the possibility of such conditions are developed. Where experiencing is the only goal, or where the group is a theater for an agent-participant dyad, less understanding develops, and distorted perceptions are more likely to be reported. The fact remains, however, that the norm of free expression of feelings and ideas is a powerful deterrent to totalitarianism, and both the usual solidarity and the usual interpersonal conflicts of group members are powerful deterrents to autism.

There is a related but more subtle danger. The participants' expectations and anxieties combine with the symbols of the situation (dress, language, even furniture or the lack of it) to create pressures toward disinhibition, expressiveness, and spontaneity that appear to be widely permissive but are in fact quite exacting social norms. As a result, some people who would prefer to be quiet become loud, some who would prefer to analyze and intellectualize become zestful wanderers, and some stoics are badgered into expressing feelings that they simply do not experience.

Added to the expectations and symbols may be the agent's acts—acts that unintentionally imply to participants that certain things are appropriate for discussion and others are not. The clearest of such acts is the close attention the agent gives to some interactions as compared to others. By their responses, agents can legitimate certain jokes, feelings, and expressions, which may come to be felt as pressures and constraints. The danger lies in the fact that it is difficult for agents to be aware of all the implications of their acts to the participants. In the interest of truth, agents must try to act authentically and openly. In the interest of both freedom and welfare, they must be aware of how their acts subtly imply unintended legitimate standards of conduct.

What are the feasible duties of the agent to the participant? Agents have a duty to the participant to set some advance limits on the sacrifice of the participant's short-term welfare, to intervene to protect any participant from group pressures, and to explicitly articulate the norms they intend to legitimize, to acknowledge that their acts may have unintended implications, and to regularly review and analyze the implications of their acts.

Agents often do not perform as I maintain they should. The most simple explanation of this fact is that it may be to the agent's advantage not to perform the duties outlined here. Examination of the implications of some agent's acts may reduce their welfare and jeopardize their reputations. On the other hand, participants are sometimes quite capable of protecting themselves from threats to their welfare or freedom. Sometimes groups are remarkably protective of their members. Sometimes particular members become specialists in protecting those seen as vulnerable. But there is a broader conceptualization of the agent's duties within the context of the duties of the participant and of the interested society.

## Participant to Agent

What is needed from the participant? If the agent is to provide information, opportunity to act, incentive to review and analyze, and representation of reality, what must participants do to realize their potential development? At a minimum, participants must consider the information, analyses, and disconfirmations.

If the agent has a duty to set advance limits on sacrifices of freedom or short-term threats to welfare, the participant has a duty to accept those limits or to negotiate changes in them as experience makes individual vulnerabilities more clear and precise. If the agent must intervene to protect the participant from group pressures, participants have a duty to accept that protection. If they do not, they release the agent from any liability for a loss of welfare. If the agent has a duty to make legitimate norms explicit, the participant has a duty to conform to those norms or to explicitly negotiate a change in them. If agents have a duty to review their acts and their implications, participants have a parallel duty to review their inferences about the agent's acts and the bases of those inferences.

All of this implies an interdependency. If the developmental goals of the group are to be attained, agent and participant must find a combination of resources that will generate development and limit the costs of it. The combinations are not remarkable: explication and consideration, limitation and negotiation, protection and acceptance, regulation and conformity or challenge, and analyses of implication and analyses of inference.

## Agent to Society

Society is interested because the resources to be developed by the participant are resources later to be employed in the joint interests of the participant and the society. Thus the agent's first duty is to return to the society a participant with enhanced resources. Because this development has a cost in welfare, the agent has a minimum duty to do no harm, that is, to limit the welfare costs as discussed earlier.

Further, because there is only limited communication between an encounter group and its environment, agents have a duty to make their activities open to careful scrutiny by representatives of the society. This duty entails a new conflict of the values of freedom and welfare and development. Encounter group participants and their agents require wide freedom to explore and negotiate the terms of their relationship. Participants often have commitments to significant others in the environment of the group. One of the functions of the limited linkage of encounter groups and their environment is the minimization of conflicts between the temporary, experimental commitments within the group and the more lasting and tested commitments outside the group. Accordingly, the group's openness to scrutiny by the society must be limited to scrutiny by disinterested parties, in order to protect the freedom of the participants to make temporary, experimental commitments.

## Society to Agent

While the society has an interest in protecting participants from exploitation or from the agent's failure to protect them, it also has an interest in the protection of the agent from unjust complaints of exploitation. Agents' performance of their duties does not eliminate some risks and liabilities taken by the participant. Where there is conflict in the claims of the agent and participant, the society must provide some adjudication of those claims. In that adjudication, the society has a duty to ascertain by careful scrutiny whether the agents have performed their duties and, if they have, to protect them from unjust accusations. The value is placed on justice, and losses of welfare are deemed just if the loss was in an experience properly limited by the agent and chosen by the participant with full knowledge of the risks involved.

## Participant to Society

The participants' duties to the society are primarily to make use of their new resources in socially valued action. But the society also depends in part on the participant to report any dereliction of duty on the part of the agent.

Encounter groups cannot be kept under constant scrutiny. The participant is thus the basic link between the society and the group.

Participants also have a duty to articulate the nature of their encounter experiences. It is not enough to say, "You must experience it to understand it." The freedom to remain silent and the privacy that entails must be sacrificed in the interest of truth. The question remains, how much freedom and privacy must be sacrificed in the interest of the access to the truth about any encounter group experience?

## Society to Participant

Perhaps the first duty of society is to provide participants with information about an agent's practices—by reputation, by reports of careful scrutiny, and by more systematic evaluations. In addition, the society has a duty to adjudicate disputes about dereliction of duty between participants and agents.

Even though the participant must accept losses justly suffered, the society has a duty to provide some partial, sustaining compensation for such losses. When the society supports a risky system, it enters a joint risk with participants. Thus, society has a duty to provide some partial compensation to members who take the losses required by the system.

In summary, the issue is the clarity and authenticity of the negotiation of agreements among the agent, the participant, and the society. On entry, and by a repeated renegotiation, experience makes greater truth available. Greater foresight and enhanced capacity to make reflective choices follow. Thus, all become more and more clear about the real limits on the sacrifice of welfare in the interest of other values, such as truth, freedom, or development. The duties in this regard are summarized in Table 4.

To repeat for emphasis, the basic rationale is that, as competence develops, true foresight becomes more available to all. Such enhanced foresight increases capacity for reflective choice, and thereby freedom. Freedom of choice promotes justice in allocating the goods and harms of encounter group activities among agent, participant, and the society. Such justice promotes a fair allocation of welfare and ultimately enhances life.

## ON THE ASSESSMENT OF CONSEQUENCES

If agents accept the duty to make actions in their groups open to public scrutiny, and if the society upholds its right to such scrutiny, then assessment of the consequences, anticipated and unanticipated, is in the hands of all three parties. The most competent party is the agent. Agents, however, must be suspect, because any negative assessment endangers their monetary and psychic rewards. Participants are also suspect because they are unsophisticated or, at least, subject to a short-term emotional confusion that limits their

**TABLE 4.** Rights and Duties Involved in Agent's Acts in Encounter Groups

| | Right to expect | | |
| --- | --- | --- | --- |
| Duty to supply | Agent | Participant | Society |
| Agent | | Limits on the sacrifice of short-term welfare<br>Protection from undue group pressures<br>Articulation of intended norms<br>Review and analysis of the implications of agent's acts | To do no harm<br>Return of participant with enhanced resources<br>Openness to public scrutiny |
| Participant | Accept limits on the sacrifice of short-term welfare or negotiate new limits<br>Accept agent's protection or waive agent's liability<br>Conform to norms set by agent or negotiate new norms<br>Review and analysis of the inferences drawn from agent's acts | | Utilization of enhanced resources<br>Articulate description of experiences<br>Report of agent's violation of limits on short-term welfare |
| Society | Protection from complaints about agent's acts within limits accepted by participant<br>Adjudication of disputes | Communication of agent's reputation<br>Disinterested scrutiny of encounter group<br>Enforcement of limits on sacrifice of short-term welfare<br>Partial compensation for loss of welfare within limits<br>Adjudication of disputes | |

objectivity. The society may mount—or induce the agent to mount—the resources of careful and sophisticated observers. Any group of scientists having an interest in an unconventional and diverse approach to purposeful human development may design controlled experiments or other evaluation efforts. By many means, given public scrutiny, careful assessment of consequences is feasible, but as specified earlier, not without costs in values sacrificed. Controlled experimentation, for example, may mean that some individuals have their crucial entry and exit—fully informed though they may be—controlled by a table of random numbers.

One of the most vexing aspects of assigning the responsibility for assessing outcomes of encounter groups is the wide variation in the extent to which the agents claim arcane knowledge on which to base the design of such assessments. If agents say they are professional practitioners with arcane knowledge, they imply a special responsibility to extend that knowledge and to improve the practice by relating their acts to modifications in their participants' behavior. If the agents say that they are simply reformers who are prepared to invest special amounts of time and energy but who have no special knowledge, they must demonstrate the efficacy of their actions to the satisfaction of their followers. In addition, they must neutralize or contain the defenses and counterattacks of those whose activities they hope to reform. If they say they have some religious or special humanistic faith, they must both satisfy their followers and adhere to the social constraints against coercion to perform religious practices. If they make no claim at all, they avoid responsibility for outcomes, but they also waive their right to compensation in money or esteem. Except for the case of the disclaiming agent, there is a basis for expecting agents to take a special responsibility for assessing the outcomes of their interventions. If they fail to perform this duty, public scrutiny will reveal the failure, and social sanction will likely follow. Note, for example, the action of the Russell Sage Foundation in supporting Back's (1972) analysis, which includes, among other things, a strong censure (justified or not) of encounter group agents for failing to give enough attention to assessing the outcomes of their actions. Another example is the controversial report of Lieberman, Yalom, and Miles (1973).

A more difficult task is to assess outcomes that not only were unanticipated but also struck at values that at first were not seen as affected. By definition such a sacrifice of values was not anticipated. The duty involved, then, is one of long-term follow-up of encounter group activities. If there are insidious encroachments on freedom, justice, or welfare, such outcomes can be discovered only by observation of participants and agents for some time after their encounter group experiences. While wholesale follow-up is probably impractical, following a sample of participants for long-term intermittent observation is a joint duty of the agent and the society.

The rights and duties involved in assessment of consequences are summarized in Table 5. The rationale by now is faimiliar. Assessment of outcomes

**TABLE 5.** Rights and Duties Involved in Assessing the Outcomes of Encounter Groups

| | | Right to expect | | |
|---|---|---|---|---|
| | | Agent | Participant | Society |
| Duty to supply | Agent | | Follow-up observation Compensation of unexpected losses of welfare Clarification of own motives, based on public scrutiny | Design of approaches to assessment of outcomes<br><br>Modification of goals and means based on the assessment of outcomes |
| | Participant | Report of unexpected consequences Cooperation in assessment of outcomes within limits of accepted sacrifice of welfare | | Report of unexpected consequences Cooperation in assessment of outcomes within limits of accepted sacrifice of welfare |
| | Society | Support competent assessment of outcomes | Follow-up observation Ensure freedom in choosing to cooperate in assessment of outcomes Enforce limits on the sacrifice of welfare in the assessment of outcomes | |

depends on competence, competence enhances the recognition of truth even in unexpected outcomes, truth leads to enhanced foresight and thus to improvement of practice. The enhanced foresight also leads to anticipation of future outcomes and, thus, to greater justice in the allocation of goods and harms from encounter groups. That new allocation contributes to welfare, and ultimately to life, its sustenance, its dignity, and its meaning.

## SUMMARY

In the foregoing discussions some specific duties of the parties involved in encounter groups have been advocated. Suppose that the agent performed those duties well, the participants did their duties loyally, and the society watched over it all, informed and adjudicated with wisdom and justice. Everybody knows that they don't, but what if they did? Would everything turn out for the best? No.

The encounter group undertaking contains inherent value conflicts. Between the agent and the participant there is an issue of justice in the exchange of the participant's short-term welfare (money, privacy, anxiety) and freedom for both the truth about and the development of the participant's capacities. The vulnerability of the exchange lies in the particular possibility that the participant acquires an enjoyable but false sense of having struggled and developed, and in return quite willingly pays the agent for that acquisition. The cliché is, "It was the most important experience of my life. ... In what way? ... You have to experience it to understand."

The society loses values in such an exchange, especially justice, but also welfare, freedom, and truth. The society—those persons having an interest—may, however, accept the risk of an unexamined testimonial (why argue with satisfaction?) in preference to the cost of examining it—the cost in time, effort, and risk of denouncing a popular avenue to development. A society will often maintain a myth to protect an ideal of enablement and to relieve an anxiety about its abuse.

In general terms, my position is that the ethical challenge to the proponents of encounter groups is to provide an unflinching exposition of the value conflicts that surround their use of groups to develop human resources. In the long term, such developmental attempts undertake to enhance the truth about the self and the world; to extend opportunity, capacity, and incentive to make reflective choices and act on them in freedom; to thereby promote justice in the distribution of the welfare of individuals; and ultimately to enhance life itself. In the short term, however, welfare can be endangered by wondrous new opportunities and incentives to make choices for which one lacks the capacity. Justice and freedom can be endangered by frightening new truths that intensify anxiety and impair both capacity and incentive to make reflective choices. The resolution of these conflicts takes several forms. Short-term sacrifices of values are accepted within specified limits in a belief in the long-term enhancement of the same values. Within the short term, freedom, justice, and welfare may be sacrificed in the interest of truth and development, in the hope that the truth will lead to new freedom, justice, and welfare. A sacrifice of any one value endangers the others: A sacrifice of development endangers truth; a sacrifice of truth endangers freedom; a sacrifice of freedom endangers justice; a sacrifice of justice endangers welfare; a sacrifice of welfare endangers life; and a sacrifice of life endangers individual development. Throughout the entire system of values and actions the vital force is life and the possibility of the development of foresight.

## REFERENCES

Back, K. W. *Beyond words: The story of sensitivity training and the encounter movement.* New York: Russell Sage, 1972.

Benne, K. D., Bradford, L. P., Gibb, J. R., & Lippitt, R. (Eds.). *The laboratory method of changing and learning.* Palo Alto: Science and Behavior Books, 1975.

Bradford, L. P., Gibb, J. R., & Benne, K. D. (Eds.). *T-group theory and laboratory method: Innovation in reeducation.* New York: Wiley, 1964.

Casey, M. T. An exploration of a risk-taking group. Unpublished paper available from the author at the First National Bank of Chicago, May 30, 1972.

Glidewell, J. C. A social psychology of mental health. In S. E. Golann & C. Eisdorfer (Eds.), *Handbook of community mental health.* New York: Appleton, 1972.

Glidewell, J. C. A social psychology of laboratory training. In K. D. Benne, L. P. Bradford, J. R. Gibb, & R. Lippitt (Eds.), *The laboratory method of changing and learning.* Palo Alto: Science and Behavior Books, 1975.

Gouldner, A. W. The norm of reciprocity: A preliminary statement. *American Sociological Review*, 1960, *25*, 161–179.

Lieberman, M. S., Yalom, I. D., & Miles, M. B. *Encounter groups: First facts.* New York: Basic, 1973.

Population Task Force of the Institute of Society, Ethics, and the Life Sciences. *Ethics, population, and the American tradition.* A study prepared for the Commission on Population Growth and the American Future. Hastings-on-Hudson, N.Y.: The Institute of Society, Ethics, and the Life Sciences, 1971.

Rogers, C. R. *On becoming a person: A therapist's view of psychotherapy.* Boston: Houghton Mifflin, 1961.

Schutz, W. *Joy.* New York: Grove, 1968.

Warwick, D. P., & Kelman, H. C. Ethical issues in social intervention. In G. Zaltman (Ed.), *Processes and phenomena of social change.* New York: Wiley, 1973.

# 5
# AN ETHICAL CRITIQUE
# OF ENCOUNTER GROUPS

KURT W. BACK

Duke University

Encounter groups have flowered and decayed for some time. It is no longer enough to talk about them only in programmatic terms or as an ideal to be achieved. One can look at the way encounter groups work, how the encounter movement is organized, and how it affects the individuals involved and the larger society. From a different perspective, one might inquire how the claimed long-range gains compensate for the acknowledged short-term injuries.

The values John Glidewell lists as important in encounter groups—life, welfare, justice, freedom, truth, and development—derive their meaning from events in Western history. The position of encounter groups in relation to these values is a result of these events and a reaction to them. The history of ideas in the last few centuries has been concerned with the relation of society to the individual. Society as a whole may be said to pursue two kinds of aims in controlling the individual. One is to reach certain social goals, such as rebuilding a community, pursuit of a certain foreign policy, or provision of a labor force. The other is to change individuals so that they will be healthy, happy, or involved with a particular ideology. The first deals with changes in society, which require certain changes in the behavior of individuals. The second deals with changes in the individual's attitudes, beliefs, values, and needs. Societies during recent times have evaluated the legitimacy of intervention differently in each case.

The development of democratic ideals during the last few centuries has produced certain safeguards against the first type of intervention, perhaps summarized best in the phrase *government by consent of the governed*. The aim is to protect the individual against society's intervention for its own goals through definite rules of behavior limiting the intervenor, the political power. Acceptance of these rules in an intervention program is reflected in the concern about consent of the target group in setting goals, about limiting the means of intervention, and about ensuring genuine participation. In the second type of intervention, however, there has been a trend in the opposite direction, which can be described as totalitarian, perhaps as a reaction to the first trend. This type of intervention has legitimized indoctrination techniques in the name of health, sanity, or correct ideology. It has ostensibly been directed at the individual, but has actually been used to further social aims. It looks almost as if a compensatory principle were at work: While individuals are freed from outward compliance, social pressure on common internalization increases.

Historically, the interaction of these two trends can be seen in the development of the concept of freedom of religion. As this development is crucial to an understanding of encounter groups, I shall discuss it briefly here. Traditionally, the state has required observance of religious forms of a particular kind from all citizens or at least from those citizens who wanted to participate in the rewards of the state. Looking back at the past three centuries, we can see that the original requirements consisted mainly of participation in ceremonies—the obligation to perform the correct rituals and to abstain from other rituals—but that these requirements placed little emphasis on belief. Relaxation and abolishment of these requirements are the main features of the rise of civil liberties and of tolerance. While the state withdrew from religious tests of citizenship, we also find the rise of mass movements, religions, and ideologies that required not so much outside conformity but deep emotional commitment to the tenets of the group and the goal of change of individuals. Terms such as rebirth, revival, or reeducation have become familiar to us.

In either of these ways, the aim of religious control is control over the emotional life. Ritualistic conformity can prevent the expression of emotions from affecting social structure and can keep a tight rein on individuals by making them take a very long-range point of view: in eternity their wishes will eventually be fulfilled. The individual, expressive kind of intervention keeps emotion within the group situation and makes people change toward a unified kind of personality, which is easily manipulated and controlled by leaders who supposedly know the way to salvation. In both cases, emotional life is seen as the enemy to be controlled and is even personalized in demons that must be suppressed.

Foucault (1976) has shown a similar development in the public control of sexuality. Earlier control of sexual behavior has given way to a pervasive strain toward conformity in sexual attitudes, which are being defined more widely and which involve more and more different areas of social and personal life. Encounter groups that accept many varieties of sexual action but insist on being in agreement on sexual liberation as a value would be an extreme case in point.

The shift of emphasis to individual freedom has been accompanied by a shift away from old concerns. Intense emotions are no longer held in awe, considered as unavoidable dangers to be controlled for the public good. Positive attitudes toward emotions, perhaps first expressed in a sentimental way by Rousseau and the Romantic movement, were later justified in the study of modern psychology and psychodynamics. Further understanding of emotionality through the work of Freud and other depth psychologists gave legitimacy to claims for accepting emotionality for its own sake. The affluence of large parts of the population was also important, as it made it possible for many people to concentrate on their emotional development rather than merely contend for survival. The conjunction of all these forces sets the stage for the development of intervention techniques in which the uninhibited expression of emotions could be seen as an unqualified good.

The success of encounter groups seems to be, therefore, a product of a combination of circumstances: the mistrust of political intervention, the appearance of intensely emotional mass movements, the rise of social science, and the general affluence and availability of leisure for part of the population (Back, 1972). This unusual conjunction of several trends has also exacted its price. The different sources of the success of encounter groups have left inherent contradictions creating technical as well as ethical problems. Some of these contradictions are as follows:

1.  A belief in democratic ideology while using, at the same time, totalitarian techniques to ensure internal conformity.
2.  An exaltation of leaders into saints or gurus while at the same time claiming that each member is just a voluntary participant who can leave at any time.
3.  A feeling of sacred awe in response to an essentially commercial enterprise.
4.  A claim of social responsibility and social concern in an activity deriving from upper-middle-class problems and directed toward this group.
5.  An attempt to use a variety of psychotherapy in an essentially religious framework (we are all sinners, hence patients).
6.  An aura of scientific respectability, use of scientific language, and claim of derivation from group dynamics and social science coupled with an anti-intellectual outlook.

These and similar problems arise in many encounter groups and discussions about the encounter movement. They are the results of the confrontation with reality of such vague and exalted goals as self-expression, joy, self-awareness, self-respect, interpersonal competence, and sensitivity. This confrontation has undermined the ideal interrelations of the rights and duties of the parties concerned in two contrasting ways. For some participants—members of an affluent, leisured population that still pays lip-service to the Victorian gospel of self-improvement—encounter groups have become a novel kind of recreation. For the other participants, who really come for help, encounters hide uncontrolled dangers. Similar dangers are present in the import of encounter groups for the society at large, as an instrument to facilitate establishment of totalitarian democracy (Adler, 1972).

## PROBLEMS OF LEADERSHIP

The central position in encounter groups is that of the leader. The participants see little of the commercial and organizational structure of an encounter center. They see only the leader of their group. Similarly, the sanctions and expectations of society may be nominally directed toward the encounter movement in general or some branch of it, but in fact they relate to the control of the claims and the behavior of the encounter group leader.

Thus, as Glidewell also implies, many of the ethical problems of encounter groups revolve around the leader (or agent). Along the lines of the issues raised in the Introduction to this book, we must ask to what extent the leader shares in the goal setting, how much he[1] accepts the participation of others in the conduct of the group, and what efforts he makes to avoid unforeseen consequences.

In spite of the leader's crucial role, the rhetoric of the encounter movement plays down the leader's importance. The essence of encounter groups is the right of any group member to the free expression of feeling and to the attention of the whole group, precluding a special position for the leader. The rejection of norms of everyday activity, of any structuring of society, would presumably also include rejection of leadership. The fact is, of course, that encounter groups have leaders and that these leaders usually have a definite program planned for the conduct of the group. Recent research has shown that the personal style of the leader, not the system he professes to use, is probably the most important variable in the conduct of groups and their effect on their members (Lieberman, Yalom, & Miles, 1973).

An expression of the ambiguity and conflict inherent in the leader role has been the long search for a term designating the leader in an encounter group. Glidewell has devoted some thought to this. There has been a tendency, in general, to use terminology to blur the distinction between leaders and the rest of the group. From such strong terms as "teacher," "leader," "trainer," or "doctor," on the one hand, and "pupil," "follower," or "patient," on the other, encounter people have turned to more neutral terms such as "change agent," "agent," or "intervenor" and "client" or "the ongoing system."

---

[1] In cases such as this, *he* can refer to a person of either sex.

These problems of terminology are more than purely semantic games. They reflect a real search for the basis of legitimation of the leader's power. In fact, the leader may be, at one extreme, a social director and, at the other, the charismatic guru who can do harm as well as good. Frequently, leaders are both or play one role while they advertise the other. In both roles, however, society has a stake in the leaders' activity, as does the client. Following Glidewell, we can analyze the three possible relationships among leader (agent), group (participants), and society.

## LEADER–GROUP RELATIONSHIP

Because of his overlapping position, the leader is forced to stress that he is just a member of the group, that he has no more power than any other member, no more rights, and hence no more responsibility. However, the group depends on its leaders and on the traditions of the movement they represent. Sometimes leaders must even exert their power forcefully because of ambiguity in a particular situation. If the regulated means of social control are unavailable, leaders must resort to more direct and dictatorial tactics. The seeming abdication of the leadership role creates a vacuum with some quite curious results.

Leaders are relieved of any democratic procedures in setting the group's aims, in limiting the means of achieving them, and in securing the cooperation of the group. An effect of this lack of structure is that the personality of the leaders, their style of conducting and developing the group, becomes all-important. This has been shown in the study by Lieberman, Yalom, and Miles (1973), which also shows the importance of a warm, supportive personality as against a strong, charismatic leader who may hurt as much as help.

Leaders of encounter groups have in their hands a great arsenal of means for dominating individual members. The feedback technique, which gives the encounter group its strength, the high emotional pitch, the ban on intellectual discussion, and the use of physical methods of interaction make it possible to exert any amount of pressure on group members. It is the plasticity of the approach in the hands of a skilled leader that makes groups so impressive to their members. The group experience will be remembered as tremendously important after a long time, even if no change or little change can be measured by any conventional means.

Criticisms from group members, as expressed in personal letters, usually center around this fact. Group members are exposed to unrelenting pressure and attacks by the leader, which result in their eventual dependence on the leader. Group members who did not accept the leader's position to begin with frequently resent this pressure (Maliver, 1973). Deleterious effects do not necessarily take the form of spectacular breakdowns, which are relatively rare. The experience of being forced to drop defenses under group pressure for a prolonged time without any guidance in finding substitute defenses is the most common cause of negative consequences. An investigation of the use of encounter groups in psychological training drew attention to hidden casualties, those who felt rejected, dropped out of the group, and thus were not noticed by the leader or mentioned in reports. "By far the worst trauma is to be ignored" (University of Michigan, 1969).

Inquiries to a number of encounter centers organized according to the Esalen model have revealed a variety of backgrounds among their leaders. A large proportion came from the traditional helping professions, especially clinical psychology, social work, and adult education, but there was also a significant number of leaders without any relevant professional training. Responses from the centers showed little concern with this difference and low regard for qualification for leadership.

The threat posed by a leader who does not accept or finds unnecessary the safeguards that exist in many institutions becomes especially important under conditions where encounter groups function within these institutions. Many encounter groups are separate from real life, serving mainly as forms of recreation or personal adventure, and thus do not interfere with the social structure. However, some occur in the regular institutions of society, for instance, as instruments in labor and personnel relations. Normally, safeguards are established within these institutions to protect workers' rights to maintain privacy, to have representation, and to oppose management interests. Also, institutional mechanisms are established for resolving conflicts. Encounter groups, however, tend to bypass these safeguards. In management training or personnel relations, for example, encounter groups may be introduced under the guise of self-expression, letting nature take its course; and, by adoption of the rhetoric of natural groups, many of the safeguards that have been established for workers may be lost. There are other institutional contexts in which encounter groups may allow leaders to use influence techniques that would otherwise be considered inappropriate. Thus, school systems may conduct training groups that deal with the personal feelings of members toward each other, even though these expressions may later hamper their relationships. The institution of new policies may also lead to the use of encounter techniques to expose and reeducate people opposed to this policy. For instance, encounter groups have been used to change interracial attitudes in governmental or private agencies. We can accept the positive value of a policy of nondiscrimination and racial integration and recognize that encounter techniques may be an effective way of changing personality characteristics and ingrained habits opposed to integration, and yet we may ask whether an agency is entitled to use this intensive, personal, and emotional technique in trying to make the policy function better. Here again, no holds are barred in encounter groups because supposedly they represent the action of the group itself and not the action of the employer. This assumption sets aside the legal safeguards that have been developed against enforcement of conformity. These legal procedures may be clumsy and not very helpful in efforts to institute a morally superior policy, but bypassing them through the use of encounter groups may lead to a totalitarian acceptance of attitude conformity. The encounter techniques, of course, are not so well developed that they always lead to positive results, but they may be sufficient to produce discomfort.

The same problem arises when group techniques are used in some labor-management conflicts. Again, these techniques may not, in fact, succeed. They may backfire and lead to greater conflicts and to strikes that are even harder to settle. But, even if they are successful, the question is, do they really represent opportunities for the members to express their potential or for the leaders to use their strength to push through their views? The fact that techniques depend so much on the characteristics of the leader would suggest that the latter is probably true.

Finally, what is the responsibility of the leader? Encounter leaders have been trying to avoid this problem by stressing the client's responsibility. They have become more and more explicit in claiming that people coming to a group are expected to know what they are doing; therefore, whatever happens to them in the group represents their own choice and thus their own responsibility. This is frequently interpreted to mean that if both parties to the contract, the leader as well as the participant, promise to do their best, everything will turn out well. Other defenders of encounter groups claim that many of the untoward happenings, breakdowns, or even suicides might have come about anyway, and thus the group should not be held responsible for them. It is pointed out that those things happen in the course of daily living as well, that there are other events in society that may lead to the same result. Finally, it is proposed that some of the events that may look untoward, like psychotic episodes, may really be blessings in disguise or at least lead to an acceptance of therapy as a way of working through problems. All these arguments may be true in some cases, but they show a real confusion about the effects of abdication of responsibility in the conventional sense. They also disregard the uneven distribution of power between leader and participants. Even the least experienced leader has already seen several groups and knows what can happen, while most participants have much less experience. Many participants also come because of a serious personality problem and place themselves in a dependent position. In short, the whole assessment of responsibility turns out to be a doctrine of *caveat emptor*, which is the opposite of consumer protection.

## LEADER-SOCIETY RELATIONSHIP

Different kinds of leaders not only exert influence differently, they also have different kinds of impact on others. Professionals concerned with change follow different models of human nature, the nature of influence, and the context of the relationship, and perform different roles in society. The social-psychological research on causal attribution can help in understanding ethical dilemmas.

Social psychologists have subjected the conditions of attributing responsibility to others to intensive analysis, both theoretical and empirical. It is clear that there are certain conditions under which we assume that people have acted on their own and were responsible for their acts, and there are other conditions under which we assume their acts were determined by circumstance or were the consequence of other people's actions. This evaluation depends not only on the circumstances under which the action is performed but also on the set of the perceiver. In experiments in which this set has been manipulated, it has been shown that evaluation as well as perception of the same acts will vary, depending partly on the perceiver (Jones et al., 1972).

It is somewhat risky to extrapolate this analysis to social situations and social movements, but it is worthwhile to attempt it. Thus we have, on the one hand, the religious point of view, which holds people responsible for themselves and all they might do. Thus, people may be guilty and deserving of punishment even if the origin of their objectionable actions is not produced by themselves but inherited from their ancestors. This has given way to the medical and sociological point of view, which assumes that people are really victims of social circumstances and, therefore, cannot be held responsible for their actions. Each of these points of view ties its beliefs to an impressive model or central myth. The myth of Christianity, of the original Fall and salvation, stresses the importance of individual choice: People can be saved by their own election. The mythology of psychoanalysis, by contrast, is based in part on the Oedipus complex and shows the individual as the victim of early childhood upbringing and the stresses of socialization. This is the essential human tragedy that can only be alleviated by trained analysts.

The myth of the encounter group, which can be gleaned from the writings of various group leaders, draws on the models of both religion and science (Back, 1972, Ch. 4). It pictures the individual as a fallen soul or fallen angel: The human soul is strong, healthy, and good, but is imprisoned in several layers of the body, convention, law, and other restraining mechanisms. Thus, the essential human mind is not able, at least in our society, to fully assert its own potentiality. Everything bad in life is outside the human essence and is the consequence of its imprisonment in these diverse layers. However, if these layers can be removed—and this appears to be the goal of encounter groups—then the original self will achieve freedom and happiness for the individual. This model can easily lead to self-absorption (Schur, 1976).

The models and mythologies are related to the different professions and their ways of changing human action. Models of human change distinguish the locus of causes of human action, the conditions under which personal change can occur, and the proper role for each participant in the process. Many professions are involved in human change, but the principal models one can consider before turning to encounter groups are the legal, the religious, the medical, and the social reform models.

These models differ in the extent to which their intervention is based on an appeal to higher principles. The religious approach justifies change by the claim of beneficial effects to be achieved at later times and, in some cases, the promise of eternal happiness. Legal practitioners claim the authority of the political community that has set up the rules that they are bound to enforce. In both of these cases, the practitioners claim a higher authority, which enables them to intervene and change people without their own initiative. By contrast, both the helping professions and the reformers take the individual's point of view. They offer to help a person to achieve a better state. All the person has to do is follow their advice. Their own authority is their claim to superior skills and training to effect the desired changes. The two models differ from each other in the locus of emphasis and hence also the assumed locus of control. The medical approach typically liberates the individual from an assumed deficiency, while the social reformer believes in changing social conditions that can effect individual change indirectly.

The greater the authority of the general rules on which practitioners depend, the more justification they have for being the sole agent of the change and the more independent they are of the consent of the client. The goal is set *a priori*, and the means are "objectively" necessary. If society accepts the necessity of religious salvation in a particular way, it will give the religious practitioner authority to interfere with private lives. The same is true for political ideologies and law enforcement. Individual and civil rights have been designed to protect the individual from the overwhelming claim of institutions of this kind and are based on the idea that the outside goal is not overwhelming and immutable. Hence, there is no absolute authority over the individual. The physician as well as the social reformer find the emphasis on individual rights congenial to their own approach. The physician is entitled to make only those changes that the patient desires. Doctors thus tend to think in terms of their individual responsibility to the patient and accept the necessity of civil rights for the patient. In fact, physicians try as much as possible to avoid legal proceedings, such as commitment procedures, which would interfere with the doctor-patient relationship. Similarly, social reformers, such as community organizers, try to obtain legitimation through the participation of the people with whom they deal. The physician's scientific ideology and the reformer's political ideology are embedded within a framework that upholds the civil rights of the individual.

The physician and the reformer may believe that they are merely interpreting immutable laws of nature or society and trying to adapt individual and social behavior to these laws. Conversely, the lawyer and priest may try to address the concerns of the people with whom they work. Thus, the difference in ultimate sanction is not always reflected in the behavior of the professionals themselves. But their behavior is at least partially based on their model of human responsibility and their attribution of causes for human action. The religious model postulates an overwhelming power and norms established by that power. Individuals are free, within certain limits, to find their way of conforming to these norms. The legal model assumes a rational human being who can be changed or deterred from antisocial acts by threat of punishment or possible reward. Medical and especially psychiatric practitioners postulate a desirable normal state that they help their patients to attain. Social reformers see certain social forces, usually manipulated by power groups, as hindering the development of the individual. Their model assumes essentially healthy beings who can be helped by collective action to reach their proper and satisfied state.

What is the role of the encounter group within this classification of professions? In a certain sense, encounter groups are a further development of psychiatry. Treated as psychiatric theory and method, encounter groups are discussed in textbook chapters on new techniques of group therapy. Encounter groups are, however, more than a new technique of psychotherapy, even if they are used as such. The emphasis on expression of emotion and on finding a new myth of human behavior links them more closely to the religious point of view on human change. Encounter group leaders talk of eternal verities, which, unfortunately, present civilization has forgotten. Thus, they follow the model of the professional who can intervene on the basis of eternal truths that do not need to be justified. In this sense, encounter groups are in decided contrast to the two models (medical and social reform) that assume a reciprocal relationship between leader and public and thus place some obligation on the leaders in their relation to the client.

Here we see the basic contradictions of the encounter movement and the ambiguous role of the encounter leader in society. The refusal to assume leadership gives the encounter leader the illusion that he is free of responsibility. This idea is particularly applied at Esalen by William Schutz and Richard Price. Thus, leaders assume the authority not only of the physician, but also of the priest or shaman. In fact, encounter leaders are neither. They do not have the advantage of the professional training of the physician, and they avoid the claim of dealing with the sick. Nor do they accept the long-range personal and social responsibility of a religious leader. In the background, however, encounter leaders have a definite ideology, as shown in the writings of the movement. What is more, many people who come to sessions realize what encounter groups represent and are aware of the new culture they claim to develop.

Encounter group leaders try to maintain a balance between the characteristics of the different professionals discussed here. They try to borrow, in part, the metaphysical aura of the religious leader and the knowledge of curing of the medical doctor, but they also try to lead a social movement and produce long-range social changes in a certain part of the population. Perhaps they are best described negatively by the one model they do not take, that of the law, which requires an exact *quid pro quo* and detailed investigations of evidence.

## GROUP-SOCIETY RELATIONSHIP

The ambiguity of encounter groups extends not only to the role of the leader but to the social definition of the enterprise—the place of such groups in society. Justification of a proceeding can be made by rational means, by the detailed scientific procedures of trial-and-error and experimentation, on the one hand, and by the inspirations and faith of religion, on the other. As justification of the theory underlying encounter groups, a combination of the two is conveniently offered. It helps to find facts that corroborate the theory, but in the absence of such facts one can always appeal to inspiration and feeling. However, the justification used determines the constraints society imposes on the conduct of the program itself. As social controls on group processes have developed, they have been most strongly exerted on pure experimentation, next on therapy, and least on religious exercises. An act that may occur in an encounter group would be difficult to carry out in the context of an experiment. Full consent would have to be obtained, after giving the person an account of the procedure and the risks it entails. If therapy is involved, much greater risk would be justified, as long as the procedure conforms to the ethical code of the medical profession (although it has been pointed out that most therapy is experimental to some degree). In religious exercises, even more dangerous practices may be allowed under the guise of protecting freedom of religion.

It becomes important, therefore, to examine the purposes for which people enter encounter groups. Probably many enter for recreational purposes, and they neither know nor care very much what will happen, as long as they have a "great" experience. Many people are also searching for something that is missing in their lives, responding to a sense of alienation from their culture and general malaise. One also has the impression that many people participating in encounter groups have a tortured religious background and have tried many different religions in an attempt to find a place in the world. However, research has shown that many of the people venturing into encounter groups are either undergoing psychotherapy, or have undergone it, or are considering it. This suggests that many group members are really patients who are trying to find a substitute for or alternative to therapy. Contrary to most therapy, of course, encounter groups provide no contract or promise of betterment. Most encounter leaders explicitly refuse to make such contracts. Exceptions are those practitioners who combine psychotherapy with encounter (Gestalt therapy, transactional therapy, and allied methods).

Fernandez (1977) has shown the difference between the integrative change techniques, modern and traditional, and the process of encounter groups. Rites of passage of all kinds occur in three steps (Turner, 1969). In the first one, initiates leave the old or sick status. In the second, the initiates are neither in the old nor the new status; this is called liminality. Here the initiates relate only to their group or to their mentor. In the third stage, the initiates are reintegrated into their new status as different members of society. In encounter groups, only the first two steps are performed. The members are left in their dependence on the group, their liminality, and the leaders refuse to take responsibility for showing them the way to apply the experience. The diverse addicts of group processes, who attend one program after another or take marginal jobs in encounter centers, are the most obvious victims of this truncated process.

Many encounter group members apparently have a hidden agenda behind the overt one. The overt agenda describes people who want to spend some time with a group to find themselves and discover what encounter groups are. Such people are free to come and go and to do whatever they wish. The hidden agenda, however, very often suggests people who are in distress and who had heard from others or from the mass media that their distress may somehow be alleviated through encounter groups. Most of the propaganda of the groups hints that this is possible. Thus we have the spectacle of a periodical refusing notices of encounter groups on the grounds that medical advertising is unethical. When *The Village Voice* did so, encounter leaders argued that their groups were primarily recreational or educational. The editor of *The Village Voice*, however, produced encounter group advertisements that promised cures for a whole range of ills.

Prospective participants are influenced by this image. A group of introductory psychology students were given an opportunity to fulfill their requirement for research participation by attending a T-group. Of the 81 who agreed to attend, more than half (54 percent) had either considered going to or had actually gone to a psychiatrist, psychoanalyst, psychologist, mental hospital, or mental health clinic. Of the 246 students who did not want to attend a T-group, less than one-third (32 percent) had considered or actually experienced some form of therapy.

Because of these expectations of the clients, it may be appropriate to inquire into the qualifications of the leaders. Here the bogey of professionalism appears. Encounter groups are in favor of freedom from society and from traditional, academic confinement and opposed to such constraints as professionalism would impose. There is a general feeling that some people are good encounter leaders, and that the elusive quality of charisma may excuse everything. It is interesting to repeat that, in studies of encounter groups, the charismatic leaders had the least success and their groups accounted for most of the breakdowns (Lieberman, Yalom, & Miles, 1973). Glidewell expresses the hope that there will soon be professional control of encounter centers. This recognition of the problem with a hopeful solution in the future points to the very core of the dilemma: The objection to outside control fits into the outwardly democratic ideology of the encounter movement, but totalitarian control can easily be established under this shield. Even if one of the organizations cited by Glidewell could establish norms, it would be in the old ambiguous position of trying to be progressive and thus would be helpless against a new leader who would denounce the rigid professional standards of the now traditional establishment.

The implication of the ambiguous social definition of encounter groups, which results from combining the medical and religious models, becomes evident when encounter groups are evaluated as medical treatment, similar to a new drug. In such an evaluation, the ratio of success over danger would not be great enough to allow the new treatment to be introduced, at least not without adequate safeguards or definitions. In a new religious movement, which simply promises to increase general joy in life, these kinds of strictures would not apply. As an alternate way of feeling, which people are free to pursue, encounter groups would be as valid as any other kind of life style advertised in our best sellers. What is dangerous, however, is to combine the aura of the medical profession and its standards with the civil and religious freedom of pursuing alternative life styles.

## THE OUTLOOK

Verplanck (1970), in a survey of psychologists on problems with encounter groups, reports a feeling of general unease. There is little evidence of direct danger and few stories about people actually being hurt, but many psychologists feel that something untoward may be happening in encounter groups and that some danger may exist.

Encounter groups do not promise anything. If you do not have a goal, how can you be accused of misrepresentation? Why do you need to make a contract with people about the direction or course of a procedure that is merely designed to release emotion and to enable participants to become themselves? How can one apply medical standards to a religious movement, moral standards to a recreational activity, and the requirements of community action to an individual, expressive experience? Few people are badly harmed and, in any case, what procedure is completely harmless?

On the other hand, we know that people who enter encounter groups are not really that naïve. They bring definite expectations to the sessions, many of which are created by the publicity of the encounter movement. People do not simply express themselves, they are part of a society. The idea of a community where people just do what they want is open to many interpretations. It generally means that the leaders do what they want and express themselves through the members. Some of the bizarre behavior in groups is clearly more expressive of the desires of the leadership than of those of the members themselves, although the members may feel that their violations of normal social taboos may reflect what they really want.

The moral uneasiness persists. It cannot be tied to any specific procedure or danger, as the whole movement is immersed in ambiguity. Specific extremes, of course, can be exposed, and the movement has been involved with the legal system when physical or mental injuries could be proven (Church & Carnes, 1972; Maliver, 1973). The threat of damage suits or unauthorized use of well-known training centers has confronted encounter leaders with the realities of society and increased their interest in the legal safeguards of society. However, the problem with encounter groups is that their exact effect cannot be pinpointed as being either positive or negative, as can more readily be done with drugs. With so little positive evidence for encounter groups, can we sacrifice truth for freedom, freedom for justice, justice for welfare? When will we recover truth, freedom, and justice?

Perhaps the answer cannot be found inside the groups but in the image they present to society. Encounter groups may be a symptom of a disease that is part of our present-day world, a symptom that appeared when rigid systems began to disintegrate, new social movements suddenly arose, and leaders became capable of propelling their followers into extreme actions.

The similarity of encounter groups to the beginnings of millenarian and related mass movements has been pointed out (Back, 1973). Such movements frequently hold out the promise of eternal happiness here on earth, with complete freedom of the senses, once the last enemy is overthrown. They are based on recognized defects within the society and thus attract many people with reasonable grievances. In our society, they may be based not on economic deprivation but on boredom within affluent groups. A promise to alleviate boredom appeals to members of the middle class and mobilizes a passionate following among people who, in an economic sense, are most advantaged within this society. Thus, the safeguards that this society has established against abuses of power may seem trivial to these people, once they are persuaded of the great aims of the encounter movement. However, most of the movements in history that have done away with such restraints have resulted in greater oppression rather than greater freedom. Encounter groups may reflect a new yearning for giving up restraints in a new kind of millenarianism. The encounter movement may be one symptom of a general unease within the society and one expression of a longing for a new, all-engulfing, mass movement.

## REFERENCES

Adler, N. *The underground stream: New life styles and the antinomian personality.* New York: Harper & Row, 1972.

Back, K. W. *Beyond words: The story of sensitivity training and the encounter movement.* New York: Russell Sage, 1972.

Back, K. W. The experiential group and society. *Journal of Applied Behavioral Science,* 1973, *9,* 7–20.

Church, G., & Carnes, C. D. *The pit.* New York: Outerbridge and Lazard, 1972.

Fernandez, J. W. Blood is thicker than water: A comparative study of the search for community. In K. W. Back (Ed.), *In search for community.* Boulder, Colo.: Westview Press, 1978.

Foucault, M. *Histoire de la sexualité*. Vol. I, *La volonté de savoir*. Paris: Gallimard, 1976.

Jones, E. E., Kanouse, D. E., Kelley, H. H., Nisbett, R. E., Valins, S., & Weiner, B. *Attribution: Perceiving the causes of behavior*. Morristown, N.J.: General Learning Press, 1972.

Lieberman, M. S., Yalom, I. D., & Miles, M. B. *Encounter groups: First facts*. New York: Basic Books, 1973.

Maliver, B. L. *The encounter game*. New York: Stein and Day, 1973.

Schur, E. *The awareness trap: Self-absorption instead of social change*. New York: McGraw-Hill, 1976.

Turner, V. W. *The ritual process*. Chicago: Aldine, 1969.

University of Michigan, Department of Psychology. *Report of the Clinical Area Special Commission on T-Groups*. Ann Arbor, 1969.

Verplanck, W. How do you track down rumors? *American Psychologist*, 1970, *25*, 100–107.

# III
# ORGANIZATION DEVELOPMENT

# 6
# ETHICAL ISSUES IN THE PRACTICE OF ORGANIZATION DEVELOPMENT

### RICHARD E. WALTON
Harvard University

## ORGANIZATION DEVELOPMENT IN CONCEPT

The concept of *organization development (OD),* referring to certain professionally led activities intended to "change" or to "improve" organizations, gained currency in the early 1960s. Organization development was first initiated in business, subsequently in government and education, and more recently in work organizations as diverse as military units, hospitals, and religious groups. Today, it is an international phenomenon.

Early practitioners generally came from sensitivity training programs and relied on laboratory training methods. Today practitioners of organization development are drawn from diverse fields and employ a growing number of change strategies. While the early practice was confined to process interventions intended, for example, to promote interpersonal dialogue, current practice includes the redesign of "structural" features such as division of labor, coordinative mechanisms, reward schemes, and career paths.

The research for this chapter was supported by the Division of Research, Graduate School of Business Administration, Harvard University. I wish to acknowledge helpful suggestions from Professors Chris Argyris and Paul Lawrence, Dr. Steve Ruma, and Robert Walton, M. D.

How do ethical dilemmas arise in the practice of organization development? How are they handled by the OD practitioner (OD-P)? What guide, if any, can be offered? My purpose in this chapter is to stimulate personal reflection, discussion, and debate within the ranks of applied behavioral scientists. I therefore raise questions about practices when I myself can offer answers only tentatively.

Ethical issues can arise for the OD-P as a result of the following types of inconsistencies:

- if he[1] assists an organization whose goals and strategies he morally disapproves
- if he associates himself with managerial actions of questionable justification and fairness
- if his interventions employ means or produce consequences not consistent with his own personal values
- if his actions vis-à-vis his clients violate standards that normally govern the professional-client relationship
- if his interventions produce consequences not consistent with the values generally attributed to OD

## ORGANIZATION DEVELOPMENT
## IN VALUE ORIENTATION

There are two broad categories of organization development practitioners: (a) external consultants, who typically hold doctorates in a discipline such as psychology or in a professional field such as business administration and are affiliated with universities, although a growing number are independent consultants; and (b) internal consultants, full-time employees, often drawn from the personnel department, who are usually without advanced degrees.

This chapter discusses external consultants whose relative independence and professional training promote the development of ethical codes. Although there are no precise data, I would estimate that the rapidly growing number of individual consultants who claim to practice OD in the United States alone is several thousand.

At least three value orientations may guide an external professional engaged in changing organizations:

1. The person may seek improvement in the organization's capacities to achieve its goals (for example, profit for a business firm and delivery of services for a government agency). This orientation to organization achievement identifies with the traditional concerns of managers.
2. The person may seek to improve the quality of work life for organization

---

[1] The writer intends in cases such as this to refer to a person of either sex.

members in order to increase self-esteem and personal growth, to ensure justice, and so forth. This is a particular outgrowth of a growing humanistic concern in our society as a whole.

3.  The person may wish to change organizations in ways that make their effects on other institutions or communities in the larger society more positive.

The first two orientations are more relevant and are more commonly involved in OD, although, as will be illustrated later in this chapter, the question of external consequences is sometimes raised by changes pursued through OD.

The dominant value orientation of OD is reflected in the formal definitions of the field. For example, Beckhard (1969) defines OD as

> an effort (1) *planned*, (2) *organization-wide* and (3) *managed* from the *top*, to (4) increase *organization effectiveness* and health through (5) planned interventions in the organization's processes, using *behavioral science* knowledge (p. 100).

Others would include in OD planned change efforts that are not "organization-wide" and not "managed from the top." In fact, Beckhard is one of the relatively few OD practitioners who consistently work from entry at the top of the organization. Nevertheless, Beckhard's definition does accurately reflect the aspirations of most other OD practitioners who believe that OD *should* start at the top, *should* have the latter's active endorsement and involvement, and *should* be organization-wide.

Organization development is also known by certain characteristic activities. For example, Burke and Hornstein (1972) identify five major classes of interventions: team building, management of conflict, technostructural, data feedback, and training. For these authors, the ultimate goal of OD is to create a self-renewing organization. The "social technology of OD" is utilized to enhance the "social functioning of organizations" and "for adapting to needed changes on a day-to-day basis." According to Burke and Hornstein, "the primary focus in OD is normative change; individual change is simply a by-product" (p. xi).

Beckhard (1969) further clarifies the hierarchy of values in OD when he emphasizes the following as a condition likely to produce failure:

> Confusing "good relationship" as an *end* with good relationships as a *condition*.
>
> Some behavioral science organization-change programs imply that when effective, open, trusting relationships exist among the people of the organization, you have organization health. They imply that an end goal of such a program is to establish this type of climate and relationships. . . . Good relationships are an important condition in an effective organization but they are not an *end state* (p. 95).

These definitions of OD reflect a primary concern for the efficacy of organization processes. Indeed, with few exceptions, the OD-P is hired by management, which typically expects improved quality of working life to be treated as a means rather than an end. If there were no more to it than that, OD would simply be a form of management consulting. However, the OD practitioner typically has personal values concerned with the quality of human experience. For example, many OD practitioners value authenticity and openness in human encounters regardless of their efficacy for organization achievement and thus give OD humanistic overtones not reflected in these definitions.

OD has a primary emphasis on organization achievement and a secondary emphasis on quality of working life. The OD-P is often a management consultant in his concern for organization achievement and a social reformer in his concern for humanistic values in the work place. Embracing two evaluative frameworks greatly increases the likelihood that value dilemmas will arise.

Many potential value dilemmas are avoided, however, by the tendency of OD practitioners to focus on only a few attributes of organizations that affect quality of work life. Specifically, OD attends to the use and development of human capacities and social integration in the work place. These are particular areas where OD-Ps believe change can simultaneously improve organization achievement and the quality of work life.

Other organization conditions have been outside the action arena of OD. Organization development has not dealt with issues of due process, articulating and advancing individual rights vis-à-vis the organization, matters of equity, and income distributions within the organization—all of which have a direct bearing on the quality of work life. These quality-of-work-life issues more frequently involve trade-offs between the interests of an organization and at least some of its members.

Having broadly characterized the values of OD-Ps, I wish to state my own values and concerns. I have a basic interest both in improving the effectiveness of organizations that produce useful goods and services and in enhancing the quality of human experience in the work place. Both improvements are urgently needed. Many U.S. industries must increase their productivity if they are to continue to compete in the world market; hospitals and municipalities must become more effective if they are to meet the rising demand for services at a reasonable cost.

Turning to the quality of work life, many of our working population are alienated from their work and the employing organization. Today in the United States, I believe humanistic concerns are especially in need of planned change efforts. Therefore, I confine my OD activities to those that have a net positive effect on quality of work life. And I accept the standard almost always held by clients that my efforts should enhance organization effectiveness. Fortunately, there are many opportunities to improve both effectiveness and quality of work life.

## ORGANIZATION DEVELOPMENT
## IN ACTION: ILLUSTRATIONS

Seven sample OD intervention cases are described in this section. Each provides a concrete context for identifying one or more of the ethical issues that arise in practicing OD. Together they illustrate a wide variety of interventions as well as a wide variety of value orientations held by OD practitioners.[2]

### Implementing Top-Down Change

Beckhard (1969, pp. 45–56) described a case involving an OD strategy for changing a firm from a family-owned and managed culture to a professional one.

The company's market position had slipped in recent years and an influential member of the family (Mr. A) called on the OD-P for help. However, "most of the management and work force were long-term employees and were generally satisfied with this state of affairs," that is, the "royalist" pattern, with family members in all top positions. The OD-P's diagnosis was that (a) "the change in management would be very dramatic and probably traumatic for a number of management people" and (b) "it would be necessary to prepare the division-management group for the change, to get out some of their feelings and attitudes about the new leadership, and to find ways of getting their commitment to making the new mode work" (p. 47).

Subsequent interviews confirmed that there were psychological and social costs. The human trauma involved "loss of status in both the firm and the community" and "loss of contact and upward influence with the power center" (Beckhard, 1969, p. 49). It also involved many career casualties. According to Mr. B, the division head, "We are running a business now that's considerably bigger and more complex and more active, with something just over a third of the people we had before" (p. 54).

This case illustrates OD as an instrument of top management with exclusive attention to organization achievement. First, in taking the assignment, the OD-P did not question the conclusions of his sponsor, Mr. A, that drastic action was necessary and that professionalization of management was the appropriate action. Second, there was no mention of any attempt to weigh the human cost for some against the expected gain for others and the firm. Third, The OD-P appeared to agree with Mr. A and Mr. B that the culture in which position and status are based on competence was superior to the culture it

---

[2] However, the examples provide neither an adequate nor representative sample of OD interventions. For example, the team-building case given (Kuriloff & Atkins, 1966) is only one of several different types of OD interventions focusing on work teams. The case included here emphasizes interpersonal relations and personal learning. Other team interventions emphasize substantive tasks, such as long-term planning, or organization procedures, such as the mechanics of interdepartmental coordination. The latter raises fewer ethical dilemmas.

replaced—where position and status were influenced by family membership. Although the majority of the management and work force were generally satisfied with the earlier culture, the consultant did not hesitate to help effect the change.

### Building a New Work-Role System

Clark (1972, pp. 46–49) described a case set in the Danish shipping industry where social psychologist Hjelholt assisted one crew in anticipating and coping with the social problems caused by the transition from a traditional tanker to one of the most automated tankers. Automation was viewed as a way for Danish shipping to become more competitive. The OD consultant did not question this analysis.

Management was the primary sponsor for the change. The unions opposed it. The government was enlisted as a second sponsor to give management permission to conduct an experiment for one year.

Hjelholt took as given certain features of the new work system: dramatic reduction in crew size, with its implication for employment; and reduced turnaround in port and extended time at sea, with their disruptive implications for the crew's onshore life. He also accepted the new automated technology which would radically change the traditional system of tasks, roles, and work relationships and cause the obsolescence of many skills. He saw, however, that within the constraints imposed by these givens, there were the possibilities of relatively satisfying work structures and rules governing work, nonwork, and private time. For example, the reduced crew could fragment the social system and isolate members, a potential that might be avoided by innovative planning.

Hjelholt was given a free hand in devising the training for the crew in the months before the tanker was ready. He planned two one-week conferences involving representatives of the new crew and proceeded in the spirit of "maximum feasible participation." He used the conferences to build up a new work-role system that would fulfill the needs of those who worked on board the new tanker. The group identified various areas for planning: meal arrangements, alcohol regulations, location of quarters, use of leisure, safety, and maintenance (role of deck hands, and so on). Hjelholt's role was to analyze and facilitate group processes. Decisions were made largely by consensus.

After the new tanker was commissioned, Hjelholt traveled with the crew, observing, articulating tensions, and ensuring that the job enlargements were working. The results were reported as satisfactory in terms of both the quality of work life and the organization achievement:

> When the reports of the success of the experiment were circulated, there was some hostility and opposition to the innovation, but the crew was not deterred. Hjelholt attributed the success to "participative planning" (p. 49).

Hjelholt reflected humanistic concerns about the impact of the new technology, as if minimizing the social and psychological costs of the new work system was a worthy goal in and of itself, even where the consequences for organization effectiveness were problematical.

Management had to be reasonably satisfied with any solution proposed before it would be accepted, but the consultant greatly increased the influence of those who were the targets of change. Hjelholt sought participation by those *directly* affected in the planning process. However, he utilized a representative structure other than trade unions. As a result, the union might well argue that some general interests of the workers were sacrificed even though the workers directly involved negotiated conditions satisfactory to them.

### Strong Emotionality in Team Building

Kuriloff and Atkins (1966) report a case involving the top work team of a small manufacturing firm. Kuriloff was the president, and Atkins was one of two OD consultants utilized.

When Kuriloff became president, he found a lack of trust and confidence among three of his key subordinates: Rod, the chief engineer; Hans, the production manager; and Earl, the purchasing manager. After five months, he concluded "that the time was ripe for a more intensive and powerful attempt to resolve the problems of interpersonal conflict" (p. 65). He reported how his subordinates were approached.

When the time came to tell my people about the T-group, I approached each person individually. "We've got a chance to go through special training, paid for by the company. It'll be partly on company time, partly on your own. We'll go for five days straight from three in the afternoon 'till ten at night, with an hour break for dinner. The objective is to help us learn how we appear in the eyes of others, so we can improve our ability to get along with one another and improve our business.

"Attendance is voluntary, and if you choose not to come, it won't be held against you.

"This is a chance for all of us to get a valuable education at no cost to us, except the time we take out of five evenings. I plan to attend myself."

Admittedly there was a kind of covert coercion in this approach. Yet I was sincere when I said that attendance was voluntary. I hoped my sincerity would show and be believed, and that the conditioning of five months of meetings with my key people would, in some measure, allow them to trust me.

My feeling that I had establised trust seemed justified when all the key managers and supervisors showed up for the T-group (p. 67).

The stage was set by the physical setting, the expectations of the two consultants, and their introductory statement of ground rules:

> Fifteen brave people would be confronting one another in this circle, finding it very difficult to hide, even behind silence or bright, facile talk. The wide space in the center of the circle would be the dumping ground for people's misconceptions, for untested assumptions about one another that caused confusion, for unstated resentments. . . .
>
> Jack, the co-trainer, a tall, slow-speaking, mild-mannered man of few words, explained that the purpose of our getting together was to explore our feelings and relationships. Projecting a quiet strength, he said, "It's important to express feelings about one another, including us trainers. No holds barred." He added, "However, everyone should also feel free *not* to respond if it becomes too difficult or too uncomfortable. Openness is valued, but so is the right of privacy" (pp. 70–71).

After the naturally tentative beginning, the group got down to business and began confronting some of the interpersonal difficulties among its members—sometimes involving superior and subordinate relations and sometimes peer relations. At some point the discussions began to focus on Hans who, along with several other people, had not been able to attend this first meeting. Mounting resentment was being expressed toward Hans.

> The group was skeptical about changing Hans. His general reputation, even among people in other companies in the community, was that of a Nazi-like, unfeeling, relentless man who would hurt people to advance his own interests (pp. 74–75).

Hans also was absent from the session the second day. He had not been at work in the morning either:

> Someone said he called in and said he had the flu. The group laughed, knowing Hans's cleverness and knowing he would have anticipated a confrontation and exposure of his past "crimes." His absence was not surprising. They went on without him. . . .
>
> Jack presented the problem of Hans's absence and how it seemed to be holding back the group's progress. The problem was posed: how to get Hans back, when in all probability he was perceiving the group as a tribunal or even an inquisition (pp. 75–76).

On the third day Hans was there. When he finally was confronted he revealed his own personal background and suffering in a way that enabled others to emphathize with him. According to this account Hans appeared to be emotionally liberated by his personal revelations and the group's acceptance of them.

Earlier this third day, the group had focused on Helen, a young woman, and Bob, the elderly man who was her boss. Helen initiated the issue, describing her problem in general terms. The group knew whom she was having difficulty with, but they waited for her to identify him. When she did, Bob responded with defensiveness and tenderness. He recounted lapses in her performance and in her respect for elders. Finally, he described the enormous work pressures he was feeling. Shortly after that the consultant addressed Bob. He reported this intervention:

> I asked Bob why he felt so responsible for everyone—Helen, the men in the field, production engineering. Giving my further impression, I said to Bob that it appeared to me that he had strong fear of failure and shouldered responsibility that was not rightfully his. "Why do you try to make everything perfect?" I asked.
>
> "That's enough, laddie. I've said my piece," Bob concluded with finality. "No more. I have to leave for school in a few minutes and now I'm all upset."
>
> I backed off (pp. 77–78).

The fourth day's work included further attention to Bob and his relationships:

> Bob . . . seemed cold and disconnected from the warmth of the group. I tried to help him back in by reflecting this.
>
> Giving warning, Bob said, "Don't try to pull your tricks on me again, laddie. I won't fall for it!"
>
> If technique did not work, I had recently learned that there was nothing more powerful than being myself. "I feel as frustrated as Helen must feel with you, Bob. You just won't let people in."
>
> Bob turned away. I tried again. "What does a person have to do, Bob? Get on his knees and plead? . . . I was thinking all morning at my hotel, wondering how I could get through to you. You remind me of how hard it was to get through to my father. He never let me in—like you. It's hard to take."
>
> Bob looked directly at me with a kindly stare, but he said nothing. The subject was dropped (p. 81).

Again, the account reports that Bob had an emotional breakthrough with the group that resulted in his becoming more accepted by the group and more comfortable in it.

If "all's well that ends well," further analysis of this case may be irrelevant, because both Hans and Bob reportedly gained from their participation a rich personal experience and greater understanding between themselves and others with whom they work. However, in similar in-company situations the outcomes are frequently unsatisfactory—participants may regret their involvement, may become less effective in the organization, and may suffer a decline in their self-esteem.

Achievement of benefit rather than harm depends not only on the competence of the OD-P and the attributes of the participants, but also on the processes by which participants are involved. This case illustrates several questions about these processes.

First, Kuriloff was not entirely open about his intent. He decided to schedure a session when the time was ripe for an intensive attempt to resolve the conflict among his key subordinates—Rod, Hans, and Earl. Yet when he explained it to the invited participants, he stressed the educational value for individuals. At best, the phrase "so we can improve our ability to get along with one another" was an oblique reference to the conflicts about which he was directly concerned. In the language of OD, he had a "hidden agenda."

Second, the choice was not an informed one. Few of the members had been through anything like this before. Only those who had at least attended a T-group with strangers would have been in a position to anticipate what they were getting into. The authors do not describe any major effort to acquaint the people invited with the processes and the range of possible consequences—a step that would have been minimally necessary for an informed choice.

Third, participation was not a matter of free choice. Kuriloff wanted attendance to be voluntary, but admitted there was coercion. No matter how Kuriloff wanted it and phrased it, the situation had the character of a command performance. Kuriloff tried to reassure himself by interpreting the fact that all key managers and supervisors showed up for the T-group as confirming evidence that he had established trust. If some had shown they felt free to decline, Kuriloff would have had better evidence of their trust in his sincerity about the voluntary nature of the session. The OD-P could have provided checks and balances for these perceptions and actions of the client manager.

The same contradiction continued between a stated standard of individual choice and the reality of strong social pressure. At the outset, for example, the co-trainer said, "everyone should feel free *not* to respond if it becomes too difficult. . . . Openness is valued, but so is the right of privacy." Yet in Hans's absence, the group agreed to confront him with their strongly felt resentments. When Hans didn't show up for the second session and they speculated that he was exercising a choice not to participate, they set out to induce Hans to attend.

Similarly, the consultant pursued Bob, endeavoring, first in one way and then another, to get Bob to open up—to reveal what was going on inside himself. He tried the direct approach, but Bob countered with "that's enough, laddie." The consultant tried a Rogerian approach, but Bob warned he would not fall for the consultant's tricks. Finally, the consultant compared Bob to his own father and likened his current feelings of rejection to those he felt with his father. Still, Bob did not open up.

This discussion already has developed the fourth issue—the right of privacy. Neither the manager nor the consultants ensured respect for the right to privacy for Hans and Bob.

A fifth issue is raised by the consultant's interest in getting through to Bob, which seemed to be as much related to his own personal needs as they were based on professional judgment about what was appropriate for Bob. I do not question the consultant's choice to reveal his own feelings—that may not only have been effective but also may have served to create more symmetry and less power differential between the consultant and the target of the intervention. However, that intervention underscores the potential for consultant behavior to be self-oriented when it is being rationalized as client-oriented.

### Helping Demotees Accept Their Fate

Golembiewski, Carrigan, Mead, Munzenrider, and Blumberg (1972) reported an OD intervention that focused on the demotion of 13 field sales managers.

> As part of a broader reduction-in-force, 13 regional managers from the marketing department of a major firm were given a choice of accepting demotion to senior salesmen or terminating. The demotees were a heterogeneous lot. Selective data suggest the point: the managers ranged in age from 33 to 55; they had been with the company from nine to 24 years; and they had been managers for periods ranging from six months to 17 years. Moreover, although most of the demotees would suffer a major reduction in salary, reductions would range from less than $1,000 to approximately four times that amount (p. 37).

The 11 who accepted the demotion rather than terminating knew that they probably would be required to participate in the OD experience that had been discussed with several levels of management.

The intervention was intended to ease the pain for the demoted men and to preserve valued resources for the organization. Demotees met together half the time and met individually with their new supervisors for the rest of the time. The first day allowed for a ventilation of issues and an exploration of ways to cope with problems faced by the demotees. Some expressed "the complaint that the demotees did not see themselves being trusted as adults, or the feeling that they were men enough to take the demotions without the integrative experience" (Golembiewski et al., 1972, p. 141). All the demotees except one emphasized the positive meaning of the intervention; one resented it as "hand-holding" and "coddling."

The intervention included a test "which would provide valid measures of three clinically relevant negative affects: anxiety, depression, and hostility" (Golembiewski et al., 1972, p. 143). The results of this test and other observations led the authors to conclude that the intervention was effective in its own terms.

Commenting on this study in a published letter to the editor of the *Journal of Applied Behavioral Science,* Kramer (1972) wrote:

I wonder, however, whether the article does not point up some moral dilemmas. . . . First, the etiology of this reduction or demotion in the marketing force is unclear. Was it the product of a thorough analysis, of the situation, or was it the product of organization edict by some agent of hierarchical authority? And does the morality of making demotions less painful convert the applied social scientist into an agent of management, an anaesthetist, or a "cooling out" functionary? Does conversion of group demotion into a "more/more" proposition create a tenuous illusion that ought to be challenged? In addition, tactical questions such as "Who was the client?" also need to be made clearer (p. 63).

The case had raised the same questions for me. In their reply to Kramer, the original authors confirm the pertinence of these questions, but assure us that they had no intentions of cooling out anyone (Golembiewski, Carrigan, & Blumberg, 1973).

While the OD consultants were concerned with both organization achievement and the alleviation of human pain, their concern for the quality of work life was relatively narrow. A broader humanistic concern would have required attention to the *fairness* of the decisions leading to the demotions, including questions about the decision criteria and the consultative review and appeal mechanisms, if any, that were used in the process. Also, it was not in any meaningful sense voluntary participation. Finally, did the tests of the "clinically relevant negative affects" invade privacy?

## A Revised Work System and an Ideological Critique

Beer and Huse (1972) report a case in which work was restructured in a small manufacturing plant. They used a team approach, replaced assembly-line methods with larger tasks, gave operators responsibility for inspecting their own work, pushed decisions down the line, and emphasized mutual goal setting and participative leadership.

To introduce the changes gradually, first one manager and then another were encouraged to experiment and then to consolidate experimental conditions that were effective. These experimental changes were imposed on workers no more unilaterally, and probably less so, than other changes that management introduced in the plant.

The reported results were improvements in employee satisfaction, motivation, and plant performance. These results were considered highly satisfactory in terms of the consultants' values and purposes of their interventions.

This OD intervention was criticized by Brimm (1972) from his own particular ideological viewpoint, one that advocates the redistribution of power and resources within the industrial organization and considers "organizations as instruments for individual fulfillment rather than valid entities in their own right" (p. 106).

Beer and Huse introduce themselves to the reader as change agents who are dedicated to helping the organization "become." Quite to the contrary, I view them as system maintainers who stabilize and legitimize existing organizational arrangements. Because they fail to recognize the latent ideological content of their concepts and methodology and its implications for the outcomes of the change process, the authors—like many other practitioners of organizational development—have begged what I consider to be the fundamental issues of organizational change. . . . Thus, questions concerning the legitimacy of organizational purpose, distribution of power, allocation of rewards, and the relative primacy of organization welfare vis-à-vis that of the individual are not considered in this case study and analysis. Failure to consider these issues yields an approach which limits the potential scope of change to minor adjustment or "fine-tuning" of the organizational system (p. 102).

This criticism does not make sense to OD practitioners who have no quarrel with the existing patterns of power and the resource allocation within the firm. Even if one agrees with the need for more egalitarianism in these areas, as I do, one need not accept Brimm's hypothesis on the stabilizing effect of the intervention. Nevertheless, the comment effectively raises the possibility that OD work will inadvertently stabilize conditions that the OD-P believes should be changed.

### Consciously Coping with Value Dilemmas in Intergroup Work

I was involved in an OD effort to bridge the gap between managers drawn from the two cultures in a foreign subsidiary of a large multinational firm. Half were black nationals of the local country; the others were white expatriates. The two groups were equally represented in the OD workshops. It was assumed that more open intercultural dialogue would decrease instances of misunderstanding, improve current effectiveness, and hasten the rate of training of nationals who could replace expatriates in key positions.

The workshops promoted both effectiveness and social integration in the workplace. However, there was a quality-of-work-life dilemma involving career concerns of the two groups. The more one promoted the careers of black nationals, the more quickly one displaced white expatriates, many of whom felt that this country was home. I responded to the career concerns of both black nationals and white expatriates by ensuring that their superiors were aware of them. I could have better discharged my responsibility to the targets of this change effort by arranging for more direct communication with those who could act on these issues.

Another value dilemma existed because many black nationals experienced internal conflicts. On the one hand, their careers with the international firm enabled them to utilize their skills and to advance on the basis of professional merit; many also desired equal status contact with whites. This orientation led them to work on lowering barriers and facilitating the effective transfer of management control to blacks within the current ownership structure, thereby avoiding nationalization by the government. They feared nationalization would change the rules of the career game favoring political connections versus expertise and force a choice between a career with the international firm and staying in their native country.

On the other hand, many of these people were also oriented toward a national identity and hoped that their country would become more politically and economically independent of foreign firms. This orientation included a desire for more solidarity in the black managerial group and alliances with elite nationalistic groups in the country. It was feared that closeness with whites would lead to co-optation by the firm and estrangement from their fellow countrymen.

I sympathized with both of these conflicting orientations. I could appreciate the black nationals' career aspirations and their desire to build open relationships with white expatriates but I also could appreciate their fears about co-optation and could see how the workshops might work in that direction.

Thus, this case takes the value dilemmas at stake in OD beyond the question of organization achievement and quality of work life. One could argue that OD interventions in this case had the potential of serving the interests of client organization where they were in conflict with the interests of the host country. However, I was not convinced that the conflict of interest was inherent. I wanted to help find ways for firms of developed countries to bring capital, technology, and managerial know-how to bear within less-developed countries in a way that would be profitable and at the same time promote the economic well-being and political independence of the host country. Therefore, I had hoped that the government would not consider nationalization necessary for the advancement of the interests of the country. (As it turned out, the government did nationalize.)

At the time, I considered how to promote constructive management of the mounting conflict between the host country's government and the multinational firm. Specifically, I had in mind a problem-solving workshop such as the one that I helped design and implement on the border disputes in East Africa (Walton, 1970). Although I never made a direct initiative at the right time, a high official of the country in question later learned of the African workshop and estimated that the idea might have been acceptable and the process effective. Apparently the breakdown in negotiations between the firm and the government was in neither party's interest.

Noting these two missed opportunities only serves to strengthen my typically preferred approach to apparent value dilemmas—namely, when value dilemmas are raised by one's interventions at one level, one ought to try directly involving those whose interests are apparently in conflict, because trade-offs are not always necessary and integrative solutions are sometimes possible.

### Focusing on "Personal Growth" of Managers

I know a behavioral scientist who was in the process of deciding to leave a consulting firm to do only what he felt like doing. His OD work focused on individuals who, like himself, were struggling with their ambivalence about working for an organization. They were attracted by the status, compensation, and security offered them, but they deplored the constraints on life styles and self-expression that accompanied the employment relationships. This consultant, because of his unconventional dress, behavior, and utterances, made these ambivalences more salient for managers he worked with. They were encouraged to dissent more openly and to adopt life and work styles that were more deviant from the organization.

The OD-P offered the rationale that freer self-expression would enhance effectiveness. However, the real meaning of the work appeared to be related to an interest in personal exploration. One manager and the OD-P jokingly referred to "ripping off" the organization on whose time and in whose context the consultation was occurring.

I understand that the consultation culminated in several cases with the decisions by managers to quit their jobs and in two cases to choose radically different careers. What was the effect on the organizations that lost these talented managers? What were the consequences of these career decisions for their wives and children? Inevitably, there were new strains on the families. Were some broken? How many were better off if and when the breaks came?

The case here is admittedly an extreme form of one of the dilemmas it is intended to illustrate—those that arise from giving primacy to the self-defined "growth" interests of employees in the context of OD consultation.

The client manager and the OD-P should openly acknowledge to the manager's supervisor the primacy they give to personal "growth" versus organization effectiveness and state the relevant secondary consequences (for example, career decisions) that may result. However, openness with organization superiors does not touch the issue raised by the possible secondary consequences for the families of managers whose life styles change.

## ETHICAL ISSUES IN THE PRACTICE
## OF ORGANIZATION DEVELOPMENT

Some of the OD-P's responsibilities to the sponsors and the targets of change are similar to those involved in any professional-client relationship. However, many issues discussed below are especially significant because of the particular belief system associated with OD, which holds that organizations will be more effective if they manifest:

- participation and mutual influence
- openness about one's plans and intentions
- opportunity to make informed choices

- autonomy
- human versus impersonal process

These conditions set standards against which the professional activities of OD-Ps are judged.

### Disapproved Organization Goals and Strategies

An OD-P may be invited to help increase the effectiveness of a firm or agency that he has moral reservations about. He may be asked to do OD work for the military at a time when it is engaged in a war that he seriously disapproves of, for a large multinational firm when he morally disagrees with the firm's attempts to influence the White House in domestic matters and the CIA in foreign affairs, or for a firm that systematically defies environmental protection laws.

The OD-P who is concerned strictly with organization achievement defines himself as a technician. He does not need to evaluate the morality of an organization with which he works. He keeps the performance of his specialty at work separate from his moral judgments as a citizen.

An OD-P may accept an assignment despite reservations. He may reason that his work is sufficiently independent of the disapproved goals so that his actions will not affect them. Or he may argue that as OD opens up influence processes in the organization, the morally questionable goals will come under more scrutiny, thereby increasing the forces for change from within. Still another rationale is that regardless of an organization's strategies vis-à-vis its environment, its members deserve a work context in which they can develop their abilities and relate openly to each other.

Each professional needs to have developed standards in this area of choice. Our society needs fewer narrow technicians who do not ask questions about purposes and more professionals who are concerned about the values of their activities for humanity.

### Questionable Managerial Actions

I refer here to actions that do not meet certain minimum standards of justification and fairness. The cases of "top-down change" and the "demotees" help frame a particular variation of this issue: If an action that adversely affects the lives of members of the organization is taken because an executive concludes that action is necessary for organization survival or growth, the following questions arise:

- Does the OD-P test the executive's conclusions before he associates himself with the action?

- Does the OD-P insist that an explicit attempt be made to weigh the social and psychological costs and gains before he plays a part in implementing the action?
- Does the OD-P insist that decisions about how human costs are distributed among employees meet certain procedural standards (such as an absence of capriciousness or the presence of due process) or substantive standards (such as consideration given to past contribution or difficulty of adjustment)?

The OD-Ps should have affirmative standards with respect to these questions and should be able to communicate them.

### Unwanted Secondary Consequences

The OD intervention may have the intended direct effect, but its secondary consequences affecting those other than the client organization may be contrary to some value held by the OD-P. Specific possible unwanted consequences of the OD interventions reported earlier in this chapter include:

- weakening the union that was bypassed in the tanker crew intervention
- stabilizing the existing power structure in industry by designing more satisfying work systems
- co-opting black nationals by an international firm and weakening the independence of the host country
- disrupting families of managers who were the targets of "personal growth" interventions

Not all of these potential consequences were necessarily unwanted by the OD-Ps involved in the cases. However, they would be unwanted by many practitioners.

The OD-P is advised to generate more awareness of possible secondary consequences, accept a greater sense of responsibility for those consequences, and ensure larger influence from those who bear the brunt of the consequences.

### Responsibilities to Client-Sponsors

Several issues relate to abuses in the OD-P's relationships with the "client-sponsor," that person to whom an OD-P feels most accountable—not uncommonly the individual or group who brings in the OD-P. The OD-P may fail to live up to his responsibilities to his client-sponsor in any of a number of respects—overselling, making inappropriate interventions, giving too little commitment to the client, generating too much client dependency upon himself, and allowing a second interest such as research to interfere with action requirements.

### Confidence-Competence Gap

A client may invest greater confidence in the OD-P than is warranted. In the end, the client may not get an adequate return on the time, energy, and money invested, or worse, the OD-P may create more problems than he solves. The OD-P who knowingly allows the client to have exaggerated expectations is behaving unethically. Solutions include increased sophistication of clients, more use of references based on prior professional practice, and more accurate and realistic self-representations by practitioners.

### Force Fit of Standardized Interventions

An OD-P may be qualified to implement what he prescribes, but the prescription may not be tailored to an adequate diagnosis. The practitioner who has prepackaged interventions may unconsciously define the problem in ways that meet his own constraints—competencies, time avilabillity, and so forth. Unfortunately, this practice is not uncommon in OD. For example, some practitioners will recommend either team building or intergroup confrontation for every organization problem in a way that is analogous to a doctor who prescribes penicillin for every minor ailment.

The problem lies in part with OD clients, who, too often, want to bypass the diagnostic step, believing that there is a simple, patent, all-purpose remedy. Therefore, the solution also lies in part with the client. The sophisticated client will require adequate diagnosis and will explore the fit between the diagnosis and the intervention with the OD-P.

The greater responsibility for a solution lies within the profession. It should be widely regarded as poor practice, even as unethical, to intervene without an on-site diagnosis. There is a promising trend for practitioners to expand the repertory of OD skills and interventions available to them. However, consider the person who remains a narrow specialist in the sense that he intends to implement only a very limited set of the possible interventions. Should he be encouraged not to rely solely upon his own diagnosis but to rely upon general practitioners for referrals or for a confirmation of his diagnosis?

### Projected and Other Distorted Diagnosis

The self-oriented needs of the OD-P may be confused with the realities of the client's situation. I have observed practitioners who project their own preferences for openness, affection, affiliation, and the like, onto their clients or targets and then design OD to meet these needs. I have also observed practitioners who create a stage for *acting out* their own needs. One internal OD consultant had a habit of arranging confrontations between subordinate groups and their superiors and then playing an active role in challenging the latter's authority. From all indications, he was acting out his own needs.

These abuses are fewer when practitioners have more insight into their own psychological needs, when they understand the practical necessity (which some seem to forget) of denying themselves some self-expression, and when they work in teams in which each member is alert to the others' biases.

### Client Dependency versus OD-P Commitment

This is an extension of a problem I first encountered in the sensitivity training context at "stranger labs."[3] Occasionally a T-group would help an individual to open up psychological issues that could not be worked through in the two-week period of the laboratory. Members of the T-group who reported, for example, that they felt "unglued" would pack up and return home without the appropriate professional help to follow through. In some cases trainers were highly qualified clinicians, but their commitment to the group members was *time*-limited, not *need*-limited. In fact, from my observations, significant numbers of sensitivity trainers are attracted to temporary systems, as if they prefer short, intensive experiences in which they feel highly needed.

In the 1960s, many T-group trainers became concerned about the tendency for a person's behavior to return to prelab patterns within a few months. They concluded that individual change could be sustained only if T-group methods were used to simultaneously change the culture of the organization and the behavior patterns of individuals.

However, the professionals who shifted from sensitivity training in "stranger labs" to organization development did not always modify the nature of their commitment. Many continued to see themselves as promoting short, intensive experiences.

A two-week stranger laboratory is sufficient time to create the kind of learning about oneself and group processes for which T-groups are well suited. Thus, it was appropriate for T-group trainers to measure their commitments in weeks (as long as they were not opening up issues requiring therapy); but the life span of organization development efforts are measured in years rather than weeks.

Many client managers and internal OD practitioners have criticized external OD consultants for their short attention spans, which makes them unreliable in many OD roles. When an OD-P initiates a change effort and creates significant client dependency on his resources, does he have a responsibility to follow through, if possible? And if the consultant doubts that he will have the interest or ability to commit himself to follow through on what he starts, does he have a responsibility to the client to explore in advance the potential concequences of this more limited time commitment?

Abuses in this area are becoming less frequent. Many T-group trainers who tried OD work have since returned to training. Others have adjusted their work styles to fit organization contexts.

---

[3] "Stranger labs" are residental workshops in which the participants are drawn from different organizations and typically have no prior or subsequent contact with each other.

### Perpetuating Client Dependency

An ethical issue is created when an OD-P creates and preserves a dependency relationship that retards the client's capacities for self-sufficiency.

This abuse can occur in the more readily appreciated form of economic exploitation. Or it can take the form of "psychic exploitation" in the sense that the OD-P's psychic needs, rather than economic interests, are being met at the expense of the client's welfare. Consultants and clients can minimize this possibility (in which both may unconsciously collude) by periodically reviewing the conditions under which the relationship will be ended or phased out.

### Role Contamination—Consulting versus Research

Behavioral scientists who combine research and OD practice may confront dilemmas similar to those associated with research and training hospitals in the medical profession.

One risk is that the research objective will cause some neglect or distortion of the needs of the client-subject. This problem can be reduced by keeping the two roles separate in any given setting or by a clear understanding that one is practicing OD, unless he specifically announces that he is "putting on his research hat."

The second risk is that concern about the welfare of the client-subject will produce distortion in the research findings. This risk is especially great if the behavioral scientist is reporting on material that could be highly damaging to the image of the organization or could otherwise jeopardize the consulting relationship. Conversely, the risk is minimized where criticism is not likely to be a relevant aspect of the material, where the subject organization can be completely disguised, and where the behavioral scientist is not especially dependent on continuing the consulting relationship.

### Responsibilities to Client-Targets

The group of issues discussed next relates to adverse consequences of OD processes for "client-targets," those members of the client organization whom the OD-P attempts to influence. Of course, an OD sponsor may also be the target.

### Violating Privacy and Overloading Targets

Organization development frequently involves intensive interviewing. Members of a managerial work team may have their feelings about work, peers, and superiors explored in depth, summarized, and reported back to the team in order to help identify organization issues. Alternatively, similar data can be gathered and fed back in "real time" in a group setting, as in the case reported earlier by Kuriloff and Atkins.

An OD-P can go too far in eliciting from a person expressions of his feelings, perceptions, and beliefs. A good OD-P is skilled in encouraging a person to lower his defenses. Moreover, a person feels relieved after having ventilated strongly felt, but unstated, emotions and opinions. The self-disclosures may have net positive value to the person. However, as is sometimes the case, when a person subsequently feels anxiety because he said too much, or chagrin because he was seduced into revealing things about himself, then one can question the ethics of the data-gathering procedure. Similarly, an OD-P can go too far in feeding back the feelings and perceptions that are directed toward a particular member. "Overload" occurs when an individual gets more adverse feedback than he has contracted for or than he can use constructively. Some diagnostic insights that are useful for the organization are not necessarily good for a given work team and some information that is useful for the total work team is not necessarily in the interest of a particular member.

When does diagnostic data gathering become an invasion of the privacy of individuals or of small groups? When does potentially useful feedback become an overload and constitute psychic "battering"? Inasmuch as the abuses stem in part from the OD-P's enthusiasm, greater practitioner insight into ethical issues may be sobering and induce more caution. Many OD-Ps alert clients to the issues and encourage them to monitor their own involvement accordingly. Similarly, most OD-Ps are very sensitive to controlling feedback according to the readiness of the recipient. Such standards as these need to be fully accepted by the profession.

### Not Ensuring Informed Choice

Organization development interventions may be manipulative or coercive. Most OD-Ps attempt to be neither and strive to allow participants informed choice. But practice does not always conform to that ideal. The two cases of demotees and team building raised these issues. One could say that the targets were coerced into participating. Also the OD-P in the team-building case was manipulative in trying to get Bob to reveal his inner feelings.

There are no easy solutions to the problem of informed consent. Nevertheless, I offer the following tentative guideliness. First, serious attention should be devoted to more accurate labeling of OD services, including activity ingredients and possible harmful effects of particular interventions. Second, informed consent and voluntary participation are both more likely when the targets of change have had a voice in the decision about whether OD should be undertaken. While it may be difficult to say "no" to a session ultimately proposed by the boss, the early expression of reservations can, on the one hand, alert the superior to sensitive areas and, on the other, give the employee greater confidence in holding back. Third, where advanced and direct participation is less important or more difficult to achieve, OD programs can use pilot projects. In other words, they can be "market tested" for employee response. If reactions are neutral or negative, management and the OD-Ps could decide not to extend the process, and even to eliminate it in the pilot unit.

### Depersonalizing Members Who Provide Data

The procedures used to gather diagnostic or evaluation data from organization members affected by an OD project may further depersonalize members when their working life is already deficient in this respect.

Argyris (1973) presents a persuasive analysis of how the properties of the temporary system of researcher-subject may be remarkably similar to the properties of formal organizations. Rigorous research designs may have some of the same consequences for subjects that they experience from organizational structures and controls. Both may create a sense of incompetence, decreased autonomy, increased dependency, depersonalized identity, and narrowed understanding of the relevance of one's tasks. Argyris's proposals are also pertinent. He recommends providing the research subject with greater influence in the research project.

### Not Reporting to Those Who Provide Data

Many OD-Ps accept an obligation to report back to all who provided them with diagnostic data. Thus, they would not interview or administer a questionnaire unless there was a prior understanding that the employee population from which the participants were drawn would be informed of the findings. They feel that to do otherwise would be exploitative. I find this application of the reciprocity ethic a reasonable one, although here, as in other areas, I cannot say that I have always met the standards advanced.

### Not Providing Influence for Targets

Organization development processes often encourage people to articulate their grievances and to formulate ideas about changes that could improve their lives. If they cannot present their views directly to those who can respond to their perceptions and act on their grievances, then the process may serve to heighten their frustration and sense of impotence. Many OD consultants ensure that organization superiors will agree to some upward influence mechanism to serve the purpose described here. They believe the failure to ensure these conditions would violate an important ethic of reciprocity.

### Violating the Norm of Confidentiality

Generally, the OD-P is expected not to reveal information gained from one person if it may work to the latter's disadvantage. The norm is sometimes violated.

Not infrequently a manager will invite an OD-P to help him assess a subordinate. If the OD-P has not worked in a confidential relationship with the subordinate, he may feel free to offer his own observations. However, if he has worked with the subordinate in a way understood by the latter to be confidential, the OD-P is constrained. But what if the OD-P is confident that his observations would not only assist the superior to understand the subordinate but also work to the latter's advantage? Many times an OD-P will have negotiated an understanding with all parties concerned that enables him to exercise judgment in such situations. In some cases that consultant establishes a "no-confidentiality norm" whereby he is free to report any data provided to him.

It is important that all parties have the same understanding of the ground rules. Nevertheless, the OD-P's sense of responsibility to the larger client system (for example, the firm) may override his prior commitment to a particular individual with whom he had worked. One OD-P related a case to me in which the incompetence of a manager was contributing largely to the failure of the division, yet his superiors did not recognize his weaknesses. The OD-P was feeling mounting responsibility to bring these weaknessess to the attention of the man's superiors, even though he appreciated that if he participated in the evaluation process, his access and effectiveness in other situations could be badly hurt.

### Shifting Clients without Warning

Who is the client? Is an OD-P more committed to the welfare of the particular manager or group of managers who sponsor him than to other employees in the organization? Should an OD-P always take a total organization viewpoint? If so, should this viewpoint support the existing policies of the chief executive or substitute for what the OD-P believes should be the policies of the chief executive?

The kind of access and influence an OD-P seeks in order to perform his function effectively often involves shifting the focus from one group to another and from one level of the organization to another. If the movement is from a subordinate unit to a higher level, how can the OD-P avoid having the subordinate group fell threatened?

The OD-P must be clear and open about his own concept of the scope of the client system for which he feels immediately accountable.

## CONCLUSION

Some types of ethical issues reviewed here relate to the values, standards, and beliefs held by the particular OD-P, not to the profession. Thus, what is considered an ethical dilemma will vary from one practitioner to the next.

Each OD-P needs to clarify his own values and test their fit with the goals and strategies of organizations and the possible consequences of his own actions. The OD-Ps are encouraged to attempt to translate their values into more operational standards, for example, a standard regarding the justification and fairness of a managerial action with some adverse human consequences.

One type of ethical issue arises from inconsistencies between the consequences of an OD-P's actions and the values generally attributed to OD. But there is not yet consensus about values. Some would liken OD to operations research where the objective is to employ systematic knowledge and technique based on that knowledge to improve the performance of the client organization. In sharp contrast, a few would be primarily concerned with the quality of human experience and relatively indifferent about organization achievement. The illustrations in this chapter present a broad spectrum in this respect. The most common tendency is to combine OD work with changes that increase both organization achievement and the quality of working life. Common standards for ethical behavior will become possible as consensus develops about the value premises of the practice.

The consensus on value premises will not be static. For example, the basis of legitimacy for managerial actions has been traditionally based on ownership and some concept of management autonomy, such as managerial prerogative. The basis of legitimacy is shifting, deriving increasingly from communities that are outside the organization but are affected by managerial actions—ecological neighbors, consumers, and minority groups. The shift in the basis of legitimacy is accompanied by a reordering of societal values from almost exclusive emphasis on self-expression to the simpler joys of human encounter and a greater appreciation of the earth's natural endowments. As the criteria for managerial actions are responsive to these shifts, so too will the dominant critieria for OD shift, presumably in a way that will lead managers in its concern for humanistic values.

Another type of ethical issue involves violation of standards for professional-client relationships. This area deserves more attention, not only in OD but in other professional practices.

I regard as encouraging the OD profession's relative openness about its practice and self-criticism. A major journal in the field, *The Journal of Behavioral Science,* regularly publishes detailed accounts of OD interventions and specifically asks authors to be clear about the value premises of their efforts.[4] Invited comments on the cases often focus on issues of ethics as well as efficacy. This is an institutional manifestation of a more general professional ethic of openness and forthrightness about practice. The availability of data is both a testimony of the profession's openness to questions and is the best protection against ethical issues going unattended. Therefore, my major recommendation to myself and my colleagues in OD is for us to keep reporting on our work and to remain open to questions about what is effective and what is appropriate.

Finally, a comment on the nature of the world of action as distinct from academia. To intervene is to take risks. Action inevitably produces multiple consequences, not all of which can be anticipated. Action inevitably occurs within practical constraints: limitation of human skills, cognitions, and

---

[4] Another positive factor in the profession is The International Association of Applied Social Scientists, Incorporated, established in June, 1971, which is attempting to promote the development of ethical standards for OD along with its primary goal of accreditation for OD practitioners.

resources. Action is always subject to error, much of which will appear avoidable on the basis of hindsight.

This is the hazard of getting involved. However, the response of withdrawal to avoid error has its own moral cost—it is to accept the status quo. And then one must cope with the dilemmas and problems of nonintervention. As Martin Luther advised, those who intervene in the affairs of man must be willing to "sin bravely."

## REFERENCES

Argyris, C. Some unintended consequences of rigorous research. In B. J. Franklin & F. Kohout. (Eds.), *Social psychology and everyday life.* New York: David McKay, 1973.

Beckhard, R. *Organization development: Strategies and models.* Reading, Mass.: Addison-Wesley, 1969.

Beer, M., & Huse, E. F. A system approach to organization development. *The Journal of Applied Behavioral Science,* 1972, *8*(1), 79–101.

Brimm, M. When is change not a change? *The Journal of Applied Behavioral Science,* 1972, *8*(1), 102–107.

Burke, W., & Hornstein, H. A. *The social technology of organization development.* Fairfax, Va.: NTL Learning Resources Corporation, 1972.

Clark, P. *Action Research and organizational change.* New York: Harper & Row, 1972.

Golembiewski, R. T., Carrigan, S. B., & Blumberg, A. More on building new work relationships. *The Journal of Applied Behavioral Science,* 1973, *9,* 126–128.

Golembiewski, R. T., Carrigan, S. B., Mead, W. R., Munzenrider, R., & Blumberg, A. Toward building new work relationships: An action design for a critical intervention. *The Journal of Applied Behavioral Science,* 1972, *8*(2), 135–148.

International Association of Applied Social Scientists. *Policies and Procedures for Membership.* Washignton, D. C.: Author, 1973.

Kramer, H. A letter to the editor. *The Journal of Applied Behavioral Science,* 1972, *8*(1), 63.

Kuriloff, A. H., & Atkins, S. T-group for a work team. *The Journal of Applied Behavioral Science,* 1966, *2*(5), 65–83.

Walton, R. E. A problem-solving workshop on border conflicts in Eastern Africa. *The Journal of Applied Behavioral Science,* 1970, *6*(5), 453–496.

# 7
# MORAL DILEMMAS IN ORGANIZATION DEVELOPMENT

## DONALD P. WARWICK
Harvard University

The field of organization development (OD) suffers from many of the same definitional and moral ambiguities seen in psychotherapy, encounter groups, and programs of economic or social development. In each case, someone decides that there is a problem, and that something should be done about it. The resulting interventions then attempt either to rectify organizational conflicts, poverty, or some other negative condition, or to promote an idealized positive state, such as mental health, personal growth, or development. Very often, in an effort to get on with practical action, the values underlying both the definition of the problem and the terminal state are treated as obvious or are glossed over as matters of science. Closer analysis usually shows that from an ethical and a political standpoint these questions are considerably less obvious and neutral than they are made out to be.

Consider the case of OD. Neither Richard Walton's discussion in Chapter 6 nor other writings in the field have come to grips with the notable ambiguities in the word "development." The term implies an orderly unfolding toward some end point regarded as desirable, whether adulthood, psychological maturity, or self-sustaining economic growth. The definitions cited by Walton suggest a variety of possible end-points, none of which are

A joint presentation of the major arguments in this and the previous chapter appeared in Walton and Warwick (1973).

conceptually clear: the enhanced social functioning of organizations; increased ability to adapt to change; normative change; increased productivity; improved quality of work life; and more open, trusting relationships among people in the organization. For Walton, the goals subsumed under the label "development" are some combination of improved productivity and increased quality of human experience in the work place.

Such definitions, particularly those using terms like "organizational health," are amenable to widely varying conceptual and operational definitions. This ambiguity gives rise to serious ethical dilemmas. What is health for the manager or owner may well be disease for the worker. These definitional problems are compounded by disparities in power within the organization. In the typical OD intervention, some parties, especially management, are in a much better position than others to impose or sell their own interpretations of these polymorphous end-states.

My own experience with OD has been mainly in the U.S. Department of State and the U.S. Agency for International Development. In 1965 the State Department's Administrative Area launched a massive OD effort for the entire department and the Foreign Service. Under a contract with the National Training Laboratories in Group Development (NTL), this program, called Action for Organization Development (ACORD), undertook such activities as sensitivity training, team building, and problem solving. At roughly the same time the Deputy Under-Secretary for Administration attempted to improve organizational performance through a reduction of hierarchy and the decentralization of administrative operations. In 1966 he invited a team from the University of Michigan, which I headed, to evaluate these structural changes and to conduct a more general study of the morale and effectiveness of the Administrative Area (cf. Warwick, 1975). During this study, which brought us into frequent contact with the NTL effort, we were able to observe client reactions to OD in a public agency. In 1972 I served on a team that evaluated the OD program undertaken by the Agency for International Development. Most of my work centered on the outcomes of OD at a medium-sized AID mission in Latin America. Hence my view of OD is strongly conditioned by its successes and failures in a relatively new arena, the U.S. federal government. This perspective has suggested several ethical issues relating to the total organizational context of the intervention.

Apart from the definitional questions already noted, most of the ethical dilemmas in OD fall under three generic headings: power, freedom, and responsibility. In any concrete intervention these issues are tightly interwoven, but the ethical issues that they raise are sufficiently distinct to merit separate attention.

## POWER

Any serious ethical analysis of OD must squarely confront the question of power in organizations: Who gets what, when and how? The issue of power relations raises two ethical questions in itself and provides a political backdrop for the discussion of freedom and professional responsibility.

The first question is one of justice. Is it fair that those who already possess power and control wealth have disproportionate access to the techniques of OD? This point is particularly important because effective OD interventions will almost always change or reinforce the balance of power, influence, and authority in a system. Some individuals and groups will gain in the ability to pursue their interests and intentions, while others will lose. The resulting distribution need not be zero-sum, but it is rarely even across all participants. The cases cited by Walton, particularly those of the family-owned firm and the Danish shipping company, clearly illustrate situations in which the benefits of OD have been unequally distributed.

A crucial factor shaping the power relations in OD is the immediate source of sponsorship and the ultimate point of accountability. With few exceptions, the OD practitioner (OD-P) gains access to the organization through management, which also pays for the services involved. While many OD-Ps insist that they are working for the entire organization, and may indeed try to do so, the fact remains that they most often enter the system as management consultants. Without stereotyping a wide variety of situations, it is fair to say that in most OD interventions the issues of sponsorship, point of entry, and accountability are highly germane to power relations.

The second question centers on the degree of openness of power differentials in the OD effort. Are the power consequences acknowledged or, as is often the case, are they masked by benign, neutral language such as "team building," "problem solving" and "improved effectiveness"? One could argue that, even when there are initial inequalities stemming from sponsorship and related factors, OD is ethically more acceptable if the game is played in the open so that all participants (such as the unions) can make informed moves. The following are some specific ways in which OD can affect power relations in the organization.

## Definition of the Problem

A core component of OD is the collective identification of one or more problems as the focus of subsequent action. What gets defined as a problem is one of the most politically salient aspects of the intervention. There are two common patterns of problem definition, both of which can alter the balance of power.

First, the OD-P may simply go along with the definition of the problem presented by the sponsor. The OD-P thus becomes essentially a technician applying the tools of social science to ends specified by others. The case cited by Walton of management changes in a family-owned firm illustrates this stance. Beyond its power consequences, such a role definition by the OD-P implies significant abdication of professional responsibility.

Second, OD-Ps may serve as midwives in helping the organization or some part of it to define the problem. As skilled group leaders, they can exert a strong but often covert influence on the outcome of the discussions. By raising or disapproving of certain kinds of questions, and by selectively reinforcing or ignoring comments from within the group, they can channel attention in the preferred directions. A single query from the leader, posed with disarming innocence at an opening session, may set the pattern for an entire day. To create a good impression with the sponsor and perhaps to retain a lucrative consulting contract, the OD-P may be under considerable pressure to have the group focus only on problems that are acceptable to management, such as morale and communications, rather than to more volatile issues, such as wages, job hours, and authority structures.

## Choice of Target for Intervention

Decisions about precisely where to intervene in OD depend partly on the definition of the problem and partly on strategic considerations—where can change realistically be brought about with maximum benefit and minimum damage? In the U.S. Department of State in the late 1960s, a major problem for the Foreign Service was the ceiling placed on promotions by an "age lump" in the upper ranks. Several points of entry might have been appropriate for dealing with this problem. Some of the senior officers could be fired to create more room at the top. The annual quotas could be increased to broaden promotion possibilities. Wages or other employee benefits could be increased to compensate for the frustrations of slow promotions. Or, a series of discussions could be held with disgruntled junior officers to provide them with an opportunity to express their concern and ventilate their hostilities. An OD consultant brought in by the junior officers might be more inclined to choose the first two alternatives than an OD-P working for the senior officers would be. This is, of course, a caricature of most real-life interventions, but it illustrates both the arbitrariness and the political ramifications of the choice of a target.

## Intelligence Gathering

OD often involves gathering data on the political life and emotional underbrush of an organization. Diagnostic sessions often examine such internal conditions as openness, trust, and effective communication. But these benign terms are applicable only in benign situations. During times of internal crisis or external attack (a normal state in some government agencies), these seemingly neutral data may easily become instruments of battle or administrative repression. Interviews, problem-identification sessions, and confrontation meetings—the stock-in-trade of OD—quickly uncover pockets of discontent or inept leadership in the system. Organizational surveys may further show which managers are liked or disliked by their subordinates, which units are judged to be efficient or effective, and where morale is lagging.

In the typical OD scenario, such information is to be collected in an atmosphere of trust; no one is to be harmed by honesty or by revelations made by others. But trust has its limits, and administrators are human. If the data show that three division chiefs are roadblocks to effectiveness, transfer or dismissal rather than discussion and rehabilitation may be the order of the day. More seriously, if the entire OD effort should collapse, the data may be used for less than noble purposes. The chances for such abuse are greatest in organizations such as the State Department, which are run on a top-down, chain-of-command basis and are constantly subject to external monitoring and attack. Even with the best of intentions and the most careful preparations, the trust built up during the information-gathering stage may be shattered by a change in top management. A nonbeliever replacing an OD enthusiast may conclude that the best use of the data is for a general housecleaning. Unfortunately, there is no legal privilege attached to such information, nor are there any binding ethical standards to prevent the punitive use of data.

### Appraisals

The issue of power arises dramatically when the OD-P is asked to help management in appraising employees. As Walton has written:

> Not infrequently a manager will invite an OD-P to help him assess a subordinate. If the OD-P has not worked in a confidential relationship with the subordinate, he may feel free to offer his own observations. However, if he has worked with the subordinate in a way understood by the latter to be confidential, the OD-P is constrained (p. 142).

OD-Ps obviously must choose sides in these situations. Will they be consultants to management about subordinates, to subordinates about management, to rank-and-file employees about supervisors (for example, by sharing survey data on leadership styles), to all parties on an equal basis, or to none? When management is paying the bill, the temptation will be strong to help out on such practical matters. As Walton has rightly observed, taking a direct consulting role can involve a breach of confidentiality and therefore of professional responsibility. Moreover, to the extent that OD-Ps carry weight in the organization, whether from the prestige attached to their scientific credentials or from their access to confidential information, they can become political actors by selectively bolstering the position of one or more power contenders in the system.

These power implications may be obscured when OD is cloaked in the garb of science. The introduction of the OD-P as "Dr. Smith, a social scientist who is an expert on organizations" may create an image of impartiality and scientific neutrality that is not justified by the circumstances. Union leaders and employees in the organization would be well advised to look beyond such professional camouflage to the gritty realities of sponsorship and latent agendas.

## FREEDOM

Some of the most serious ethical questions about OD lie in the area of human freedom. Individuals can be said to be free when they have the capacity and the opportunity to make reflective choices and to act on these choices (Warwick, 1971). The essential components of freedom are an awareness of options for choice, knowledge of their respective consequences, and the ability to act on a decision. Freedom may be reduced or destroyed by coercion, environmental or psychic manipulation, and certain kinds of deceptive persuasion (Cf. Warwick and Kelman, 1973). As Walton's paper has made clear in Chapter 6, all of these conditions can arise in OD interventions. Four problems deserve particular emphasis: informed consent, coercion versus voluntary participation, manipulation, and misuse of information.

### Informed Consent

I would question whether most participants in OD, particularly in programs including some version of sensitivity training, are adequately informed about the nature and consequences of these activities. One dilemma, which also arises in behavioral and medical research, is that full information about the process and likely effects of the intervention may undercut the possibility of producing those effects. The practical moral question, then, is whether the personal and organizational benefits of OD justify ambiguity or even concealment in the advance explanations provided.

My own view, which Walton shares, is that significant concealment is not ethically justified. While there is no need to spend five hours detailing every conceivable form of psychic damage or career liability that may follow from OD, the initiators are obligated to explain in straightforward language what is entailed in the intervention and what major effects—good or bad—are likely to occur. Since the aim of OD in most cases is to promote greater openness and trust within an organization, it would be ironic if the very presentation of the intervention were marred by equivocation and mistrust of the participants.

Walton has offered three useful suggestions for improving the chances of informed consent in OD: (1) more accurate labeling of both the activity ingredients and possible harmful effects of the intervention, (2) greater participation by those affected in the initial decision about undertaking OD, and (3) more extensive use of pilot projects or market testing to determine employee responses.

There are, however, enormous practical barriers to achieving a genuine advance understanding of the OD process, as distinct from formalistic consent procedures. Informed discussion is often impaired by the cryptoscientific language used to describe OD, by the mystery in which its operational aspects are shrouded, by the difficulty ordinary employees have in imagining how group discussions might damage their personalities, and by the absence of a familiar calculus for assessing other consequences, such as the impact of the intervention on one's promotion prospects. If, on the other hand, the more sophisticated employees do grasp the nature of the process and its potential for harm, they may be so frightened that they choose not to participate at all. The practitioner therefore must often engage in either a veiled exercise of power, telling the employees in velvet tones that "the boss wants you here," or in a form of seduction, telling them enough to intrigue them but not enough to frighten them away. Walton's third suggestion is especially significant. Much more experimentation and pilot testing should be done to find ways of explaining OD in terms that are understood by all participants. Much can be learned from similar processes now being developed to improve informed choice in medical experimentation (Fletcher, 1967, 1973).

### Coercion

Whether or not employees are adequately informed about OD, they may be coerced or manipulated into participation through sundry techniques. The most common and ethically offensive is direct pressure from superiors. This situation is most likely to arise in the federal government or other traditional line organizations in which authority is enshrined at the top. Consider the following case from the federal government:

> The Director of [Unit A] accepted OD readily and thus influenced selection of his division as an initial target. The Deputy Director of [Unit A], heavily involved in daily operations of the office, perceived himself as "shut out" of the OD process. Whether this was actually the case is difficult to verify, but his perception strongly influenced his attitude toward the Director's mandate. OD became identified as the Director's pet project, a serious handicap when he was succeeded by the Deputy in March. . . .
>
> When the former Deputy became Acting Director, he immediately indicated his lack of interest in pursuing the OD effort. The consultants ceased work in March, 1971 and did not return until September when, as Director, he responded to a strong suggestion by his superiors and permitted them to return (American Technical Assistance Corporation, 1972).

Such top-down pressure is most common in line organizations where promotions depend heavily on cooperation with senior managers rather than measurable aspects of output.

Related problems of coercion or strong persuasion occur in the selection of individuals for sensitivity training, sometimes an ancillary part of OD. Between 1965 and 1967 the ACORD program in the State Department provided such experience, usually at off-site laboratories, for some 200 employees. I attended one of these in 1966 to acquire a better understanding of the entire OD effort. It was soon apparent that one of the participants in my group was acutely uncomfortable with the process, and had he been able would gladly have withdrawn into the upholstery. When his discomfort persisted for several days, I asked him privately how he happened to have come all the way from Europe to Maryland for this exercise. He replied that he had been sent by his immediate superior, who had attended an earlier T-group and thought it would be "good for me." Given the promotion system in the Foreign Service, which leans heavily on efficiency reports prepared by immediate superiors, refusal to attend would have been masochistic, if not suicidal.

While the OD profession cannot legislate or regulate the internal factors that lead to such command performances, OD-Ps should, as a minimum, refuse to take part in activities where there are indisputable signs of coercion. The practitioner who asks no questions about how the recruits were conscripted becomes the amoral "hired gun" of social science.

### Manipulation

This term covers deliberate attempts to change personal qualities or the structure of the decision-making environment without the knowledge of the individuals involved. By its very nature OD is manipulative, and OD-Ps are usually hired for their skill in group manipulation. To say that OD is inherently manipulative is not to say that it is intrinsically unethical. In many situations, such as attending lectures or movies, we choose to be manipulated for the sake of learning or entertainment. In counseling and psychotherapy, the clients are usually aware that the practitioner will carry out certain manipulations, psychic or environmental, to alleviate their problems. Whatever one thinks of their content, such cases at least have the advantage of being done for the person's welfare. In OD, by contrast, the manipulations are usually directed toward increased organizational effectiveness, morale, or other group conditions. The key ethical question is whether the individual participant has a right to know about and control the content and intensity of such manipulations.

Let me illustrate this issue with a personal experience. Some years ago I was employed by an organization that was extensively involved in both organizational research and OD. At one point the directors decided that it would be good for all the staff to participate directly in OD. Weekly sessions were scheduled, and all were asked to attend. After a few introductory presentations, the meetings quickly became T-groups. With little warning I found myself one evening in a sensitivity training session with about six other people.

The trainers—graduate students in social psychology—announced that this was an unstructured group, and that they were there only as helpers. After some initial groping about, the discussions began to center on the personality characteristics of individual participants. At this point, I questioned the ethics of the procedure, jarring the trainers out of their passive, so-called helper, role. None too subtly, one tried to turn the question back on me: "Aren't *you* being defensive? Isn't this your way of not facing yourself?" I said that I could see his strategy (I, too, had read books on sensitivity training) and did not accept it. I repeated the ethical question and suggested that we face it rather than try to discredit the questioner. The trainers again sought to mobilize pressure against such questions, but the tactic did not work. This seesaw pattern persisted for several weeks, after which I decided to withdraw. My point is not to justify my own tenacity but to illustrate the techniques commonly used to steer discussions in acceptable directions. In this case it was apparent that, despite their protestations, the trainers did have a hidden agenda, and that my questions about ethics were not on it. This point is further illustrated in the cases cited by Walton, particularly the remark made by one participant in a similar group: "Don't try to pull your tricks on me again, laddie. I won't fall for it."

### Misuse of Information

Many OD exercises use group processes to elicit expressions of hostility, anxiety, and resentment, as well as positive feelings. In the name of authenticity and trust, participants are encouraged to tell all. This is precisely what the OD-P was brought in to do, and most OD-Ps are quite good at it. The open expression of emotion raises two serious ethical questions: What is the impact of the revelations on the revealer, and what are the effects of overload on the target of hostility?

Walton has addressed both questions, but omits some important issues. On the first he states: When a person subsequently feels anxiety because he said too much or chagrin because he was seduced into revealing what he did about himself, then one can question the ethics of the data-gathering procedure. Beyond simply questioning the procedure, specialists in OD should investigate how often and under what conditions anxiety and chagrin arise, and with what intensity. It is difficult to discuss the ethics of a phenomenon whose dimensions are largely unknown.

An even more serious problem is the potential backlash effect of hostile or critical reactions to others in the same organization. Differences of power and authority give some members of the system an opportunity to retaliate later for unpleasant revelations or attacks. Let me again cite a personal experience.

The sensitivity training sessions held in the research organization mentioned earlier involved staff members at all levels, from the director to first-year graduate students and some secretaries. Despite the obvious power differentials and the ongoing organizational relationships, all were encouraged to participate as equals and to be totally candid in their reactions to each other. Such openness seems fraught with danger, especially for those whose career position is precarious. I was totally honest in revealing my reservations about this matter to the director, who was totally honest in telling me that I was being troublesome. The matter did not stop there, however. The combination of my nonconformity in the T-group and my questioning of the director quickly earned me the reputation of being a boat-rocker. My relations with the director and one other senior staff member suddenly became quite frosty, while friends reported that comments were being made among the senior staff about my lack of cooperation. I cannot honestly say that I suffered any career damage from this incident, for I had already decided to leave the organization for other reasons and had good prospects elsewhere. But the picture would have been quite different had I been a first-year graduate student whose employment network and letters of reference depended on the beneficiaries of my candor.

In a situation such as the Foreign Service, where promotions hinge on the ratings of one's immediate supervisor, openness can be disastrous. It is well known that some of the senior officers who participated in ACORD were emotionally scorched by the T-groups. One man, later to become an ambassador in South America, was reported to be still fuming six years later and wanted to hear nothing about OD at his post. In a system that exalts the role of the ambassador, it is hard to imagine that there would be no backlash against junior officers who gave vent to their hostile feelings. Moreover, with the frequent rotation of Foreign Service officers to overseas posts, it is quite possible that a ranking diplomat who suffered abuse in a "stranger's" laboratory could settle scores when the assailant was later assigned to the same mission. I would seriously question whether it is ethical for an OD-P to promise trust and nonretaliation in work groups or single organizations when there is no way of knowing if these guarantees will be honored. In the U.S. Foreign Service of the 1960s, there was certainly ample reason to believe these promises would not carry over to real-life situations involving the same participants.

Walton has pointed out the ethical difficulties arising from overload, a situation in which "an individual gets more aversive feedback than he has 'contracted for' or than he can use constructively." It would be helpful to know more about the kinds of contracts that are struck in OD, and how well they are observed. If there were genuine contracts, based on participation in the initial negotiations, informed choice, and reasonably complete knowledge of what might occur, the ethical questions would be less problematic. From what we can see, however, OD rarely involves contracts that are worthy of the name, and little advance effort is expended in determining how much feedback the individual can use constructively. Such an assessment would require considerably greater time for individual consultation than is normally available in OD.

## RESPONSIBILITY

In Chapter 6, Walton has given good coverage to the ethical issues deriving from the OD-P's obligations as a professional. I would like to expand on one of these, the failure to adapt OD to the concrete realities of a given organization.

It is generally conceded that, measured against its own objectives, the OD effort in the U.S. Department of State (1965–1967) was largely a failure. There were modest successes for certain individuals and scattered work groups, and the program may have facilitated subsequent reforms in the Department, but it brought about little permanent or deep change. There were three basic reasons for this failure, all traceable to the organizational system surrounding the reforms (cf. Warwick, (1975).

First, the political leadership of the department is highly transitory. A study of 1,000 political executives appointed between 1933 and 1965 shows that their median tenure in office was about two years (Stanley, Mann, & Doig, 1967). Significantly, the State Department had the shortest average tenure among major cabinet departments. This fact would be less crucial for OD if there were not a second complicating factor: the tendency of the top leadership to be new brooms for a few months, sweeping out the pet ideas of their predecessors in order to establish their own authority. Third, the permanent impermanence of the top echelon breeds suspicion and protective reactions in the middle and lower levels of the bureaucracy. Given the authority structure of an agency such as the State Department, a major change program will normally have to be initiated by or at least have the blessing of the senior appointed leaders. To succeed, however, it will have to be institutionalized or take root at lower levels, where resistance is often maximal.

The State Department's OD program was initiated by the Deputy Under-Secretary for Administration, William J. Crockett, on the advice of several leading social scientists. It was largely a top-down decision to promote bottom-up democracy (as one critic put it, Theory Y by Theory X methods). ACORD generated a flurry of activity during the two years of its existence, but was almost entirely scuttled when Crockett resigned in 1967. In a 1970 interview, Crockett commented:

> The rotation of top officials in State . . . does produce casu-
> alties to programs left by an outgoing official, especially if the

program is either difficult to carry out, controversial, or in trouble. . . . If we can't command the time frame to get it in place then we should think carefully about starting it in the first place. At least this is the way I feel now, but I frankly didn't even think of this matter at the time.

From all indications neither did the OD team. The ACORD/NTL effort could thus be criticized for failing to take account of the total context of the State Department, and for force-fitting interventions developed in other kinds of organizations. It could be argued, on the other hand, that it was precisely the mistakes made in ACORD that brought out the distinctive features of that environment. I would personally not be too hard on the ACORD program, but I do feel that more of an effort could have been made by all concerned to carry out a prior analysis of the unique features of the State Department and, indeed, of the entire federal executive system. This example underscores Walton's point about the dangers of focusing on techniques rather than on the total situation.

Another problem in the State Department arose from the attempt to induce attitudinal and behavioral change greatly at variance with the prevailing norms in the system. The culture of the Department emphasizes the accountability of officials up the line, particularly to Congress and the White House, and the need for obedience by those below. The basic thrust of the OD effort, on the other hand, was to democratize relationships in the system by promoting bottom-up communication, openness, and similar qualities. The ethical dilemma concerns the advisability of encouraging change in individuals that may ultimately work to their disadvantage in the organization. Specifically, is it professionally responsible to foster confrontation in a system that normally punishes such qualities? One could argue, of course, that the only way to change the system is to develop a critical mass of employees who will eventually spread the leaven of openness. But the difficulty in the short run is that some of the more credulous acceptors may be singed by applying the right behaviors to the wrong situation. This point relates to the earlier discussion in that the constant rotation of political appointees may increase the chances of a poor fit between managerial expectations and employee performance. If OD changes the norms, expectations, and behaviors of an entire work unit, such as an AID mission, and if that unit has a good chance of remaining together, the ethical difficulties would be minimal. But if both employees and managers are in constant rotation, as is true of the Foreign Service, and if there is little possibility of altering the entire system in which they work, one could question the efficacy of piecemeal OD in single units. Their ultimate effect may be to raise employee expectations, only to have them dashed on the shoals of leadership change. This discussion suggests that professional responsibility calls for attention to the broader context of organizational change, especially to the hazards accompanying frequent reassignments and rotation.

Walton concludes his chapter by posing two ethical alternatives for the practitioner: nonintervention, with the risk of accepting the status quo; and getting involved, with the liability of unanticipated consequences and errors. His final recommendation is to take action and be prepared, with Luther, to "sin bravely." Both his comments and mine, however, suggest a third course falling between retrograde inaction and mindless intervention. This is the strategy of advance contextual analysis followed by constant attention to direct and indirect consequences. Rather than plunging immediately into confrontation, team building, and other group exercises, the OD-P would spend a fair amount of time analyzing the power setting of the organization, the understandings and suspicions of the groups affected, possible side-effects of the intervention on vulnerable individuals, and the likelihood that any changes produced will be permanent. If the cost of such caution and foresight is a slower pace of change and even a few lost contracts, so be it.

As a counterpoise to Luther we might heed Samuel Johnson: "Without prudence fortitude is mad; without justice it is mischievous."

## REFERENCES

American Technical Assistance Corporation. *Organization development in AID: An evaluation.* Washington, D.C.: 1972.

Crockett, W. J. Personal communication, 1970.

Fletcher, J. Human experimentation: Ethics in the consent situation. *Law and Contemporary Problems,* 1967, *32,* 620–649.

Fletcher, J. Realities of patient consent to medical research. *Hastings Center Studies,* 1973, *1,* 39–49.

Stanley, D. T., Mann, D. E., & Doig, J. E. *Men who govern: A biographical profile of federal political executives.* Washington, D. C.: Brookings Institution, 1967.

Walton, R. E., & Warwick, D. P. The ethics of organization development. *Journal of Applied Behavioral Science,* 1973, *9,* 681–698.

Warwick, D. P. Freedom and population policy. In Population Task Force, *Ethics, Population, and the American Tradition.* Hastings-on-Hudson, N.Y.: Institute of Society, Ethics, and the Life Sciences, 1971.

Warwick, D. P., in collaboration with M. Meade and T. Reed. *A theory of public bureaucracy: Politics, personality, and organization in the State Department.* Cambridge, Mass.: Harvard University Press, 1975.

Warwick, D. P., & Kelman, H. C. Ethical issues in social intervention. In G. Zaltman (Ed.), *Processes and phenomena of social change.* New York: Wiley, 1973.

# IV
# COMMUNITY-CONTROLLED EDUCATIONAL REFORM

# 8
# THE SEATTLE URBAN ACADEMY PROGRAM: AN EXAMPLE OF SOCIAL INTERVENTION

**C. P. HUEY, J. C. LITTLE, AND P. SMITH**

Seattle Urban Academy

**R. J. BROUNS, H. HARTY, J. W. JOHNSTON, AND R. D. WIDRIG**

Battelle-Northwest

**W. M. HARRIS**

Visiting Student, Battelle-Seattle Research Center

**C. MILLER**

Washington State Board for Community College Education

**J. L. WARE**

Former Chairman, Central Area School Council, Seattle

## INTRODUCTION

The Seattle Urban Academy (SUA) program began during the fall of 1968, a time of severe racial strife and home/school alienation in Seattle. Continuing disruption of the schools, slacking discipline, and a fall in the quality of instruction were the trends in the schools. The Academy idea was conceived that year by John C. Little and Charles P. Huey, co-directors of the Community Talent Bank, a program designed to help students by bringing central area homes and schools closer together. They saw, first-hand, the inability of the existing educational system to meet the needs of many inner-city youths, particularly those who, for one reason or another, were repelled by, or unable to cope with, the present school environment, and who did not find anything in that environment to stimulate them. The pattern in the inner-city schools of Seattle was typical of inner-city schools across the country.

Current affiliations of the authors are listed on page xi.

The Urban Academy program was an effort to bring about change in the educational system serving Seattle's predominantly black central area. The scope of the effort can be gauged from the facts that it took place over a three-year period, involved more than 100 meetings with community groups, had a permanent staff of ten people, and expended about half a million dollars. The program's impetus came from the community[1] and its funding from Battelle.[2] The goals of the SUA effort were to design and put into operation an educational system based on the needs of Seattle's inner-city community. The education system that was developed did not reach the operational stage. The SUA effort did, however, produce a methodology for developing an educational system based on: (1) the community's educational objectives, (2) the methods the community wanted used to attain the objectives, and (3) successfully demonstrated inner-city education programs. The results of this developmental effort are summarized in "The Seattle Urban Academy Program Plan" (unpublished), which contains the outline of the design, organized into logical groupings of "activity write-ups." A complete activity write-up contains a goal statement, assigns responsibility for goal attainment, describes methods to be used in attaining the goal, and gives scheduling and cost estimates for the activity. Some activity write-ups are quite complete; others are merely titled to provide a place for future development. The SUA effort can be summarized as an attempt to meld the community's input with Battelle's methodologies and the education profession's expertise, and, through a series of phases, pass the initiative and responsibility from the SUA team back to the community.

In this chapter, we describe how the effort began and progressed and discuss some of the problems and ethical issues encountered. Despite the fact that the Urban Academy never became an operating school, it is hoped that the communication process, which was the core of the developmental methodology, can provide social scientists and educators with an expanded scope, if not a model, of what is required for community involvement.

## An Overview of the Seattle Urban Academy Program

Huey and Little brought the idea for changing the school environment to Battelle, for whom they became part-time consultants, and requested assistance in developing it. Battelle, recognizing the need for educational change and the merits of the Urban Academy proposal, agreed to provide staff assistance for developing the concept in more detail and exploring ways to implement it.

---

[1] The community referred to in this paper was composed of the population (60 percent nonwhite, 40 percent white) that elected the Central Area School Council, plus the students residing in that area, and others in the greater Seattle area who exhibited an interest in the SUA program.

[2] Battelle Memorial Institute is a private research organization, home-based in Columbus, Ohio. Other Battelle facilities involved in the SUA program are Battelle-Northwest in Richland, Washington, and Battelle-Seattle Research Center in Seattle, Washington.

A team composed of Huey, Little, several other Seattle central area residents, and Battelle staff members worked on the concept for several months. They solicited suggestions from other community people and educators, acquired background information about educational innovations, and prepared a written description of the proposed Academy. During this preliminary development process, the team decided to expand the concept from simply a school for drop-outs to one for all inner-city youth. This decision was motivated by the recognition of the need for fundamental changes in philosophy, attitudes, and teaching approaches in the educational system of inner cities rather than the need for remedial programs. The overall objective of the Academy became "to develop and demonstrate an educational system which is effective in educating urban youth who are underachieving in the present system, while not compromising but rather enhancing educational opportunity for achieving youth." The final Academy concept was to plan and implement a comprehensive and full-scale inner-city education system (3,000 or more students of ages 3 to 20). The concept incorporated with the Academy team felt were the things inner-city students, parents, and teachers most wanted in their educational system.

The Academy program was carried out in several phases (Figure 1). Following the development of the concept by Huey and Little (concept phase), the first major phase was termed the "preliminary design" phase. This phase was an orientation for the participants and a deciding phase for the Academy concept, that is, what the Academy should become and how it could be realized. It became apparent that what was needed in subsequent phases was to pass the

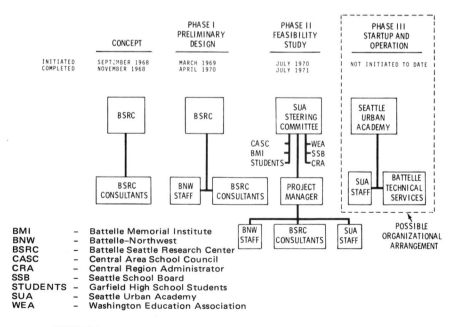

**FIGURE 1.** Groups involved in the phases of the Seattle Urban Academy program.

initiative and responsibility back to the community for implementation and operation of the Academy, based on the conviction that the people in inner-city communities must have more control over the administration and the teaching in their schools.

In Phase I, the originators of the Academy concept (shown as Battelle-Seattle Research Center consultants in Figure 1) were assisted by five part-time engineer/scientists from the Battelle-Northwest Laboratories and several additional short-term community consultants. More than 100 meetings with student groups, teacher groups, and parent and community groups occurred during this phase. These meetings were generally chaired by a person selected by and from the group rather than an Academy team person. The discussions were very open, candid, and often vigorous. Minutes were kept, usually supplemented by audio- or videotape recordings and the Academy team drew many of the Academy ideas out of these discussions.

The end-product of the preliminary design phase was a tentative plan for proceeding and a program plan describing the Academy in considerable detail. The preliminary design phase was completed in the spring of 1970. During these months the team was developing an understanding of the problem, evaluating the potential role and commitment of Battelle, and simply getting to know each other and where each was "coming from" and "going to." Meetings were also held with educators, the Seattle Superintendent of Schools and his staff, and the School Board, and numerous innovative educational facilities were visited.

During the same period (spring 1969 to spring 1970), the Central Area School Council (CASC) was formed as the result of another community action effort, and in July, 1969, the CASC selected a Central Region School Administrator. This administrator requested and received assistance from some of the SUA program team members and from Battelle in organizing and developing procedures and systems for the Central Region Schools. This experience, as well as the fact that Huey was a member of the CASC, provided the SUA program team with valuable insight and background information. It also increased the visibility of the Academy's working group and the acceptance of the Academy effort with the CASC and the community.

The objective of Phase II, broadly stated, was to determine the technical, economic, and political feasibility of implementing the Academy concept (Phase III). Phase II was initiated in mid-1970 and completed in mid-1971. It had become apparent during Phase I that the SUA program could become a major divisive factor in the central region community if an attempt were made to bring it into being apart from the CASC. In addition, because of its political and policy-making capabilities, the CASC seemed to be the logical and most direct vehicle for involving the community in a substantial way in the Academy implementation. Thus, a major decision was made to ask the CASC to carry out Phase II. The CASC set up a steering committee: community adults and high school students were in the majority; Battelle staff members, representatives of a teachers' professional organization, and the Seattle School Board made up the rest of the membership. The steering committee hired the Phase II project manager and several staff workers. These persons were supplemented by the above-mentioned BSRC consultants and Battelle staff.

Based on the feasibility study, it was determined that the economic and political requirements for implementing Phase III could not be met. Phase III was not initiated because adequate support from financial, community, and other interests did not materialize. A number of factors were involved, including the concerns that the Academy program might conflict with new educational programs being implemented in the central area, that the program might conflict with school system desegregation plans, and that the Academy might lead to fragmentation of the school district. Failure of the state legislature to pass legislation to make programs like SUA possible was another major factor.

## Composition of the SUA Team

The inner-city people who were major participants in the program had been extensively involved in community activities for years. They included two city utility department employees who had been loaned to the school district in 1967–1968, during a period of severe disruption in the inner-city schools, to conduct a home-school liaison program; a lawyer; a student who had been actively involved in such community action efforts as formation of the Central Area School Council and a Black Student Union at a Seattle university; a former Battelle employee (a physicist) on leave as a student; an elementary school teacher; a school principal; and several short-term participants, including two housewives and a retired career military man. Nine were black; one was white. Two law students were also involved, doing legal research on the specific problem of subcontracting the operation of public schools. As previously indicated, some of the inner-city people were consultants to Battelle for all or part of the three-year period; others were employed by the Seattle Urban Academy.

The Battelle people involved in the program had these backgrounds: one was a nuclear engineer; two were chemists; one was a chemical engineer with an MBA; one was a statistician; and one was a physicist. Most of them were long-term Battelle employees with extensive management experience. Other Battelle people with skills in such areas as public relations, finance, and systems engineering were used in short-term assignments.

## THE SEATTLE URBAN ACADEMY PROGRAM'S APPROACH TO SOCIAL INTERVENTION

So far, in this chapter we have stated the context of the problem attacked and the progress of the solution proposed. For the most part, the SUA team looked upon the Academy program not as a social intervention effort but as a problem-definition and problem-solving effort—much as one views scientific or engineering problems. The team was not comprised of sociologists, and little formal sociology entered into the problem-solving efforts.

A description of a program like this in retrospect often has the effect of "filling in the hollows and knocking off the peaks"—that is, of making the program seem better planned and executed than it actually was. The Academy program did not proceed in an orderly manner like most engineering projects. There were many starts, stops, and pauses. The phases referred to did not become clearly defined until the inception of Phase II. A complicating factor was the fact that the traditional sponsor-client relationship did not exist. Thus, decisions and directions were not readily forthcoming. The authority to establish the Academy and the source of funds to operate it were not clear in the beginning.

### Context and Goals

The general context of this example of social intervention is urban education. Using the definition of social intervention given by Warwick and Kelman (1973), education itself is the most pervasive example of social intervention in our country. Its basic goal is to alter the characteristics of each individual in such a way that he or she has a common basis for relationships with other individuals and with agents of our society. Although education has traditionally been considered the socialization agent for our society, its real impact on upward social mobility is being seriously challenged (Greer, 1970). Its responsibility to educate everyone, not merely provide the opportunity for education, is being more universally accepted. The ethical affront the educational enterprise gives to some social activities is exemplified by the exhortation to de-school society given by Ivan Illich (1970, 1971).[3] Irrespective of the position one takes on the elitist to least-common-denominator continuum of educational policy, the fact remains that education is a massive form of social intervention which Kenneth Clark (1965, 1970) and other critics of education have observed to produce devastating infringements on individual freedom and self-esteem, particularly among the urban poor.

The approach the team took in developing the SUA program was influenced by a number of factors. The objectives the participants held as individuals and as members of groups were a major factor. These objectives may be considered under the three groupings of participants:

- the objectives of Battelle
- the objectives of the blacks who participated in the program
- the objectives of the community the SUA would serve

[3] Ivan Illich is the founder and head of the Center for Intercultural Documentation, Cuernavaca, Mexico.

Battelle's chief objective for the program was to innovate improvements in the educational opportunities for inner-city (mostly black) youth by serving a community with the research and development resources of Battelle. Additionally, Battelle hoped to utilize this experience to better understand the ways of change in social systems; to conceive and evaluate other possible new roles for Battelle in education; and to find better ways for coupling the skills and perspectives of natural scientists, engineers, and social scientists to the urgent needs for improving the quality of living in urban communities.

It is important to note that these objectives are process-oriented, and not end-product-oriented. From the black participants' point of view, Battelle's goals tended to be organization-centered and not client (black community)–centered. Battelle had no preconceived idea about the outcome. The Battelle participants exercised caution because of their inexperience in this sort of activity and because they wanted to ensure that Battelle did not become involved in activities that might be inappropriate to Battelle's charter (for example, lobbying for legislation) or that would create significant unfavorable publicity. The Battelle participants were genuinely concerned that they hear the messages from the community and accurately translate or assist in the translation of these messages into an educational plan or design. They tried to play the roles of expeditors and resource persons and to avoid imposing on the team their preconceived, white, middle-class concepts of a good education system. In addition, Battelle was concerned that its involvement in the effort might alienate the community (that they might regard it as another effort by a large white organization to solve the blacks' problems for them) and thus hamper getting the broad community input that was needed. Therefore, Battelle appeared—and was in some cases—timid or placid in striving to implement the SUA program.

The blacks' objectives tended to be end-product-oriented. For the most part, their concerns came from the frustration felt by the black community toward unresponsive, unproductive schools. This frustration, coupled with the high value they put on quality educational achievement by their children, led to the establishment of community goals for education. The black community's primary goal was to bring about institutional change in the educational establishment. This change would be realized through schools that were responsive to and productive for the community.

The black community's image of a productive school is one in which children achieve. No excuses such as family status, socioeconomic conditions, and race are acceptable reasons for poor student performance. Blame for failure in school is shifted from the student to the school itself. Thus, the blaming-the-victim philosophy of the educational system is counteracted. A responsive school is one where parents and students have a real communication link with the administration. That is, these two groups are genuine partners in the decision-making process of the school. For example, they have a voice in staff selection (and dismissal), school program evaluation, and the teaching process.

The Academy objectives were intended to be synonymous with the community's objectives, although it was recognized that such unity is seldom attained in reality. The major objectives were as follows.

*Overall Objective:*

The overall objective of the Academy is to develop and demonstrate an educational system that is effective in educating urban youths who are underachieving in the present system while not compromising, but rather enhancing, educational opportunity for achieving youths.

*Subobjectives:*

1.  To involve the community actively in the education process.
2.  To develop an improved understanding of the teacher-learning process for urban youths, including those who in some respects are under-achieving in the present system.
3.  To demonstrate convincingly the effectiveness of the proposed educational system in a nonlaboratory, real-world system.
4.  To duplicate or replicate the educational system that is developed.

Many meetings of the SUA team and of team members with community groups were devoted to developing these objectives. The fact that the community was concerned about institutional changes and their acceptance and understanding of the research-demonstration-replication methodology for bringing about changes are reflected in the last three subobjectives. The community's immediate concern was with its own local problems, but it saw the value to itself and others of applying the educators' own paradigm for change.

The Academy could have taken many forms. The team periodically considered and reconsidered applying its efforts to (1) creating street academies and (2) assisting the present school system. Both of these were done, but the main effort remained an educational system standing somewhat apart from the existing system. The major reason for rejecting applications 1 and 2 was that neither promised to have any lasting effect on the educational system. A broader effort was needed if the SUA's objectives were to be attained. An actual community school was threatening to the existing educational system and difficult to finance; yet a high degree of autonomy was needed to bring about the changes deemed necessary. This played an important role in formulating the concept of a community corporation operating the Academy for a fixed time period.

The objectives held by other important entities, such as the school district and the teachers' education association, were very important too. Their educational objectives were factored into determining the overall program approach.

As the SUA program team members began to interact, several additional factors became important in determining the course that the program took. First, and perhaps most important, was the fact that both the blacks and Battelle had a problem-solving orientation. The blacks had this orientation for reasons stated earlier; Battelle had this orientation as a way of doing business. A major conflict would have occurred had Battelle primarily approached the effort on a "search for knowledge" basis, as many academically initiated programs do. This mutual orientation was largely responsible for the selection of a specific end-product by the SUA team—the Academy as a functioning institution. The second determining factor was the observed fate of small efforts at educational change. Members of the SUA team visited the sites of many meritorious efforts at educational change. Most of these efforts were quite small, and it was often noted that when the key person in the effort left, or the federal financial subsidy ended, the program would die out. The third factor was that neither Battelle nor the community had control of an educational system. Fourth, Battelle could not commit the financial resources required to operate the SUA. The fifth factor was the criteria believed necessary for successful operation of the Academy. These were:

- The Academy must have the authority to control its own program within a broadly stated charter.
- The Academy must have adequate resources, including funding, to carry out the necessary parts of its program.
- The Academy must strive for real community, teacher, and student involvement.
- The Academy must maintain a thorough and open planning and evaluation program.
- The Academy must select, train, evaluate, and restructure teachers' job responsibilities and assignments to help teachers meet the challenges of the Seattle Urban Academy system.
- The Academy must offer educational opportunities to all children living in the community it serves.

During Phase I, it became apparent to the team that the problem went much deeper than the failure of the schools to teach the urban poor to read: the schools were actually having a detrimental effect on the socialization of many urban poor. That is, rather than providing the urban poor with easier access to the good things of society, the educational system turned many off to the pursuit of the ethical goods traditionally valued by our culture. Thus, the program's goal became one of restructuring the educational system.

### The Communication Process

The major working tool of the SUA effort was the process of communication. One party to the discussion would state his interpretation of desired ends or means, the other party or parties would react to the postulated ends or means and alternatives would be generated. A conscious effort was made to consider all potential alternatives, even if their realization might be improbable. Discussion and analysis of the alternatives were also directed toward the potential implications of each on other desired ends. The output of these discussions (which varied from a few hours to weeks on a particular topic) within the SUA team was the alternative or, frequently, alternatives on which consensus was reached. These alternatives were then used as postulates to initiate the same type of reactive discussion between the SUA and other groups in the community. The process was interactive and iterative; it worked because it was open, it was not constrained to come up with unanimity on a single alternative, and there were minimal hidden agendas. When two or more alternatives were required to express consensus, both were included in the program plan as postulates for further development or consideration.

The SUA effort was based on the development of this communication process on two levels: first, within the working team—between white, middle-class engineer/scientists and black community representatives (including educators)—and second, between the SUA team and the broader community interested in education. The process was similar at each level and can be characterized by the following chain of activities:

This process was used at every stage of the program, from problem definition and goal selection through any methodological details that developed. The SUA plan was designed to facilitate this type of communication between people with differing or undefined goals. The rationale was that if real objectives can be clearly stated and agreed to, then methods to attain the objectives can be intelligently discussed and selected. A key to the overall success of the approach was that the discussion included the impact of the focus topic on other aspects of the whole problem. This is where the structure of the systems engineering approach was a valuable tool, permitting piecemeal discussion and solution of problems without losing sight of the overall picture.

To illustrate, Huey and Little's original description of the problem was interpreted quite narrowly by educators at early meetings as expressing a need for an alternative school for drop-outs or drop-out-prone students.[4] While that

---

[4] Largely due to Huey and Little's efforts, such a school now exists in the central region of Seattle. This alternative school, the Extended Services Program (ESP), serves those

type of alternative was sorely needed, the SUA team reached a consensus—after months of discussion and analysis—that the high drop-out rate experienced in the central area, along with the in-school floaters, was a symptom of a more basic deficiency in the system itself. Further application of the communication process with teachers, parents, and student groups resulted in the realization that the deficiency was also manifested in the system's inability to respond to the human needs of its own staff, particularly teachers, and that the system was consequently insensitive to the human needs of students and was unable to respond to those needs, should they be recognized. Thus, the solution was to change administrative methods and the role of the teacher. The system itself, not the drop-outs it produced, became the focal point of the social intervention.

The communication process helped the team to avoid the major ethical problem encountered in getting many social interventions under way: namely, getting started without compromising the freedom of choice of the eventual participants in the program. In addition to the communication process, the fact that Huey and Little were involved from the beginning—indeed initiated the joint effort—helped avoid an unfortunate kind of preplanning that often preceds community involvement. Such preplanning often sets up boundary conditions, or a prejudged framework for acceptable solutions, that result in the community's being a rubber stamp, and often the community does not even realize it. This preplanning approach may have a rationale that is valid from the preplanner's point of view but not necessarily from the community's. In fact, such preplanning is often the cause of the community's standpoint: the preplanning activity, to which the black community is highly sensitive, comes through at best as distrust of the community's ability to know what it wants and at worst as outright manipulation.

Communication was facilitated by the organization of objectives. There are many levels of objectives in any program. If the program is large and well designed, the objectives should fall into a hierarchy with lower-level objectives contributing to higher-level objectives. An attempt was made to arrange the SUA objectives in a hierarchy. The first two levels—the overall and subobjectives of the SUA—have already been discussed. Third-level objectives were prepared for each grouping of activities comprising the nine "systems" of the SUA, and some fourth-level objectives for selected activities were prepared using the communication process previously described. Preparation of all fourth- and lower-level objectives would eventually require participation of the teachers, students, and parents who would comprise the SUA. One could

---

students that the regular public school system experiences great difficulty in educating. The ESP employs many of those concepts and procedures that were part of the proposed SUA program. The ESP has been in operation for more than three years as part of the Seattle School District.

expect lower-level objectives to affect already written higher-level objectives, and they frequently did, resulting in modification of the higher-level objectives.

## Means of Intervention

The communication process described earlier is retrospectively classified as the "means of intervention." But it is informative to discuss how the program's activities fit into one typology of intervention means. The typology of means suggested by Warwick and Kelman (1973, p. 40) classifies means on a freedom continuum, ranging from coercion through manipulation and persuasion to facilitation. Application of this typology to the SUA program is difficult because the classification scheme has the implicit assumption that the change agent has the power to set limits to the freedom of the change target. A further complication arises when there are multiple targets or when targets change as the program unfolds. As there was a hierarchy of goals, there was also a hierarchy of targets in the SUA efforts.

The process of communication we described earlier was the key to developing the program of change, and it was planned to be the means for bringing about change in the major target of the effort. This process was based upon equal status of the individuals or groups who stated and discussed postulates in an attempt to come to consensus on alternatives. The process required true mutual respect for the contribution each party could make to the discussion and an admission (at least implied) by each party that the problem was beyond his or her capability to solve. Each party needed the other, and consequently, no party set any limits to the freedom of any other. The only tag we could put on the process would be the "iterative-interactive-mutually-educative" means of social intervention. The process comes closest to "facilitation" (Warwick & Kelman, 1973, p. 57). The "completely honest and open" example (Warwick & Kelman, 1973, p. 59) is a good parallel to the relationship between Battelle and the community representatives on the SUA team, which represented a cross section of the community and not a particular organized faction. As the program developed, a formal association was made with the CASC.

The Seattle Urban Academy team had the role of change agent, and the major target was the educational system. Although the team had no sponsor in the usual sense in which a change agent is hired by a sponsor to help bring about a particular change, the team acted as though the community were its sponsor. The team was, organizationally, outside the school system. (However, its members had, or took on, working responsibilities within the system in roles other than change agents. These roles no doubt influenced many changes but not to the degree nor in the systemic way envisioned by the SUA effort.) The team was, necessarily, a double-edged change agent in that its community development work was intended to change the community, while its basic target was change in the school system. The skills of each person on the team were used to the best advantage of the effort. The control of the team, as far as the direction of change goes, was in the hands of the community members of the team. Battelle's funding limited the resources available for the planning effort, but it did not limit the scope of the solutions that emerged. Battelle provided its problem-solving skills for use as the community saw fit.

The community was ready to make substantive contributions to the education of its youth, contributions that transcended those available from confrontation. The community had exercised its muscle and was ready to do more than simply force correction of conditions that made discipline in the schools impossible. In the absence of manipulation by social activists, it takes a situation viewed by the community as a crisis to get out the pickets and bring on the boycotts. Such manipulation is frequently practiced by social change agents with apparently no more justification than that it is *easier* than the extensive community development work that could result in getting the community what it wants instead of what the agent wants. The SUA effort was intended to make the basic types of changes that do not have the high emotional impact of getting drugs and knives out of junior high schools. It required a long-term effort based on reason and "soul," not on emotion. The maturity of the Seattle central area community is evidenced by the continuing interest, support, and input it gave the SUA effort over the three-year life of the program. It is likely that the support and input would have dramatically increased and been sustained over the five years of community work yet remaining had the project continued to be funded. Unless the maturity of the community is a controlling factor in the selection of means, a social intervention project can be extremely wasteful of the pool of skills available.

The SUA team had hoped that the communication process would work with teachers and educational administrators. It appeared to work initially because of school district policy supporting community involvement. The educators did not go against that policy as long as the SUA program appeared as powerless as other community involvement groups. But when the educators became aware of the developing power base that could result in violation of the unwritten boundaries they set for community involvement, SUA's postulates became infringements on their right to make educational policy. In such a defensive posture, they could not interact during subsequent iterations of the process and the possibility for an iterative-interactive-mutually-educative process was lost. Subsequent dealings with the target (the educational system) were attempts at persuasion or manipulation. The SUA's means of interventions were then reduced to:

- Facilitating the community's access to educational policy-making groups
- Persuading educators enamoured of the status quo to allow basic changes to be made in their system
- Manipulating the environment of the educational system by providing an alternative system of schooling

(Note that each of these means has a different target and that each interacts with the other.)

## ETHICAL ISSUES ARISING IN THE SUA PROGRAM

Ethical problems in the social intervention context arise when an intervenor and a target of the intervention have a conflict in the priorities each places on the elements of its value set. In what frequently passes for social change on the level where the relationships to be changed are between an agency providing a service (for example, the education system) and the users of that service (for example, students, parents, and the community), problem recognition, need definition, and program planning are all at the discretion of the serving agency, at least in substantive matters, and the users are persuaded, manipulated, or coerced into changing to better fit the system. Little change is made in the serving agency.

In retrospect, the Seattle Urban Academy program was an attempt to reverse the way social intervention usually operates, that is, to reverse the usual agent and the target. The problem that initiated the SUA effort was the same as that recognized by many educational policy makers, namely, that the urban poor were not being adequately educated. The main goal was to get the educational system to cope effectively with the needs of the urban poor.

The salient features of the SUA approach to social intervention and those of a frequently observed approach are compared in terms of primary agents at each major activity in Table 1. The after-the-fact characterization of the SUA

**TABLE 1.** Comparison of "Agents"—The SUA Program Approach versus the Usual Approach

| Activity | SUA primary agent | Usual primary agent |
|---|---|---|
| Recognize problem | Huey and Little | Policy makers |
| Define needs (desired "good" not being realized) | SUA team, central area community involved in education | Academic theoreticians |
| Determine objectives (who or what is to be modified—target group) | SUA team, central area community involved in education | Policy makers, academicians |
| Operate program* | Program Director, with SUA and community corporation | Program Director |
| Evaluate program* | SUA, academicians, policy makers | Academicians, policy makers |

*These activities were planned, but were never implemented in the SUA program.

approach detailed in Table 1 is given to provide an organized basis for answering the critical questions in the evaluation of ethical implications at each activity: Who is the agent initiating the activity? and How does the target of the intervention have an impact on the activity? The ethical success of the intervention can be gauged by how well the value conflicts that arise in the intervention are resolved.

At each stage in the sequence of activities, these questions should be answered. In the SUA effort, there was a hierarchy of targets as well as a hierarchy of objectives. Thus, the nominal targets and intervenors changed. We now discuss some of the problems avoided or encountered in each activity.

### Problem Recognition and Need Definition

In the SUA approach, the problem was recognized by two individuals (Huey and Little) who could be characterized as urban poor and who were in a position to communicate their understanding of the problem to the noneducational agency (Battelle) that became interested in the problem. The most immediate perceived need was not to promote literacy, although that was important, but to stop the destruction of self-esteem and intellectual curiosity of the urban poor by the educational system.[5] The cold and deterministic nature of the systems engineering techniques used by the SUA program was permeated and kept responsive by this sensitivity to the personal needs of the expected participants.

The problem was recognized by those who personally felt the effects of the problem and who were thus able to go beyond symptoms to arrive at the underlying needs that had to be satisfied. The frequently encountered problem of applying narrow expertise, which limits the range of potential solutions, to an ill-defined problem was thus avoided.

The preplanning problem, previously alluded to, was also avoided. The starting point of any discussion was a postulate—a tentative statement of personal opinion. The simple words "I think" preceding a statement apparently did two things. First, they put the statement on a tentative basis, and, second, they invited others to state what they thought.

To ensure that problem recognition and need definition were not limited only to what the SUA team thought, additional input was obtained from a series of visits to innovative educational facilities in other urban settings. Also, the Urban Academy team did involve and employ experienced educators and educational change specialists. Discussions had been held with people such as Offie Franklin and Rodeh McCoy, as well as a number of white educational specialists. Information gained from these discussions was applied to the program where it was deemed appropriate.[6] The educational system (the target)

---

[5] Documentation on this argument can be found, for example, in Sizemore (1972).

[6] It is not clear, however, that there are any successful educational change specialists to pattern one's efforts after. Change in the educational system is rare, despite the many remedial programs or, perhaps, because of them.

also had input into the problem recognition phase through the involvement of local educators in the SUA advisory groups.

Throughout the program it was recognized that the SUA program efforts would cause some conflict. Some of the conflicting values that could cause ethical problems follow.

1.  Self-esteem of urban poor versus elitist educational policy
2.  Parental freedom of choice versus self-esteem of educators
3.  Teacher's security/survival versus expansion of their freedom with consequent increase in responsibility
4.  Administrator's security/survival versus freedom of choice of teachers, parents, and students
5.  Survival/self-esteem of schools versus values of broader social justice
6.  Self-determination of students versus ease of educational system operation

This list was drawn up retrospectively, but the potential for conflict in these areas was recognized and efforts made to resolve it in the direction of providing more freedom of choice to more people.

## Objectives and Methods

An ethical issue arises when the target and the broader community have not had ample input to the program. By way of illustration, using the input to objectives development, we focus on the typical application of the methods that the SUA team used to get input for one objective, namely, a third-level[7] objective dealing with administration of the SUA. Over a period of time (weeks), we developed a number of options, including the CASC, Battelle, a subsidiary of Battelle, an education corporation, a community corporation, and the School Board. We listed the advantages, disadvantages, and unknowns. These options were discussed informally with a number of groups and with members at the community. The community corporation (with an undefined, but predominantly community, membership) began to emerge as the organization that would be most consonant with the objectives and with certain necessary conditions (listed above) that had to be met for the SUA to be successful. The points to note are that input was not directed and that the community had its wishes written into an objective, the objective of establishing a community corporation.

The overall program management methodology was that of a phased project, as indicated in Figure 1. In the situation within which the program operated, phasing was a given, necessary way of proceeding. From the Battelle point of view, no program exists without phasing. Phasing may be formally

---

[7] The first two levels of objectives were discussed earlier. The community corporation is subsumed in Subobjective 1.

stated, as in the case of the Academy program, or may be a hidden agenda item. In the case of the Academy program, Battelle made clear its intention to phase the program. This was stated to all participants and in all presentations. Even though the implications of phasing were stated, there is still the ethical issue that the community may not really have heard the statement because of its total commitment to success. Thus, phasing could provide options only for Battelle and not for the community.

Phasing worked to the advantage of all parties in the Academy program. For instance, the Central Area School Council clearly stated that it did not know whether it wished to continue participation with Battelle and the Academy team beyond Phase II. It was possible that there could be certain outcomes from Phase II that would not be in their interest. Thus, it was mutually agreed that either or both parties could step out at the end of Phase II.

The Battelle staff found it very important that blacks on the team had the opportunity to talk to Battelle Laboratory directors, the president and senior officers of Battelle, and occasionally to members of the Board of Trustees, so that they could state their concerns and their positions. This was accomplished throughout the entire program. Indeed, the team believes that the effort could not have hung together without the blacks' having this option to talk to senior Battelle officials, because through communicating they were able to feel assured that a real commitment was behind Battelle's efforts. The black community, however, never believed that Battelle had a genuine commitment to central area education.

Phasing did create the basic problem that each component involved directly or indirectly in the effort waited for some other component to make a total commitment. This was impossible without predetermining the outcome.

A question that naturally arises is, Who called the shots in the Academy program—the blacks or the whites, the project manager, the steering committee, Battelle? It is difficult to describe the decision-making process that operated in the Academy program accurately and succinctly. It was a subtle process. Unilateral decisions were not feasible. Decision making evolved through an enormous communication effort and constant discussion of alternatives and responses. Essentially, the results of the communication process led to the final decisions that were made in the Academy program.

## ASSESSMENT OF CONSEQUENCES

### Attainment of Major Goals

There is no edifice that we can point to as being the Seattle Urban Academy. The concrete end-product of our efforts is the "Seattle Urban Academy Program Plan," which explains the nature of the Urban Academy and how it could be brought into being and managed. The program plan is not a cookbook that gives step-by-step directions, but rather a framework within which an educational program responsive to changing local needs can be developed and controlled.

The SUA program failed in its goal to bring about systemic institutional change. Throughout the program's duration, the community was involved in the more immediate priority of the desegregation movements of the Seattle School District, so the broad-based support needed did not develop. Busing to desegregate schools and reorganizing the central region subdistrict created other areas for community involvement with a more immediately perceived value impact. (The children of central region parents were going to be bused to a potentially hostile environment in schools outside the central region.)

Some overall positive results of the SUA effort are:

- Many issues that needed it were tackled openly—issues ranging from productivity in education to overhauling the management structure.
- Increased credibility was given to a number of educational innovations or changes that might have been delayed or laid aside for lack of a confirming opinion.
- Many innovative programs being carried out elsewhere in the country were identified and have subsequently been incorporrated into Seattle schools.
- Many ideas developed by the SUA team have been adopted or are being tried in the present system.

In conclusion, it appears that the most basic reason the efforts did not produce a school is that the team was not able to sufficiently involve the major target of the intervention, namely, the teachers and administrators. They recognized the validity of the SUA program's objectives for the system insofar as these objectives related to students, but changing the role of the teacher, even with extensive input from teachers, was not to be a postulate for discussion between the SUA team and teachers.

Despite failure to come to consensus on this basic conflict between teacher interests and the team's interpretation of student and community interests, the decision was made to go ahead in the hope that the needed educational process of teachers could be accomplished through extensive (one-year) involvement of carefully screened and committed teachers in the development of the operational form of the SUA. Educators were involved in subsequent development, but their conscious effort was to help develop program components, not to change the roles of administrators and teachers.

### Community Perspectives on SUA Program Consequences as Viewed by the SUA Team

The following perspectives are the SUA team's view of community responses to the program, based on the team's association with community elements that came in contact with the SUA effort.

A number of impacts were felt by the community as a result of the SUA program. First, parent-student involvement in educational planning increased.

Second, community members became more widely used as nonprofessionals in classroom work. For example, parents were used in teaching a science demonstration program at one of the local elementary schools. Third, a small cadre of black people from the community received training and acquired skills in modern management and planning methods. These skills have subsequently been used in other community projects. Fourth, a major consequence of the SUA program was to provide the community with new and more thorough ways of questioning and challenging proposals that concerned them. The community has expressed, as a fifth result of the SUA program the raising within the community of expectations that failed to be realized when SUA failed to materialize. The opportunity for community people to interact with educators on a nonthreatening basis was a sixth impact of SUA on the community. This differed from the confrontation dialogue experienced by parents and educators in other settings. Finally, community people became more aware of additional sources of support for their educational proposals. Members of the CASC participated in soliciting funds from Battelle Memorial Institute, the U. S. Office of Education, the Seattle School District, and other organizations.

Out of Phase II came the development of a nonprofit firm, Urban Academy, Inc., formed by community people who participated in the Academy effort, to provide for continuing the Academy concept. That firm has worked with the school district of another city (East St. Louis, Illinois) in developing an Academy there.

### SUA Program Impacts on Battelle as Viewed by the Community

The community had its own perceptions of SUA program impacts upon Battelle. Generally, the community (central area Seattle) felt that Battelle achieved its objectives. Battelle staff members expressed increased confidence in understanding the ways of change in social, especially educational, systems. Likewise, Battelle management gained significantly in its ability to deal with social issues arising in the inner city. Second, the community felt certain that Battelle was able to investigate possible new roles for Battelle in education. On the strength of its knowledge acquired during the SUA effort, Battelle became involved in the evaluation of other educational programs on a contract research basis. Finally, the community believed Battelle's scientists would be better able to employ their skills and methods in working with social problems.

### SUA Program Impacts on the Seattle School District as Viewed by the Community

Community people have responded that the SUA program had impacts upon the Seattle School District in four major areas. First, a result of the Academy program was to introduce several new educational methods and programs into some central region schools. For example, the elementary school science demonstration project was started. Coupled with the science project was a staff training component. Second, the SUA program meetings became a new forum, outside of the traditional settings of the Seattle School District, for teachers, parents, and students to discuss and review educational ideas. Several high school departments revised departmental meetings to reflect the openness advocated by the SUA program. In meetings held by the SUA staff, educators were exposed to the idea that educators are *responsible* for educating youth; that is, educators must do more than simply provide an opportunity for youth to acquire an education. Third, as central region educators worked with SUA staff, these educators increased their ability to plan school activities. Educators experienced the method of curriculum and program planning in which teachers and administrators jointly resolved issues. For example, teachers would no longer be handed a curriculum package without participating in its development. Finally, the SUA staff trained several central region educators in the use of modern educational planning techniques.

### Battelle Perspectives on SUA Program Consequences

#### SUA Program Impacts on Battelle

It appeared to the Battelle staff participating in the SUA program that there was an element of disappointment within Battelle that more was not accomplished. This disappointment came in large part because the Academy was not realized as an entity. This may be somewhat surprising in light of the Battelle Institute's objectives for the program, which were of a process nature rather than an end-result nature. To understand this disappointment, one must understand what kind of company Battelle is. In any given year, Battelle processes and completes hundreds on research contracts. In a vast majority of cases, the contracts are fulfilled completely within the objectives stated for the program. Consciously or unconsciously, any program that does not meet its objectives is looked on with some disappointment, akin to a sense of failure. The Seattle Urban Academy program did not reach the program's implicit objective of becoming an operating school, thus, the source of disappointment with respect to the outcome of the Academy program.

There are many voices within Battelle, and any one of several perspectives can be obtained on the outcome of the Academy program. Some members of Battelle were glad to see the program completed because it was a high-risk program through which Battelle could have obtained a great deal of negative publicity. There were Battelle members who felt that a greater and more aggressive involvement was appropriate; they were disappointed that the program did not continue beyond Phase II. Others who would have invested the funds used in the Academy program for physical research or other activities may have felt that the money could have been spent better elsewhere.

On the whole, the Battelle staff believes that Battelle wishes to obtain more perspective on the Academy program and other efforts similar to it before evaluating what a Battelle-type organization can bring to social intervention efforts. It is not expected that this perspective will be gained for several more years.

Participation by an organization like Battelle in as volatile an area as inner-city education was not nearly as hazardous as it appeared from the "outside." It appeared to the Battelle staff that there were conscious efforts by blacks, both in the program and outside the program, to protect Battelle from unfavorable publicity that might cause it to withdraw or decrease its effort. This is not to say that its "toes were not held to the fire" in many meetings. But such times were mainly those when there was a minimal chance of significant publicity. The blacks appeared to understand the community's concerns and needs, and each helped the other stay out of pitfalls that could destroy the joint effort or render it ineffective.

Team building in the Urban Academy program was based on the mutual respect that evolved during the effort. One can best understand the circumstances by considering the factors involved in any problem-solving effort, including development of the Seattle Urban Academy concept. These include cognitive knowledge, a process, and team building and maintenance. In the Academy effort, the cognitive knowledge about inner-city education was supplied primarily by blacks from the inner city. The process part of problem solving, systems engineering methodologies, came primarily from the Battelle staff. Team building and maintenance had to be a joint effort. The fact that both primary participants, those from the inner city and those from Battelle, needed the other to develop meaningful approaches to resolving the problems built a mutual respect. It was not a case of each helping the other, but of each supplying to the effort something of value that could not be supplied by either alone and which was valued by each. The principle that seems to be involved here—that in a joint effort all parties must feel they are benefiting and contributing for there to be respect and understanding—is probably not new; we simply experienced it in another setting. It seems that in problem-solving efforts in the social arena, one-way helping is not a viable option. Mutual help is a necessity.

The systems engineering methodologies applied during the Seattle Urban Academy program proved to be excellent working tools in the highly sensitive social area. These methodologies appeared to promote openness and helped focus communication, and they were solution-oriented—all very important attributes in a setting like this. These methodologies have to be applied with some sensitivity or else they become too rigid—even ends in themselves. It must also be recognized that all values cannot be quantified by systems engineering methodologies and, thus, the methodologies should not be pushed beyond their limitations.

## SUA Program Impacts on the Community

It seemed to the Battelle staff that the Seattle Urban Academy effort simply stretched the credibility for the community too far. This kind of a working relationship, in which a sophisticated research and development company attempts to work with a community, and not through organizations of the community, has not been experienced by many inner-city blacks or whites. Since the usual sponsor-client relationships did not exist (there was no contract between the parties), an aura of disbelief constantly surrounded the program. One impact on the community, then, was the realization that such efforts can exist. It expanded the community's understanding of what is possible.

A second impact on the community related to technology transfer. A number of the techniques, both of systems engineering and of sound management practices, have been adopted by members of the community as well as by members of the Seattle Urban Academy staff. It is believed that these techniques have benefited the community. For example, the number of people actively interested in changing education was increased through the many meetings and task forces initiated by the SUA team. The team was conscious of the danger of raising expectations and not producing results, but any fears along this line were not confirmed by events. Apparently, expectations were not inordinately raised although the postulates' discussion expanded the range of the possible.

We believe that the Academy effort had several beneficial results on the educational system, although it is not possible to show causal relationships. The SUA team brought speakers and consultants to the community for conferences and discussions of educational concepts. These contacts and the many SUA-related meetings of teacher, student, and parent groups promoted open discussions, interchanges of ideas, and stimulation of new interests and concerns. Several program innovations in central area schools followed and were, it is believed, significantly influenced by the SUA program. Examples are greater parent involvement, wider use of community persons as nonprofessionals in classroom work, some new math and vocational education programs, and a new approach for drop-out-prone youths. Some school administrators began using systems approaches in program management—particularly in setting goals, using time schedules and check-pointing, and articulating objectives. Finally, many parents have come to recognize and use the power of asking, "What are the objectives?"

## SUA Impacts on the Education System

How the SUA program affected the educational system is difficult to describe from the Battelle staff's perspective. Some educators, both in the central area and in the school district office, appeared to feel very threatened by the academy program. Thus, they were probably glad when the program ended.

Others appeared to have held high hopes for educational change through the Academy program, and these were probably disappointed when the next step in the program was not taken. The Battelle staff believed that the Seattle School Board was relieved to have Battelle and the central area community terminate the Seattle Urban Academy program, because it appeared to interfere with on-going programs of the Seattle School District.

## SUMMARY OF CRITICAL ETHICAL ISSUES

The primary objective of this book was "to explore some of the broad ethical issues raised by social intervention."[8] Three questions were asked in an attempt to provide a unifying framework for the chapters included here. Explicit answers to these questions will serve to summarize this chapter.

1. *In setting the goals for the intervention, who speaks for the group that is the target of the change effort?*

Urban school systems were the target of the change effort in the SUA program. Effort was focused on developing and demonstrating a process for enabling urban school systems to cope more effectively with the educational needs of an urban population. The origin and context of the demonstration was the central area of Seattle.

The target was articulate, and many spokesmen had an impact on the effort. In the early conceptual phase, Dr. Roland Patterson (then principal of the central region's junior high school, subsequently Assistant Superintendent for the Seattle Central Region Schools and Superintendent of the Baltimore School District) was quite active. He remained a concerned and helpful sounding board throughout the SUA program effort. Dr. Forbes Bottomly, Superintendent of the Seattle School District, was kept informed of the SUA effort through formal meetings with the SUA team and informal communications with Charles Huey and John Little. Writings of the many critics of education, most of whom are educators, and visits to operating innovative and alternative schools also provided input to the development of goals. The most direct spokesmen for the target were the teachers from the central region and other schools who formed the teachers' advisory group. During what turned out to be the final year of effort, an elementary teacher and the high school principal from the central region were assigned to the Urban Academy team for six months.

The target group thus had much more opportunity to have an impact on goal formation than is usually the case when the community is the target of a social intervention. The target group availed itself, sometimes vehemently, of

[8] From the letter of invitation to the conference from which this book developed.

this opportunity. Its major contributions to the effort were those goals relative to changing current administrative structures that made the teachers subject to the arbitrary decisions of bureaucrats, forcing the teachers to transmit this oppressive atmosphere in the classroom. The teachers had many ideas for improving urban education, but it cost them too much personally to fight the curriculum, materials, and facilities battles required to bring the changes about.

In the sociologically topsy-turvy world of the SUA effort (the usual roles of intervenor and target being reversed), the question of who spoke for the intervenor was more critical than who spoke for the target. The intervenor was the community, specifically that part of the community interested in educational changes. As pointed out by a teacher at one of our meetings, teachers have other roles than "teacher": most are parents, and all are members of the community. The Urban Academy team accepted this. Also accepted was the fact that persons representing a multitude of other skills were present in the community, including attorneys (one was an active member of the team), college professors, artists, contractors, reporters, mailmen, and research workers. Most important, the team recognized that it had three men from the community, at least one of whom could communicate with any segment of the target community. Charles Huey, John Little, and Carl Miller were the major spokesmen for the community. The Parent and Student Advisory Groups also had the function of speaking for the community. There was close liaison with the community-elected education board—the Central Area School Council—which had a strong impact on the program. Informal contact with representatives of the black separatists led to an agreement that they would not interfere with the project. (They could not, of course, support an effort funded by a representative of the white power structure.) It cannot be said that all community elements and positions were represented, particularly those people who were satisfied with the status quo or those who were simply unconcerned, but the team was aware that such people existed and designed efforts to get them involved in the preoperational year of the effort.

The source of the intervenor's authority was the community. The community's authority derives from the application of the principle that the community transfers part of the family's responsibility to educate its children to the educational system. When the community feels that the system is not doing the job it wants done, it has every right and, in fact, a duty to reassert its ultimate authority.

2.　*In selecting the means, how is genuine participation in the change process by the target of the change assured?*

In reply to this question, again the problem of participation of the intervenor in the definition of the means of intervention arises.

First, with regard to the formal target of the change, the school system's facilities, staff, and money were to be used, which placed external constraints on the effort and at the same time ensured that the system's self-interest would bring genuine participation. Built into the demonstration itself were ample communication procedures to ensure that SUA teachers would obtain quick response from SUA administrators; ample time for staff interaction in the development of curricula; use of academic consultants in development of curricula, teaching methods, and administrative practices; periodic reports to the sponsoring school district; and evaluation of results by the sponsoring school district. Participation by the target was thus, almost by necessity, assured.

The major question here becomes: how could the intervenor ensure that the target would not take over the effort and effectively exclude the intervenor? During the developmental phases, Battelle had put its skills and name at the disposal of the community. Battelle assumed that the school system would do the same. The concept that evolved as the major solution to this problem was that of the community corporation. This corporation would be developed in more detail (explicit composition, method of selection of members) by the community when the operational phase proved feasible and would execute a contract with the district to operate the SUA. Also built into the demonstration itself were "community teachers"—noncertified full- or part-time classroom teachers who could offer educational experiences in or out of the SUA facilities—parent and student paraprofessionals who would tutor, drill, correct papers, schedule use of resource centers, and generally free the certified staff for more professional activities; parent and student advisory groups; more effective student government; and student businesses. In addition to the particular, obvious goals of the listed activities was the common goal of bringing more of the community into the life of the school to keep up, in turn, a continuing input to the change process by the intervenors. The community had to be kept more intimately aware of what the educators were doing, so that they would have a solid focus for any pressure they felt necessary to exercise.

3. *In assessing the consequences of a social intervention, how does one account for unintended effects?*

Since the SUA effort terminated before the demonstration subdistrict could become a reality, the project had little discernible impact on the target of change—the educational system. In particular, there were no significant systemic changes in the target system. There were, however, many unintended effects of an incremental nature, similar to the remedial changes common in education. These have already been elaborated and are not the major issues here. What is at issue are those unintended effects that contributed to a deterioration, rather than an improvement, in the relationships among the principal elements in the effort. These relationships can be considered on three levels: impact on individuals, impact on the specific agents involved, and impact on agents who might get involved in future similar efforts. For the purposes of this chapter, it will suffice to focus on the specific agents involved.

Battelle could have done more had the Urban Academy effort achieved a higher priority among the many projects competing for Battelle Institute funds.

Just as certainly, Battelle could have done nothing. The point is that the effort was in the real-world position of having to compete on a scheduled basis for the funding that would continue its life for the next budgeting period. The impact of this fact will become apparent in what follows.

Just as important for any analysis of unintended effects is an understanding of the maturity of Seattle's central area community. The community had had considerable experience in "dissensus situations"[9] and had used confrontation strategies with good success. The community had also participated in and experienced disappointment with numerous programs to remedy their situation and make them able to cope. They knew these remedial programs failed because they were designed and imposed from without their community. Battelle was frank about both its altruistic and business motivations. The community was mature enough to perceive the limited extent of Battelle's commitment. They were prepared to feed the turkey as long as the personal commitment of the Battelle members of the team was evident. (The meaninglessness of organizational commitment alone is quite evident to the black community.)

Let us consider an analysis of the relationships that may have suffered negative unintended effects. The relationships at issue are those among urban communities, their educational systems, and a business organization with appreciable skills and financial resources.

The major danger, recognized and discussed by the Urban Academy team, was community backlash from being led down a path that resulted in raising expectations without fulfilling them. Such backlash would be demonstrated by increased skepticism in the community about the possibility of change, increased distrust of the educational system, and a fear of getting involved with Battelle, or similar organizations, again.

The Urban Academy team's view was that such backlash was certainly possible—common sense, past experience with Seattle's central area, and sociological literature warned against it. The team recognized two alternatives, since it did not have the resources to ensure success. The first was the unproductive option to drop the effort. The one selected was to be completely frank to the community about the contingencies of Battelle's commitment and about the obstacles to success. In Battelle's view, the outcome of this course of action was to expand the community's concept of the possible, which lasts to this day, despite failure to bring an operating Seattle Urban Academy into being. The community had an opportunity to exercise its hard-won freedom in the forum provided by the SUA effort. The Academy effort was not "the only game in town." Dr. Patterson's development of the 4-4-4 plan for the central region schools and the School District's desegregation planning provided opportunities

[9] See Warren (1971, p. 13). Warren defines issue discussion as occurring when "important parties to the situation either (a) refuse to recognize the issue or (b) oppose the change agent's proposal."

for those more interested in within-the-system remedial changes to exercise their skills. Again, the team was involved with a mature community.

The SUA team's view was that the community and Battelle were partners in selecting the path to be followed, not that Battelle had to select a path for the community. Battelle provided people and contacts the community could not muster, not limits to the scope of the effort. The existence of the effort was in the hands of Battelle, but it is doubtful that the community perceived this as a sword over its head, since it had control over the direction to be taken and recognized that only remedial programs had come out of the application of confrontation strategies. It appears to us that the feared backlash did not result because the community understood and accepted the long-term effort required to produce systemic change. They valued being recognized as a mature force with broader skills than carrying picket signs or keeping their children home from school.

In summary, the SUA effort gave the community the opportunity to become a change agent through simply putting the SUA team's skills and resources at the disposal of the community. Battelle provided money and technology; the community provided soul and inner-city life-style knowledge. It was a partnership.

## REFERENCES

Bermant, G., Kelman, H., & Warwick, D. Letter of invitation to the Conference, "Ethics of Social Intervention," held at Battelle-Seattle Research Center, May 10–12, 1973.

Clark, K. *Dark ghetto: Dilemmas of social power.* New York: Harper & Row, 1965.

Clark, K. Alternatives to urban schools. In F. F. Korton, S. W. Cook, & J. R. Lacey (Eds.), *Psychology and the problems of society.* Washington, D.C.: American Psychological Association, 1970.

Greer, C. Public schools? The myth of the melting pot. *Education Digest,* 1970, *35,* 1–4.

Illich, I. False ideology of schooling. *Saturday Review,* 1970, *53,* 56–58.

Illich, I. Alternative to schooling. *Saturday Review,* 1971, *54,* 44–48.

Sizemore, B. A. Social science and education for a black identity. In J. A. Banks & J. D. Grambs (Eds.), *Black self-concept: Implications for education and social science.* New York: McGraw-Hill, 1972.

Warren, R. L. *Truth, love, and social change.* Chicago: Rand McNally, 1971.

Warwick, D. P., & Kelman, H. C. Ethical issues in social intervention. In G. Zaltman & R. Schwartz (Eds.), *Perspectives on social change.* New York: Wiley-Interscience, 1973.

# 9
# ENGINEERS, SYSTEMS ANALYSIS, AND EDUCATIONAL CHANGE: SOME ETHICAL IMPLICATIONS

**ALAN E. GUSKIN**

University of Wisconsin–Parkside

## INTRODUCTION

The Seattle Urban Academy project was an attempt at social intervention into the school systems of Seattle through the creation of a new school as a demonstration of what could or should be done in educating inner-city, primarily black, youth. Most of the professional staff of the project were from Battelle-Northwest, and the project was financed by Battelle. It involved a number of community people in a very significant way in the development of plans for the school and had community control of the school as one of its primary objectives. The development of the school never materialized and the entire project was aborted because of a lack of financing expected from a contract with the School Board and because of political difficulties in the community and within the school system. While it is not totally clear whether the School Board would have let out such a contract, even if legally possible, state law did not permit it, and the legislature failed to enact a special law to enable the Board to do so.

Writing a critical discussion of a project such as this is a difficult task. First, the final report of the project (Chapter 8) was written following the conference at which the material in this chapter was discussed. As expected, that final report was responsive to that discussion and as a result contains information that seemingly counteracts some of the criticisms of this chapter. Second, there is always a great deal of difference between observing an ongoing project and reacting to a report of those responsible for the project's development. One always wonders whether one is reading rhetoric or actual observation. Third, in a change project such as this it is difficult to assess whether the original objective of system change was a strategy and the resultant incremental change the natural compromise between desire and reality or whether the incremental change resulted from a naïve approach to reality itself. As will be seen, I favored the latter interpretation: that the change agents fully expected that if they were successful, system change would have occurred and that they were naïve about the nature of system change in the very complex Seattle school system.

To deal with these problems, I have decided to divide this chapter into two parts: the first part is my original analysis of the project as I assessed it on the basis of a few preliminary reports; the second part is an epilogue in which I discuss the issues of incremental change as they relate to the development of new programs of which I was unaware when I wrote the first part. I have chosen this approach because I trust my "analytic antennae" and believe that my guesses may be accurate even if some of them are seemingly contradicted by the changes in the project report as it appears in Chapter 8. As does anyone who has been involved in school change efforts, I react to case studies of these activities by reading between the lines as much as by understanding the actual words. This is not a statement of mistrust but rather, I believe, a facing of the fact that there is no objective way to define reality and that, when we attempt to write such descriptive accounts, we are always doing so from our particular value orientations (Guskin & Chesler, 1973).

When I read the original proposal (written in December, 1970) for the establishment of the Seattle Urban Academy, I was struck by its attempt to apply "systems analysis" (these words were used in the planning document) to school problems. The application of the concept appeared to be merely a facade or rhetoric used by someone recently grown enamoured of systems analysis. The final paper indicates the reality: in effect, the primary skills of most of the professional change agents were in the engineering–systems analysis area and one of the less obvious, though stated, major goals of this project was a testing of the feasibility of using these engineering tools to bring about educational change.

This analysis of ethical implications focuses first on the change agents involved—their orientations to change and how their skills and perspectives affected the project. Second, it deals with the effects of the sponsoring agency, Battelle. Following this, I discuss the implications of a demonstration project, on the premise that such a development was the primary intermediate goal of the entire effort.

## THE EFFECTS OF THE CHANGE AGENTS

Because of their backgrounds as engineers, physical and mathematical scientists, and systems analysts, the strong tendency of the Battelle change agents, and as a result their co-workers, was to assume a rational, nonpolitical model for the change process. This perspective does not reflect the nature of change in human organizations, particularly educational institutions. Schools are developed around sets of values about the proper behavior and cognitive patterns for individuals: students who graduate with high marks are assumed to be properly socialized beings who have internalized the standards the institution has stated as being the most desirable. The values implicit and explicit in the socialization process are not usually open to question. In fact, the very problem the change agents in this project wanted to correct was a function of these sets of values—namely, a set of standards that do not permit different cultural styles and that reject non-middle-class, non-white perspectives. I would maintain, as Colin Greer (1972) does, that American schools have been organized to facilitate the integration of minority youth into the society as equals with white middle-class individuals.

Such a socialization process, based on rather limited and inflexible sets of values, usually does not change through rational discussion, no matter how much anyone desires it to. Our school systems are built around such values and the administrative structure will not willingly permit exceptions.

In effect, there is a set of values that discriminates against minority youth; the socialization process through which these values operate are supported by the vested interests of professional school people and powerful nonschool elements. To change these processes and the values embedded in them means dealing with the political vested-interest process. It is this political process that is essential to changing school systems and with which the Battelle people had difficulty. The rational communication orientation that was at the base of their skills did not permit them to be concerned with the very essence of changing organizational structures or gaining a foothold within them—namely, dealing with human beings who have strong vested interests in maintaining the status quo.

Furthermore, the Battelle engineers and scientists (and too many social scientists) seem to have believed that their aspirations were the same as those of the school system's and, hence, all they had to do was reason together. This was not the case—the values and orientation of the Battelle and SUA change agents were in dissensus with the implicit and explicit values and interests of the school system. In simple terms, they wanted to make the Academy responsive to youth, not to make youth fit into the middle-class white school system.

Roland Warren (1971) states that there are very different strategies that have to be utilized in situations in which the underlying values and interests of the change agents and target groups are in dissensus, difference, and consensus. When there is an underlying consensus, "collaborative" strategies are most effective—people reasoning together after overcoming their initial apathy about the issues. When there is a difference, which may lead to consensus, the strategies to be utilized are "campaigns"—educational campaigns, persuasion, and so forth. When there is a dissensus situation, one should use "contest" strategies, which are typified by a group organizing in order to get the opposition to move toward the desired end-state.

My reaction to the literature I have read on the Battelle project indicates a dissensus situation, while the strategies seem to reflect a collaborative or campaign orientation. The collaborative orientation reflects their primary concern for communication and rational statement of objectives; their campaign orientation is reflected in their attempts at persuasion.

Another key issue was that the change agents were not really aware that they were change agents, nor that their efforts were social intervention. This was stated at one point in Chapter 8:

> For the most part, the SUA team looked upon the Academy program not as a social intervention effort but as a problem-definition and problem-solving effort—much as one views scientific or engineering problems (pp. 167–168).

It seems that the Batelle group failed to recognize the following:

1. The meaning of changing a social institution—the complexity of a school system, the ways in which roles interact with each other to form organizational structures, the effect of tradition, the manner in which roles are structured to maintain the present operations, the effects of administrative structures on the organizational climate in schools, and so on. Before one can undertake serious change efforts, a considerable understanding of these and other variables is required; that is, assuming the target of change is truly the school as an institution.

2. The politics of educational change. The Battelle group did a commendable job of involving the community in the planning process. The problem seems to be, however, that they were not able to carry their project beyond the rudiments of community involvement. While the Battelle change agents did become aware of the politics of change, they never quite adjusted to its implications. An example is the following statement:

> The educators [that is, school people] did not go against that policy as long as the SUA program appeared as powerless as other community involvement groups. But when the educators became aware of the developing power base that could result in violation of the unwritten boundaries they set for community involvement, SUA's postulates became infringements on their right to make educational policy (p. 173).

I sense from this statement a lack of strategic analysis and planning by the Battelle group. Did they expect this situation to occur, and what were they prepared to do about it? My guess is that they did not prepare themselves; they were not prepared to enter into the kinds of tactics required, either to change the school system or to create an alternative public school.

Since they were serious about changing the school system, one could expect that they should have been aware of the implications of their actions—this could have meant using "contest" or more political strategies (in Warren's terminology) at the local school system level. They also might have thought of alternative strategies if their primary orientations failed. After all, community involvement should mean more than conferring or working with parent groups; it means utilizing the strengths of community resources to reach specific ends.

My major concern is that the freedom or integrity of the community people may have been potentially seriously impaired by this project while that of the Battelle people was not. The parents assumed an expertise on the part of the Battelle staff that was only partly present. They assumed the potential success of the project, yet the Battelle people seemed unaware that they were even in a social intervention process and, therefore, would have difficulty achieving that success.

For me, the major ethical implications of this project are, first, a lack of accountability of the change agents to the community, and second, the community's implicit assumption that the Battelle people were experts, which seems questionable. The lack of accountability resulted in the lack of a search for alternative routes when the main one failed; the lack of an intense, concerted effort to change the school system or to establish an alternative one. It is no doubt true, as is stated in the final report, that the Battelle group "acted as though the community were its sponsor" and felt that "the control of the team, as far as the direction of change goes, was in the hands of the community members of the team." But the reality is that Battelle controlled the funding of the project and most of the change agent staff were Battelle employees. The Battelle change agent team may have had a great deal of good will, but they were in a very basic sense ultimately accountable to Battelle and not to the community.

Relative to the second point, while the Battelle people were expert in engineering–systems analysis methods, they were not experienced in educational change. While the authors disclaim any single-minded concern for utilizing their engineering analysis, their lack of experience in social institutional change seemed to cause them to fall back on their process skills. Such skills are not consistent with the objectives outlined, namely, institutional change in schools. In effect, one of the goals of this project for the Battelle group was to test the applicability of their skills to school change.

The community people devoted enormous energies to this work, yet seemed to gain little of their major objectives. Was their freedom constrained by this effort? Possibly even more important are the feelings these parents and community people may have about future change attempts. Have they become more cynical about school change as a result of their experience in this project? Will they and their children become more cynical about schools?

A corollary of the disenchantment of community people about change as a result of this failure is the backlash effect of the SUA work within the school system, without any significant offsetting gain by the community people. As reported in the original draft of Chapter 8:

The major negative impact, although a causal relationship is not definite and certainly not exclusive, is that the school district has deleted the hard-won power of the CASC [Central Area School Council] by encouraging other areas to develop school councils and limiting the power of such councils to advisory only. On the positive side, some educators were helped to become more sensitive to the human needs of students and more aware of alternatives they could try in their classrooms.

The question still remains: Why didn't the Battelle people and other change agents utilize their money for immediate change by establishing a school themselves: given a half million dollars, such an effort might have been feasible. While there are considerable problems in such a demonstration project—which I will discuss—their own plans and skills seem more attuned to such a venture.

The ethical issue here is the lack of self-awareness, among the Battelle staff, of the limitations of their skills. This lack of awareness is all too common in social intervention efforts and raises serious questions about first steps in such a process. I would suggest that some deep reflection by the Battelle group could have helped them to clarify their own conceptions of what they wanted, how they could have achieved it, why they were involved, and what the likely results would be.

## THE EFFECTS OF THE SPONSORING AGENCY

A second major issue I would like to discuss is Battelle's involvement in the project. While I respect the good intentions of Battelle and its staff, it is important to look at the effects of this huge research corporation on the SUA project. While Battelle seemed to concerned with future involvement in such projects, a number of statements in the report indicated that the reputation of Battelle was an important issue. They refer to "restriction on Battelle," blacks' attempt to protect Battelle from unfavorable publicity, the relationship between the organization and the community, one of the justifications for not paying community people being the necessity of their being independent of the organization when it was attacked, and so on. It seems to me that the Battelle people were too concerned with their own "company," as they called it. This is consistent with their allegiances—they were, in the end, accountable to Battelle and not to the community.

It could have been possible that the Battelle people did not follow the implications of their change effort because it might have interfered with their loyalty to their company: for example, organizing parents to put pressure on the School Board or other organizing tactics. I suggest that such conflicts in loyalties have serious ethical implications. Battelle is not unique in these conflicts of loyalties. It was common to OEO, Model Cities, and other community agencies that hired change agents to work with community people to change community structures. Usually, the OEO or Model Cities group was pressured by the established powers to cool off their community organizers. The loyalties of the organizers were not in question; the structural dependence of the community agency on city and county agencies was the issue. In Battelle's case, the conflict seemed to reside in the minds of the change agents—so much so that they communicated this to the community people who may have gone easy in the change process in order to protect the reputation of Battelle with the established powers in Seattle.

One senses that this project was a major breakthrough in the Battelle organization toward the establishment of a sense of community responsibility and involvement in community change projects. Such an effort by an organization as large as Battelle is very desirable. Yet, I feel such efforts must be closely analyzed to assess the positive and negative consequences of the intervention. The major issues regarding Battelle, as I see them, are:

- Battelle wanted to maintain control over the project and did so by short-term commitments of money—the project, at times, was funded on a six-week basis, even though it lasted for three years.
- Battelle did not utilize their informal influence to achieve benefits for the SUA (for example, legislation) when such was probably possible.
- Battelle's very limited commitment was not perceived or heard by the community and their own consultants. This may have reflected the community members' desire not to hear Battelle, but it also resulted from Battelle's naïvete in dealing with the community—they may have been giving double messages to indicate their desire to help and their fear of hurting their reputation.

## THE IMPLICATIONS OF A DEMONSTRATION PROJECT

A third major issue relates to the major middle-range goal of the project—the creation of a new school as a demonstration project. While this goal was never achieved, I would like to analyze the implications of such a project.

The main purpose of a demonstration is to develop a new technique or structure and to test this technique or structure independently of the system into which it is going to be integrated, so that it has a chance to succeed in experimental form. The SUA strategy, and the most common strategy for implementation of a demonstration project in the target system, was modeling—namely, the acceptance by the target system of certain elements of the demonstration project because these elements seem desirable.

One of the most basic and common problems with demonstration projects, and those that seem to exist in the SUA planning document of December, 1970, is the tendency to promote the case for the demonstration project in such a way that the technique or operations are overdetermined; the amount of financial and human resources allocated to such a project were well above the maximum amount that the target institution could afford. If the resources needed to model the demonstration are not available to the target system, it is unlikely that adoption of significant parts of the demonstration project will occur unless there is an active dissemination-utilization process. Such a process would require careful planning during the early phases of the planning of the demonstration project itself.

My reading of the literature on demonstration projects indicates an avoidance of such an active dissemination effort. It also indicates a great deal of failure on the part of the target system to adopt the important elements of the demonstration. The SUA plan, following most of their predecessors, had not worked out detailed and active dissemination-utilization procedures.

But what is the target of this social intervention effort? The stated target was the institutional structure of inner-city schools in Seattle. Yet since there was a lack of detailed preparation for such a transfer from the demonstration project to the school system, is it not possible that this demonstration project, like most others, if implemented would have focused mainly on aiding those students and faculty who were in the experiment rather than on the larger "target" population? I have no basic objection to doing this, but I am concerned about the behavioral confusion regarding the project's goals. Since I define the goals of the project by its proposed or actual functions, I feel that the change agents were unclear in their planning about their target; they lacked the instrumental means to achieve change in the target system (their major stated goal), while they had the ability to affect positively the youth in the demonstration program.

Significant ethical issues could be raised. Is it legitimate to spend such a large amount of money and human resources on a few students while keeping other students in their present predicament? The answer to this question would have required an analysis of the standards that would have been involved in the Academy's admissions process. Are we providing more resources to help a few because we cannot help any more at present? If the latter is the case, then perhaps there should be limits on the amount of financial and human resources used to help a few students in order to spread it out over more of them.

I have no simple answers; what is most important is that these questions be raised. Personally, I have been involved in too many projects that were to change the world or even whole school systems when in reality our behavior indicated we were concerned *only* with those with whom we were directly involved. Such work was good work, but we confuse ourselves and those we aid or work with when we are not clear about our real targets, as reflected in our activities rather than our rhetoric.

## CONCLUSION

I have been strong in some of my statements because of my concern about the ethics of conducting change efforts when one is not fully prepared for the job. For too long, too many people have tinkered with social systems (and thereby large numbers of individuals) when their own training has barely given them minimal insight into a diagnosis of the systems. I have been there myself, as were the Battelle change agents.

We would not think of tinkering with the physiology of a person or the development of a weapons system unless we were trained to do so. Yet, when dealing with the most complex forms of human organization, so many people are willing to be expert with little or no training or prior experience. The organizational change process is a delicate one that:

1. Requires careful self-reflection about one's values, motives, abilities, and present resources;
2. Requires a team of experienced personnel along with some novices;
3. Requires some indication that success is likely;
4. Requires the potential availability of financial and human resources (or the means to get them) prior to embarking on the project;
5. Requires a careful diagnosis of the particular system to be changed at about the time at which the change process will begin; and
6. Requires that individuals involved in the change process be, at a minimum, somewhat accountable to those who have the most to gain or lose by the project's success or failure.

One key ethical implication of all change efforts at any level is that the individuals proposing the change be conscious of the human and financial costs and benefits of the project, aware of why they are involved, and able to communicate these to the people they are trying to benefit. I find many educational change projects do not start or end this way. The SUA project is no exception.

## EPILOGUE

As I noted earlier, after having written the first part of this chapter, I was informed that there were a number of positive changes in the Seattle inner-city schools that may have been the result of the planning work carried out be the SUA group. These changes seemed to center around new and special remedial activities in the schools. The exact details of these changes are still unknown to me.

However, the real question is always what caused such program changes that were not directly related to the original project? The Seattle school system has a reputation, I believe, as a progressive system. A group that I was involved with worked in a Seattle high school found the leadership of the system and teachers' association quite open and experimental.

The issue, then, is not whether there were small, incremental, progressive changes in the school system—changes that may have resulted from many different forces, among them the SUA team—but whether these effects were the direct result of the SUA team, directly related to the SUA design.

Since the SUA never came into being, one must ask how the SUA team could have achieved these changes. One possibility is that the process created, in order to accomplish Phases I and II of the project, did create an atmosphere in which the incremental changes would be more likely to occur. Such activities as the group meetings in black and white communities to facilitate the creation of the Urban Academy could have helped the process. This process could be described as the "softening-up" phase.

A second possibility is that the potential existence of the Urban Academy pushed the inner-city schools to think of alternatives to their present activities. This is quite possible and a decent strategy.

The problem with either of these possibilities is that they depended less on community involvement and control than on the goodwill of the Seattle school system. The major problem, however, with the Seattle schools and other school systems is not goodwill but the manner in which schools are structured. A remedial reading program is a desirable activity, but it will not alter the ways in which schools operate to make minority youth feel incompetent and less skilled than middle-class youth. The major goal of the SUA group was to alter in a significant way the inner-city school system of Seattle. This was not done and, I would maintain, could not be done given the strategies employed, the skills and experience of the change agents, and the nature of the experiment itself, which was a demonstration project.

Given the positive spin-offs that may have come into existence as a result of the SUA planning effort, the community had more at the end of the project than when it began; in comparison to what could have occurred—given a half-million dollars and three years of work—the community might have expected more.

We are thus left with many desirable incremental changes in the Seattle school system as a result of the SUA planning activity. This is good, and the change agents should be satisfied that their work of three years had some successful outcomes. Their final report reflects these feelings.

The involvement of the Battelle staff in the project also had desirable outcomes. Given the initial resistance of Battelle's leadership to involvement in educational and community activities, the fact that they eventually allocated a half-million dollars and three years of staff time is a major development for this huge research organization. Many Battelle people risked a great deal to begin the slow process of reorienting the organization. It seems that they were successful, in that Battelle lost very little, the community received new services from the school system, as well as being sensitized to future actions, and Battelle's image remained untarnished.

There remains the problem of control: Battelle got involved and was willing to lend staff and money to help the community, but with their controlling the ultimate decisions about the allocation of resources. Battelle needed to keep this control and protect its image; and, in the end, it was these acts that helped limit the type of strategies that could have been employed. Ultimately, whoever controls the resources controls the project.

Also, the collaborative design employed by the change agents was successful in producing the incremental changes achieved. Such a strategy is desirable for achieving these kinds of gains; it is not a good strategy for achieving system change when the goals of the community are in conflict with those of the school system. But the collaboration also achieved community-wide involvement (that is, beyond the black community), which may lead to considerable payoff in the future.

Throughout this project, the change agents seemed to be limited in their ability either to diagnose the system problems or to understand the kinds of strategies needed to achieve their objectives within the particular school system that was their target. Their final report further indicates this lack of understanding. In this report, they imply that on a few occasions "contest" strategies would not have produced system change because of its threat to the school system. They further imply that contest strategies are the same as the conflicts and turmoil common to many communities in the late 1960s. But when there is dissensus between the objectives of a community and the operations of a school system, there are many different "contest" strategies besides conflict and turmoil. Resolution of differences in dissensus situations could result from the use of the political processes, an everyday means to which the school system is continually responding. Organizing, political pressure, the implicit threat of new voting patterns, the political power of selected sympathetic individuals—all of these could be employed effectively in pushing the system to change. Obviously, these will not lead to change overnight, but they could very well produce greater incremental changes than were achieved in this project and, hopefully, lead in the direction of sytem-wide change. There is no easy path to significant change, but directing one's attention solely to a collaborative strategy, as was done in Seattle, assures only very modest changes that are acceptable to the already established educational authorities.

Clearly, the incremental changes wrought in Seattle are desirable in their own right, but they are very different from system change. System change is concerned with the control of resources and redirecting the allocation of resources in new and desired ways; incremental change accepts the established control of resources and seeks to achieve, following standard procedures, a new allocation of resources to a small number of desired projects. Those who desire incremental changes seek to persuade the controllers of the allocation of resources that it would be desirable to establish new programs; they do not challenge the legitimacy of these controllers, that is, their objectives or the procedures used to allocate scarce resources.

This does not mean, however, that producing incremental change is undesirable; the reality is that many of the gains made by seeking such change have led to significant new services, while system change attempts have been notably unsuccessful. Why is incremental change in schools desirable?

1. It usually creates better services for the dispossessed sectors of the community.
2. It can sensitize people to the potential for change within a system.
3. It may, over time, lead to a "critical mass" of new programs that might produce significant school change. This might occur by proving to the system's leadership the necessity for major changes in a school or even in the system itself. This is not often the case, but is a possibility.
4. It may show authorities that change is not necessarily disruptive, and such adjustments could lead to results they would consider desirable. It may sensitize authorities to the desireability of change.
5. It could whet the appetite of community people for seeking more significant changes in their school or in the system itself.

But incremental change will be most successful when it is consciously sought and when it faces the reality of the collaborative development of new services combined with attempts to achieve slow but methodical changes in the composition of the authoritative bodies through the political processes. Then, the objectives of the system's leadership and the means of allocating scarce resources will be acceptable to the community most affected by a school and by the system as a whole.

## REFERENCES

Greer, C. *The great school legend.* New York: Basic Books, 1972.
Guskin A., & Chesler, M. Partisan diagnosis of social problems. In G. Zaltman (Ed.), *Process and phenomena of social change.* New York: John Wiley & Sons, 1973.
Warren, R. *Truth, love and social change.* Chicago: Rand McNally, 1971.

# V
# INTERVENTION IN COMMUNITY DISPUTES

# 10
# THE ETHICS
# OF INTERVENTION
# IN COMMUNITY DISPUTES

**JAMES LAUE**

University of Missouri–St. Louis

**GERALD CORMICK**

University of Washington

Disputes involving two or more groups or organizations in a community have been very much in the news and on the minds of Americans in the last 15–20 years. Such confrontation as the lunch counter sit-ins of the early 1960s, Birmingham, Selma, Watts, Chicago, Detroit, Newark, Ocean Hill–Brownsville, the 1968 and 1972 political conventions, and Wounded Knee have signaled the politicization of grass-roots groups aiming to wrest their share of the power and resources away from politicians, lawyers, bureaucrats, and other professionals.

Attempts to intervene in community disputes have grown accordingly, with a variety of goals on the part of intervenors, and with a wide range of outcomes of intervention. Since the mid-1960s we have intervened in numerous such disputes, and more recently we have been studying them on a national basis and monitoring the emergence of the new field of "community conflict intervention." Our aim, through the Community Conflict Resolution Program at the University of Missouri–St. Louis and the Office of Environmental Mediation at the University of Washington, has been to develop a language, a network of intervenors, and an awareness of the ethical implications of their work on the part of intervenors.

In this chapter we first define community disputes and present a composite case of a typical dispute. Then we turn to the development of a typology of five intervention roles commonly assumed by intervenors in community disputes: activist, advocate, mediator, researcher, and enforcer. The nature and problems of the intervenor role most frequently seen in community disputes—the mediator—then are analyzed.

In the concluding sections of the chapter, we outline the basic assumptions, values, and criteria of a system of ethics for intervention in community disputes. These criteria are applied to case vignettes drawn from our studies of disputes. Finally the system is summarized in the light of common problems facing intervenors and the groups with whom they work.

Proportional empowerment, justice, and freedom are the root values of the ethics we propose. Because the issue in all community disputes is each interest group's ability to advocate its own needs, power becomes the central reality. Unless all parties to a dispute have some negotiable power, joint determination of the outcome is impossible. This chapter is aimed at developing the implications of this position for intervenors in community disputes in the light of the questions of target group participation and intervention consequences posed in the Introduction to this book.

## COMMUNITY DISPUTES: A DEFINITION AND A TYPICAL CASE

Community disputes are a form of social conflict. Lewis Coser's (1968) widely accepted definition of social conflict is:

> a struggle over values and claims to scarce status, power, and resources in which the aims of the opponents are to neutralize, injure or eliminate their rivals. Such conflicts may take place between individuals, between collectivities or between individuals and collectivities (p. 232).[1]

*Community disputes* are a form of social conflict having the following characteristics:

1. They involve two or more *parties*.
2. These parties have differing *goals*.
3. These goals relate to mutually salient *issues*.
4. The disputes occur at and between differing *system levels*.
5. They are of varying *intensity* and *duration*.
6. They result in widely varying kinds of *termination*.

---

[1] Other recent works on social conflict that have been valuable in providing a basis for development of the concepts of *community* conflict intervention include Angell (1965), Barnard (1957), Boulding (1962), Brickman (1974), Coleman (1957), Deutsch (1973), Kahn and Boulding (1964), Kramer and Specht (1969), Kriesberg (1973), Mack and Snyder (1957), Walton and McKersie (1965), and Williams (1947, 1972).

Each community dispute represents a particular combination of these dimensions. Community disputes emerge when traditional mechanisms of social control such as ideology, media, laws, custom, police, or religion no longer adequately keep natural interest-group competition in equilibrium. Equilibrium—often called "community stability" or even "peace"—is maintained as long as two crucial conditions are met:

- *Power* (the control over decisions about allocation of resources) is perceived as legitimate by sufficiently large numbers of persons in the system.
- *Resources* (goods, services, jobs, facilities, land, etc.) are defined as adequate and their distribution as equitable.

The everday life style of communities and their institutions may be characterized in terms of these two conditions as falling somewhere along a continuum that ranges from cooperation to crisis:

COOPERATION ←——→ COMPETITION ←——→ CONFLICT ←——→ CRISIS

When power is seen as legitimate and resources as adequate, *cooperation* is the dominant mode of interaction. When the legitimacy of established authority and the adequacy of existing resources or the equity of their allocation are questioned, *competition* exists. *Conflict* represents intensified competition, of which large proportions of the system members affected are aware. It arises when the existing power arrangements are seen as non-legitimate and resource allocation as inadequate. *Crisis* occurs when the holders of power ("in parties") being challenged by subordinate groups ("out parties") define the situation as serious enough to take new and unusual action to avoid or minimize what they perceive to be severe costs (see Cormick, 1971a; Laue, 1971).

The system level at which the conflict occurs distinguishes community disputes from others treated in this book. There are five levels of social organization within and between which conflicts may take place: an organization, a neighborhood, an institution (the educational system within a city, for example), a community, or a transcommunity (a Standard Metropolitan Statistical Area or region, for example). Assorted clients, consumers, constituents, employees, and other out parties challenge service professionals, providers, representatives, employers, and other in parties for inclusion—student/school, patient/health care system, welfare recipient/welfare system, black neighborhood group/white controlled planning department, tenant/landlord. The focus of intervention for this chapter is most often a dispute within a commmunity rather than a community-wide dispute.

It is important to recognize that this framework makes a fundamental distinction between personal or interpersonal problems (which are often defined and treated in terms of individual pathology or difficulties in communication and relating to others) and systemic problems (which have their root in the distribution of power and resources within the system). This distinction, and problems associated with inappropriate applications of intervention across system lines, are treated in greater detail in the section on ethics.

Race and racism are factors in many, if not most, community disputes. Racism is pervasive and particularly malicious in the United States. Because racism has meant the historical exclusion of racial minorities from decision-making processes in American communities, the axis of many community disputes is white/nonwhite, and the issue is power. We have observed that whenever different racial groups are involved in a community dispute—or whenever the projected outcomes will change the shape of the power distribution between whites and nonwhites—race or ethnicity becomes the controlling dynamic in the dispute (Laue, 1968).

In sum, every community dispute is a game of power. Power is the issue, power is the goal, and the effective use of power is the strategy for all sides in any conflict. And if race is involved, the power struggle becomes more intense, the stakes higher, the sensitivities greater, the duration of the dispute longer, and the outcome less predictable.[2]

Intervention in community disputes refers to deliberate attempts by outside or other organizations, persons, or forces to influence the course of events in a conflict or crisis situation. Generally, the intervenors perceive their role as helping the disputing parties resolve their differences in what the intervenors see as a positive or socially desirable manner.

There are a number of persons and organizations who practice community dispute intervention, among them human relations commissions, religious groups, government agencies at all levels, psychologists, civil rights groups, and university research and training centers. They include such organizations as the Community Relations Service of the U.S. Department of Justice, the Federal Mediation and Conciliation Service, the Institute for Mediation and Conflict Resolution (New York), the Community Disputes Services Division of the American Arbitration Association (New York), the Community Conflict Resolution Program at the University of Missouri–St. Louis, the Center for Teaching and Research in Disputes Settlement (University of Wisconsin), the Department of Law, Justice and Community Relations of the United Methodist Church (Washington), and the Office of Environmental Mediation (University of Washington, Seattle).

Individuals and organizations practicing community dispute intervention have brought with them a variety of backgrounds and approaches to the field,

[2] For a more detailed analysis of the nature of community and racial disputes, and of the application of innovative intervention techniques, see: *Crisis and change* (1971-1975), Abner (1970), Chalmers and Cormick (1970, 1971), Cormick (1971a, b), Laue (1965, 1970, 1971, 1978), and Nicolau and Cormick, (1972).

including labor-management bargaining, psychological and psychiatric models, sensitivity and encounter approaches, models from international relations, and intergroup and human relations approaches. The somewhat limited applicability of these approaches to community disputes is a major focus of the remainder of this chapter.

## A Typical Case: Elmwood Hospital
## and the Chicano Community Coalition

The important structural and dynamic characteristics of community disputes may be illustrated by the following composite case, based on a number of situations in which the authors have intervened.[3]

> Elmwood is a medium-sized, 450-bed private hospital. It is well equipped for inpatient care and has an open-heart surgery team which is a matter of special pride. None of the trustees lives in the hospitals's service area, although some of their parents once did. Most of the trustees are professionals or businessmen, and their main function is to help in fund raising.

> Until five years ago, Elmwood was in the middle of a white, working-class community. Now, however, it is on the edge of an expanding Mexican-American barrio that has crossed the expressway and is moving eastward. A part of the Mexican-American community is served by a public hospital on the west side of the highway. Those on the east, however, are turning to Elmwood. Few private physicians remain in the area, and Elmwood and its outpatient clinic are the main source of medical care for the new minority group residents.

> The new residents now make up approximately 65 percent of the hospital's service area. Most are in low-paying service jobs or on public assistance. Infant mortality is three times as high as in the rest of the city. Malnutrition is a problem, as is tuberculosis, lead poisoning, and other diseases associated with a deteriorating urban environment. Most cannot afford to enter the hospital when sick, and consequently rely on outpatient treatment in what is now an overburdened facility.

> Like most private hospitals, increased costs have put Elmwood in a financial squeeze. It has become increasingly difficult to attract interns and residents and harder to retain present professsionals. Although the hospital's director is somewhat sympathetic to the medical care problems of the surrounding community, he sees his first priority as building the hospital's institutional strength.

[3] This scenario was adapted from a teaching case developed by the Institute for Mediation and Conflict Resolution, New York.

Citizens in the surrounding community would like the hospital to increase its almost nonexistent efforts in preventive medical care, to improve and expand outpatient facilities, to establish a satellite health center with day-care facilities, and to train a mobile Spanish-speaking paraprofessional health team to provide diagnostic services throughout the community. "This is what a neighborhood hospital is all about," they say.

A neighborhood group, the Chicano Community Coalition (CCC), sent a letter to the director asking that the hospital initiate these efforts and requesting that he meet with them to discuss how the community and the hospital could work together. Although the community is deeply concerned about its medical problems and resents the fact that an Anglo institution has not acted before this on its own initiative, the letter was not unfriendly.

The letter was not answered immediately.

A few days after receiving the letter, the Elmwood board of trustees announced the acquisition of a site on which it said it would build a heart research facilitiy, a six-story nurses' residence, and a staff parking lot.

On learning of these plans, the leaders and members of the Chicano Community Coalition were incensed. About 50 coalition members came to the director's offices and vowed not to leave until the hospital agreed to meet the following demands:

1. Replacement of the board of trustees with a community-controlled board
2. A 100 percent increase in outpatient facilities
3. Establishment of a neighborhood health center and day-care facility on the newly acquired site
4. Establishment of a preventive diagnostic mobile health team, consisting of neighborhood residents chosen by the coalition
5. Replacement of the director by a Chicano chosen by the community
6. Making the hospital a bilingual institution at all levels

While the director indicated that he would gladly meet with the group's leader to discuss the matters raised in the letter, he also stated quite forcefully that he considered the new demands arrogant and destructive, and that, in any event, he would not meet as long as the *de facto* occupation of his office continued.

The coalition repeated its intention not to leave until a meeting took place and the demands were accepted.

This description offers a broadly representative example of the type of community dispute that is becoming commonplace as citizens' groups compete with established institutions (and, often, with one another) for control over the allocation of the scarce resources available—whether health care, jobs, space, recreation, housing, education, or other goods, services, and statuses. The Elmwood case contains the following characteristics, which are typical of most community disputes:

- It involves an ethnic minority, historically a victim of discrimination based on linguistic as well as physical characteristics.
- It involves a facility that delivers service to the community and is staffed by professionals who believe they are doing good and important work.
- The dispute is affected by demographic and physical changes in the urban environment which are little understood and certainly cannot be controlled by any of the parties involved.
- There is not only a multiplicity of issues, but of parties as well (the board of trustees, the administration, the various segments of the coalition, and soon, we may assume, additional parties such as physicians, nurses, service staff, police, etc.).
- The resources—hospital beds, availability of professional personnel, space and money for research and/or patient care—are perceived as scarce.
- At least one party is considerably weaker than the others in terms of organizational structure, staying power, and the ability to influence the decisions of the others.
- A simple yes or no solution of the type provided by litigation will not serve the various needs of the parties, and a package in which all win something is called for.
- Unilateral determination of the immediate outcome (by the most powerful party, as is typically the case) will not provide a lasting solution; clients and community as well as care givers must be involved if any solution is to "stick."
- The situation now has escalated to the point where the establishment representatives likely would define it as a crisis.

Given the situation, what are the next steps? What avenues to solution to the dispute are available? How can options for settlement be kept open for all the parties? These are the questions to which intervenors initially would address themselves. Any move taken by an intervenor in such a situation would be subject to ethical inquiries about its impact on the lives and well-being of all the parties, their organizations, the institution, and the quality of health care in the community.

What types of intervention might ensue? Using the Elmwood case as a vehicle, an intervention role typology is presented and analyzed, and one role, the mediator, is discussed in greater detail in preparation for our discussion of the ethics of intervention in community disputes.

## INTERVENING IN COMMUNITY DISPUTES:
## AN ANALYSIS OF INTERVENTION ROLES

Our work has identified five roles that intervenors in community disputes may play: activist, advocate, mediator, researcher, and enforcer. They are differentiated in terms of three variables:

- The intervenor's organizational and fiscal base
- The intervenor's relationship to the parties—the degree of identification with one party and range of empathy for, and access to, the other parties
- The skills the intervenor brings to bear on a conflict situation

The five intervention roles types are defined and analyzed below in the light of some aspects of the Elmwood case. They are represented spatially in Figure 1, which builds the role types on concentric circles around each of the disputing parties, beginning with the activist.[4]

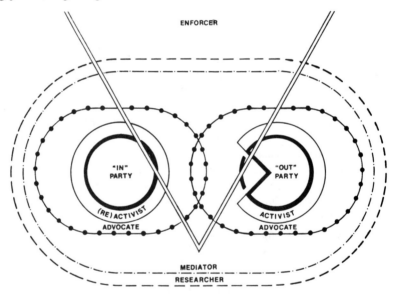

**FIGURE 1.** Intervenor roles.

### Activist

An activist most frequently works closely with the powerless or non-establishment party in a conflict. A variant of this role, the reactivist, may appear in a dispute aligned with the party of the establishment. Both the

---

[4] This analysis and illustration of intervenor roles is adapted from Laue, Cormick, and Cohen (1973). For further analysis of the roles and their applications, see especially Cohen et al. (1972), Cormick (1971b), Laue (1971), and Laue et al. (1971).

activist and reactivist may either become members of the group or be so closely aligned with it that they become directly involved and take the group's goals fully as their own. They have little or no ability to empathize with any party other than the one with which they are identified. In fact, the activist role is drawn to indicate that the activist may, on occasion, fully merge his or her identity with the powerless party. Activists' skills usually include organizing, public speaking, devising strategy, and the ability to rally a following.

At Elmwood there would have been a number of activisits present. Frequently coalitions such as the CCC are the result of the efforts of live-in community organizers to define issues, suggest courses of action, and organize the community. Our experience has been that physicians, particularly chiefs of staff, often act in a reactivist role, using their influence to prevent what they fear will be a sell-out by the hospital administration.

### Advocate

An advocate is not a member of a disputing group, but serves as an advisor or consultant to that group. Advocates support the goals of the group and promote its cause to the opponents and to the wider community. They are better able to extend their boundaries than the focused, more committed activist. The typical advocate for the establishment party is the management consultant, while the community organizer is the most frequent type of out-party advocate. A negotiator representing any of the parties also exemplifies this role type. Requisite skills include those of the activist, plus the ability to envision and achieve conflict termination and arrange contingencies so it can take place on what the advocate's party defines as good terms. The slight overlap of role lines between in- and out-party advocates designates the area where negotiations may begin as the advocates reach out to the other sides. Sources of support for the advocate's work may include any of the parties, as well as foundations, religious bodies, public agencies (Legal Aid, for example), and the like.

During confrontations such as those at Elmwood, which involve professional organizations with high levels of technical expertise, there usually are a number of advocates present. Often public health students and faculty at local institutions will enter such disputes to provide the client groups with the expertise necessary to negotiate technical issues. Some of the demands (the community health center and roving diagnostic team, for example) suggest the contribution of such advocates in this case. Should the board's attorneys seek an injunction to remove the CCC members, a legal advocate would probably come forward to represent the coalition.

Most urban hospitals have a community relations officer or staff, a large part of whose function is to advocate its cause to the surrounding community and the wider public. In addition, a frequent institutional reaction in cases like Elmwood is to engage a consultant to run communications workshops or other sensitizing programs for staff to improve their working relationships with the protesting client group, the result of which often is deflection of community pressure.

### Mediator

Mediators do not have their base in any of the disputing parties and thus have a more general, less party-parochial view of the conflict. (The dot-and-dash line representing this role in Figure 1 encompasses both of the parties, rather than being centered on one of them, as is the case with the activist and advocate roles.) The mediator is acceptable at some level of confidence to all of the disputing parties. A fiscal and organizational base acceptable to the disputing parties (and ideally, in most situations, independent of them) is crucial. Mediators assist the parties in reaching a mutually satisfactory settlement of their differences, usually by means of face-to-face bargaining sessions. Mediation skills are too numerous and too well known to catalogue here, but a brief analysis of the nature and problems of this role in community disputes follows this section.

> At Elmwood, a mediator might have entered the dispute in a number of ways. The mayor of the city might request that the parties meet with a mediator in the interest of the total community. One or the other of the parties might have felt it to be in its interest to seek a settlement and may ask a mediator to enter the dispute. The mediator would have to find a way to be invited in or accepted by the opposing party. Should the parties begin negotiations on their own, they might jointly request the intervention of a mediator. A mediator or mediation agency might attempt to enter the dispute through its own contacts and on its own volition. Or, should an injunction be sought, the courts might "suggest" mediation. The authors have studied or intervened in similar disputes in which each of these entry modes has occurred.

### Researcher

The researcher may be a social scientist, a policy analyst, a media representative, or (as is increasingly the case in confrontations arising from a planned event such as a demonstration or political convention) a trained lay observer, who provides an independent evaluation of a given conflict situation. The researcher perceives the conflict in its broadest context and is able to empathize with all positions. The impact of the researcher's intervention is determined by the interpretation and importance accorded his or her findings by the parties and by the wider public. It is difficult, however, for the researcher to stay uninvolved. Researchers may find themselves subpoenaed by one party to testify about alleged law violations by another party. They may also be used by the out party to analyze the power structure of the in party in preparation for conflict.

At the Elmwood confrontation there is little doubt that the news media would have a strong impact on the situation. If street demonstrations evolved, there might have been visible independent observers on the scene such as the observer committee established by the New York City Bar Association.[5]

### Enforcer

The enforcer represents power to enforce conditions on conflicting parties irrespective of their wishes. Enforcers often take the institutional form of a formal agency of social control in the larger system within which the conflict is set—the police or the courts—or perhaps the form of a funding agency or an arbitrator. In Figure 1, the role is illustrated as a double line intersecting the other four roles to indicate that the enforcer alone brings formal coercive power to the situation. The enforcer brings the right to specify behavior that may support the goals of any or all of the parties, or to provide a baseline of legality and, flowing from it, a sense of the superordinate power realities to which disputing parties must respond. One rarely sees a true arbitrator in community disputes. The web of issues and parties usually is so complex that no single person or agency has an appropriate base to command allegiance to an imposed solution, and no statutory process for submitting such disputes to arbitration currently exists.[6]

We have already speculated on the possible role of the courts at Elmwood. There is little doubt that a contingent of police would be on the scene during the entire confrontation. Public officials such as the mayor, depending on the current state of his popularity, might bring sufficient independent leverage on the situation to enable the police to perform as *de facto* arbitrators of the immediate course of the conflict (but probably not of the final package).

[5] In planned crisis events there is a growing tendency to establish such observer forces. During the political conventions at Miami Beach in 1972, for example, local and national religious bodies organized Religious and Community Leaders Concerned, which had an extensive observer corps with widely publicized daily synopses of their observations. At the Republican Convention in Kansas City in 1976, religious leaders formed Watch, Inc., for the same purposes. In addition to New York, the local bar association in Washington has trained teams of lawyers to serve as observers at mass demonstrations.

[6] The best illustration of a true enforcer's role that we know of was the activity of Mayor Richard Daley in terminating the protracted conflict between black leaders, the contruction unions, and contractors in Chicago in 1969.

Each of these intervenor roles tends to appear in every community conflict situation. Usually, any individual intervenor or intervention organization can play only one role in any dispute. In fact, once an intervenor is typed in a particular role in one dispute, he or she may be unable to play a different role in another dispute. However, we have observed skillful intervenors playing two or more roles in the same dispute. The advocate-mediator is the best example. In this role, an intervenor combines mediation skills with the work necessary to organize and strengthen the weaker party so a settlement that will stick can be achieved. The key to this kind of role mixing is the perceived integrity and judiciousness of the intervenor.

There are a number of widespread misconceptions and problems regarding roles for third-party intervention in community disputes, among them (a) the indiscriminate labeling of all intervenors as "mediators," (b) the notion that mediators in community disputes are or ought to be neutral (as the concept has developed in labor-management relations), and (c) the failure of many intervenors to be aware either of the fact of their intervention (activisits and researchers are the most typical examples) or of the implications of their particular skills, biases, and power base on the parties and the dynamics of the dispute. These and other problems receive more extensive treatment in the section on ethics below.

## The Nature and Problems of the Mediator Role

The role most often associated with intervention in community disputes is that of the mediator. Many who in fact are performing other intervention roles tend to call themselves "mediators."

The experienced mediator performs a number of different functions in community disputes and crises, each designed to further the negotiations and the resolution process. It is particularly important to remember that the mediator is an *aid* to the negotiations and does not replace the joint decision-making process.

Mediators do not serve as a netural third party when they enter a dispute. Merely by advocating the negotiation or joint decision-making process as a way of dealing with a conflict, the mediators are advocating, in our view, positive change rather than repression. Their decision on when or whether to intervene is an important factor affecting the outcome of a dispute. So is the way they report one party's issue-saliency to another.[7]

The negotiation process itself determines the extent to which a mediator

---

[7] Often parties in a dispute wish to use a mediator to gain a sense of the importance conflicting parties place on the issues under dispute and on their various goals and demands. What, for example, is negotiable for the other side(s), and what is truly nonnegotiable? For a discussion of this question as it relates to community disputes in particular, see Chalmers and Cormick (1970) and Cormick (1971b).

can favor one party over another. Obviously, the parties would not accept the assistance of a mediator who had a reputation for unfairness. If a party felt that a mediator was acting unfairly during negotiations, it could require him or her to withdraw from the negotiations.

As a tool for achieving change, mediation has both advantages and disadvantages. Negotiations convert power and potential power into a settlement that reflects the relative strength of the parties. Community groups choose to negotiate when they wish to solidify the gains they have made so far, or when they want to buy some time to reorganize, develop new strategies, or further develop their power base. Mediators will assist change only if they understand and respect these motives.

Mediation and the negotiation process are often the quickest routes to gaining concessions from the opposition, for established institutions are coming to recognize and accept these processes. Indigenous leaders who develop good negotiation skills, who understand the mediation process, and know how to use mediators can help achieve the goals of their organizations.[8]

Mediation may also be the best route to achieving legitimation with the established institutions, and a way of setting up direct communication in an otherwise noncommunicative or chaotic situation. In this context, a mediator often helps grass-roots or citizens' groups gain recognition, overcome internal problems of representation and leadership, establish new contacts, cut through red tape, locate new resources, or use the resources they already have to the best advantage.

Mediation is not suited to all conflicts and disputes. Disputing parties always need to carefully weigh all of the pros and cons before pursuing this course of action.

## THE ETHICS OF INTERVENTION IN COMMUNITY DISPUTES

The ethics of intervention in community disputes center on the nature and quality of decisions made by the intervenor, and whether those decisions promote the core values outlined in this section: freedom, justice, and empowerment.

From this standpoint, the single ethical question that must be asked of every intervenor in community disputes at every decision-making point in the intervention is:

> Does the intervention contribute to the ability of relatively powerless individuals and groups in the situation to determine their

---

[8] One of the critical issues in the emerging field is the availability of the processes of negotiation and mediation to all parties, especially those without experience or skill in these areas. Establishment parties generally are able to secure highly skilled negotiators, while out parties often cannot.

own destinies to the greatest extent consistent with the common good?

This question flows from a basic assumption about human nature and three values derived from that premise. Ethical principles supply criteria for decision making. Ethical criteria are implemented in specific intervention situations through the decision-making process of the intervenor. The framework and flow of our ethical system regarding community dispute intervention may thus be diagrammed as follows:

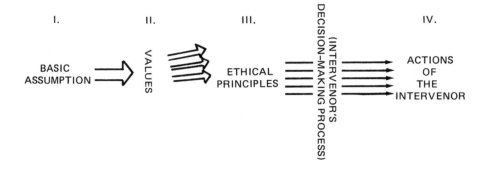

## Basic Assumption

Any consideration of ethics must be based on assumptions about the nature of human beings. Our basic assumption is that persons are by nature fallible, decision-making creatures who seek meaning. Human beings are, of course, many other things, but these are their most important characteristics, and this basic nature ought to be honored and fulfilled. Persons seek meaning through their interaction with others. Persons are, and ought to be treated as ends in themselves.[9]

## Values

Three core values concerning appropriate goals for human beings and the social systems within which they live flow from this doctrine of persons. The three values may be summarized as empowerment, justice, and freedom. Empowerment is the requisite condition of individuals and groups to achieve the desired end-state of society—justice. A just society is prerequisite to the maximum attainment of freedom by all individuals in the system. The freedom to make responsible choices among a number of options and live

---

[9] The Preamble to the Code of Ethics of the American Sociological Association (1971) cites the recognition of people as ends-in-themselves as the ultimate value toward which the work of sociologists should be directed.

with the consequences of those decisions is the process whereby the deepest forms of personal meaning are realized.[10]

### Freedom

A person's nature is most fully honored—the person finds deepest meaning—when he or she has the maximum degree of freedom to determine his or her destiny consistent with the common good. Freedom for the individual exists only when the individual and the groups he or she belongs to have adequate power to negotiate rights and interests vis-à-vis their fellows.

### Justice

Justice is the ultimate social good.[11] The just social system would be one in which power (control of decisions) is diffused, decision making is participatory, accountability for decisions is visible, and resources are adequate and equitably distributed. Justice can only result from the continuous interplay of individuals and groups adequately empowered to represent their own interests, with a minimum of superordinate umpiring to prevent power concentrations and, therefore, abuses. Given human fallibility, a system of justice cannot be constructed and implanted on a social system by wise and/or powerful outsiders. It must emerge from the interplay of empowered, meaning-seeking individuals and groups.

### Empowerment

Assuming that all individuals and groups have a right to seek justice and freedom, empowerment for all is essential. To be fully human, individuals and their groups must make their own decisions and live with the consequences. Self-determination is impossible without negotiable power. Ultimately, no one speaks for another. Thus, individuals and groups must represent their own interests. Proportional empowerment becomes a crucial value. It refers to a condition in which all groups have developed their latent power to the point where they can advocate their own needs and rights, where they are capable of protecting their boundaries from wanton violation by others, where they are capable of negotiating their way with other empowered groups on the sure footing of respect rather than charity. Given the fallibility of judges, sociologists, politicians, philosophers, and theologians, we can only trust that

[10] Empowerment may be viewed, in Rokeach's terms (1973), as an "instrumental value," one that is essential to the achievement of social justice and personal freedom. Justice, then, becomes a "terminal value," but freedom remains instrumental in our system, its exercise leading to the ultimate terminal value: human fulfillment.

[11] In our view, justice subsumes the other two first-order values (in addition to freedom) identified by Warwick and Kelman (1973): welfare and security/survival. If social groups are proportionately empowered to represent and negotiate their own interests in the marketplace of societal decision making, their welfare and survival needs will be served vis-à-vis those of all other groups.

true substantive justice will flow from the procedural safeguard of proportional empowerment.

Applying this scheme of core values to intervention in community disputes, we conclude that in a situation marked by a high degree of power imbalance among the parties, any intervention must enable the powerless party or parties to increase their power. Empowerment—and justice and freedom—are ends in themselves so long as all individuals and groups are equipped to advocate their interests to a similar degree. If only certain persons and groups are empowered, then other people cannot protect themselves and speak for themselves, and they inevitably come to be wrongly treated as means rather than ends.

It should be clear by now that we believe the coinage of community disputes is power—the ability to make or at least influence the decisions that affect one's life in the community. The single ethical question, which must be put to every intervenor—whether the intervention contributes to the ability of relatively powerless individuals and groups in the situation to determine their own destinies to the greatest extent consistent with the common good—now comes into sharper focus.

Social change toward justice thus becomes the proper general goal for intervenors in community disputes, and empowerment of relatively powerless individuals and groups becomes the immediate ethical mandate.

Settlement of community conflicts and crises per se will not do as the overriding goal for community intervenors. When power imbalances are great—as is the case with most of the community disputes with which intervenors deal—a focus on settlement per se usually contributes to the strengthening of the status quo. Justice is only approached when all the parties involved in a dispute over power or resources have a share in shaping the settlement, that is, when joint determination rather than unilateral determination is the mode of operation. Joint determination is not possible unless all parties have negotiable power.

### Ethical Principles

Ethics refers to a set of principles defining the rightness or wrongness of acts. Ethical principles flow from basic values about desired end-states and processes for achieving them. The desired end-states we posit regarding community life are the core values of social justice and personal freedom, and the procedural absolute for achieving these end-states is represented in the core value of proportional empowerment.

We have identified eight principles that we believe translate these three core values into operational criteria to guide intervenors in making decisions about intervention. They are stated in brief form here and applied to case examples near the conclusion of this chapter.

1.  The actions of the intervenor (whether in entering a dispute, timing of intervention moves, selecting strategy and tactics, or helping fashion agreements) should contribute to proportional empowerment of powerless groups for social change.

2.  The intervenor should promote the ability of the weaker parties to make their own best decisions through helping them obtain the necessary information and skills to implement power. The intervenor should assess the relative level of information, negotiating skills, and analytical ability of the parties and, if there is a considerable differential, help even the odds through training or other forms of advocacy.[12]

3.  The rationale for an intervenor's decisions should be conscious, explicit, and (where consistent with the basic values of freedom, justice, and empowerment) public. Such decision-making requires the intervenor to engage in interchange on several levels (cognitive, between principles and anticipated action, with colleagues, etc.) and thus works to inhibit unilateral, uncritical decisions that may adversely affect the weaker parties in a dispute.

4.  Since neutrality or claims to neutrality on the part of an intervenor in a community dispute almost always work to the advantage of the party in power, the intervenor should not claim to be (or worse, actually feel) neutral. Such a stance is evidence of the intervenor's failure to make conscious, explicit, and (where possible) public decisions.

5.  The intervenor should be intimately familiar with the dynamics of power and, where the situation involves race, the realities of racism. If this is not the case, the intervenor's actions (even if well-motivated) will result in damaging the position of the weaker party and strengthening the hold of the party in power.

6.  The intervenor should consistently advocate resolution of conflict or crisis through a process of joint decision making by the parties, because, in community dispute situations, the more powerful party virtually always has the ability to terminate the dispute through sheer physical or military force (a practice that violates the values of freedom and justice through empowerment).

7.  Intervenors trained in one conceptual approach (one-to-one psychotherapy or labor-management bargaining and mediation, for example) should not transfer their intervention models uncritically to a different system setting (a racial/community dispute involving multiple parties, for example). To do so is to increase the probability that issues will be diverted and that

---

[12] As Kelman has observed in reviewing this manuscript, proportional empowerment refers to the intervenor's contributions to structural changes, while the intervenor's role referred to in point 2 involves the development of particular skills or capacities on the part of the weaker parties.

the outcomes will not meet the most basic needs of the disputants. "Improving communication" or building temporary trust rather than building power for influence on decisions inevitably results in cooling out the disadvantaged parties or unnecessarily exacerbating the conflict in the long run.

8.  While empowerment of the powerless is a premier value in our system, intervenors should not lend their skills to empowering groups who do not hold the values of empowerment, freedom, and justice for all peoples, regardless of race, sex, religion, or national origin. In fact, an intervenor should place a high value on working *against* such groups. Thus the value positions and ethical criteria outlined herein do *not* call for invervention activities that will further empower racists, sexists, fascists, militarists, or religious bigots, for to do so would be to contribute to violation of the very premise of human fulfillment from which these principles flow.

### Action as Translation of Principles through Decisions

The flow from basic assumption to values to ethical principles is not fulfilled unless it culminates in action in specific concrete situations. The translating mechanism between principles and action is the decision-making process. The personal decision is the unit act of social ethics.

Every facet of intervention analyzed in this chapter flows from a decision or combination of decisions by intervenors or intervention agencies. Not to decide is to decide; to act without consciousness or comprehension of one's decision-making process is to decide. The actions or inactions of intervenors in community disputes have an impact on parties regardless of the decisional etiology of the act.

*Decision* is the linking concept between intervention ethics and intervention actions. Only by clearly tracing intervention decisions can we assess accountability, measure the actions against ethical criteria, and stimulate wide discussion among intervenors about their own actions. We focus on decision because we have encountered literally dozens of naïve, well-motivated intervenors who never comprehended the detrimental impact of their decisions and actions on subordinate groups in a dispute.

Throughout this chapter, there have been numerous examples of the kinds of decisions intervenors must make. We may now summarize them in four basic categories, with examples of the types of questions an intervenor faces:

1.  *Entry decisions.* Whether to intervene. What is the potential for enhancing the power of weaker parties by intervention? What are the prospects for successful termination of the conflict through one's intervention? What impact will the intervenor's entry make on the legitimacy of the weaker parties? On the power of the stronger parties?

2.  *Timing decisions.* When to enter. Whether to enter at the start, or to let

the process "cook." How to avoid the tendency to try to get weaker parties to the bargaining table before they are ready. How to relate one's own intervention to existing mechanisms for conflict resolution in the system.

3. *Process decisions.* Whether and when to allow, oppose, or promote escalation and system disequilibrium. Developing contingency plans for decisions should violence arise or escalate. Making decisions regarding shifting roles in the course of a dispute (from mediator to advocate for a weaker party, for example).

4. *Termination decisions.* How to recognize a good settlement. Determination of trade-offs. Dealing with nonnegotiable demands. Criteria for decisions regarding the importance of procedural versus substantive issues. Assessing practicality and cost of proposed settlements.

We now turn briefly to illustrating the application of the eight ethical principles to difficult decisions faced by intervenors in actual dispute situations. Some situations are disguised for obvious reasons; some are not. Some offer the obviously correct answer to the intervenor's decisional dilemma; others end with a question.

## Proportional Empowerment

A young black psychologist was hired by the Harvard Community Health Care Plan in 1970 to help organize a Community Advisory Committee whose manifest purpose was to advise the physicians and administrators of the plan on the nature and delivery of health care needed. His greatest difficulty was in dealing with several black welfare mothers who stressed neighborhood health care centers. He met with them extensively, took them to lunch, and eventually hired them as paraprofessional aides for the plan. The women now had steady income, and the advocate had his package for his employer. But he had perceived himself as an advocate for the *community*, not the plan.

Did this outcome contribute to proportional empowerment? In the short run, probably not, for it in effect co-opted some of the strongest activists in the Community Advisory Committee and undercut the organizational base of the group. But minor redistribution of resources did take place (for example, the new jobs as paraprofessionals), and one could scarcely argue against securing the financial life of the families of the women who were hired, some of them probably for the first time. In the long run, it seems clear that power may have been added to the powerless group in the situation, for some of the women have functioned as inside advocates with the kind of experience and base in the community that the professional psychologist could not bring to the organization.

## Promoting the Ability of the Parties to Make Their Own Best Decisions

A dispute arose between a major private urban university and members of the surrounding black community over planned cutbacks in a substantial and highly valued community program sponsored by the university. The program included, among other benefits, hard-core job training and technical assistance for promoting minority economic development. It had been established partly in the hope that it would ease growing tensions between the university and the community.

Following an overt confrontation that included an effective sit-in by members and supporters of the program's community advisory board, both parties to the dispute invited mediation.

It became apparent to the mediator that the protesting community group had agreed to engage in a process with which it was unfamiliar. Their lack of skill in negotiation could be expected to lead to their settling for something less than their relative power and influence would seem to indicate. If this should happen, the mediator could realistically predict heightened frustration that could lead to renewed tensions in the near future.

Accordingly, prior to the beginning of negotiations, the mediator engaged in informal training sessions and developed a lengthy draft of a "how to negotiate" pamphlet for the community-based group. Their understanding of the process improved, and their new skills led to an eventual settlement that the parties believed served the needs of both the community and the university.

### Promoting Conscious, Explicit, and Public Intervenor Decisions; The Issue of Intervenor Neutrality

The following vignette dramatically illustrates these two ethical principles. In 1969 two private consultants, in collaboration with an official of a major religious denomination, ran a laboratory confrontation exercise for 10 police officers and 10 black community members in a large midwestern city. The exercise was planned to last for five days. The aim was to improve working relationships between the police department and the black community. On the second day the police, after refusing the blacks' request to leave their hand-guns and holsters at the door, walked out, claiming foul language as the reason. The blacks, most of whom had taken leave from work for the week to engage in the laboratory, sat until Friday, but the police did not return. All three intervenors made efforts to persuade the police to return to the sessions, but the police chief and the mayor ordered them not to return.

As the end of the week approached, it became clear that money for the honoraria verbally promised the black participants by the consultants would not materialize because the workshop had not proceeded with both parties present. The two private consultants made no efforts to secure the money and did not consult with the group about the problem. The religious official assumed the responsibility for paying the black participants and secured the money on an emergency basis, making himself personally liable for the money.

The two consultants did not adhere to the suggested openness of exchange with colleagues and with the weaker party in making their decisions about payment to the black participants. This action is closely related to the consultants' perception of their own role as simply neutral facilitators of the laboratory confrontation between blacks and police. A serious moral dimension involving the valuable time and the raised expectations of the black participants was at stake, but later conversations indicated that the consultants did not even recognize it as such, for they lacked (in our judgment) a basic understanding of the power differentials involved and the impact of their intervention on the situation.

### Understanding the Realities of Power and Racism

Cormick, Laue, and another consultant were called for a one-visit intervention in an ongoing conflict surrounding a desegregating K–12 school in a blue-collar neighborhood in a large southern city. Our sponsor possessed good legitimation with the superintendent and the school board and felt that the time was appropriate for outside expertise to help move the situation along. In the course of the three-hour consultation, all three outsiders independently determined that:

- The problem was largely *outside* the school, among the white parents rather than between the students.
- What several of the school personnel perceived as a breakdown in school spirit in reality was a redefining of school spirit to encompass the needs and styles of the newly arriving minority students.
- The superintendent of the system was forward-looking, and the lawyer for the school board was a recalcitrant racist who was exacerbating the problem.

It became clear that the superintendent agreed to our sponsor's calling us in as consultants because he wanted support for recommendations he no doubt had made previously, to provide him with sanction to move. Without any formal communication among the three of us during the course of the meeting, each apparently decided to allow the superintendent to use us in this way, for we all perceived the problem in the system in the same way and believed the approaches he was advocating were appropriate. Our understanding of the dynamics of power and racism in these types of communities and situations—and our joint recognition of the positions of the superintendent and the attorney—made this outcome possible. If any one of the consultants had been naïve, the scenario that developed could have been disrupted and the initiative turned back from the hands of the superintendent to the school board attorney and others with his views.[13]

---

[13] Note the relevance of this example to the operational criterion regarding relations with antidemocratic groups and its illustration later in the chapter.

### Advocating Joint Determination

The Wounded Knee crisis of Spring 1973 is the most dramatic example of intervenors' understanding and promoting the principle of joint determination. At Wounded Knee, representatives of the National Council of Churches and of the Community Relations Service of the U.S. Department of Justice literally helped prevent a massacre, this time of certain U.S. citizens (Indians) by U.S. Justice Department marshals, U.S. Army troops, local law enforcement officials, and vigilantes. They did so by the relentless running of communications back and forth between the American Indian Movement (AIM) and federal bunkers; by insisting that all parties thoroughly check out rumors rather than fire first, and then helping them to do so; by drafting the original 15-point agreement that led to the cease-fire by participants, and working in the *de facto* demilitarized zone at great personal risk to see that it was implemented; by standing up to military and other officials who publicly declared they wanted to "clear those savages out of here"; by facilitating negotiation; and by assisting in provision of food and basic medical services to the various parties in the dispute.

The unspoken (and probably, at the time, unconceptualized) aim was to keep the dispute negotiable rather than to permit its unilateral termination by the more powerful party through military force. The link to the core values of freedom, justice, and empowerment is dramatically clear in this case.

### Inappropriate Application of Intervention Models

Two brief examples illustrate the importance of the ethical mandate concerning application of intervention models in inappropriate setting.

In a major Northeastern city in 1970, a new organization set up to intervene in community disputes was seriously and deservedly discredited because of inappropriate wholesale application of a highly rationalized model, originally developed for white-dominated labor union elections, to the process of composing a neighborhood housing board in an all-minority area. The insensitivities of the white officials were many. They ignored the importance of working hours of the election participants; low-income black styles of political participation and communication; the realities of the neighborhood's informal political organization; the people's orientation to time and deadlines; the people's natural resistance to an all-white, all-male, tersely professional election staff. The result was an election process that failed, that had to be redesigned and rerun, and that set back the parent organization in its attempts to develop intervention in racial and community disputes.

The second example represents the more typical case: the application of psychological, psychiatric, or encounter models to community disputes, where the problem is essentially one of imbalance in power and resources rather than individual psychopathology. In this case, a highly paid private consultant hired by only one of the parties dramatically flew in to a medium-sized eastern city after arranging to bring city officials and black representatives to a secluded location during the height of a racial disorder in the early 1970s. The predictable scenario took place: verbal catharsis for both groups, eventual discussion of issues, inability of city officials to produce needed resources for the changes demanded (because the consultant had not educated them about the realities of urban racism and the inequities underlying disorder), heightened hostility and suspicion on the part of blacks after finding raised expectations cruelly dashed, and return of the participants to real life where existing political and economic power arrangements continued to control decisions. Establishment interests inevitably use such experiences to gather additional intelligence on minority community perceptions and groups before the temporary early euphoria of the communications/encounter gives way to a clearer perception by minority representatives of the political realities of the meeting.

An article on this intervention later quoted the consultant as referring to himself as a "doctor to the cities" and as saying that all the parties "seem to feel a little better" after they talk to him.

### Intervenor Relations with Antidemocratic Groups

A serious dispute arose in a large city over construction of scattered-site low-income housing in a predominantly white blue-collar neighborhood. The neighborhood residents saw the project as designed for blacks and Puerto Ricans. The dispute escalated quickly. Major private and public leaders entered the verbal fray, and a series of large demonstrations by whites against the proposed housing were held.

A mediator was asked to intervene by the mayor. He succeeded in building good rapport with both the white residents of the area and the major civil rights spokesmen supporting the proposed new housing.

Both sides soon pushed the mediator for his position on open housing. He tried to avoid a complete break-off of negotiations by focusing on problems of planning the implementation—a strategy that indicated his position on the issue all the same. The white anti-housing group secured an injunction to stop the construction, some of which was being destroyed by arson and other vandalism, and the mediator was required to testify in court. A decision was required from him at this point as to whether he could continue to work with the antihousing group. He testified that he not only was morally committed to the right of individuals to live where they chose, but recognized that it was the law of the land. He then initiated a series of meetings with federal and court officials because of his rising concern over police handling of civil rights and minority demonstrators. He succeeded in having the proceedings transferred from civil to federal courts, which eventually resulted in the use of federal marshals at demonstrations rather than the essentially antiblack local and state police.

The choice had been put to him by the situation: Is it more important to continue as a mediator in the dispute, or to risk one's credentials with one of the parties by taking a strong and public advocate's role for open housing? The intervenor's values were clear; the choice was easy.

## SUMMARY AND IMPLICATIONS:
## THE INTERVENOR AND
## THE TARGET OF THE INTERVENTION

Our aim in this chapter has been to analyze the nature of community disputes and the emerging field of community dispute intervention, to offer a sense of the multiplicity and complexity of intervention roles, and to develop an ethical framework for assessing this type of intervention and its outcomes. Our own values and the ethical principles flowing from them have been stated, and we have returned at many points in the chapter to focus on intervenors and their decisions, organizational bases, skills, and biases, and their understanding of and sensitivities to race, power, and process.

The core values of freedom, justice, and empowerment lead us to demand of all intervenors a conscious self-questioning about whether their intervention in specific situations will empower weaker parties and lead to joint determination of outcomes. We find that, given the fallibility of even the wisest of outside "princes and experts" (Benveniste, 1973), proportional empowerment is the only safeguard we may ultimately trust in the pursuit of justice and freedom.

The implications of these value positions for the three general questions posed in the introductory chapter regarding goal setting, target group participation, and intervention consequences are clear, we believe, and this summary section is organized around those questions.

*In setting the goals for any social intervention, who speaks for the person, group, or community that is the target of the change effort?* This question does not pose a problem regarding the powerful groups in community dispute situations. They are used to speaking for themselves and have the means to do so. Our ethical system, properly implemented in intervention, would empower weak or powerless community groups as well to speak for themselves through the ability to negotiate their own rights and interests. The intervenor's efforts to obtain empowerment and to even the odds through training or other approaches offer two important guidelines for response.

The tendency of intervenors to see and present themselves as professionals is a pervasive problem in intervention at all system levels and is especially crucial for intervenors in community disputes. This tendency is reflected in the working definition of social intervention offered in Chapter 1, which refers to "deliberate attempts *by professionals* to change the characteristics of individuals or groups, or to influence the pattern of relationships between individuals and/or groups" (italics added). The essential point is that a concern with the professionalism of the intervenor may presume the inability of the target group to cope with self-determination.

A subquestion posed for contributors to this book was, "In deciding whom they will 'recognize' as spokespersons for the target group, how can the intervenors avoid conferring power on some segments of that group at the expense of others and taking on themselves the role of 'kingmakers'?" We believe a more important question is, "Why should the intervenor have the right to make such a determination at all?" The very essence of self-determination is the right of the individual or group to select its own spokespersons. The parties involved make that decision. Accurate and updated assessment of the viability and legitimacy of the relationship between the spokesperson and the constituency is the critical demand on the intervenor.

Ambiguities arise when intervenors attempt to give their goals the same priority as those of the target. When personal goals (for prestige, publication, change in clients or target, for example) strongly conflict with the goals of the parties who need empowerment in a dispute, intervenors should disengage themselves or not become involved initially. Many community-based health groups are now insisting that there be no health professionals on the governing boards of community health centers. Their position is that the necessary medical knowledge can be provided by doctors engaged as their consultants, that health-care recipients should decide where they are going, and the professionals' duty is to help them get there. Similarly, the responsibility of the intervenor is not to determine goals but to provide the technical assistance needed by the parties in achieving their self-determined goals.

Achieving self-determination requires the empowerment of the powerless—those individuals and groups of individuals who are disadvantaged and disenfranchised. It is only from this proportional empowerment that other desirable values of freedom and justice and, only thereafter, peace can flow. More important, the power of self-determination can preclude professionals such as ourselves from imposing our own definitions of justice on others.

The basic responsibility of the intervenor, then, is to use skills, position, and power to further the empowerment of the powerless. Proportional empowerment will prevent license without responsibility. It furthers the confrontation-interaction process through which groups ultimately discover their common as well as conflicting goals. Otherwise the powerful will continue to exercise their power and unilaterially impose their will, justify it as truth, manifest destiny, the white man's burden, God's will, "technical expertise on problems too complicated for average citizens to understand," or the "reasoned judgment of the City Planner's office."

*In selecting the means of intervention, how does one assure genuine participation in the change process to the people who are its targets?* Again, proportional empowerment is the only lasting, nonpaternalistic answer. Yet our concern grows that, now that the overt large-scale disorders have at least temporarily run their course, many intervenors working in the aftermath approach intervention with a token economy model rather than a political model. That is, they perceive their role as one of aiding in the process of making certain concessions in the allocation of resources rather than in helping to significantly empower powerless groups. In this regard, many professionalized intervenors are similar to most establishment parties: They wrongly see resources alone rather than power as the arena for change.

The empowerment goals of our ethical framework may be phrased somewhat differently in response to the second basic question: How can community intervenors help powerless disputants regain their sovereignty from politicians, government agencies, and professionals so they can make their own basic decisions? Wresting the process for dispute settlement away from lawyers and the litigation scenario in particular is a major objective if the goal of genuine participation in the change process for the target population is to be realized.

*In assessing the consequences of social intervention, how does one take account of higher-order or unintended effects?* Our approach to intervention practice and ethics is not very helpful in dealing with this question, for several reasons:

- The systems, parties, and issues involved in community disputes are so numerous and so complexly related that determining causal relationships between individual acts (by intervenors or others) is extremely difficult if not impossible. What causes, for example, the settlement of an Elmwood Hospital dispute that results in a community-controlled board of trustees?
- Success is hard to define in community dispute intervention. What may be success to one intervenor, may not be to another or to one, any, or all of the parties with whom that intervenor has worked. We have our yardsticks of empowerment and joint determination, but they may not be sufficient in the eyes of the target group.
- Unintended or higher-order effects cannot be controlled, because the web in which community disputes are set is no smaller than the world. Illustrations of such effects are the impact of a health-care settlement in one city on plans in another city; the movement of an Alinsky organizer or a community mediator from one area to another trying successful models; or the impact of the writings of a HUD professional trained in Boston and working in Washington on Chicanos organizing in San Diego to oppose a freeway location defined as the best by all professional criteria.

In this context, intervenors in community disputes must recognize that their role is generally catalytic rather than directly causal, but they must keep themselves visible and ever available to groups with whom they have worked in the past to assess and share responsibility for higher-order or unintended consequences that may develop.

A final word must be directed to ourselves and other intervenors at all system levels. Intervenors must be on guard at all times against ideological captivity by the professional/client therapy model of intervention where the professional holds at least implicitly the assumption that the client or target group is sick. Disadvantaged groups are not sick. We do not have to protect them for their own good. Most especially, they do not need our definitions of what constitutes their best interest.

We believe that the most effective method of ensuring that intervention is not unethical is to give the clients or target groups the tools with which to protect themselves from the intervenor. The Institute for Mediation and Conflict Resolution, for example, has worked particularly hard to ensure that in every dispute in which it becomes involved there are people in the weaker groups familiar with and trained in the negotiation-mediation process, and who know what that process can and cannot achieve for them. Intervenors are not permitted the opportunity to be unethical. Expressing a similar commitment, the Community Conflict Resolution Program has published a series of pamphlets, including "Preparing for Negotiations" and "Evening the Odds through Training" to help disadvantaged groups cope with professional intervenors, especially establishment advocates posing as mediators or advocates of the weaker group. Grass-roots groups are then able to use the intervenor as a tool in the quest for their own definition of their goals and how to achieve them.

We conclude that, in addition to developing ethics of intervention, it may be time for us to learn how to make our ethics irrelevant by ensuring that the objects of our intervention have the wherewithal to protect themselves and their interests from our efforts—however skilled, sincere, and well-motivated we may be.

## REFERENCES

Abner, W. *Annual report to the Ford Foundation.* Washington, D.C.: National Center for Dispute Settlement of the American Arbitration Association, 1970.

American Sociological Association. *Code of ethics.* Washington, D.C.: Author, 1971.

Angell, R. C. The sociology of human conflict. In E. B. McNeill (Ed.), *The nature of human conflict.* Englewood Cliffs, N.J.: Prentice-Hall, 1965.

Barnard, J. The sociological study of conflict. In *The nature of conflict.* Paris: UNESCO, 1957.

Benveniste, G. *The politics of expertise.* Berkeley, Calif.: Glendessary, 1973.

Boulding, K. *Conflict and defense.* New York: Harper & Row, 1962.

Brickman, P. (Ed.). *Social conflict.* Lexington, Ky.: Heath, 1974.

Chalmers, W. E., & Cormick, G. W. *Racial negotiations: Potentials and limitations.* Research Report to the Ford Foundation. Ann Arbor: Institute of Labor and Industrial Relations, University of Michigan–Wayne State University, 1970.

Chalmers, W. E., & Cormick G. W. (Eds.). *Racial conflict and negotiations: Perspectives and first case studies.* Ann Arbor: Institute of Labor and Industrial Relations, the University of Michigan–Wayne State University, and the National Center for Dispute Settlement of the American Arbitration Association, 1971.

Cohen, A., Cormick, G. W., & Laue, J. H. *The Community Crisis Intervention Project: October 1, 1970 to September 20, 1972.* Final Report to the Ford Foundation. St. Louis: Washington University Press, 1972.

Coleman, J. S. *Community conflict.* Glencoe, Ill.: Free Press, 1957.

Cormick, G. W. *Power, strategy and the process of human conflict.* Doctoral dissertation, University of Michigan, 1971. (a)

Cormick, G. W. *Year-end report to the Ford Foundation.* New York: Board of Mediation for Community Disputes, 1971. (b)

Coser, L. A. Conflict: Social aspects. In D. L. Sills (Ed.), *International encyclopedia of the social sciences.* Vol. 3. New York: Macmillan, 1968.

*Crisis and change* (1971-1975), 1-5. Boston: Harvard Medical School, and St. Louis: Washington University, Community Crisis Intervention Center.

Deutsch, M. *The resolution of conflict.* New Haven: Yale University Press, 1973.

Kahn, R. L., & Boulding, E. (Eds.). *Power and conflict in organizations.* New York: Basic Books, 1964.

Kramer, R. M., & Specht, H. M. (Eds.). *Readings in community organization.* Englewood Cliffs, N.J.: Prentice-Hall, 1969.

Kriesberg, L. *The sociology of social conflicts.* Englewood Cliffs, N.J.: Prentice-Hall, 1973.

Laue, J. H. *Direct action and desegregation: Toward a theory of the rationalization of protest.* Doctoral dissertation, Harvard University, 1965.

Laue, J. H. Power, conflict and social change. In L. H. Masotti and D. R. Bowen (Eds.), *Riots and rebellion: Civil violence in the urban community.* Beverly Hills, Calif.: Sage, 1968.

Laue, J. H. *Third men in new arenas of conflict.* New York: Ford Foundation, 1970.

Laue, J. H. Urban conflict: What role for negotiations and mediation? Paper prepared for seminar on community disputes settlement, Institute for Mediation and Conflict Resolution, New York, 1971.

Laue, J. H. (Ed.). Intervening in community conflicts. *Journal of Intergroup Relations* 1978, (in press), whole issue.

Laue, J. H., Cohen, A., Lee, W., Mann, H., Schultz, P., & Cormick, G. W. *Report from a national workshop on community crisis intervention.* Boston: Community Crisis Intervention Project, Harvard Medical School, 1971.

Laue, J. H., Cormick, G. W., & Cohen, A. Intervenor roles: A review. *Crisis and Change,* 1973, *3,* 3-4.

Mack, R. W., & Snyder, R. C. The analysis of social conflict—Toward an overview and synthesis. *Journal of Conflict Resolution,* 1957, *1,* 212-248.

Nicolau, G., & Cormick, G. W. Community disputes and the resolution of conflict: Another view. *The Arbitration Journal,* June 1972, *27,* 98-112.

Rokeach, M. A. *The nature of human values.* New York: Free Press, 1973.

Walton R. E., & McKersie, R. B. *A behavioral theory of labor negotiations.* New York: McGraw-Hill, 1965.

Warwick, D. P., & Kelman, H. C. Ethical issues in social intervention. In G. Zaltman (Ed.), *Processes and phenomena of social change.* New York: Wiley, 1973.

Williams, R. M., Jr. The reduction of intergroup tensions. *Social Science Research Council Bulletin,* 1947, *57,* 1-153.

Williams, R. M., Jr. Conflict and social order: A research strategy for complex propositions. *Journal of Social Issues,* 1972, *28*(1), 11-26.

# 11
# COMMENTS ON "THE ETHICS OF INTERVENTION IN COMMUNITY DISPUTES"

PRESTON N. WILLIAMS

The Harvard Divinity School

During the past 20 years the United States has passed through alternate periods of activism and quiescence, of energetic government and lethargic government, of liberalism and conservatism. Fortunately this movement was more akin to the to and fro swing of the pendulum than the lurching of a ship in heavy weather or the convulsive spasms of some afflicted muscles. The arc, even if not accurately regulated, had to do with the participation of U.S. citizens in the decision-making function of their government, and the pendulum's sweep had to do with the extent of inclusiveness to be permitted. When activism, energetic government, and liberalism prevail, the number of people participating is enlarged. When quiescence, lethargy, and conservatism are dominant, an elite excludes many who should enjoy the opportunity to participate. A better regulation of the movement is needed to provide continuity and progress to the process of participation.

In Chapter 10, James Laue and Gerald Cormick deal with the institutionalization and professionalization of a procedure that regulates participation by citizens in government and society. Whether the citizens are, as the chapter suggests, civil rights, ethnic, and working-class groups, or the contemporary, largely white middle- and upper-class consumer, environmental, and health-care groups, the intervenor in community disputes is a much-needed and required profession in our society. Laue and Cormick encourage the development of this new vocation and offer a helpful description of the types, nature, and problems of the intervenor in community disputes. Their typology provides great insight into the variety of ways in which one may intervene to secure social change and the several variables that determine the intervenor's role.

Chapter 10 represents a genuine contribution not only because of its technical discernment but also because of its value orientation. The authors seek to structure a profession and a procedure that will maximize participation of all groups seeking inclusion in societal or governmental decision making. The pendulum's swing is not to encourage extremism but to provide a balanced, inclusive, and properly functioning communal process. The authors' superb analysis of the nature of community disputes and the emerging field of community dispute intervention as well as their description of the multiplicity and complexity of intervention roles do not require extensive comments. What does need further elaboration is the ethical framework used for assessing this type of intervention and its outcomes.

Laue and Cormick's assumption is clear and frequently stated. The injustice that incites community disputes has its source in the imbalance of power and resources within the community, and its redress requires that every community dispute intervenor at every decisional point in the intervention ask a single ethical question:

> Does the intervention contribute to the ability of relatively powerless individuals and groups in the situation to determine their own destinies to the greatest extent consistent with the common good? (pp. 217–218).

The context in which this question is asked indicates that the authors' point of reference for ethics demands that the intervenor always say yes to this question, even if it is an equivocal yes. With this desire most people would have no quarrel, but we might ask whether this is an adequate ethical framework. I think it is not. The difficulty stems from the fact that we are not told what it means "to determine their own destinies" and how we can know that that has been done "to the greatest extent consistent with the common good."

The authors seem to believe that a group determines its own destiny when it has a bit more power and a bit more of the community's resources. Yet even when both of these are achieved, the group may be as little in control of its destiny as it was prior to the favorable intervention. This is no doubt the experience of a number of powerless groups, especially racial minorities, that made meaningful gains in the settlement of community disputes during the late 1960s. I certainly would not want to claim that the advances made were not real or that the intervenors did not act ethically. But even when we acknowledge that these advances had an impact on the destinies of the powerless groups, the authors' conception of the task of the intervenors is exaggerated. It is necessary to underscore the exaggerated nature of their claim because part of their ethical energy and motivation is derived from the overstatement of the significance of the decisions made by the parties to the dispute.

Powerless people in a society are quite frequently indifferent or apathetic to their own best interest. Sometimes they are motivated to action by leaders who overestimate the significance of some event. Such actions by partisan leaders may be right and proper. Yet one wonders if it is also the task of the intervenor to see in every decision some great and momentous outcome. Ethically the action is just as praiseworthy or blameworthy when it leads to something other than a greater measure of control over one's destiny. Martin Luther King's unsuccessful campaign in Albany may have been as morally praiseworthy or blameworthy as his later successful campaigns in Selma or Birmingham. Yet we cannot assert on the basis of the criteria suggested by Laue and Cormick that the participants in Albany gained greater control over their destiny even if we were persuaded that their deeds were ethically as right as those performed by King's followers in Selma or Birmingham. I would urge, then, that the ethical obligation of the intervenor consist on occasion in informing the powerless (and the powerful) that the specific issue about which controversy rages is only marginally relevant to the powerless group's quest for greater control of its destiny. The use of the term "destiny" is not casual but a vital part of the description of the ethical disposition Laue and Cormick seek to instill in the intervenor. As such, it is misleading because it seeks to derive ethical energy from what is on most occasions a misstatement of the main issues in the dispute. Intervenors are right to bend justice in the direction of the weak, but they also need to inform the powerless that most incremental changes do not lead to significant redistributions of power or resources. Conditions may be improved and destinies seldom significantly altered even though the life of the participants may have been changed for the better as in Selma or Birmingham. On the other hand, destinies may be changed even though acts of empowerment fail or turn out to be blameworthy. My point is that Laue and Cormick's understanding of power and its relation to the control of one's destiny is too simplistic. The notion of control of one's destiny should not be abandoned; it and its operation should be more subtly elaborated.

Self-determination of an individual's or of a group's destiny is a desirable end-state, but it needs to be considered in relation to the definition of the common good or the just society and not simply to a single situation in which some change is taking place. The problem of the transfer of power and resources needs a broader canvas than has been suggested by the community dispute outlined in Laue and Cormick's chapter. The authors themselves know this and on one occasion excellently sum up the issue: "The web in which community disputes are set is no smaller than the world" (p. 230). What is implicit here is the notion that the destiny involved in the situation is apt to transcend the incident and community that hold the attention of the community dispute intervenor. Such a person cannot, of course, attend to all these ramifications. But any intervenor does need to keep in mind the national or universal dimensions of the problem—for example, the ideal national and international policy regarding health care and medical research, race relations, or criminal justice. This, in turn, presupposes explicit introduction into the dispute of a more sufficient understanding of the just society.

A constant source of concern, therefore, of the intervenor in community disputes should be the fashioning of a conception of the common good or just society. Without it the noble intent of redistributing power and resources can go awry. Laue and Cormick fail to point out that the disputes are not about the adoption of their core values or basic assumptions, but about their interpretation and implementation. They have written that "empowerment is the requisite condition of individuals and groups to achieve the desired end-state of society—justice. A just society is prerequisite to the maximum attainment of freedom by all individuals in the system" (p. 218). But they have not provided an explicit sketch of that desired end-state. The dispute between the powerful and the less powerful is not centered on the acceptance or rejection of ethical principles but rather on their interpretation.

A step in the right direction is taken when Laue and Cormick affirm justice to be the ultimate social good and assert that, "the just social system would be one in which power (control of decisions) is diffused, decision making is participatory, accountability for decisions is visible, and resources are adequate and equitably distributed" (p. 219). In another context, they assert: "While empowerment of the powerless is a premier value in our system, intervenors should not lend their skills to empowering groups who do not hold the values of empowerment, freedom, and justice for all peoples, regardless of race, sex, religion, or national origin" (p. 222). In both instances, the movement in the direction of enunciating a clear conception of the just society is too truncated to provide the necessary ethical guidance for power redistribution and resource reallocation. Participation will not guarantee justice for any minority and self-determination in the competitive world described by the authors seems to mean that one party is always free to take from the other what it thinks it needs. Neither participation nor competition, as provided by the authors' procedures, will significantly alter the stigma of race and the burden of poverty. Only if greater attention is given to formulation of an adequate conception of the common good or just society will the possibility of significant change emerge. In addition, a notion of the common good or just society would act to limit the misuse of power or coercion by the community or the parties to the dispute. Competition has replaced cooperation and conflict has ensued precisely because, as the authors themselves state, the conception of the legitimacy of power has broken down. Consequently one aspect of the ethical responsibility of the intervenor is to restore a notion of the common good that both parties to the dispute might come to acknowledge as valid and that can serve to set limits to the aspirations of all community members as well as provide a normative definition of the just society.

Martin Luther King, for example, sought always to discipline his followers and to sketch a vision of the good society toward which their efforts were directed. Prior to his campaigns, he planned some means for reconciling the parties to the conflict after the empowerment of the disadvantaged had taken place. As a consequence, there was always an attempt to have everybody win something and when conflict became violent there were guidelines for restoring peace and harmony among the several parties. The intervenors to whom Laue and Cormick speak may bear a different relation to their parties than King did to his followers. Nevertheless, the model for intervention should embody an idea of a common good. What is implicit in such typologies as activist, advocate, mediator, researcher, and enforcer must be given a minimal, but explicit, conception of substantive justice that is situationally specific. Knowledge of the intervenor's character or past patterns of settlement should not be accepted as sufficient. The intervenor should be urged to formulate over against the parties some general conception of what seems fair or right in a particular situation. Such a tentative conception of a common good would not prevent joint determination by the parties in dispute. It would suggest instead some reasonable expectations about the transfer of power that ought to occur in the negotiations. Granted that the number and variety of disputes make it exceedingly difficult for intervenors to be precise about their assumptions concerning society and the relation of various groups to the resources and power present in society, intervenors need to be able to provide some substance to the understanding of the core values of justice and proportional empowerment. Laue and Cormick's typical case, "Elmwood Hospital and the Chicano Community Coalition," should thus be framed in such a way as to indicate not only what roles an intervenor might play but also the necessity of creating some tension between the goals of the two parties and some minimal conception of justice or common good that might be required if ethics alone, and not ethics and power, were the major ingredient in finding a solution. Only when ethics or norms are thus explicitly stated can groups and individuals be expected to transcend politics and self-interest.

One reason why Laue and Cormick did not proceed further in this direction is their strongly held conviction that groups must make their own decisions. They believe that a strong statement about the common good or just society would rob the parties in a dispute of an opportunity to determine their ends themselves. This concern is misplaced because resolving community disputes involves several different systems of activity and requires clarity about goals at levels above that of the immediate situation. In these matters the intervenor should not be neutral, but should seek to formulate conceptions that suggest the desirable power balance and resource balance that should exist among the disputants. This would not rob the parties of the opportunity to make their own decisions, but it would better enable them to place their decisions and strategies in the context of what sober and objective reflection perceived to be the requirements of a just institution or a just society. Just as empowerment of those who seek to discriminate on the basis of race, sex, religion, or national origin is ruled out, so also would certain undesirable patterns of social organization be discouraged. While this might seem to be paternalistic, I would urge that it is more akin to the authors' proposal to instruct the powerless in the procedures needed to participate in negotiation and decision making. It is a method of empowerment in which one further illumines the decision-making process and the ability of the powerless to make wise decisions on behalf of themselves and society. Moreover, by attempting to formulate a conception of the common good or just society, the intervenor might cause both parties to think more seriously about the cohesion needed to keep disparate groups working in a harmonious relationship. Such thought might provide greater flexibility for the process of conflict resolution by modifying the exclusive concern with group self-interest.

In addition, stress on the common good or the just society is much needed in order to make clear the relation between the political and ethical dimensions of community dispute resolution. This is necessary because Laue and Cormick have adopted a basically political procedure for resolving disputes. On numerous occasions they state that the essence of their enterprise is the manipulation of power:

> Because the issue in all community disputes is each interest group's ability to advocate its own needs, power becomes the central reality (p. 206).
>
> In sum, every community dispute is a game of power. Power is the issue, power is the goal, and the effective use of power is the strategy for all sides in any conflict (p. 208).
>
> It should be clear by now that we believe the coinage of community disputes is power (p. 220).

The stress placed on power cannot help but obscure the authors' emphasis on justice unless there is an opposing and equally weighted concern with constraining the group advocacy of the parties to the disputes. The self-righteousness of all interest groups is sufficient evidence for putting forth a notion of the common good that suggests limits to the power distribution and resource allocation requested by either the powerless or the powerful. What Laue and Cormick need to undertake is a more precise differentiation of ethics and politics. Unless this is done, much of what they call ethics can be more accurately and properly described as strategies for social change.

My criticism of Laue and Cormick's overemphasis on power should not cause the reader to believe that I seek the abandonment of an approach stressing the significance of power. Power is important and must be considered, but one needs to remember that it, like one's anger, indignation, or resentment, must be controlled. The disadvantaged suffer oppression because the advantaged have not properly regulated or distributed the power that they possess. The cure for this injustice is not, therefore, the cultivation of more unregulated power or the creation of a countervailing power. Since it is unlikely that any negotiation will result in a just balancing of power between groups, it is important to seek the regulation of power according to some just norms. The conception of a common good can serve as such a regulator. Even though the norm, like the Ten Commandments, is violated, it will serve to establish true norms for community. One gain from this procedure will be the education of both the powerful and the powerless to a greater recognition of what the just sharing of power entails, as well as providing them with knowledge about political decision making.

The essential nature of our emphasis on the common good and the creation of a tension between ethical norms and the politics of power is evident from the great confusion present in the section of the chapter treating the movement from the enunciation of ethical principles to specific actions by means of decisions made by community dispute intervenors. Laue and Cormick's eight ethical principles tend to be advice concerning tactics and strategy rather than ethical principles. A brief restatement of their alleged principles follows. Intervenors should:

1.  Contribute to proportional empowerment of powerless groups for social change
2.  Promote the ability of the weaker parties to make their own best decisions
3.  Make the rationale for their decisions conscious, explicit, and public
4.  Not claim to be (or worse actually feel) neutral
5.  Be intimately familiar with the dynamics of power and, where the situation involves race, the realities of racism
6.  Advocate resolution of conflict or crisis through a process of joint decision making
7.  Not transfer their intervention models uncritically to a different system setting
8.  Not lend their skills to empowering groups who do not hold the values of empowerment, freedom, and justice for all peoples, regardless of race, sex, religion, or national origin

Of these principles only 1, 2, 6, and 8 seem to qualify, and they can be reduced to two principles:

1.  Act always so as to enhance the ability of the least powerful group in a dispute to make their best decision and to participate in decisions affecting their destiny.

2. Do not discriminate and do not aid groups who discriminate to increase their power.

Principles 3 and 4 do not seem to me to qualify as ethical principles. At best they are an operating rule that suggests that intervenors should always make decisions based on critical rational reflection upon the issues of the dispute and these decisions should be clearly communicated to the parties involved. The desire to avoid the neutrality of some labor mediators may be commendable, but it is not well formulated as a principle nor is it easily transformed into one. Moreover, the end is not to be biased or unbiased but to do justice. If it is true that the disadvantaged have been treated unjustly, the intervenor will have to act on behalf of their interest. Finally, 5 and 7 can be rendered "know the facts, act and decide on the basis of the facts, and do not make a mistake." Sage advice, no doubt, but not what one would call an ethical principle.

The point of our observations concerning the common good and ethical principles is to alert people to the fact that the ethical must act as a restraint on power and serve to properly guide the use of power. This cannot be done unless both are cultivated, clearly distinguished, and set in tension with each other. Laue and Cormick have not done as well as they might. They have exhibited wisdom in their stress on power, but show great confusion in their thinking about ethical principles. The source of their problem was well underlined in a statement by Reinhold Niebuhr in his classic work, *Moral Man and Immoral Society* (1949):

> The relations between groups must . . . always be predominantly political rather than ethical, that is they will be determined by the proportion of power which each group possesses at least as much as by any rational and moral appraisal of the comparative needs and claims of each group. The coercive factors, in distinction to the more purely moral and rational factors, in political relations can never be sharply differentiated and defined (p. *xxiii*).

Laue and Cormick have sought to do what Niebuhr saw as a necessary and exceedingly difficult task, and in a measure they have succeeded. Their accomplishment is to be celebrated but not without speaking also of their failure. This failure is in part the result of a too great concern to let oppressed parties determine their destinies and to the fact that they, like Niebuhr, have overemphasized power and human fallibility and underemphasized moral, rational factors and the human capacity to do good. They have not yet learned what Martin Luther King always practiced and what Malcolm X discovered in Mecca, namely, that no one ascription can be made about groups of people. Groups and individuals possess possibilities for both good and ill. In group relations, then, one discovers more than power and coercion.

Laue and Cormick record this fact in their several vignettes, but they do not make it a part of their basic assumptions or ethical principles. To speak of the Anglos and Chicanos in the Elmwood Hospital case as people seeking only to grasp or hold power is to trivialize the issue of community health care versus research/training hospital needs and to misrepresent the real concerns of the parties. For both parties something more was at stake than power or self-interest. The health of the Chicano community and the professional standing of the hospital cannot be treated simply as aspects of power. Intervenors must perceive this and act on these additional factors. We have other illustrations of this "more than power and self-interest" dimension in the disputes between the major private urban university and the black community, as well as in the K-12 school dispute. In both situations, one is impressed by the fact that individuals take risks for something other than power and for something that can be termed the common good or fair treatment of others. Laue and Cormick need to account more adequately for this reasonableness and good will that at times are found among parties to a dispute. I think it can only be accounted for when one acknowledges that injustice may result from good intentions and genuine mistakes, and that some people and groups are truly seeking to do good deeds.

Laue and Cormick begin their own continuum characterizing the everyday life style of communities with cooperation and competition—modes of interaction that could be designated positive or good. At this point on the continuum group decisions are acceptable to all parties and seem to depend as much on mutuality and reason as on power factors. Presumably also in these cases, the strong voluntarily consent to empowerment of the weak because of rational moral factors and not simply as a result of power. The powerful and the disadvantaged can cooperate and compete because both possess the human capacity to use right reason and to pursue the good. This positive potentiality and (not only human) fallibility permits the construction of models of the common good and the just society as well as encourages voluntary consent to societal systems of power redistribution and resource reallocation. Any ethic for intervenors should seek to recognize and strengthen these moral, rational elements in decision making. Laue and Cormick need to make this explicit in their ethics of intervention. Stronger assertion of individual and group potentiality for goodness is needed in order to make group interaction and relations more significantly ethical. If they could see this truth, they might come to see that some differences among groups are resolved because individuals and groups can know better the right and good and can transcend what might be defined as narrow self-interest.

Toward the end of their chapter, Laue and Cormick make the very strong statement that "proportional empowerment is the only safeguard we may ultimately trust in the pursuit of justice and freedom" (p. 228). I have challenged the accuracy of that statement. We can teach people as individuals and as members of a group to use their freedom to procure a justice that transcends group self-interest because they possess the potentiality for goodness as well as the quality of fallibility. When Laue and Cormick speak of the ethics of the intervenor they need to put more stress on the moral, rational factors in decision making. Proper appreciation of these factors will lead in addition to a modification of the almost sole reliance on power balances. More equity is needed among community groups, but ideally this need not come only through power and coercion.

My disagreement with the authors on this point should not obscure my agreement with them concerning the importance of power and the wisdom of seeking to develop a social ethic that deals with systemic problems while insisting on integrity and judiciousness in the intervenor. My position seeks not to lessen concern with proportional empowerment, justice, and freedom, but to ensure their development in a context that is supportive of the common good and the just society.

## REFERENCE

Niebuhr, R. *Moral man and immoral society*. New York: Charles Scribner's Sons, 1949.

# VI
# INCOME
# MAINTENANCE
# EXPERIMENTS

# 12

# SOME ETHICAL IMPLICATIONS OF THE NEW JERSEY-PENNSYLVANIA INCOME MAINTENANCE EXPERIMENT

## PETER H. ROSSI
University of Massachusetts

## MARGARET BOECKMANN
American University

## RICHARD A. BERK
University of California

## INTRODUCTION

The dismantling of the Office of Economic Opportunity (OEO) brought the ' war on poverty symbolically to an end. What began as a crusade with high goals, strong presidential support, and considerable enthusiasm among an army of poverty warriors has limped off the scene. Like the other war of the '60s, it was never clear whether the enemy was fully identified. Just as no battles were ever decisively won in Vietnam, so OEO programs were never decisively effective. In both cases, peace with honor was declared by fiat, but neither peace nor honor was attained in fact.

On the domestic scene, the effects of both wars of the 1960s will be felt for some time to come. Much can be written on the broad, long-run consequences; however, such a discussion is beyond the scope of this chapter. For the social sciences, one of the more important consequences of the war on poverty may well be the legitimization of large-scale social experimentation, with the New Jersey–Pennsylvania Income Maintenance Experiment forming a critical basis of that legacy. It is clear that this field experiment is an important precedent,

The research reported in this paper was supported by a grant from the Russell Sage Foundation to the senior author for the purpose of conducting an overall evaluation of the New Jersey–Pennsylvania Income Maintenance Experiment (reported in Rossi and Lyall, 1977).

because it has made it possible for social scientists to obtain a more favorable hearing when suggesting field experiments as a mode of social intervention.

The New Jersey–Pennsylvania Income Maintenance Experiment is a unique departure from the policy-oriented researches of the past in several important ways. First, it brings experimentation out of the laboratory and closed institutions into open society. Earlier attempts to assess social programs through controlled experiments had been centered on relatively isolated and autonomous institutions such as schools and prisons. With such captive populations, researchers were easily able to use experimental designs to evaluate the relative effectiveness of a variety of interventions. Hence, there is a vast, though not especially conclusive, literature on the effects of various teaching techniques and classroom arrangements and a less rich literature on rehabilitation treatments.

The Income Maintenance Experiment, however, was not attempted within the confines of such a total institution, but in the far more complex milieu of the larger society. Second, earlier work was typically on a much smaller scale in terms of dollar cost, complexity of design, and administrative overhead. Third, the Income Maintenance Experiment drew on considerable contemporary sophistication in experimental methodology and statistical analysis, employing an eclectic blend of research techniques borrowed from psychology, statistics, and economics. Consequently, the research represents a peak in the present state of the art and will become an important exemplar for future studies. Indeed, its impact is already being felt in four additional income maintenance experiments and in experiments to be undertaken shortly on health insurance and on housing vouchers for the poor. Fourth, the Income Maintenance Experiment has established an important precedent for a role to be played by social science in the *development* of policy. Earlier social science contributions to policy formation involved providing general orientations (such as those in OEO's Community Action Program) or evaluations of programs already under way and constructed almost exclusively by policy makers. In contrast, the Income Maintenance Experiment was developed primarily by persons sophisticated in social science theory and methodology. Social scientists were heavily involved from its inception in far more than an advisory capacity. Finally, the policy issues addressed were of a far larger magnitude than earlier work. The purpose of the research was to aid in the restructuring of our national welfare policy by testing a new program as innovative for today as social security retirement benefits were in the 1930s. In short, the stakes were very large.

## A DESCRIPTION OF THE INCOME MAINTENANCE PROJECT

The New Jersey–Pennsylvania Income Maintenance Project (IMP)[1] involved experimental treatments that were combinations of guaranteed income levels and tax rates. The income levels were yearly incomes below which people could

---

[1] For the sake of brevity, we will refer to the experiment as the "Income Maintenance Project" or "IMP" throughout this chapter. The additional experiments were the Rural

not fall, and the tax rates reduced payments a certain proportion if incomes were above the guaranteed levels. The population was composed of households in five locations in New Jersey and Pennsylvania, selected by area probability sampling methods from among households that were intact, in which there was at least one employable male (between the ages of 18 and 58),[2] and whose income levels were below 150 percent of the 1967 poverty level of $3,300 for a family of four. Eligible households were randomly assigned to treatment and control groups, with treatment groups given checks bringing their incomes up to guaranteed levels (or above, less tax rate) upon submission of monthly income reports. Some of these families had outside income; some had previously subsisted on welfare. Both treatment (experimental) and control group households were visited quarterly for extensive interviews for which both were paid. In addition, experimental groups were paid for each income report filed.

A schematic outline of the experimental design is shown in Figure 1. Note that treatments vary the level of support and the rate by which payments are reduced as households exceed support levels through their own work efforts. The guaranteed levels are sensitive to household size, ranging in 1968 from a low of $1,000 for a one-person household on the lowest (50 percent of poverty line) guaranteed level to $5,750 for a family of eight or more on the highest guaranteed level (125 percent of poverty line).

As we said earlier, families were allocated to treatment groups or control groups at random, the number of families in each stratum being determined by an allocation formula[3] that took into account the total funds allocated to the experiment, the policy importance of a stratum, and several other assumptions concerning the shape of the distribution of responses to treatments. At the outset of the experiment, 724 households were in the experimental treatment group and 650 in the control group. Attrition from both sets of groups periodically reduced these numbers somewhat.

The experiment ran for three years, the first group starting in August, 1968, and the last in November, 1969. Few rules were imposed on the households other than the prompt reporting of income. Households were kept in the experimental groups unless they failed to file income reports or they elected to go on welfare.[4] Income received under the IMP plan was tax exempt, according to an IRS ruling.

---

Income Maintenance Experiment (Iowa and North Carolina rural areas), the Seattle Income Maintenance Experiment (SIME), the Denver Income Maintenance Experiment (DIME), and the Gary Income Maintenance Experiment (G-X). All of these additional experiments were variants on the New Jersey–Pennsylvania Income Maintenance Project, differing in populations covered, treatments administered, and in additional services offered (as in Gary).

[2] This rule mainly eliminated female-headed households.

[3] The final allocation model is described in Conlisk and Watts (1969), pp. 150–156.

[4] In the initial few months of the experiment, before New Jersey changed its welfare rules to include households with males present, as eligible under AFDC, participation in both welfare and IMP was allowed, a ruling that made for some trouble, as we shall discuss later in this chapter.

**FIGURE 1.** Schematic outline of design of New Jersey–Pennsylvania income maintenance experiment.

I:  Income strata[a]:
    Stratum I   = Below poverty line ($3,300 for family of four)
    Stratum II  = 100% to 125% of poverty line
    Stratum III = 125% to 150% of poverty line

II:  Treatments within income strata: guaranteed levels and tax rate combinations:

Tax rate (reduction in payments for income exceeding guaranteed levels)

| Guaranteed Levels (in % of poverty level) | 30% | 50% | 70% |
|---|---|---|---|
| 50% | X[b] | X | |
| 75% | X | X | X |
| 100% | | X | X |
| 125% | | X | |

III:  Control groups:
      Three control groups are used, drawn from each of the three income strata.

IV:  Total number of treatment groups:
     The design calls for 27 treatment groups (8 treatments for each of three income strata and 3 control groups). Families are selected first for income strata and randomly allocated to treatment groups (including controls).

[a]Based on 1967 BLS definition of poverty, adjusted for price level changes. Households of greater or smaller size than four get respectively higher or lower guaranteed income levels.
[b]"X" indicates treatment used. Blank cells indicate omitted treatments. For example, in the "50–30" cell, a family would be guaranteed 50% of the poverty-level income based on household size, and then would have payments reduced 30% for income exceeding that level.

Households were recruited to participate in the experiment by sampling small areas (census tracts within each of the five sites) whose average income levels were such as to ensure a relatively high "take" of eligible households. Probability samples were taken within such areas; a short screening interview determined eligibility, according to the criteria outlined earlier. Once a household was determined to be eligible, it was assigned to a treatment group or a control group according to probability ratios that would ensure proper stratum sizes in the 28 household groups shown in Figure 1.

Once assignment was made, the plan was explained to households (if they fell into a treatment group) or they were asked to cooperate in a survey of urban life (if they fell into a control group). Considerable effort went into explaining the plan and the conditions surrounding participation. Households were given pamphlets and other informational materials as well as being told that they were being asked to participate in a longitudinal study of urban life; they were promised compensation for cooperating in answering quarterly surveys.

It is difficult to determine just how much the experimental households were told about the experiment. The pamphlet left with each family described the plan as "experimental," but did not describe guaranteed levels and tax rates in specific terms. Most likely, households were not told of alternative treatments, and only their own particular treatment was explained to them in detail. Households that decided to participate were asked to sign a consent form indicating that they understood the plan and the requirements for continued eligibility.

In summary, the intervention consisted of the following acts:

- Supplementing earned income to bring household incomes up to designated levels with bimonthly payments
- Monitoring household income through monthly income reports
- Interviewing household members concerning labor force participation, assets and savings, and a host of specialized inquiries centering around variables considered of interest by the research staff

It should also be stressed that no additional treatments were given in IMP. In particular, households were not offered any social services, although, if requested, field representatives would refer households to existing local social services. Furthermore, during most of the experiment, households were given the option of remaining on income maintenance or going onto welfare rolls; but income supplementation and welfare could not be obtained simultaneously.

It would be surprising if a program with such critical potential policy implications did not involve a variety of value-laden decisions. Indeed, the Income Maintenance Project was based on rather specific expectations concerning the negative income tax concept. As David N. Kershaw (1972), the project director at MATHEMATICA, noted,

Its virtues include simplicity of administration (it is a self-administered program which makes use of forms similar to those used by the Internal Revenue Service), equity, (it is paid to all whose incomes fall below a prescribed level), dignity (there are no indiscriminate or compulsory "services" provided), and the creation of conditions conducive to individual initiative (the negative tax grant is not taken away from a recipient dollar for dollar as his earned income increases) (p. 222).

## SETTING THE GOALS

The detailed history of the Income Maintenance Project is yet to be written.[5] At this point, enough is known about the circumstances of its origins, design, and implementation to explore several ethical issues, to which the reminder of this chapter is devoted.

The main goal of the Income Maintenance Experiment was to estimate to costs of a national program of income maintenance, especially those costs incurred by the work-leisure trade-off behavior of households under an income maintenance program. The experimental treatments were variations in the levels at which income would be maintained, combined with variations in the rates at which additional income would be taxed. The households studied were picked to represent those whose response was deemed most problematic—households in which an employable adult male was present, and whose incomes were distributed in a band around the poverty line. The main question was whether workers would drop out of the labor force under income maintenance, trading leisure at slightly reduced income levels for work at slightly higher income levels.

In addition, there were many subsidiary goals of IMP, from examination of the problems that might arise in the administration of income maintenance to assessment of the impact of IMP on a range of social psychological variables. The fact that these were subsidiary goals can be seen in the experiment's design, which was dominated by the work-leisure trade-off question and was therefore considerably less efficient for obtaining answers to the subsidiary questions.

The main goal was chosen because the planners of the experiment and the staff of OEO anticipated that the work-leisure trade-off would be the paramount issue debated by public officials when income maintenance plans were considered for implementation. The experimental treatments were chosen as the best bets for what might eventually be considered as public policy. For example, the poverty levels chosen were those established by the Bureau of Labor Statistics. The supplementation rates were fixed to cover the anticipated range of politically viable proposals. In addition, work-leisure trade-off was an important question in static equilibrium economic theory[6] concerning work incentives. Since most of those involved in the design of the experiment were economists, this issue was of considerable interest, regardless of its policy implications.

Whether work-leisure trade-off would be the question uppermost in policy maker's minds was in fact problematic, as we indicate later in this chapter, but there were more important implications that flowed from the choice of this focus for the experiment. To begin with, the emphasis on trade-offs implied that work is more important than leisure. If any significant portion of the population

[5] Margaret Boeckmann has compiled a detailed account of certain critical periods in the history of IMP, under a grant from the Russell Sage Foundation to the senior author.

[6] For a summary discussion of the static theory, including the preexperimental empirical evidence, see Green (1967), Chapter 8.

began to withdraw from the labor force to enjoy leisure at a lower level of income, the intervention would be judged a failure. To be sure, this value most likely reflects the modal views of the American population, but one may question whether it represents the value positions of all Americans, and especially the value positions of those who constitute the target population of the policy.[7]

In addition, defining IMP in terms of the work-leisure trade-offs to some degree limits discussion to this issue, flagging it as the critical point in the arguments pro and con. This would be particularly important as a constraint if the experiment uncovered a significant amount of trade-off behavior. Proponents of a guaranteed income plan, whose endorsement rested on the assumption of insignificant amounts of trade-off behavior, would find their position untenable with no alternative justification to support of the policy. And there could well be alternative justifications.

These considerations raise the issue of whose interests were being represented in the formulation of the issues of IMP and the design of the experiment. From the viewpoint of the planners of IMP, the experiment addressed the needs of the general society. In their view, it was in the public interest ("public interest," as defined by "mainstream" America) to put a floor under household income without deteriorating the will to work. Furthermore, IMP reflected public policy as seen from the precincts of the presidency, an executive-centered perspective.

From a much larger political perspective, it is possible to envision a set of interested actors including more than the executive and legislative branches of the federal government. First, there are the poor who are to be the targets of guaranteed income. Second, there are employers who may be concerned with the impact of guaranteed income on the supply and price of labor. In addition, there are all those groups who are bound up in the present welfare system—social workers, government employees, municipal and state administrators—whose organizations and jobs would be either aided or threatened by the adoption of a guaranteed income strategy.

Of course, one of the obvious interests being directly served by the experiment was that of academic economists to whom the empirical test of this

---

[7] This value position can also be seen quite clearly in the widely held judgments that AFDC is a failure and that the present welfare system is a mess. The growth in welfare rolls, especially AFDC, in the period from 1960 to the present is seen as a clear index of failure. Something must be wrong if so many households become dependent on welfare payments because household members are clearly trading leisure at subsistence income levels for paid work. An alternative value position might regard the same phenomenon as an indicator of the program's success: more households were being supported by the welfare programs, indicating the uncovering of previously unmet needs, or households were shunning low-paid work in favor of welfare payments, or some women with dependent children preferred to spend their time in child rearing than in such low-paid work. There are alternative ways of looking at the same phenomenon—the increase in welfare rolls—dependent on how one views the relative importance of work in relation to other values. For a long-winded exposition of the conventional viewpoint, see Moynihan (1973).

particular aspect of static equilibrium theory was of some concern. How strong such an interest is, in fact, is hard to judge. Certainly, careers could be advanced on the basis of making scientific breakthrough; whether the results of this experiment would be such a breakthrough seems unlikely.

Of course, a major obstacle lying in the path of taking these interested constituencies into account is the difficulty of precisely determining the boundaries of these groups and who can represent them. Later on in this chapter, we suggest the establishment of a mechanism that could aid in removing this obstacle.

### INVOLVING THE POLICY MAKERS

Although substantial consensus existed among the economists involved that the work-leisure trade-off was of crucial importance to policy makers, there is very little evidence[8] that any policy makers (for example, representatives and senators) or officials in the executive branch above OEO were consulted about this assumption, let alone any representatives of the groups to which the IMP was to be administered. In short, this was to be an intervention designed to answer a policy question that was so obviously critical to the designers that it seemed unnecessary to ascertain whether, in fact, it would be critical for those who had to approve or disapprove of income maintenance as public policy or those who might be interested partisans. Indeed, our questions on this score addressed to the major actors have been uniformly met with bewilderment, suggesting that none of these parties had faced that issue either as individuals or in discussions with others.[9]

In addition, there are strong indications in the responses of the major actors that asking anyone outside the group of designers, proposers, and OEO staff members might have jeopardized IMP. Funds for the experiment were taken from the Community Action Program budget, and the experiment was gotten under way with a minimum of publicity. Indeed, the administrative structure of the experiment was designed to minimize exposure. The Institute for Research on Poverty at the University of Wisconsin, a research center funded by OEO, was the prime contractor, and MATHEMATICA, a private, for-profit, research firm located in Princeton, New Jersey, was the subcontractor with operating responsibilities.

---

[8] This conclusion is based on interviews with people involved in the design, approval, and implementation of IMP, conducted by Margaret Boeckmann as part of a research project on IMP supported by a grant from the Russell Sage Foundation to the senior author of this chapter.

[9] The political and philosophical sympathies of the people involved were mainly on the side of income maintenance as a policy. Implicitly, they hoped that the null hypothesis would be upheld, that there would be no appreciable effect on labor force participation that could be attributable to IMP. Their expectations, however, were that IMP would show a small amount of work reduction, considerably lower than is the case (presumably) in current welfare policies.

Given this description, it is clear that setting the goals of IMP was accomplished by a relatively small group primarily composed of economists within OEO and associated organizations. They hoped to settle what they considered an important policy question that would be raised when income maintenance moved onto the agenda of national politics. The goals of IMP were thus oriented toward an anticipated program that would be debated in the future and that would have at least some discernable chance of being enacted as public policy.

One must conclude that the design, approval, and implementation of IMP was elitist within a very narrow definition of elites. Those who had to propose social policy (legislators and executive officers) were not consulted on the relevance of the experimental design. Certainly, the poor were not consulted. Nor were representatives of the poor. In effect, a cloak of secrecy was placed over the experiment, and its existence did not become a matter of common knowledge until well into the experiment's life.[10] Therefore, a fairly strong objection can be raised about the lack of participation in the design of IMP by some potentially partisan groups (for example, the poor). In addition, since IMP sought to provide information for policy makers, the absence of their input seems especially strange. Is work-leisure trade-off the most important issue to be solved by empirical research? Did the design fairly represent questions policy makers might raise when income maintenance was considered? If the experiment was to be of relevance to senators, representatives, presidential counselors, and secretaries of departments,[11] it is striking that none were consulted.

As for groups who might be thought of as partisans of an income maintenance policy, it seems clear that their participation in designing the experiment would have been quite relevant as well. The treatments tested in IMP are scarcely generous levels of income maintenance and were certainly far below levels advocated a year or so later by the National Welfare Rights Organization. Conservative groups may have been concerned with the impact of income maintenance on recruitment of workers to low-paid occupations, an issue that can scarcely be addressed with the present design of IMP. Similarly, other potential partisans, such as social workers, might have been more concerned with such issues as family stability and their own careers than with work-leisure trade-off.

---

[10] This is not to say that its existence was classified. Rather, the mode of getting the experiment under way did not expose the experiment to widespread publicity. For example, because the experiment was channeled through the Institute for Research on Poverty, it was not necessary to issue an RFP. Nor was the experiment a secret from the social research fraternity.

[11] Indeed, a good case could be made that the experiment should have been conducted by HEW, the agency that would have the responsibility for carrying out any income maintenance policy (of course, Wilbur Cohen, then Secretary of HEW, although in principle sympathetic, was opposed to advocating income maintenance as a policy issue, since he felt that it was not politically viable).

In defense of the planners of IMP, it should be emphasized that a single experiment can scarcely be expected to address all relevant issues. Hence, criticism of the failure to be comprehensive per se is clearly a cheap shot. The main vulnerability in setting the experiment's goals was the absence of widespread input from decision makers and partisans. But a careful consideration of the political milieu suggests that the planners were heavily constrained by factors essentially beyond their control.

The experiment was designed at a time when there was extensive controversy surrounding antipoverty programs. Several of OEO's pet programs were under severe attack both from those who felt they had gone too far and from those who felt they had not gone far enough. Congress was faced with rising inflation generated in part by President Johnson's guns-and-butter policies. Confrontation politics was employed on campuses and in America's inner cities, and the atmosphere in Washington was not one in which any major change in domestic or international policy was likely to receive a calm hearing. Furthermore, the domestic conflict was superimposed on considerable uncertainty about the nature of the next regime in the White House and in Congress. Given these circumstances, the designers of IMP were faced with the real possibility that encouraging public airing of the concept of a negative income tax and related experiments of its effects would eliminate any chance of the program's being seriously considered, let alone implemented. In short, had they chosen to worry about their failure to be more democratic, it is far from clear what their best strategy could have been. They were faced with what may become an increasingly common dilemma in which the use of wide input in the planning of experiments may make reasoned debate of its merits impossible and ultimately lead to acceptance or rejection of an experiment, based on arguments essentially irrelevant to its real issues.

Even if the planners had chosen to widen the input into IMP, there were no ready mechanisms to facilitate such an exchange. In 1967, who could have spoken authoritatively for the decision makers, the poor, welfare bureaucracies, and fiscal conservatives? The very identification of groups to which invitations should be extended would have been problematic. And, if a large number of groups were able to provide representative input, in what institutional context could such hearings have occurred? How could the varying views have been sorted out, evaluated, and ultimately reconciled? It should be clear that no institutional forum was available, and to encourage a more democratic procedure in designing the IMP would have mired planners in a political and bureaucratic swamp from which they might never have emerged. In summary, a less elitist process might well have doomed the experiment, not only because of the political atmosphere but because of the organizational chaos open hearings would have probably produced. Clearly, if one wishes to generate more varied input into such experiments in the future, some sort of institutional mechanism will have to be developed, a point to which we will return.

## THE ISSUES OF SUBJECT CONSENT AND PARTICIPATION

Over the past decade the principle of informed consent has been developed and widely adopted in the social sciences as a safeguard for human experimental subjects. Certainly, to the extent that IMP is regarded as experimentation on humans, the principle is applicable. Yet, IMP was more than research; it was also the trial run for a potential social program, which complicates the issue considerably.

When one speaks of informed consent, the situation typically involves a proposed intervention into the lives of individuals. The intervention has not been solicited by the subjects and is usually administered by an outsider, presumably possessing special expertise unavailable to the subjects. Under these circumstances, protection of the subjects is a justifiable concern, since they may lack the skills and knowledge to act in their best interests. When this occurs, the main way to foster a fair outcome is to implement the intervention only after subjects have been made fully aware of the potential benefits and costs of the intrusion and after they have agreed to participate. Once these two criteria are met, the burden of responsibility is shifted somewhat from the intervenor to the subject, who may choose to utilize or ignore the information provided. Note that the intervenor is not obligated to make sure the the subject acts wisely but only to provide the tools for wise action.

The Achilles' heel of informed consent is the degree to which the subject is considered informed. Obviously, the subject can never be completely informed because, for virtually all interventions, many of the outcomes are unknown. The debate about informed consent actually revolves around the degree of "informedness" judged sufficient.

In practice, most observers would agree that potential subjects of an intervention must be at least provided with an accurate description of the intervention and its likely consequences. Disagreements develop on the following two types of questions: first, how complete must the list of potential consequences be; second, how well must the subjects understand the information provided? It should be obvious that neither issue can be addressed using any absolute criteria: none exist. Rather, debates develop in relative terms.

Among the many relativistic standards used to judge the sufficiency of informed consent, the most important probably is the amount of possible damage of a proposed intervention. Eyebrows are properly raised when there is a poor fit between the potential risks and the degree to which subjects understand the outcomes of an intrusion. More dangerous interventions require more thorough understanding; standards for less risky intrusions need not be as demanding. It is important to emphasize again that, since understanding can never be complete, disagreements are always in terms of the appropriate level of understanding. The issue of informed consent should be distinguished from the structure of an intervention's rewards and costs. A proposed intrusion may provide so many rewards and so few costs that a potential subject may readily agree to participate. As long as reasonable effort is made (given the intervention's potential seriousness) to facilitate subject understanding, informed consent is not violated.

Informed consent must also be distinguished from the kinds of inducements used to gain participation. An offer a subject can't afford to refuse would not be a violation of informed consent as long as the consequences of a refusal were detailed in advance. Of course, other ethical issues would be involved, but these concern normative assessments of the sanctions being applied. (And again, these must be evaluated in the context of the kind of participation desired. Few people object to forcing a child to visit the dentist.)

How well does IMP stack up on attempts to gain informed consent? Looking at IMP just as social experimentation, we think it fares pretty well. Given IMP's relatively benign character, considerable effort was directed toward participant understanding. However, assessing IMP as a prototype of a massive social program, the issue of informed consent becomes more complex. Probably the crucial problem is the lack of information available to all parties, participants and administrators alike. It would seem unreasonable to criticize the planners of IMP for failing to inform subjects about unknown outcomes.

The administrators of IMP—in particular, MATHEMATICA—took considerable pains to produce informed consent. The operations manual of IMP outlined a procedure in which the operation of IMP was explained in considerable detail along with the restrictions placed on the family by virtue of participation. The procedure stressed the importance of explaining to participants that they could not receive payments under IMP and from welfare at the same time. That some families violated this rule may suggest that this structure was not completely understood, or it may be the case that the temptations were too much for some households to resist.

MATHEMATICA also promised and guaranteed confidentiality about participation in IMP and any information recieved by MATHEMATICA and the Income Maintenance Project. Since such guarantees have little standing in the face of subpoenas from state courts or federal agencies with subpoena powers, the participants were subjected to some risk of disclosure of which they were not completely aware. When the Mercer County (Trenton, New Jersey) Public Prosecutor and Grand Jury attempted to subpoena MATHEMATICA's files to determine whether there was any cheating on welfare (that is, whether any IMP participants had received payments from both IMP and welfare), MATHE-MATICA's David Kershaw was prepared to go to jail rather than release the records. Fortunately, it was possible to resolve the problem without either releasing the records or jailing Kershaw through negotiations in which OEO played an important role.

In short, the procedures outlined and presumably followed by MATHE-MATICA in recruiting households and explaining to them the implications of their participation indicate a reasonable effort to obtain informed consent.

Indeed, there is little doublt that these procedures would easily pass the most finicky of university committees set up to review the use of human subjects in social scientific research.

Unfortunately, a reasonable effort may not be matched with acceptable levels of success. Members of the research team currently analyzing the results of IMP have been examining the extent to which participants in IMP in fact knew the details of the particular plan in which they participated. Although we have not seen a finished analysis of this problem, preliminary analyses indicate that IMP households understood their particular plans quite imperfectly. Especially important in this respect was their understanding of the tax rate applied to additional earnings, an important factor in the work-leisure trade-off. If households do not understand the tax rate, then it is unlikely that they will be able to correctly perceive the incentives offered for increased labor force participation. The findings indicate that only a small proportion of the households understood the tax rates being applied in their plans, a finding that casts considerable doubt on whether the tax rate treatment was strong enough to make an impact. In any event, these findings, in the face of conscientious efforts, raise the question of the efficacy of means of obtaining informed consent.

The second large issue involving subjects is the active participation of the subjects in the conduct of IMP. In this connection, it should be emphasized that there is something inherently nonintrusive in the treatments that were delivered under IMP. Under no circumstances can additional income be construed as treatment that restricts the recipient household's freedom: indeed, just the opposite can be assumed. No strings were attached to the payments (other than reporting income and participating in quarterly interviews). Households were free to save the income, spend it in any way they chose, or even to send the checks back if they wished.

Were the funds involved to be used in increasing public services or goods, for example, increasing school expenditures or expanding recreational opportunities for juveniles, a case might be made for participation in the allocation of such funds among alternative modes. But this was not the situation for IMP. Each household could participate in the decision it made about the allocation of the income payments it received; indeed, there was no one else who could participate.

We are aware that this discussion is limited to the effects of IMP on a rather narrow group of individuals, the immediate participants in the experiment. Should one choose to extend the definition of "participation," it becomes far more difficult to deal decisively with the issues. Clearly, there are a number of external effects generated by the experiment that affect the public agencies dealing with the participating households, relatives, and friends of the households, and there are "opportunities lost" to the general public. Although not a large investment of resources (given the typical sizes of federal programs), the resources channeled into IMP were considerable, and one could argue that the question of participation involved a wider range of affected parties. However, extending the definition of relevant constituencies generates complications that we feel unable to address in this chapter. Part of our hesistancy is based on our inability to specify who, in fact, the other interested groups are. Even if these groups were listed , the problems involved in arguing that certain actors should have participated and in deciding which ways were relevant to their different roles are considerations we have not thought through.

## THE ISSUES OF UNINTENDED EFFECTS AND EXTERNAL RAMIFICATIONS

Although the issue of the work-leisure trade-off dominated the IMP, the data collected from participating households provide opportunities for observing a wide variety of unintended side effects on the households. Data have been collected that address such issues as family stability, consumption patterns, use of leisure time, self-esteem, and so forth. If anything, too much data have been gathered, some of dubious quality and relevance. In short, the side-issue data cover a broad area of possible household effects and show all the stigmata of having been put together by a committee.

Although the quarterly interviews may be regarded as rich sources of information on noneconomic effects on households, it is difficult to extrapolate from all the data collected what the suprahousehold effects might be. Several issues immediately come to mind. First, what would be the effects on supply and demand for certain types of occupations? If income maintenance plans can effectively compete with certain types of low-skilled and low-paid occupations, will labor supply for such occupations dry up? And, what would the fate of such employing organizations? In short, would income maintenance act effectively as minimum wage legislation, driving up the price of labor in presently poorly paid and unpleasant occupations? One obvious consequence would be to increase motivations of employers to automate, possibly eliminating precisely those jobs for which IMP participants may be most qualified.

Second, it is easy enough to carefully and responsibly administer an income maintenance plan if one has the skill and resources available to MATHE-MATICA. MATHEMATICA's staff impresses one as having considerably more competence and integrity than any welfare department in the country. If the administration of income maintenance is put into the hands of a local welfare department, would the monthly income report, for example, become another form of the means test with all the negative stigmatizing connotations that are associated with means tests?

This may not be viewed by some as a substantial objection, since at least in some discussions of a guaranteed annual income or a negative income tax there is no role to be played by local administrative units such as welfare departments. It is our contention that such views are quite visionary. It is difficult to conceive of such a plan without local administrating offices charged with the responsibilities of providing information to beneficiaries and with policing income reporting. Indeed, it is more than a little likely that the wholesale administration of an IMP-like plan would require as much in the way of overhead and personnel as present welfare plans do. The pressures to expand administrative forces would come, as we see it, from pressures to detect cheating and from pressures on the part of the social work profession to add services to income delivery. Indeed, President Nixon's version of income maintenance, the Family Assistance Plan (FAP), did take precisely this predicted form.[12]

Third, the experiment was delivered to a group of households identified by an area probability sampling plan. Although households were somewhat clustered in space, it is still unlikely that any participating household knew more than a few other households who were also participating. Thus, synergistic effects of saturating a neighborhood with IMP cannot be observed under the IMP design.[13]

These three considerations are to a large degree defects that arise from the design and would be difficult to eliminate. Alternative approaches would likely be prohibitively expensive or less powerful in addressing the central issue of the work-leisure trade-off.

## SOME GENERAL OBSERVATIONS
## ON SOCIAL EXPERIMENTATION

The conception of IMP and its implementation are important not only because of the intrinsic importance of the experiment, but because one can learn from the history of the experiment. Some of the positive experiences generated by IMP are instructive examples of sensible, ethical social intervention. Its failures suggest ways in which one might strengthen future programs.

Unlike many other social intervention programs, IMP must be judged as relatively benign. It is difficult to imagine that providing households with more money of the magnitudes involved can do anything but affect them marginally and for the better. Since participation is voluntary, involves few restrictions, and is not intended to fundamentally change people or households in any given direction, IMP is an excellent example of a class of intrinsically benign interventions. By our values, any program that enriches freedom of choice, either by providing more alternatives or increasing resources that enlarge the scope of choice, would be similarly assessed. We have in mind such programs as housing vouchers, educational vouchers, scholarship and fellowship programs, and retirement benefits.

---

[12] See Moynihan (1973).

[13] A number of alternative designs were considered, including saturation designs and a national sample design. Saturation was given up because it would have been to dependent on the characteristics of a particular saturated area, and a national sample was given up on the grounds that administration would be too difficult to handle. These issues are discussed in Rivlin (1971), pp. 94–102.

Of course, if one strains, one can come up with malignant aspects of IMP. For example, the offering of the plan to some individual households may have enticed them wittingly or unwittingly to violate the laws and administrative rulings concerning AFDC in New Jersey. Or IMP payments may have made some households careless of their own interests in the pursuit of occupational careers, giving up opportunities with long-run large payoffs in favor of short-run income benefits under IMP. Of course, the extent to which these effects are likely to have occurred is a matter that can be empirically determined: the best bet we have is that such effects are very unlikely.

In addition, at some point, concern with the possible negative consequences of programs becomes counterproductive. Every intervention, no matter how unintrusive, risks some damage to participants. Ironically, programs designed to attack the most severe problems will likely be those for which the risks are greatest, since more dramatic change is desired. An obsession with possible risks could, therefore, delay programs where need is the greatest and limit social intervention to trivial issues requiring trivial remedies. We are not arguing against sincere efforts to anticipate and minimize damage. On the other hand, at some point, one must ignore a nagging conscience and proceed with the realization that one cannot win without risk of losing.

When serious ethical problems involved in social experiments do appear, some remedies may be found through the application of several general principles. To begin, a program evaluating the feasibility and effectiveness of a prospective benign social policy ought to address within its experimental design two main considerations: first, it should provide information that is deemed relevant to major interested parties; second, it should test the range of alternatives that might be considered when the issue is debated in the appropriate political arena.

Concerning our first suggestion, recall that IMP was designed primarily to provide hard data to assess the conservative objection to income maintenance: that workers would prefer to trade leisure for work under income maintenance. Obviously, there are a host of other policy issues that are of importance to some of the partisans. For example, is the income-reporting provision just another form of a means test? Will income maintenance force up the cost of labor and hence produce inflationary increases that would wipe out the benefits of income maintenance? That this last sort of side effect can be disastrous to the society in general is shown in our recent experience with Medicare and Medicaid. We have managed thereby to drive up the price of medical care, especially hospital costs, for everyone. At the same time, it is not clear that these two programs have materially improved access to medical care for the aged and the poor.

On the second suggestion, IMP was also found wanting because one can envision a wide variety of specific income maintenance plans. Income support can be provided at a very low level or at a very generous level. Income maintenance can be put in the form of family allowances or in the form of a negative income tax. Even the present welfare system can be viewed as an income maintenance policy. Indeed, the first income maintenance plan that came before Congress (Nixon's Family Assistance Plan) combined features of IMP, although at a lower level of income support, with features involving compulsory labor force participation.[14]

In practice, our two suggestions imply that a fuller range of issues should be incorporated within a program of social experimentation. This could be achieved through a family of experiments or through more complex designs. Thus, with respect to income maintenance, the experiment might have been expanded to include treatments that were relevant to each of a set of reasonable alternative forms of income maintenance.[15] One form might have involved looking at a broader range of income maintenance with provisions for employment in public service occupations, and so on.

The outcomes of such a family of social experiments can be more relevant to social policy in a variety of ways. First of all, by including a broader spectrum of input, there may be more serious consideration of the results by potential partisans. When alternative programs were then considered for adoption as social policy, a wider range of political support may be produced as a consequence. Second, the outcomes would be more relevant to the issue when finally addressed by decision-making bodies. The current irrelevance of IMP and the other income maintenance experiments is partly a function of the fact that the specific form of income maintenance that has been considered by Congress over the past two years bears only a slight resemblance to the plans being tested in the field. Of course, if an income maintenance plan that resembles IMP more closely comes on the agenda, then IMP will become more relevant. Relevance is obvious, relative to the issues as presented to policy makers.

It should also be recognized that some forms of income maintenance that might be considered as viable social policy (for example, FAP) may not be as benign as the plan tested under IMP. This raises the general question of how one should responsibly handle more intrusive forms of experimentation, or ones that are more clearly directed at changing individuals or households in specific ways. One approach involves the development of some sort of compromise solution of conflicting values inherent in more intrusive programs. We take a more opportunistic view. The more intrusive the program, the more inevitable that damage will be done to some parties. Further, political realities dictate that even if a forum existed in which competing values could be reconciled, the values of some groups would typically be overrepresented in any program while the values of others would be typically underrepresented. Hence, at least in the short run,

[14] So different are IMP and FAP that it is not clear that the results of IMP are at all relevant to a consideration of FAP, as several senators who heard testimony from IMP personnel remarked.

[15] In part, the subsequent income maintenance experiments were responsive to this issue. In particular, the Gary Income Maintenance Experiment combines income maintenance with intensive social services. The other experiments seem to be merely extensions of the experiment to other types of populations (for example, rural, female-headed household, and so on).

while effort should be made to provide a fair opportunity for all parties to have significant impact in shaping social intervention programs, more progress may be attained by trying to minimize the negative effects of the intrusion. It seems to us that there are several ways of handling potentially intrusive social experimentation.

First of all, it may be possible that a set of alternative social policies can be ranked in terms of potential intrusiveness. We are assuming that it is possible for partisans to agree on relative intrusiveness even if they still disagree on how much intrusiveness is appropriate. If we are incorrect in this assumption, then we would suggest that a set of experiments be started varying in intrusiveness with the implied or explicit agreement among partisans that the relative effectiveness of the intrusive aspects of the treatments are also being tested.

If such is the case, then a strategy may be followed that tests out the least intrusive first and only goes on to the more intrusive if the lesser are ineffective. Thus, with respect to income maintenance, the work–leisure–trade-off question perhaps ought to be answered first before moving to policies that would include compulsory labor force participation, as a means of preventing people from trading leisure for work. The general principle that might be enunciated here is that we should first test for that policy that achieves intended effects at minimum levels of intrusiveness.

For example, if the goal is to design a program that would materially reduce the proportion of young persons who drop out of high school before graduation, one might start with a program that tests the effectiveness of a publicity campaign that stresses the cost to the individual of dropping out. If that program proves ineffective, then one might try to effect changes in high school organization, developing new curricula that are designed to be more attractive to potential drop-outs. The next step might involve paying students to stay in high school with an incentive that increases the closer one comes to graduation. At the extreme of intrusiveness, we might test a program that commits drop-outs to residential education centers (a euphemism for reform school) and requires school attendance through completion of high school. It may well be the case that this last alternative is so unacceptable to all partisans that even if all other, less malignant alternatives prove ineffective, no one would support this treatment even on an experimental basis.

Second, when one considers potentially intrusive programs, it is necessary to specifically address the damage that one might inflict on participants. In this connection, it seems only responsible to build into an experiment postexperimental treatments that are intended to restore the status quo ante. This principle involves two considerations: first, one should try to devise interventions that are reversible; and second, one needs to provide resources to reverse the effects of such intervention in the postexperimental period. It is difficult to imagine our suggested "residential educational center" as a reversible treatment, and, hence, one would not ordinarily consider such a treatment as an experimental treatment. Much of the research on social deviance testifies to the damage done by programs that provide stigmatized labels for those the program is supposed to help. But it may be possible to provide individual tutors to students put through an unusual curriculum in high school. Tutors could assist students to make up material missed in the innovative curriculum.

Third, if one is forced to employ an irreversible experimental treatment, then it seems reasonable to compensate subjects for the ill effects of the program. The compensation may involve money, services, or simply some sort of recognition. For example, youths released under an experimental probation experiment might be provided with free legal counsel if they are indicted for crimes committed while in the program. Similarly, some of the untoward side effects might also be compensated for: victims of crimes committed by people who are under experimental probation might be compensated for their victimization.

## THE MISSING INSTITUTION

These strategies are forward-looking in their time perspective. They are predicated on knowing future social policy issues far enough in advance so that one can design experiments that provide reasonable input when needed. Social experiments, even on the small scale of IMP, require some years to develop, implement, and analyze before the findings can be useful. It seems that any program of social experimentation ought to be oriented toward the social policy issues that will be on the public agenda at least five years later.

Under the present circumstances, it appears that we are willing to undertake experiments when the issue is about to be placed on the political agenda. Thus, IMP was only in the field for eighteen months when Nixon's Family Assistance Plan was presented to Congress for the first time. Indeed, it may well be the case that the existence of the experiment itself helped precipitate movement of the Nixon administration in the direction of a guaranteed income policy to substitute for AFDC and other welfare payment systems.

If large-scale social experimentation is to play an important role in the formation of policy, it has to be accomplished within an institutional context that is free of the pressures to solve immediate short-run problems. For this reason, it would seem unlikely that the planning units of existing agencies, busy as they are in putting out every day's brush fires, are appropriate bodies to plan and carry through forward-looking programs of social experimentation. It seems particularly unlikely that the Department of Health, Education, and Welfare would develop the necessary five- to ten-year perspective. Rather, it appears that we need an organizational context that is relatively free of operational tasks and, hence, capable of developing the "futures" research that is necessary. It goes without saying that such an organizational context would need to be able to command resources and attract professional personnel of considerable competence.

For these reasons, it seems most appropriate to place the responsibility for developing, designing, and implementing such experimental programs in the hands of an organization that exists either outside the present structure of government or as a very autonomous unit within the government.[16] Perhaps an appropriate organization would be a quasi-public body (for example, The National Laboratory for Experiments in Social Policy), funded on a long-term basis (say, five to ten years) by a combination of private and public sources, ruled by a board broadly representative of major partisan groups. Alternatively, this may be a function that could be overseen by the proposed Council of Social Advisors.

There are many tough problems to be solved in the setting up of such a body. To begin with, there is the question of how to obtain the financing that will enable such an organization to undertake long-term planning and experimentation. Large-scale field experiments that are funded from year to year cannot have the necessary continuity. A staff that has to spend a good portion of the year convincing money-giving bodies that next year is worth financing is a staff that is spending too much of its time on the wrong things.

Second, there is the question of which partisan groups ought to be represented and by whom? Who can speak for the fiscal conservatives or for the poor? We leave this problem to our colleagues, the political scientists, to worry over, only noting at this point that it is our hope that enough diversity of representation appear on the ruling board of such an organization to ensure that a broad range of prospective social policies is always under consideration.

Third, how can one divine the future? Obviously, such an organization would serve our society best if it had available all the relevant information at the point when a particular social policy appeared on the national agenda. Social scientists have not been extraordinarily proficient at seeing into the future up to this point. On the other hand, they have not had much opportunity to do so. Even more important, the existence of social experimentation on a topic may itself affect what goes onto the agenda of the nation.

We are not suggesting that a National Laboratory for Experiments in Social Policy would solve all ethical, political, and methodological questions. Indeed, careless development of such an institution might replicate in miniature all the problems that currently exist. We are, however, suggesting that a National Laboratory for Experiments in Social Policy would provide a better arena in which to address the issues than presently exists. To minimize potential damage done by a National Laboratory one would have to devise mechanisms within the organization that specifically address the pitfalls involved in all social intervention. For example, within a National Laboratory one might organize several relatively autonomous divisions working on the same problems. Each division

---

[16] We are suggesting something that very much negates the present RANN Program of the National Science Foundation, which is too closely tied to serving the perceived needs of operating agencies to be able to develop a conception of the policy of the future.

would have access to the same range of inputs and be provided with equal resources. Final decision to implement a given type of social intervention might then combine three different kinds of checks and balances. First, one might institute advocacy proceedings in which each division could present its position before programs were begun. In a sense, procedures could be developed like those found in appellate courts in which the debates and decisions would be public information. Second, each division might be permitted to implement its version of a given program where methodological and/or political considerations had eliminated the possibility of fully crossed factorial designs. Finally, one could build in independent replications of each social experiment in which the host of factors not considered through controls, matching, and randomization in the research designs could be assessed, at least in a quasi-experimental format. Hence, external validity as well as internal validity might be improved.

## CONCLUSIONS

This chapter could have been divided into two sections. The first section was concerned mainly with the New Jersey–Pennsylvania Income Maintenance Experiment and the ethical problems involved in programs of that sort. We advance the argument that there is a class of experiments, exemplified by IMP, in which the ethical problems arising out of dealing with human subjects are minimized because of the benign character of the treatment and of the way in which the treatments were handled in administration. The main fault we found lies in the fact that few, if any, of the partisans and antagonists of income maintenance were involved in the design of the experiment and the determination of the policy issues to which IMP was directed.

The second part of the chapter suggested two strategies of social experimentation in general. The first strategy is designed to maximize the utility of experimental results in the determination of social policy. We suggest that single-purpose experiments be replaced by factorial experiments in which the factors are features of alternative programs that might be proposed by interested parties. The second strategy involves minimizing risks to participants in experiments and minimizing external side effects of experimentation. A program of social experimentation should be implemented by attempting to test the most benign treatment first and going on to the less benign only if the most benign is ineffective. We also suggest developing experimentation devices that attempt to restore the status quo ante.

Finally, we suggest that we are missing an important institution in our society, one that can bear the responsibility for designing and carrying out experiments that will be relevant to the social policy issues of the future. However, such an institution must be developed carefully, or the current problems with social intervention will be simply moved to a different arena and remain unsolved.

## REFERENCES

Conlisk, J., & Watts, H. A model for optimizing experimental designs for estimating response surfaces. 1969 Proceedings of the Social Statistics Section, American Statistical Association. Pp. 150–156.

Green, C. *Negative taxes and the poverty problem.* Washington, D.C.: The Brookings Institution, 1967. Chapter 8.

Kershaw, D. N. Issues in income maintenance. In P. H. Rossi & W. Williams (Eds.), *Evaluating social programs.* New York: Seminar Books, 1972. Pp. 221–245.

Moynihan, D. P. *The politics of a guaranteed income.* New York: Basic Books, 1973.

Rivlin, A. *Systematic thinking for social action.* Washington, D.C.: The Brookings Institution, 1971.

Rossi, P. H., Lyall, K. *Reforming public welfare.* New York: Russell Sage Foundation, 1977.

# 13
# ETHICAL GUIDELINES FOR SOCIAL EXPERIMENTS

**DONALD P. WARWICK**

Harvard University

Beginning in 1968 the U.S. government mounted a series of social experiments to test promising policies under fairly controlled conditions. In addition to the New Jersey–Pennsylvania Income Maintenance Program (IMP), there were income maintenance experiments in Seattle and Denver, as well as a health insurance experiment, a housing assistance experiment, an education vouchers experiment, and others. All these experiments share several characteristics: They were large, with many subjects and a sizeable administrative staff; they were complex, often involving several government agencies and at least two levels of government; they were politically sensitive, not only because they were meant to test significant public policies but also because they touched the interests of powerful actors and contending groups; they were carried out in a pressure-cooker atmosphere, which is not conducive to ethical reflection; and their effects were often unpredictable (Kershaw, 1975). All the experiments mentioned were also benign in purpose. Their principal aim was to improve the welfare of the disadvantaged, and they have all met reasonably high standards of ethics in implementation. As Rossi, Boeckmann, and Berk show for the IMP, these have not been carelessly designed forays into poor neighborhoods executed with little regard for informed consent and other protections for individual rights. On the contrary, the designers for the most part adopted stringent ethical standards and, in the case of the IMP, were willing to go to jail to honor their promises.

That having been said, it is also clear that social experiments raise a host of ethical issues requiring careful attention from program designers. Some, such as the conditions of informed consent, were well known before the federal experiments, but others, including the ethics of experimental design, were brought into sharp relief by the experiments. Perhaps the most basic moral conclusion to be drawn from this set of experiences is that ethics transcends benign purposes and the lack of harmful effects. There is still an unfortunate tendency to define ethical issues only in terms of benefits wrought or damages done to immediate participants of an experiment. This criterion is unquestionably important, but so are others, such as the adequacy of the procedural safeguards observed, the political interests served by the experiment even when no one is palpably harmed, the spillover effects to other groups, including those who might like to conduct other experiments at a later date, and the degree to which the experiment actually tests policies likely to be implemented.

From an ethical standpoint, a distinct advantage of the social experiments done to date is that their underlying benignity allows us to focus on more subtle moral questions. Because none of those mentioned is the sort of intervention that lends itself to instant proclamations of outrage, the ethical analyst can delve into procedural and other issues without major distraction from the substance of the intervention. Rossi et al. have provided a thoughtful discussion of the issues at stake in the IMP. In this chapter, I will consider the ethics of social experiments more generally and propose some tentative guidelines for future experiments. The need for such guidelines has been convincingly stated by David Kershaw (1975), who directed the IMP and participated in several of the other experiments:

> There is often a direct conflict between ethics and experimental efficacy which creates a considerable strain on social experimenters. . . .
>
> The characteristics of social experiments make the development and application of a set of ethical principles not only more difficult but, because of the large number of individuals simultaneously affected by a given decision in the experiment, in some ways even more compelling than the adoption of medical ethics has been (pp. 60–61).

One of the most knotty questions involved in this effort is deciding whose standards should be given what weight in making ethical judgments.

## BALANCING HARMS AND BENEFITS

In social experiments, as with all discussions of research ethics, there is no objective, quasi-scientific means for weighing harms and benefits. Indeed, some would claim that the very mode of ethical reasoning assumed by risk-benefit analysis is inappropriate. There are some rights, they might argue, that should not be traded off against such benefits as scientific knowledge and improved public policies. Among these might be life, liberty, and the capacity to bear children. Thus, whatever the presumptive gains, we are not free to sell ourselves into slavery, relinquish our right to vote, or subject ourselves to physical mutilation for the sake of science or social progress.

Short of those ethical extremes, the concept of risk-benefit analysis also stumbles over the problems of selectivity, bias, and political interests. The particular harms and benefits that enter into the ethical equation, as well as the weights that are assigned to them, will obviously depend on who is doing the figuring, and how. Scientists typically select the advancement of knowledge as one of the central rating dimensions and assign it a strong weight. Similarly, staff members at an agency such as the defunct Office of Economic Opportunity (OEO) place a high value on the generation of new policy options and on information about the effectiveness of such options. Civil libertarians, on the other hand, usually hold no brief against knowledge, but are primarily concerned with such values as privacy, consent, and other aspects of freedom. In like manner, political conservatives take as their central value the preservation of social order and adherence to tradition. Given such varied perspectives, it is not surprising that different groups will see different harms and benefits in a given experiment, and even in the very concept of experimentation. More often than not, social scientists will allow that there are potential costs and dangers in an experiment such as the IMP, but choose to resolve any dilemmas in favor of greater knowledge. Moral philosophers and constitutional lawyers might be less eager to move ahead with such interventions on the grounds that the dangers to liberty are too great. A mythical impartial observer could rightly argue that both are biased, but that would not solve the problem of how practical judgments are to be made about experimentation. The key question is not whether biases are present, for few would deny that they are, but how they are to be reconciled in a given case.

While there are no easy answers, we can postulate at the outset that the decision about what is at stake and how value dilemmas are to be resolved should not be left to the experimenters or researchers. As the American Psychological Association (1973) points out in its principles of research ethics:

> The investigator should not trust his own objectivity in balancing the pros and cons of going ahead with research that raises an ethical question for him. His personal involvement tends to lead him to exaggerate the scientific merit of what he is about to do and to underestimate the costs to the research participant. In addition, he may be hindered from seeing costs from the latter's point of view, because of differences in age, economic and social background, intellectual orientation, and relation to the project itself (p. 12).

Peer review, especially with social experiments, is also no panacea, for one's professional peers tend to be uncritical of research that is not patently unethical and are not an adequate surrogate for others whose interests may be at risk. It is not clear just who professional peers should be in the case of social experiments, for there is no single academic discipline or professional association that is nominally responsible for this area. Until social experimenters themselves develop a broad-based review procedure or the government establishes procedures akin to those required in more conventional research, I would suggest the following guideline:

> *Principle I.* In determining the ethical acceptability of a social experiment, its planners should establish a review committee including the major interested parties, among them the academic disciplines involved, the sponsoring or implementing agency, peers of the subjects, specialists on research ethics, and representatives of interest groups with special concern for the subjects or for the policy area covered by the experiment.

Needless to say, there would be enormous practical difficulties in organizing such a committee and in coming to a concrete decision if widely different views emerged on the merits of the experiment. But whatever the difficulties, some serious effort to follow this principle would be greatly preferable to an in-house procedure where the cards are stacked in favor of a preformed design.

## PARTICIPATION AND DESIGN

A point that is sometimes lost in debates about the scientific merits of social experiments is that they are, or can be, a strong source of political power. Other things being equal, those who can show with data that a policy option works are in a better position than those who must make their case from *a priori* reasoning. To the extent that knowledge becomes a scarce resource in the struggle for influence over public policy, social experiments raise a fundamental question of social justice: Who should have the right to design and conduct empirical tests of policy options? Do government agencies, by virtue of their official mandate to develop policies, have special prerogatives to experiment, or should access to policy testing be open to other legitimate groups? Should the experiments be of the government by the government for the people, or should the people themselves have an opportunity to influence the options tested? If so, how?

Rossi et al. make it clear that the New Jersey–Pennsylvania Income Maintenance Experiment gave distinct political advantages to the program's designers. First, the planners, working with the Office of Economic Opportunity, had the chance to conduct a large-scale experiment, a possibility that was not open to other interested groups. Second, they were able to design the IMP in such a way that it tested only the options that they considered relevant. This meant that in subsequent debates about a negative income tax they could say that, whatever its failings, their option was tested while others were not. The fact that the debate did not go as expected and that the IMP results seem to have had little effect on public policy does not negate the potential political advantage conferred by selective experimentation. Third, the designers were able to buy some of the best minds in economics, sociology, and other social sciences in conceptualizing, conducting, and evaluating the IMP. These professionals lent not only their intellectual skills but their prestige to this fledgling social experiment. While the astute use of consultants is to be applauded as a rare feat in government programs, the concentration of talent in the IMP made it a difficult act to follow or challenge at the level of data gathering. Finally, as Rossi et al. point out, the designers were able to work under a "cloak of secrecy," shielding their efforts from rivals, adversaries, legislative critics, and other interested parties until well into the IMP's life. From the standpoint of the designers, such seclusion was necessary to prevent the experiment from being aborted by hostile forces. From a larger perspective, the cloak of secrecy was also a vital ingredient of power, for it allowed the designers to gather politically salient data without effective challenge.

The key ethical questions raised by this discussion are: (1) who should participate or be consulted in planning the experiments? and (2) what range of options, reflecting what values, should be tested in the final design? The questions are closely related in the sense that who participates and how will have a crucial bearing on the options tested and the values that they represent.

## PARTICIPATION AND CONSULTATION

Few social experimenters would disagree with the broad ethical principle that those to be affected by the policies tested by social experiments should take part in their design. Yet none of the experiments conducted to date has been based on anything resembling real participation by target groups. All have been essentially elitist in design. Several standard arguments are offered against popular participation.

One is that the target groups, such as the poor in the IMP, have either no organized representation or only very partial representation. It is thus impossible or highly impractical to solicit their views on public policy, much less involve them directly in the design of experiments. Any attempt to do so may be undemocratic by opening the policy door to groups that, while organized, are highly unrepresentative of the constituencies for which they purport to speak.

A second argument, rarely stated as baldly as it is here, is that the poor and the disadvantaged are not in a position to understand the intricacies of public policy and experimental design. To let them into working sessions on social experiments would be as misguided as allowing the inexperienced to take part in the annual mark-up sessions for congressional appropriations. Not only may these people not know what is good for them, but in the process of expressing their views they may hopelessly muddle any serious efforts at sound experimental design.

A third line of reasoning is that, whatever the credentials of the participants, participation will open the way to political meddling and other delays that could ultimately kill the experiment. If legislators and representatives of interest groups are told in advance that there will be an experiment, the enemies of testing will try to stop it completely, and even its friends will cause it harm through their incompatible intercessions. The only sensible solution, therefore, is to design the trials quietly and to set the experiment in motion before exposing it to wide public scrutiny.

Even if one grants some validity to these arguments, the options do not come down to either elitist design or open but chaotic participation. As a minimum, the planners could canvass the literature of concerned groups or interview their representatives to determine the range of policy options considered salient at the time. While such surrogate consultation is two steps removed from the target groups, it is better than nothing. Moving one step closer, the designers might involve a few interest group representatives in the semisecret planning sessions. While this strategy runs the great risk of cooptation, especially if participants must agree to maintain public silence about the experiment, it is again an improvement on pure elitism. These and other, more active possibilities suggest a principle for future social experiments:

> *Principle II*. The design of social experiments should be based on an adequate representation of competing values and interests in the policy arena. Representation may come about through such direct means as consultation and participation or through such indirect means as a thorough canvass of stated policy options and values.

The ethical standard that might apply here is whether all reasonable efforts are made to have adequate representation of competing values and interests in the light of other legitima· concerns, such as the need for a controlled experiment. There is no reason why the efficacy of different forms of participation and consultation cannot be subjected to much the same kind of testing as the policy options themselves.

## OPTIONS AND DESIGN

A practical dilemma in the design of social experiments is whether to select one policy and test it thoroughly or take several and test them in lesser depth. This also becomes an ethical question when the policy chosen for testing is associated with one interest group in the society while others do not have the resources to mount comparable experiments. The notion of distributive justice would suggest that all leading contenders for influence on public policy should have access to experimentation, provided that the benefits of this approach (randomization, controlled observation, etc.) are not vitiated by excessive coverage. Thus the following might serve as a guiding principle in decisions about coverage:

> *Principle III.* Social experiments funded by public monies should test the major alternatives likely to be considered in the final deliberations about public policy. In the event of constraints arising from limited resources or experimental design, the choice of options for testing should be based on their probable salience in the policy debate.

The essential notion is that social experiments should test those policies that are mostly likely to come up for consideration by legislators or other policy makers. Experiments should not be limited to the favorite policies of the designers or their sponsors, to those that are easiest to test, or to those with the best theoretical rationale. The qualification of public monies is introduced to exclude small-scale experiments that might be conducted by special interest groups.

Judged by this principle, the IMP does not fare particularly well. The experiment tested only one policy option (the negative income tax) and focused on a fairly narrow range of policy consequences, especially the work-leisure tradeoff. The values and interests underlying these choices, as Rossi et al. have indicated, were mainly those of equilibrium economists and OEO officials, rather than legislators or the poor themselves. There was a belief, moreover, that only those options should be included that are bolstered by theoretically based, testable hypotheses. A comment by David Kershaw (1975), the IMP director, is very revealing in this regard:

> The third question creates a real problem: has sufficient theoretical work been done to specify in advance a set of carefully designed hypotheses that can be tested? In the income maintenance experiments the economists had a solid theoretical basis for measuring labor-force response, and it was relatively easy to develop a direct, efficient, and tight set of income questions. Among the sociologists, however, there was a tendency to fish for relationships. The requirement that all data gathered had to be centrally related to the impact of a guaranteed income was no restraint at all on sociologists, since it could apply to an almost limitless set of items (p. 71).

While the importance of tight theoretical frameworks is a subject of continuing debate among professionals of good will, it is difficult to comprehend why this requirement is introduced as a *sine qua non* for testing policy options. If one's goal is the advancement of economic or social theory, this approach would be understandable. But if the aim is to test public policy in terms that are comprehensible not only to theorists but also to policy makers, such stringency seems misguided. From an ethical as well as a political standpoint, the central question is the efficacy of a given policy option in producing certain effects, whether or not those effects can be explained within a neat theoretical rationale. If we can show convincingly that an income maintenance policy improves family welfare without incurring significant costs, that information seems important even if the precise reasons for the change are not theoretically clear.

The IMP case suggests an additional ethical guideline:

> *Principle IV.* In assessing any of the policy options chosen for consideration, social experiments should attempt to measure those consequences of concern to all of the major groups involved, including the target group and the decision makers.

Considerations of justice suggest that the dimensions assessed should not be limited to the concerns of the designers, their sponsors, or some other interest group. Rather, they should flow from the questions and issues likely to be most salient in the final deliberations on policy choice. This might mean, in practice, that the program designers could collect information on topics that are suggested by their critics on the grounds that their task is to provide information rather than just ammunition. This principle also rejects Kershaw's notion of theoretical relevance or derivation as a major criterion for inclusion. This critical aim is to have the experiment reflect the values and problem definitions of those with significant stakes in the policy domain, and to collect information relating to those values and definitions.

Also crucial to the ethics of design is the issue of generalizability. At root a social experiment serves its purpose only if the conditions in which it is carried out are reasonably similar to those under which the contemplated programs would be implemented. The history of social programs in the United States and elsewhere is replete with examples of demonstration projects that were judged remarkably successful upon completion, but that could not be replicated with similar success on a large scale. The possible reasons are many. The demonstration might make use of more talented administrators than are generally available in the country, or it might have better resources for fighting brushfires, or simply a bigger budget. In addition, the very fact that it is a pilot project may create a kind of Hawthorne effect in which public visibility leads to higher motivation among staff and participants alike. These points are well recognized in the field of experimental design, but they are also significant for the ethics of social experimentation. The following principle, therefore, seems both ethically and scientifically sound:

> *Principle V.* The conditions under which social experiments are carried out, including their duration, their budget, the level of administrative capacity, the availability of support services, and the overall environmental complexity, should approximate those under which a full-blown program of the same type would operate.

To state the principle negatively, it seems unethical to test a social program under conditions that are significantly more or less favorable than would normally be the case. This concern is far from academic. There have been many cases in which demonstration projects were arranged in the most favorable manner possible in order to sell the overall approach to skeptical authorities. In fewer cases, programs seem to have been rigged in a negative direction to prove that they really could not work. And then designers sometimes simply overlook key features that might affect generalizability. The IMP has been criticized, for example, for having too short a life span to appear realistic to the participants. Some would argue that a program of this type would have to last a minimum of ten years to be credible. Similarly, Rossi et al. point out that the staff administering the IMP was probably of a higher caliber than that found in the typical welfare department, and that the experiment's sampling desing precluded accurate measurement of the synergistic effects arising from many participating households in the same neighborhood. Some of these questions, such as synergistic effects, seem more technical than ethical in their implications, but overall the principle of fair generalizability seems beyond moral challenge.

At the practical level, several steps could be taken to deal with the points raised here about participation, consultation, and design. After the initial consultations, the planners might convene an advisory committee to monitor the entire intervention, from the selection of problem definitions and options for testing to the final report. This group could include several lay interest-group representatives, one or two potential decision makers or users of the information, methodological specialists of differing policy persuasions, and perhaps others. The aim would be to create an internal forum for debate about the ideological assumptions, power implications, ethical adequacy, and other vital features of the intervention. The following questions, among others, could be raised:

1. Does the basic design reflect the assumptions or serve the interests of some groups more than others? Are the hypotheses tested too narrow? Too broad to provide useful answers to policy makers? Does the design allow for competing interpretations, or is it slanted in one policy

direction? Could a critic of the major hypothesis find data to test an alternative explanation of the effects observed?

2.  Is the information gathering biased toward any policy option or ideological group? For example, will the questions lead to interpretations that "blame the victim"? This bias is likely when the preponderance of questions focuses on the attitudes and behaviors of disadvantaged persons, such as their attitudes toward work and leisure, their behavior in seeking or failing to seek jobs, and their level of initiative and entrepreneurship. Critics from the left might suggest that such questions be balanced off with others focusing on the larger structures within which the poor find themselves, such as on the lack of jobs, on poor pay, discrimination, and other forms of exploitation. Warwick and Lininger (1975) have suggested such a dialectical procedure as a means of reducing bias in sample surveys.

3.  Does the evaluation collect information from all or most of the groups known or suspected to be interested in this question? Rossi et al. have suggested that the evaluation of the IMP was slanted toward the interests of equilibrium economists and away from potential critics of the program, such as employers relying on cheap labor. A fair evaluation requires data collection from several perspectives.

4.  Do the interpretations made give evidence of ideological or policy biases? Are they loaded in favor of one or another option? Do they unfairly damage the image of certain groups, such as urban blacks or the working poor? Critical methodologists can, at a more subtle level, point out areas in which the data seem over- and underinterpreted and suggest the political implications of such reporting. They might also propose additional analyses needed to give fair representation to competing views or to test alternative explanations of the main findings. This process seems especially important when, as was true of the New Jersey–Pennsylvania experiment, the program designers themselves have a vested interest in one approach. The dialectical process suggested here could, in other words, be applied at every stage of the social experiment, from the initial formulation of the problem to be studied to the final interpretations. The aims would be both ethical and scientific. From an ethical standpoint the purpose of such continuing scrutiny would be fairness in the use of a valuable tool for testing public policy. From a scientific perspective, research subjected to exacting challenge before publication will stand up much better to later external assaults. Some will say, of course, that the procedures outlined are needlessly time-consuming and will stand in the way of rapid action on pressing social problems. In fact, several of the steps recommended would not add significantly to the time required for careful research, and any delays introduced may be more than offset by gains in policy coverage and political legitimacy. The efforts to date strongly suggest the need for more experimentation on the very process of social experimentation.

## SOCIAL EXPERIMENTS AND THE PARTICIPANT

Beyond their contents and the process by which they were designed, social experiments raise a series of questions about the protections needed for participants. For the most part, these are the same questions that arise in medical and other behavioral research involving human subjects (cf. Veatch, 1975). However, in addition to the generic issues, such as informed consent, there are distinctive features of the social experiment defining those issues. The areas particularly in need of guidelines include participant capacity to understand the experiment and the degree of understanding required, the use of inducements, long-term or second-order consequences, and the protection of confidential information.

### Protection versus Paternalism

Before turning to these issues, however, we must address the hoary issue of paternalism. On the one hand, a prime reason for ethical concern in social experiments is that they are designed to improve the lot of the disadvantaged and are tested on disadvantaged populations. These groups almost by definition suffer handicaps in understanding the details of a social experiment and in evaluating the long-term consequences for themselves and their families. Also, according to some observers, they are more vulnerable to the appeals of money and other experimental inducements. At the same time, most experimenters want to treat potential participants as citizens with normal capacities to understand and protect their own interests. To overprotect the disadvantaged would, in their view, be not only demeaning and patronizing, but also unjust, for it might, on essentially procedural grounds, deprive some qualified candidates of the right to participate.

The existing literature on the ethics of social experiments, especially the volume edited by Rivlin and Timpane (1975), clearly illustrates the dilemma of responsibility versus overprotection. For example, Peter Brown (1975), a philosopher, argues strongly in favor of protections for the disadvantaged, including the "principle of inverse selection." According to this principle, the sampling for a risky experiment should be biased in favor of those with the greatest capacity to understand it, such as physicians in risky medical experiments.

> The experimenter seeks to sample the target population, or at least some sections of it, randomly; but the ability to truly consent will vary among individuals. ... Barriers to consenting include lack of practice in making decisions, lack of education, information inaccurately conveyed or difficult to understand, the power roles between experimenter and subject being played out in the context of the consent decision, difficulty in articulating lifetime objectives, and

difficulty in rationing between present and future consumption. The principle of inverse selection serves as a heuristic device to remind the experimenter of the characteristics of persons most able to consent (p. 91).

Brown's position has not met with ready assent by other practitioners and observers of the social experiment. Writing in the same volume, Gramlich and Orr (1975) rejoined:

> Brown's extension of the accepted definition [of informed consent] raises the question of whether, in protecting short-sighted people from social experimenters, it is in turn a violation of their freedom to prevent them from participating in an experiment even if they want to for irrational reasons. This protection may be just as undemocratic as having the experimenter "simplify" a description of the rights and prerogatives of poor individuals (p. 107).

Schelling (1975) is even stronger in his rejection of protections against financial incentives:

> People who deprecate "undue enticement" are somewhat like those who explain that paying household help too much spoils them. . . . If the designers of an experiment have worked responsibly and conscientiously, maybe it isn't up to them to decide that in the interest of their potential subjects they should keep compensation down. I think that the notion that compensation ought to be kept low is usually arrogantly paternalistic (p. 174).

This debate suggests two broad conclusions. First, social experimenters should ensure that disadvantaged participants have an adequate understanding of intervention and are not sacrificing their long-term welfare for immediate inducements. A key notion behind the social experiment is that the disadvantaged are not in a position to protect their own welfare, and so need interventions designed by others. It would thus be ironic if experimenters who believed in protection at the origin of an intervention should resort to the free market, rational consent model during its implementation. I doubt very much that either Gramlich and Orr or Schelling would accept the practice of paying money to poor volunteers for kidney donations or for agreeing not to vote in a certain election, however much the participants wanted the inducement. Second, the appropriate guideline for social experiments is not full protection but reasonable protection of the disadvantaged. Brown's recommendation of the principle of inverse selection seems an extreme form of protectionism. His suggestion that individual consent be judged by actual understanding rather than information presented falls within the realm of the reasonable. The core issue, then, is not protection versus paternalism, but rather the degree and kinds of subject protections that are called for in a given experimental situation.

## Capacity

For all the reasons indicated by Peter Brown, the subjects of social experiments may be handicapped not only in their socioeconomic position but in their capacity to understand the experiment. The prospects for genuinely informed consent are further diminished when the intervention is complex and makes use of a vocabulary that is not familiar to the participants. The difficult ethical question is whether the adequacy of informed consent should be judged by the explanation as given or as understood. Do experimenters have an obligation to go beyond the provision of correct information to ensure that the participants have grasped its meaning? The following principles might serve as guidelines in answering this question:

*Principle VI.* The primary criterion for judging informed consent in social experiments is the degree to which essential aspects are understood by the subject. The experimenter is ethically obligated to take steps to ensure that key elements of the experiment are actually understood by, as distinct from correctly explained to, the participants.

*Principle VII.* The greater the potential harms to the participant, the greater the efforts required to ensure an adequate understanding of the experiment, especially with regard to the possible sources of harm.

*Principle VIII.* In cases where participants do not give evidence of comprehending the central features of the experiment, they should be dropped from the sample. This obligation to remove potential candidates from the sample increases with the potential harms at stake in the experiment.

Principle VI argues that subjects should not only be informed about, but also understand the key features of the intervention. Evidence from the Seattle income maintenance experiment underscores the difference between information and understanding. A follow-up survey showed that only 48 percent of black one-parent families, as contrasted with 80 percent of white two-parent families, gave correct responses on how full-time work affected their grant. Even more striking was the finding that only 6 percent of the black, one-parent families and 37 percent of the white two-parent families seemed to know how large a family income would reduce their payments to zero (Stanford Research Institute, quoted in Brown, 1975, p. 86). These were not trivial items about the experiment, but features of considerable importance to the participants.

Principle VII postulates that the degree of understanding required should increase with the seriousness of the risks involved in the experiment and should be most stringent in areas connected to those risks. Thus, if there were a significant chance that the subjects could suffer death or serious injury from the experiment, the experimenters would be obligated to run a series of cross-checking tests to ensure that these dangers were understood. Where the risks are slight to moderate, as has been the case with income maintenance experiments, less rigorous standards would apply. Even when there are no significant risks of physical, social, economic, or psychological damage, participants should still be expected to grasp the essentials of the intervention. This is the floor of informed consent required by human dignity. According to Principle VIII, if subjects are simply unable to fathom the experiment and repeat its critical details, they should be excluded from the sample.

How should understanding be judged? At the simplest level participants could be asked to repeat what they have been told. In more complicated or risky experiments, the interviewer could ask the person to explain the essential features to someone else in the family, especially someone (such as a spouse) who will also be affected by the intervention. In highly complex or dangerous experiments, it might be advisable to have the participants write out their understanding of what they have agreed to, rather than simply having them sign a prepared consent form. When candidates do not appear to comprehend the crucial features in the first round of discussions, the experimenters might send in a specially trained team to explain the project in other language (including a foreign language, if appropriate), and then check the level of understanding in formal or informal ways.

### Incentives

Social experiments raise anew the question of whether financial and other kinds of inducements increase or decrease a person's freedom of choice. Is it coercive to offer an income payment of $2,000 per year to a family earning $3,000? Is this an offer so attractive that it can't be turned down, and does it therefore reduce the chances for voluntary consent? Or is it an option that truly enhances the freedom of the poor by enlarging their opportunities for economic choice?

The growing literature on the ethics of incentives makes three points that bear on this discussion. First, incentives are more attractive to some groups than to others. Their compelling power will depend not only on their absolute size or value but on their attractiveness to the recipient. Second, incentives can diminish people's capacity or motivation to act in their own long-term best interest. The experience with financial inducements for sterilization in India provides many examples of individuals who would not have undergone the operation without an inducement (cf. Elder, 1972; Veatch, 1977). From a medical and psychological standpoint some of these, including individuals under 20 and men over 80, should not have risen to the bait. Third, where the potential harms at stake are not grave, restrictions on incentives can pose as many difficulties for human freedom as their use. In its discussion of ethical principles for research the American Psychological Association (1973) recognized the dilemmas posed by incentives:

> Even so conventional an incentive as money may become unduly coercive. A person in dire financial need, for example, the prisoner without money to buy cigarettes, might agree to participate in a hazardous experiment for a very small sum whereas others would ask a thousand times as much. In this case, is the exploitation of the prisoner's special situation not unethical? On the other hand, would it not be even more unethical to diminish the prisoner's freedom by withholding the opportunity (p. 40)?

The ethical debate about incentives in social experiments can be sharpened by considering three aspects of the transaction: (1) what is being bought; (2) from whom; and (3) under what conditions. The first question concerns the actual purchase made—the behaviors, goods, or services that the incentive is designed to elicit. Here we can easily distinguish between purchases that are inherently dangerous to the person or the society, such as the donation of an eye or the acceptance of indentured servitude, and those that are largely risk-free or benign, such as participation in an income-maintenance experiment. Thus it would be totally unethical, as part of a social experiment, to use financial incentives to convince individuals to vote in predetermined ways during a national election. This practice is better known as bribery. Thus, the following principle might apply broadly to social experiments:

> *Principle IX.* The ethical acceptability of incentives decreases to the extent that the object of influence is hazardous to the individual or deleterious to the society. The use of inducements to procure behaviors that are immoral or illegal is ethically unacceptable.

The ethics of incentives further depends on the condition of the individual or group to whom they are offered. The greater the attractiveness of the inducement to the recipients and the fewer the alternatives available to them for obtaining comparable inducements, the greater the danger of coercion. An extreme example would be the offer of a month's supply of heroin to a group of addicts as a means of winning their participation in an experiment on drug abuse. These comments suggest another principle for experiments:

*Principle X.* The stronger the likely attraction of the incentive to the recipients, the greater the need for explanations pointing out the risks of the experiment (if any).

This principle stresses the need for a kind of compensatory education when incentives are likely to be too strong to resist.

Also relevant are the subsidiary conditions attached to the inducements. Foremost among these in the experiments conducted thus far is the connection between the inducements and the research component. In the income maintenance experiments, there are few who would argue that offering income guarantees to poor families is itself unethical. But there are moral problems when, as a condition of continuing to receive income maintenance payments, participants must agree to a series of intrusive interviews. David Kershaw (1975) writes of these experiments:

> In New Jersey the program and research components were separated to the extent that refusal to participate in the interviews had no bearing on participation in the payments segment. In Seattle and Denver, however, subjects must continue to participate in the interviews in order to receive payments. This may constitute excessive inducement, particularly if the subject does not understand the number, length, and complexity of the interviews he must face once he is locked into the treatments (p. 67).

This point can be stated in the form of a general principle:

*Principle XI.* Social experiments relying on inducements should separate the program and research components so that the inducements are not used to pressure unwilling respondents into participation in research.

This principle does not forbid the designers to ask participants to agree to take part in the research function. Rather, the participants should understand that this is a moral agreement that can be renegotiated rather than a binding contract that will be enforced with a carrot turned into a stick. Critics might object that this approach is too soft in that it will allow participants to receive benefits while contributing little to the data generated by the experiment. But research methodologists could counter that the most valid data will come from willing and interested respondents, and that results obtained from the unwilling may contain serious distortions growing out of resentment or low motivation.

## Long-term and Second-order Consequences

Other moral issues arise from the long-term effects and the unanticipated side effects of participation in social experiments. The IMP, for example, lasted three years. During this period the research team took careful readings of the effects of the intervention on the areas of concern and was prepared to compensate subjects for any short-term damages, which seemed to be few. But as David Kershaw (1975), the project director, later pointed out:

> It is the long term that creates problems. Some participants in the income maintenance experiments might have lost their attachment to the labor force after three, four, or five years. Ineligibility for welfare or other sufficiently generous support programs could place them in dire straits. Some families in the housing experiment may find it difficult or impossible to find suitable housing after the experiment, or the experiment may have so inflated the general cost of housing as to strain all of the participants in the future. In the health insurance experiment, although considerable effort is made to insure that subjects keep a policy in force during the experiment, circumstances could arise in which subjects are uninsurable for a disease for which they would have been covered had the experiment not existed. In the education vouchers experiment, schools that cannot exist without the voucher funds may close when the support is withdrawn, leaving the community short of facilities (pp. 61–62).

The experiments may also have unanticipated side effects during the immediate period of their execution. To cite a hypothetical example, the housing experiment may have encouraged some families to move to better quarters without regard for social attachments in their original neighborhood. After the move, the families may experience a sense of loneliness and uprootedness that is not measured in the experiment. Such costs may be as real to the participants as the benefits of improved housing.

I propose three ethical principles for dealing with long-term and second-order consequences of social experiments.

> *Principle XII.* In designing social experiments, planners should take all reasonable steps to anticipate harmful side effects and to arrange the intervention so that these are minimized.

This would mean, in practice, that the planners should conduct a thorough search of the literature and make widespread consultations with experts on the subject to determine the *possible* side effects. In some cases, they might be able to work out a design that will reduce or eliminate such possibilities. At the very least, this exercise will alert the designers to areas that should be monitored during the experiment. This point relates to the next guideline:

> *Principle XIII*. When there is evidence that participants have suffered or are likely to suffer harm as a result of the intervention, the experimenters are obligated to restore the status quo ante.

As a minimum, the participants should be left at least as well off after the experiment as if it had not taken place. Thus, if they have lost their health insurance coverage or their jobs as a direct or indirect result of the intervention, the experimenters are obligated to restore their situation not only to what it was before, but also to what it would have been had they not participated. There is, of course, a certain amount of conjecture required to establish what the situation would have been like without the intervention, but the principle itself seems defensible on the grounds of justice to the participants.

The third principle looks beyond the immediate period of execution to longer-term consequences:

> *Principle XIV*. When there is reason to believe that the intervention will produce harmful consequences extending or arising beyond its conclusion, the experimenters are ethically obligated to continue the monitoring over a reasonable period of time and make appropriate compensation to the participants if harmful effects are found.

In other words, even if the intervention covers only two or three years, the evaluators should follow the participants over a longer period to see if any unintended harms as well as unexpected benefits have been produced. With the experiments done to date, the researchers were forced to say, in effect: "We are reasonably sure that there were no long-term harmful effects from the interventions, but we really don't know." Kershaw (1975) goes further to argue that we not only don't know, but we can't know:

> But the simple fact remains that if there are any long-term harmful effects, is impossible to predict their kind and extent. . . .
> I would not attempt to measure long-term benefits and harms in any systematic way because it is impossible to do so (pp. 62–63).

Coming from someone who was willing to tackle the extraordinary complexities posed by short-term evaluations, this statement reflects a surprising lack of nerve. While Kershaw is undoubtedly right that causal attribution becomes increasingly shaky with the passage of time, there are many possibilities for checking long-term effects. A well-designed follow-up survey should have little difficulty in determining whether recipients of income maintenance payments dropped out of the labor force with greater than normal frequency after the experiment. These studies could also assess the extent of other possible difficulties thought to be related to the intervention, such as ineligibility for welfare in the case of income maintenance experiments or problems of insurability for participants in health experiments. I see no more methodological difficulties in this kind of follow-up than in most surveys involving repeated interviews with the same respondents (panel studies). One study, in fact, obtained excellent information from college graduates some 25 years after the original interviews (Newcomb, Koenig, Flacks, & Warwick, 1967). At the very least, this kind of assessment, which need not involve all of the original participants, should be able to rule out the possibility of harmful effects. If there are no differences in labor force participation between recipients of income maintenance payments and others like them, it would be difficult to make a case that the experiment had produced significant long-term damage on employment.

## Disclosure and Confidentiality

Participants in sample surveys and other kinds of social research are commonly told that the information they provide will be treated as confidential. The difficulty is that unless this information is connected to the census and similar government operations, it enjoys no legal protection or privilege. The resulting ethical dilemmas are well illustrated in the IMP. Participants in this and related experiments were informed that the data provided would be kept strictly confidential and would not be released without their written permission, except as required by law. However, a prosecuting attorney bent on exposing welfare cheating requested information about individual participants in the IMP. Given the nature of the experiment, which prohibited, but did not audit for, acceptance of welfare payments, the participants were handy targets for investigation. Although the IMP was sponsored by a government agency, the data enjoyed no legal privilege and so were vulnerable to subpoena. The matter was finally settled out of court when the project agreed to provide the prosecutor with the names of income recipients and actual amounts received from the project (Kershaw & Small, 1972). Subsequently, the U.S. General Accounting Office (GAO) attempted to audit and verify the interviews from the IMP. Citing their promises of confidentiality, the project staff refused to release the names of respondents so that they could be reinterviewed to check the data. They did, however, agree to release computer data from the interviews with identifying information on individuals deleted. Once again the GAO, as an agency of the government, had a formal right to subpoena the data, but backed off in the face of resistance from the staff. Had it or the prosecutor persisted, the research staff would have faced the difficult choice between a jail term and releasing information that might place individual respondents in jeopardy.

The cardinal ethical questions raised by these examples are whether respondents should be told of the lack of legal protection for the data and, if so, how. I suggest the following guideline to deal with these questions:

> *Principle XV*. In the data-collection operations of social experiments, respondents should be given clear, accurate statements about the meaning and limits of confidentiality. The greater the jeopardy posed by the information itself, and the greater the chances of subpoena or audit of individual data, the more explicit the explanation required.

This principle argues that respondents and participants should always be given an accurate picture of the confidentiality of information from and about them, but that the level of detail should increase with the risks inherent in the data and the probability of forced disclosure. Donald Campbell and his associates (1976) offer these suggestions for possible explanations:

> Where the material solicited involves no obvious jeopardy to respondents, a vague, general promise of confidentiality is acceptable. E.g., "These interviews will be summarized in group statistics so that no one will learn of your individual answers. All interviews will be kept confidential. There is a remote chance that you will be contacted later to verify the fact that I actually conducted this interview and have conducted it completely and honestly."
>
> Where full and honest answers to the question could jeopardize a respondent's interests in the case of a subpoena, the respondent should be so informed. E.g., "These interviews are being made to provide average statistical evidence in which individual answers will not be identified or identifiable. We will do everything in our power to keep your answer completely confidential. Only if so ordered by Court and Judge would we turn over individually identified interviews to any other group or government agency. We believe that this is very unlikely to happen, because of the assurance of cooperation we have received from _____ " (p. 14).

A great practical limitation to these suggestions is that interviewers are most reluctant to open the Pandora's box of nonconfidentiality, particularly when they are being paid by the interview. In most surveys, it is hard enough to win a respondent's cooperation without evoking the triple spectre of court, judge, and jail. We may safely assume, therefore, that the more detailed the explanations required about the risks of nonconfidentiality, the less stomach the interviewers will have to make them. Thus, as distasteful as this step may be to the research organization, it may be necessary to carry out reinterviews that cover not only the substance of the survey but also the explanations given. And there is no guarantee of success, for even with the most detailed and accurate explanations some respondents will completely misinterpret what was said. Perhaps all that we can ask is a reasonable effort to alert respondents to the potential hazards at stake, and particularly strong efforts when inherent risks or the chances of subpoena are greater than usual.

## THE LIMITS OF ETHICAL CONCERN

At this point the advocate of social experiments might rightly wonder if, with this spate of ethical principles, guidelines, and worries, it will ever be possible to run another experiment. The less patient might add: "Isn't this entire exercise really making moral mountains out of experimental molehills? Isn't it a kind of liberal breast beating that would foreclose not only most social experiments but much of social research?" These concerns are well taken and bring us back to perhaps the most fundamental ethical point in the entire discussion. This is whether, on balance, the social and individual benefits of benign social experiments, such as those conducted to date, do not outweigh the risks outlined in this paper. As suggested earlier, there is no answer to this question, but it should be allowed to stand as a continuous reminder of the need for perspective on the ethics of social experimentation. There is, on the one hand, a clear danger that ethical solicitude can be used as a roadblock to very worthwhile and essentially benign experiments. It would be most unfortunate, I feel, if the entire notion of experimentation were to be put on ice until a watertight code of ethics is devised. But it would be equally unfortunate if the argument that social experiments are a useful and not very harmful source of information on policy were used to squelch ethical debate. If the experiments to date provide no cause for alarm, they do suggest grounds for legitimate concern. Perhaps the best course is to move ahead with further experimentation as well as ethical deliberation about experiments, with constant contact between the two.

## REFERENCES

American Psychological Association. *Ethical principles in the conduct of research with human participants*. Washington, D.C.: American Psychological Association, 1973.

Brown, P. G. Informed consent in social experimentation: Some cautionary notes. In A. M. Rivlin & P. M. Timpane (Eds.), *Ethical and legal issues of social experimentation*. Washington, D.C.: Brookings Institution, 1975.

Campbell, D. T., et al. Protection of the rights and interests of human subjects in program evaluation, social indicators, social experimentation, and statistical analyses based upon administrative records. Preliminary sketch. Northwestern University, January, 1976, mimeo.

Elder, R. E., Jr. *Development administration in a north Indian state: The family planning program in Uttar Pradesh.* Chapel Hill, N.C.: Carolina Population Center, Monograph No. 18, 1972.

Gramlich, E. M., & Orr, L. L. The ethics of social experimentation. In A. M. Rivlin & P. M. Timpane (Eds.), *Ethical and legal issues of social experimentation.* Washington, D.C. Brookings Institution, 1975.

Kershaw, D. N. Comments. In A. M. Rivlin & P. M. Timpane (Eds.), *Ethical and legal issues of social experimentation.* Washington, D.C.: Brookings Institution, 1975.

Kershaw, D. N., & Small, J. C. Data confidentiality and privacy: Lessons from the New Jersey negative income tax experiment. *Public Policy,* 1972, *20,* 257–280.

Newcomb, T. M., Koenig, K., Flacks, R., & Warwick, D. P. *Persistence and change: Bennington College and its students after twenty-five years.* New Yok: Wiley, 1967.

Rivlin, A. M., & Timpane, P. M. (Eds.). *Ethical and legal issues of social experimentation.* Washington, D.C.: Brookings Institution, 1975.

Schelling, T. C. General comments. In A. M. Rivlin & P. M. Timpane (Eds.), *Ethical and legal issues of social experimentation.* Washington, D.C.: Brookings Institution, 1975.

Veatch, R. M. Ethical principles in medical experimentation. In A. M. Rivlin & P. M. Timpane (Eds.), *Ethical and legal issues of social experimentation.* Washington, D.C.: Brookings Institution, 1975.

Veatch, R. M. Governmental incentives: Ethical issues at stake. *Studies in Family Planning, 1977, 8,* 100–108.

Warwick, D. P., & Lininger, C. A. *The sample survey: Theory and practice.* New York: McGraw-Hill, 1975.

# VII
# FEDERALLY FUNDED HOUSING PROGRAMS

# 14
# COMMUNITY GROUP AND CONSULTANT INTERVENE IN FEDERALLY CONTROLLED HOUSING

**CARROL W. WAYMON**

The California School of Professional Psychology
and
Mirimar Community College

## INTRODUCTION AND BACKGROUND

This chapter is about the attempts of a small group of black people and their hired consultant to acquire some federally controlled housing units and rehabilitate them for public occupancy. This group of twelve, referred to as the Corp, sought to obtain a federal grant through HUD (Housing and Urban Development, a department of the federal goverment) under a HUD program provision known as "Section 235." This provision is designed to assist local citizen's groups that have nonprofit corporation status in acquiring and rehabilitating housing units and renting or selling them, under tightly controlled government guidelines and regulations, to low- or medium-income families. The Corp was composed of "ordinary, little" people who had lived in the city for many years and were residents of the community in which the units were located.

At the time I entered the picture, the Corp had been operating for several months and was bogged down in all the typical red tape of processing the many required forms and applications, securing bids from contractors, and rounding up other resources. The Corp had exhausted its own knowledge and resources and was becoming progressively discouraged, partly because of its own internal exhaustion, but mostly from the pressures of the establishment, which held all the power over the group; that is, the Veterans' Administration, HUD, city officials, and financial institutions controlled both the units and the means by which these units could be acquired by the Corp.

It was apparent that the roles and functions of the many parties involved had become unclear; at times they were not only confusing, but also overlapping. It was understood and accepted, however, that the primary role of the Corp was that of an intervenor designed to break the cycle of poverty and economic exploitation externally imposed upon one group interested in initiating a federally funded, special housing program located in the heart of the black community. The Corp had been formed initially to accomplish this general goal, which was later translated into specific concrete objectives.

The Corp, however, was more than just a group of men and women seeking to package data to justify their being granted funds to implement a housing program. As intervenor, this group had to learn to play many different roles—some conflicting at times—while remaining acceptable as the recipient group for funds to be granted by the very establishment it sought to shake up. (The drama of this group's functioning as intervenor is discussed later in this chapter.)

It became increasingly clear to the Corp that it would need some outside technical assitance if it were going to get its project off the ground at all. So it hired the first of four consultants. The first three were dismissed for various incompatibilities between the consultants and the Corp. I was the fourth consultant hired, and I worked with the Corp successfully for a little over a year. As their technical advisor, my major roles were to provide them with technical knowledge, methods, and techniques for accomplishing specific tasks; to help them to facilitate the process involved and inherent in this kind of enterprise; and to assist them in program formulation, planning, and implementation. In general, I was to be their expert in know-how that related to the tedious and assiduous chores of moving the powers-that-be to effect the acquistion and subsequent rehabilitation of the desired housing units. Later in this chapter, I will elaborate on some of the specific functions in my role as consultant and discuss briefly a few selected dilemmas encountered by me and the Corp.

Despite the fact that the Corp had engaged and dismissed three other consultants when I was hired, I found them involved in what I call "agonizing group self-evaluation." Essentially, this was a period right after the group had, in effect, given up and decided to forget it all and go their separate ways. They had done this, but not for long, because the problem they were seeking to solve was heavy on their minds and each member of the Corp lived in physical sight of the housing units they were seeking to secure. So the group never really let go, and after being apart for a short while, they predictably rejoined.

It seems inportant to point out that this analysis of an actual human interaction is made after our concluding formal and official contractual associations. From volumes of notes and letters and minutes, I have reconstructed many of the events that occurred and have given logic and sequential order to the events and meetings that took place with the Corp and with me, and to the relationship between me and the Corp. But, of course, things did not actually happen according to a blueprint drawn up by anyone, nor did any of us ever sit down and make a detailed analysis of our own feelings, emotions, or philosophical stances on a scale of comparative values and points given to each item. We behaved, at the time, in a manner deemed appropriate and proper within the context of the objectives to be achieved at that time.

This is equally true with respect to my own record keeping: I did not write down at the time the questions that are posed herein in the discussions on ethics, morality or ethnic ideology, or survival strategies. The logic and order given to the questions and to this analysis throughout is imposed by me after the fact and was not an inherent element of our operations. This is especially significant with reference to the relationship between the Corp and me. All of these and other questions arose within a specific context of events and not as isolated items unrelated to events and conditions that had occurred previously or those anticipated for the future. We went about working together on this project. This meant conducting regular business meetings: reading minutes and reports, hearing committee recommendations, directing and authorizing people to take particular action on specific issues—just as all groups conduct meetings and carry on their business. Yet, on paper and in this analysis, it is necessary to give order and logic to this experience so that the reader may best understand and appreciate what actually happened. After accepting this imposed logic and order and the need for it, the reader may more fully appreciate the subjective experience of the analysis as simply a human involvement, a human interaction.

There were no major conflicts between the Corp and me, no power struggles, no bickering or disputes. From the beginning, there was a strong identification: we were on the same frequency, as it were, in terms of basic beliefs for the need for the project and the anticipated battles with some of the establishment representatives in our attempt to secure their assistance in implementing the project. In reading those discussions about my own ethical position and my inner struggle for answers to the questions I posed for myself, it should be remembered that I have chosen to present the issues in this particular style in an attempt to relate the human encounter with its dynamics as they always seem to operate between and among groups of individuals engaged in any enterprise. From the beginning, we recognized that such dynamics were present in the individuals as a group and in me as a consultant, and from time to time, we openly discussed some of the dynamics that were, at that moment, relevant and pertinent to achieving the objectives before us.

## DESCRIPTION OF THE CORP'S SELF-EVALUATION

The following is a description of the phases through which the Corp passed as it finally resolved to move. Of course these phases were not clear-cut, mutually exclusive time or activities frames; the description is simply my way of trying to capture verbally, in retrospect, some of the operating dynamics of a group experience.

### Phase I: Awareness of the Problem and Resulting Frustration

Phase I may be described and delineated in any number of ways and in many terms. The essential conditions in this phase were:

- An awareness and concern that created a level of deep frustration and dissatisfaction about this housing project.
- The common experience that occurred daily with these Corp members. In general, they recognized that there was a problem, without, at this time, knowing what it was; in this initial stage, the Corp was unable to describe except in general terms what was causing the frustration. This was the "complaining and bitching stage" of subjective awareness, which led immediately into Phase II.

### Phase II: Discussion and Definition of the Problem

This phase was typified by much talking about the problem and what ought to be done about it. The talk remained in general terms at this stage. What seemed to be happening was that the concerned individuals began to define the conditions generating the complaints in Phase I as a problem, and to associate the problem with some power base: the establishment, the federal government, and so forth.

It was also during this phase that a consensus was reached that some unspecified thing must be done about the problem, and through the talk and initiation of a few action-determined individuals, an agreement emerged to take action. (In our everyday experience, this is the moment someone says, "Let's call a meeting and do something about it.") The "it" is significant here, because later, in meetings and in interactions of the Corp members, the "it" was to be escalated into a series of conditions and to take on the character of a constellation of problems. In fact, much of the initial frustration sprang from *not* knowing the components of this "it." In subsequent meetings and planning sessions of the Corp, many people commonly became disillusioned and even left the group because of additional frustrations that mounted as the now-small group struggled with trying to define the problems in concrete and operational terms that would allow for concrete and incremental solutions and measurements. It was the dynamics operative at this stage that led imperceptibly into Phases III and IV.

### Phases III and IV: Implementation Plans and Actions

These two phases are grouped together because the line is muddy between the planning and the doing. Within the context of Model Cities and other government-funded projects these two phases are often programmed as distinct and separate stages. Sometimes, funds for these programs are allocated, but staff and other resources are hired accordingly as one stage ends and the other begins.

These latter programs are designed to operate in well-planned and logical order. Outside such programs, however, as in this project, the behavior was centered around pressing problems and did not follow such logical and organized stages.

Phase III was intermittently percieved as an action phase and as a time for planning because of the nature of the meetings and the production of plans, minutes, or other documents. In addition, committees were typically formed or a structure of some nature was created. Someone also took on the task of telephoning people and arranging the details of the business required to keep the group's momentum at a level high enough to maintain the interest and involvement of those who had to be active in order to carry out the projected plans. However, they were painfully aware that the action required to carry out the specific solution was of a different order. These phases are summarized below:

| Phase I | Phase II | Phases III and IV |
|---|---|---|
| Complaints | Articulation of the problem | Implementation plans |
| Frustrations | Expression of ideas about what to do | Schedules and action |
| Awareness | | |

During Phases I and II, the Corp sought additional members from practically every segment of the wider community through personal contacts and formal meetings announced in the mass media. At times, many people expressed a definite interest in joining the group. But as events unfolded and frustrations mounted, most newcomers dropped out, leaving twelve members. Nine of these twelve were originators of the project.

Attempts to engage wider community involvement were significant, since at one point HUD required concrete evidence of these attempts as a qualification for further consideration of the grant proposal. Such data as meeting notices, minutes, and even notes from conversations related to these attempts were used to meet HUD requirements. Thus, the Corp could legitimately claim that it had tried to broaden its base in the community: it was the latter that had decided not to become involved. In addition, the Corp became frustrated occasionally as it attempted to engage specific community leaders to work in its behalf without pay, when it sought bids from local contractors without being able to guarantee these contractors any work, and when trying to locate bidders who were acceptable to all parties.

These experiences served to further convince the Corp that it should try to make it on its own. As a result of all of these attempts, some fruitful and others not, the Corp, with the assistance of the consultant, spent several hours developing a position paper on the issue of rights and power, which was used internally as a base for public stances on matters relating to involvement, strategy, and ethics (although the term "ethics" was never used). These were the dynamics operating within the Corp. But there was still the city out there, the scene and target of the program itself. To understand the total context of what was happening within the Corp, it is necessary to place the Corp within the broader framework of that city.

## Bright City

### Background

    This Southern California city, which I call "Bright City," may be described as typical. There are large populations of blacks and Chicanos (Mexican-Americans) and smaller numbers of other racial and ethnic groups. Most of these racial and ethnic groups live in pockets located in the bad areas of town, with all of the other conditions concomitant with living in any large urban area. There is no point in spelling out all of these here; they are known to everyone.

    Bright City has a progressive-thinking mayor and a reasonably liberal city council (as described and accepted by most of the spokesmen of these racial and ethnic groups as well as by ordinary residents). The power establishment had worked cooperatively with the action-oriented community groups and with the many community agencies, for example, Model Cities, War on Poverty Agency, and most of the non-government-sponsored groups and projects.

    The city was aware of the important of a close association with all segments of the community because Bright City had recently experienced several open confrontations of a racial nature, all ignited around either school desegregation and busing or around typical police-youth incidents. When viewed within the context of such problems as racial confrontations and urban blight over the past eight years, there was a consensus among the many activist groups and others that this city's movers and powerholders, including public officials, were supportive and were in a mood to encourage, if not initiate, programs that spoke directly to these urban problems.

### Bright City's Housing Pattern

    Bright City's housing pattern had changed only slightly over the past two decades, not so much because those responsible for and in control of the decisions affecting housing had planned any changes or facilitated them, but because of emerging conditions related to the economic and social mobility among the black and Chicano populations throughout the United States in general and in Bright City in particular.

    The Chicano clusters were practically all concentrated in two locations, on opposite sides of town, and contiguous with a few smaller enclaves of Asiatic, Filipino, and other racial and ethnic people. Black people, on the other hand, continued to live in large enclaves on the opposite sides of town from the Chicanos in "their town." But unlike most of the other large minority groups, the blacks also lived in the many well-to-do rings around Bright City and its suburbs. On an individual basis, black families resided in all areas of metropolitan Bright City. But this degree of freedom for blacks had come only after the city had been rocked a few years earlier by a series of lawsuits relative to instances of restrictive covenants,[1] which in Bright City, as in other cities, were used as a major weapon to maintain racial and ethnic ghettos. Supported by local court orders, many blacks simply moved into previously all-white areas. The number of such families is small when compared to the total black population of Bright City, but large enough to forge new patterns of thinking and perceiving among black people in this city. Despite this, however, the vast majority of black people live and die in Bright City's "Black Belt."

Bright City continues to have a relatively large population of youths. Black youths enjoy only a limited number of outlets for their energies and interests. Especially true for those black youths who live near or in the area in which housing units are located, this simply aggravated the conditions and problems facing the Corp.

And, thus, the stage was set for the Corp to play out an intriguing drama in Bright City, California.

## STRUCTURE OF FEDERAL HOUSING POLICY

Housing is a key to improvement in a family's economic condition. Home ownership remains one of the most important avenues by which Americans acquire financial capital and leadership status. The tax advantages, equity accumulation, and appreciation in real estate all enable homeowners to build economic assets. From the assets, families may educate the children, expand the number of children, expand business enterprises, and make possible more opportunities for leisure activities. "Nearly two of every three majority group families are homeowners, but less than two of every five nonwhite families own their homes" (Civil Rights Commission, 1973). Thus, most nonwhite families are not in a position to enjoy all of the advantages of home ownership.

It is the official policy of the United States to provide fair housing opportunities for all of its citizens throughout the country. The home and the neighborhood are the physical world in which families live, raise their children, and build life-long relationships that give meaning to their lives. Few rights are as basic as that of acquiring a home of one's own choice. So basic is this right that Congress, in writing fair housing legislation into the nation's body of civil rights laws, used specific language in this 1968 Civil Rights Law relative to fair housing:

---

[1] A racially restrictive covenant was a written agreement in which the buyer of a house or property promised not to sell, rent, or transfer property to families of a specific race, ethnic group, or religion.

It is the policy of the United States to provide, within constitutional limitations, for fair housing throughout the United States (Civil Rights Commission, 1973).

Housing was the last of the major civil rights areas to receive congressional consideration, despite its overriding importance.

Housing is of special significance in securing civil rights in other areas, since residential patterns segregated along racial and ethnic lines render ineffective the many programs and efforts to enjoy equal opportunity in education and employment. The effects of these residential patterns are felt most directly by whites and nonwhites in our urban centers. Two of the regularly publicized issues that crystallize this interwoven relationship are school busing and job discrimination. The cities and metropolitan areas are divided into separate enclaves by racial groups as well as by economic factors. White and nonwhite families actually live apart and are mostly strangers to each other.

## The Role of the Federal Government

In practice, the government is a party in every decision made in the area of housing because of zoning laws and other prerequisites to building or restructuring houses, roads, and the like. Thus, it may be appropriate to briefly review the structure and role of the government as it relates to housing. There are at least five governmental mandates for fair and equal housing:

1. The Federal Fair Housing Law, Title VIII of the Civil Rights Act of 1968.
2. The Civil Rights Act of 1964, Title VI, which forbids discrimination in a variety of federally assisted housing programs, including low-rent public housing and urban renewal.
3. President Kennedy's Executive Order of November, 1962, which forbids discrimination in housing where funds are secured through federally assisted programs.
4. The 1968 United States Supreme Court decision in Jones v. Mayer Co. (392 U.S. 409), barring discrimination in *all* private and public housing.
5. Fair housing laws in more than half the states and in thousands of U.S. municipalities.

## The Legacy of the Past

Federal, state, and local governments have always been active participants in the housing industry. In theory, decisions as to where housing will be constructed, to whom it will be sold, under what conditions, and how it will be financed are made by private parties: the real estate broker, the builder, the mortgage lender or other financing institution, and the private owner. In practice, however, government is and always has been the key participant in such decisions: the government lends financial and other support to the so-called private housing industry.

### The Veteran's Administration (VA) and
### the Federal Housing Administration (FHA)

The homeowner can build only by complying with building codes, zoning, and other controlling local ordinances. Once these ordinances are complied with, the federal government alone controls the factors that determine whether the building commences or not. The VA and FHA are the federal government's agencies through which housing regulations are operated in the following manner:

1. The federal government gives the builder of homes the advantages and benefits of underwriting insurance through FHA and VA programs, and the builder must meet certain professional construction standards established by the VA and FHA.
2. The mortgage-lending agency is regulated by one or more state or federal agencies. It also receives benefits because its accounts and deposits are backed by the federal government.
3. The real estate broker is licensed by the state.
4. The National Association of Real Estate Brokers (NAREB) has influenced the housing industry perhaps more than any other one entity, except the federal government itself:
   a. Only those who belong to NAREB are called "realtors."
   b. The membership of NAREB has always been nearly all white.
   c. The manuals and textbooks of NAREB have been used in training real estate brokers. In 1922, NAREB published its "Principles of Real Estate Practices," which emphasized "racial types as very likely to diminish the value of other property." Another textbook of NAREB stated that black families were a threat to property values.

While some of the policies and practices of NAREB, mortgage lenders, and the government have changed in recent years, many of the effects of their narrow and discriminatory policies remain and account for significant problems in housing in our urban center.

### Specific Role of the Federal Government

In the 1930s, the Federal Government for the first time became actively engaged in the field of housing:

- *1932:* The Federal Home Loan Bank Board (FHLBB) was created to assist savings and loan associations.

- *1933:*     The Home Owners Loan Corporation (HOLC) was established to assist the refinancing of small home mortgages in foreclosure during the Depression.
- *1934:*     The FHA was created to protect the mortgage lender from financial loss caused by the inability of a borrower to keep up the payments on the mortgage and was thus intended as an inducement to the lender to make more money available for housing construction. (The VA, often referred to as FHA's "sister agency," instituted its own housing insurance program after World War II. Some years later, the VA and FHA were merged in those functions in the area of housing insurance guaranty programs.)

Many activities took place between 1934 and 1948. The most significant action was that of the Supreme Court, which ruled in 1948 that the restrictive covenant provision was unenforceable in the courts. The restrictive covenant was the tool used by property owners to exclude "undesirables" from owning their property by writing into the titles exclusionary clauses, which in turn became binding on all subsequent owners or occupants of the properties. Between 1948 and the Executive Order of 1962, several court cases were settled in the direction of providing legal protection for citizens' rights to purchase housing of their choice.

Most major cities over the past decades were the scene of racial confrontations and the target of legal actions brought against them by groups seeking redress because of alleged housing discrimination based on race. Large cities accept these intermittent flare-ups as inevitable and expected. Numerous smaller cities have also experienced racial confrontations in many areas, but have seldom been projected into the national spotlight. These smaller cities have settled their disputes, relegated them to the arena of "another local problem" solved, and continued as before.

Large urban-blighted cities such as Los Angeles, Chicago, Detroit, New York, and Philadelphia are accepted by the general population as breeding places for fights over segregated housing and other kinds of racial confrontations. But Bright City is not just another urban, segregated American city. It has been the subject of national concern for the past eight years or so, as it struggled to rearrange its resources to comply with the Supreme Court's orders to desegregate its schools. Bright City experienced several racial riots of minor and major intensity during these past eight years. This city, perhaps more than any other in California, except perhaps Pasadena, delayed in coming to terms with the serious problems of racial segregation in housing, until forced to do so by a series of court orders. Yet, unlike Pasadena and other large California cities, once having been ordered to desegregate its schools, Bright City moved with dispatch to comply and, in the context of the mood of the times, did so in a comprehensive manner: the School District desegregated itself, instituted special busing on a city-wide basis, and rearranged certain schools into clusters by grade levels in implementing the order. For Bright City, such events and bold initiatives by school and other public officials were indeed nothing short of "radicalism."

These early battles in Bright City were fought around the issues of school desegregation and the controversy of school busing. They served, however, to highlight the importance of equal housing opportunity, which is still considered basic to the exercising of all other civil rights. Residential segregation undermines efforts to implement policies in equal employment and educational opportunities. The controversy over busing in Bright City was intimately linked to the pattern of residential segregation along racial and ethnic lines, because the city's schoolchildren had to be transported at public expense in order to convey them from segregated neighborhoods to integrated or desegregated schools. With these school and busing issues in the foreground, the stage was set for different community groups to directly confront the issues of residential blight, segregation, and economic exploitation. The Corp was such a group, and it was ready to move.

But this meant that the Corp had to effect direct and indirect associations with all the parties, in and out of Bright City, that had anything to do with the project now being considered by the Corp. Although the Corp was aware that it existed, that it had an interest in housing, and that it had formulated elaborate plans in that area, no one else knew of the Corp. So the elements of the first giant step for the Corp were to:

- Map out plans to gather basic data on the units they had established as a target.
- Make contact with those who controlled these units and determine their status, legally and otherwise.
- Decide on a timetable for initiating a master plan of approach.
- Determine what steps to take once the basic data were in its hands.

From the Corp files, minutes, and notes and from members' memories, the following seems to be a fair representation of the data the Corp uncovered initially in relation to the history of the housing units it was interested in. It must be added that no written records had been kept of these developments as they had unfolded over the previous years. The Corp found that:

1. Originally, the 280 housing units belonged to a private developer who rented and sold to veterans, which meant that the veterans negotiated their rental or purchase transactions for these units through the VA. (The VA housing benefits are administered through the FHA, which protects the mortgage lender from financial loss.) The developer automatically became involved with the VA and FHA the moment he agreed to rent and sell to veterans, which also meant that each unit had to meet specified building codes and other federal government standards.

2. As a government policy, the VA became the mortgage holder for those units sold to veterans; this was not true for those who were renting.

3. The FHA became the holder of the mortgage insurance on those properties being purchased by the veterans (through the GI Bill) from the developer. (This is the function of the FHA.)

4. The private developer continued to own the units being rented and those not purchased. When sold, the property then actually belonged to the VA, although it was occupied by and paid for through regular monthly payments by the veteran and his or her family. This is similar to the arrangement in conventional loans: instead of a bank or savings and loan association holding the mortgage after having paid the seller off, the VA held the mortgage, protected by the FHA insurance guarantee provisions.

5. The Department of Housing and Urban Development was established to implement the 1968 Fair Housing Law, with its creation provided for as part of the 1968 Civil Rights Act. (This department [HUD] has regional offices throughout the nation, just as FHA and VA do, and in some instances, FHA and HUD share the same physical offices and regional boundaries.)

6. These units, long ago abandoned, and now owned or controlled by the VA, were available.

7. The Corp could come in and talk to the VA about their availability.

And so began the Corp intervention, which took place against a backdrop of interactions between these entities, on the one hand, and this group of citizens of Bright City, on the other.

### The History of the Housing Units

These 280 housing units, through a series of sales, trade-offs, subdivision, and resale, had ended up as two separate clusters: 180 in one and 100 in the other. The intervention centered only around the 100 units and two small vacant lots, which at one time had units on them. Specifically, these 100 units ended up being owned by the VA as a result of the owners' (buyer-occupants') abandoning them and, thus, forfeiting their payments. Since they were being purchased through VA benefits, this meant that the VA was totally and solely responsible for the units. These same units had gone through the cycle once earlier, but the VA had succeeded in reselling them to a second private developer. After refurbishing them, this second private developer had also obtained approval to rent and sell them as "VA-approved." They included one-, two-, and three-bedroom units; a garage or carport; a yard of predeterminized size with provision for clotheslines; and concrete walkways.

This last private developer was unable to keep the units rented. Less than one-third were ever rented, and these few were constantly changing tenants. Within six months after the last private developer had taken them over, *all* of the units were again vacant. The units were all vandalized regularly, until the Corp began its actions, which from the start included patrolling these 100 units.

Thus, within the heart of one of Bright City's ghettos stood units that were once occupied but that were now vacant and that were the site of ugliness, vandalism, and potential drug use and other undesirable or nuisance behavior. The nearest VA and FHA offices were over two hours away. On the other hand, the police and fire departments of Bright City were constant visitors to these units and were the immediate symbols of the establishment to the ghetto residents. The Corp, then, was composed of a small group of frustrated, angry, but determined, ordinary working men and women, unlettered, and mostly naïve about the red tape and other necessary procedures they would be faced with in just learning how to go about getting a program started.

For over twelve years, neighborhood residents had watched these presently abandoned houses change ownership several times through the strange cooperation of the federal government and private industry, while daily experiencing constant surveillance of their own neighborhood by local fireman and policemen, knowing intuitively that nothing was being done to improve this state of affairs. This group concluded that they and the community had had enough of this, and the group decided to do something about it. Obviously, the many, many other questions inherent in this kind of venture were equally crucial and immediate. They were all asked, in different ways, by different persons, and addressed in one way or another over the next year and a half.

The group began their effort by seeking information on what steps to take internally and externally in order to effect the initial requirement of owning the units legally. The group had heard that there were government programs that allowed groups or clubs or organizations to buy or build houses. No one in the group had any idea of what these programs were, but they did find one government program related to their expressed desire; it was referred to as "the 235 Program."

The 235 Program, as well as a few others, was provided for as part of the 1968 Housing and Urban Development Act (HUD-Act). Essentially, it was to be an interest-subsidy program, authorizing the government to pay up to the difference between the monthly payment of the written terms of the mortgage and the amount of those monthly payments, if the mortgage were let at a 1 percent interest rate. This amounts to having the government underwrite monthly mortgage payments for low-income families unable to keep up high-interest mortgages. This allows poor, and especially some minority, families to purchase their own homes. At least, this was the expressed intent of the legislators who passed this 1968 HUD Act. However, the FHA's administration of the 235 Program has not lived up to this original intent, according to the Civil Rights Commission's findings. In its 1970 study to determine the effectiveness of the 235 Program in opening up housing opportunities for minorities and other low-income families, the Commission found that most of the 235 Program's housing was constructed in the suburbs.

The neighborhood group learned that certain procedural conditions had to be met just in order to apply for participation in this 235 Program, which it now had decided to pursue. The group began these steps by agreeing among themselves to become a California corporation and by engaging an attorney to draw up the proper papers and complete the process of securing the necessary papers for the group's becoming a nonprofit California corporation. The group, now a corporation calling itself the Corp, learned that to meet the minimum requirements for the 235 Program, it had to demonstrate that it had the capability to administer such a program. At the time I entered the picture, the Corp had fulfilled all the initial legal, governmental, and organizational procedures necessary. The Corp had:

- Become incorporated as a nonprofit organization.
- Elected officers and assigned responsibilities.
- Broadened its base of community participation.
- Secured proper recommendations from city and other public and private officials.
- Secured financial commitments from local banks.
- Drawn up plans for rehabilitating the units.
- Hired a qualified consultant experienced in the area of housing.
- Held meetings with residents surrounding the units.
- Produced a master plan for advertising, marketing, and selling all units in time phases.
- Begun a homeowners' counseling-center class.
- Organized a youth patrol.

In addition, the Corp held numerous meetings; made many personal contacts; and produced volumes of documents and application forms, letters, replies to letters, and so forth. In short, the Corp met all the technical requirements required by HUD, FHA, and the VA to administer a 235 Program, including a separate homeowners' counseling center. But the ultimate question remained: how could a group of ordinary black citizens—very poor housewives and working men and women of little education—eventually gain control of the 100 units and, through a nonprofit corporation, receive HUD grants under the 235 or 236 title, rehabilitate, and sell these units?

## THE CORP AS INTERVENOR

### The Intervention Sequence

The Corp had begun what eventually turned out to be a long, arduous, frustrating, and ceaseless battle with the federal government by obtaining information kits from the local Model Cities offices of Bright City. This information kit gave general directions for seeking government funds for the 235 Program. The first procedure for the Corp was to become incorporated as a nonprofit organization in California. But the Corp had neither the funds nor the personnel to take even this first step. This created the first big dilemma for the

Corp, because at the time the Corp became aware of the existence of these HUD programs, there were two immediate deadline dates to be met if the Corp wished to be considered for that fiscal year's funding. In addition, there were many other procedural steps to be followed simultaneously. At this time, the Corp, without any outside or professional assistance, met and decided upon an overall general plan, briefly summarized as follows:

1.  Organize as a formal corporation, with appropriate officers and assignments.
2.  Direct the Corp president to contact and set up a meeting with:
    a.  The regional HUD office.
    b.  The regional FHA office, located in a city several miles away from the HUD office.
    c.  The local (Bright City) Justice Department Community Relations representative.
3.  Authorize the Corp president to call the HUD office in Washington, D.C., to inquire about any additional procedures not covered in the information kits.
4.  Meet every night to review progress and study the guidelines of all federally funded housing programs and to modify all plans as their feedback indicated.

### The First Big Wall

The Corp followed these general plans and were immediately instructed to file all application forms; they did this even though they were not yet incorporated: this fact was known to the director of the local FHA office, who so instructed them. At this time, they were also told that they must first get the VA to agree to sell them the units *before* any further discussions or steps could take place between the FHA and the Corp. All of these directions were given over the telephone; none of the meetings had, as yet, taken place. The Corp president then set up meetings as instructed (see the list above), and on most occasions, at least three of the members attended.

The first meeting in January was with HUD personnel assigned to the 235 Program. The HUD counselor directed them to the regional FHA office, which they visited the same day. In turn, the FHA directed them to contact the VA in Washington, D.C., and after getting clearance there, to contact the regional VA office and obtain a letter from them that in essence indicated that "the VA agrees to sell the subject units to the Corp, provided the Corp meets all the qualifications to be a sponsor of a 235 Program, and provided HUD and FHA so certifies them within the next 45 days." To the Corp, this was a bombshell and a delaying tactic, since by this time all the office personnel dealing with the Corp were quite aware of what such a "certification" entailed and that the Corp was only then completing its own formal organization. It was obvious by this time that the Corp needed professional technical assistance. Nine full weeks had passed since they had first met to draw up their general plans, and they were still not incorporated and were without funds to pay for services of any nature. They made contact with the mayor, who wrote a letter supporting the efforts of the Corp. A prominent minister and attorneys had agreed to lend their individual assistance. The minister, the Reverend Seaton, contacted the poverty program director, and, together, they arranged to have an attorney draw up all the papers for incorporation. The poverty program director allowed the Corp to use his office duplicating machines, and, after work hours, he authorized the use of his office for meetings and conferences with the local representatives of the Justice Department and other interested citizens who had, by this time, learned of the problems of the Corp. The general mood of city officials, community youth, organizations, and local residents was essentially one of attempting to facilitate the process of helping small neighborhood groups help themselves.

## Some Funds Are Found

For the next month or so, all the Corp's activities came to a stand still, except those aimed at securing enough funds to pay for technical assistance. They were fortunate, in that they experienced their first small, concrete success: one of the local poverty program directors, with whom several members of the group had been associated, was informed of their plight and arranged to have them receive a grant of $3,500. This, too, was contingent upon their securing the services of a consultant and of their becoming incorporated. They agreed to these conditions and received the $3,500. Thus, eleven weeks after the Corp had met and drawn up its overall general plan, it received its first money, contingent upon execution of a signed, written agreement with a professional consultant, knowledgeable in the area of government housing specifically and in expediting "red-tape" bureaucratic processes in general.

## The Consultant Is Hired

The Corp held its first meeting after receiving its money and directed its president to call the FHA's Washington, D.C., office the following day to inquire about possible consultants. The FHA personnel informed the Corp that it could not make referrals or recommendations on the hiring of specific people. But the Corp was given my name as one person with past experience in the general area of housing. I was contacted by telephone the following day—two days after the meeting—and arranged to meet the Corp officers at their office in Bright City. This initial meeting, which lasted for four hours, was essentially set up to:

1. Discuss the need of the Corp, with references to the services of a consultant.
2. Explore their problems in relation to the FHA, HUD, the city, builders, as well as to contracts, agreements, and other interactions and neccessities they would have to deal with.
3. Draw up a tentative agreement with terms of schedules and fees.

The committee agreed that I was to be responsible to the executive committee of the Corp, which was made up of the officers and two other board members. Additionally, the president was authorized to confer by telephone or in writing at any time with me, initiated by either of us; and the agreement was to be between the Corp and me, and signed by all of the members of the executive committee.

## THE CORP'S MODUS OPERANDI

### An Approach

Underlying many of the dilemmas facing the Corp and other parties involved were certain conditions and factors, as well as assumptions, inherent in this enterprise, which continued to crop up in the early meetings between the Corp and the other parties. Some of the assumptions related to me directly and are so indicated in the following discussion. To avoid some of the likely confusions, they are listed below as givens and assumptions. All of these are likely to operate with groups everywhere, to different degrees, since they represent, for the most part, general principles of group social behavior and group dynamics, but they were crystallized very clearly in the Corp's interactions with all parties involved, when dealing with particular issues.

- Most Corp members did not behave in a linear fashion; most behaved both irrationally and illogically at times and rationally and logically at other times—as do most people everywhere.
- Most operated from the basic stance of vested interests, which were definable and identifiable—as do most people everywhere.
- The Corp worked not just best, but *only,* for selfish reasons, which included returns that were intangible (for example, achievement, inner satisfaction, status changes, and so on), as well as tangible rewards— an assumption everyone in the group implicitly accepted.
- What was considered good or bad was relative and a function of the group at a given time, under a given set of conditions.
- The originally expressed goals of the group were to be modified as the operation was implemented—an assumption everyone accepted.
- The Corp was not neutral on issues of values.
- Roles and functions also changed (in a vertical and horizontal sense) as the operation was implemented—an assumption that also became an operational practice.
- Consultant service skills were subject at times, as a purchasable package, to the same rules and procedures in the marketplace as other professional skills—perceived by the Corp as a marketable item and accepted by everyone.
- In this housing program, there were always at least two forces involved in a power battle, with the Corp wanting something held by the VA, HUD,

and the like, which were refusing and resisting giving up anything to the Corp.

- Members of the Corp and the other power blocs engaged voluntarily in activities that promoted their better self-image, peer acceptance, and status standing, but avoided and resented those that negated these positive self- and peer perceptions.
- There was at all times an implicit value system operating. This meant that the Corp and the other parties involved always operated within some kind of social context.
- Power was seldom voluntarily surrendered; it always had to be taken through some method of threat or confrontation.

(I do not mean to imply that these assumptions or other operating dynamics were spelled out or discussed as presented here. This was not the case. True, at different times, some of these assumptions were alluded to indirectly or were single elements of a general discussion on other subjects, but they were not openly discussed and agreed on. In fact, most members were not even aware that they were making and operating on any assumptions, unless and until it was pointed out to them; this happened in a few cases, as noted later.)

### A Case in Point

One potentially explosive meeting took place between the Planning Department of Bright City and the Corp. The meeting centered around the discipline of a city employee and "who pays the salaries of the department's personnel." The Corp took the position that, since they were taxpayers and since all city personnel are paid out of taxes and other public funds, therefore, the Corp actually paid a part of the city employees' salaries. Further, with this established, the employees could be held accountable to the people who paid their wages—hence, to the Corp. The Corp was absolutely correct—but only in the theory of democratic governance. Everybody recognized and conceded the validity of this position. But the meeting came to a rapid halt when the question arose as to why, if this position were valid, the city shouldn't fire one of its inspectors for what appeared to be an obvious and blatant violation of decency and ethics. The inspector was accused of having walked, unannounced and unescorted, into one of the Corp member's homes while the wife was taking a shower; she had yelled out to him as he pushed passed her six-year-old son. The immediate issue here was that the white man had, by this action, insulted a black woman, arrogantly invaded her privacy, and disrespected her as a person; that if the color and roles were reversed, the chances were that a black man would have been locked up in jail the following day, without possibility of bail. As a result of separating these issues out along primary, secondary, and so on, strata, all parties were again able to communicate openly. Eventually, it was agreed that disciplinary action would be taken against this inspector. (We learned later that he was reassigned and placed on six-months' probation.)

But the dilemma was compounded: how, on the one hand, should the Corp handle this kind of racial issue without its becoming the spark for an incident that could be broadcast and carried by rumors to the community, thus setting off still another chain of racial disorders? And, on the other hand, how should the Corp handle this delicate matter so as not to have it become a justification for delays by the city? Other questions came up constantly during this crucial period: should the Corp compromise; should it let the black community know about these incidents, and privately seek to organize some demonstrations against the city; would the consultant utilize the incident to sell out the Corp? All of these issues were eventually handled in ways that allowed the Corp and the city to continue working to the mutual benefit of both. The answers came operationally from the nature and dynamics of the situations as they unfolded. We shall return later to this incident to view other aspects of it.

Another question raised by City Hall at this time was a direct but disturbing one to the Corp: for whom did this body of twelve ordinary black citizens speak, and who gave them the right to do so? To the Corp, it was a simple matter: they spoke on behalf of all oppressed peoples in Bright City and, specifically, on behalf of that city's black ghetto residents, but not necessarily for the well-to-do blacks. They had followed all of the ceremonial steps of incorporation required by state, federal, and city regulations; hence, they should be considered a legal entity. As such, the Corp considered itself authorized to initiate whatever means were necessary to achieve its avowed goals within the legal provisions of its charter. The Corp took the position that the state gave them the right to speak in behalf of the people, because they themselves were a part of the people. To the Corp this was clear-cut and "no big thing"!

To the Corp, their legal status also implied that the city, the FHA, and others were obligated, both legally and morally, to recognize them as having certain inherent rights by virtue of their charter. The Corp was disturbed that they apparently needed to use confrontation or threat of force to effect such recognition from these establishment agencies, in contrast to other similar, but nonpoverty, groups that had dealt with these "city halls" and had received due recognition without having had to use threats or engage in direct confrontation.

## MY ROLE AS CONSULTANT

I was hired by the Corp on a professional contract basis to perform certain tasks that could be easily enumerated and modified if necessary. For me, this arrangement was routine. But considering the nature of the Corp's program, the people involved, and what was occurring in Bright City at that time, as well as the peculiar events that had taken place only shortly before, which were potentially racially explosive, my role and function in this program qualified it as far more than just another routine consulting job.

It was soon apparent to me and the Corp that there was an important category of issues to confront and resolve in order to establish mutual trust and cooperative functioning; otherwise, neither I nor they could, in good faith, begin to carry out our contractual obligations. This other category was what might be called "general ethical, moral, and ethnic/ideological issues." In the specific context of this program, this other category of issues was far more pressing and important than my simply performing the tasks written down in the contract.

But deciding how to handle these other issues or even define them clearly was not easy. So, in order to cover these different levels of personal involvement, I have chosen to list first my assigned role and activities with little elaboration, and then to discuss the other issues in some detail. The Corp also had these same issues within its orbit, inextricably interwoven with mine, since we interacted together at all times and were independent, not in practice, but only as far as this presentation is concerned. They are separated here only as a matter of style, and this issue is discussed later under "The Corp as Intervenor."

## My Assignments

In general terms, I was hired to perform the following tasks:

- Review all paperwork done to date by the Corp and make changes if appropriate.
- Review the organizational process of the Corp, make related changes, and initiate other steps as mutually agreed upon by the consultant and the Corp.
- Review the Corp's overall plan of action and suggest any changes that seemed needed.
- Meet with the Corp not less than once a week for not less than six hours per meeting.
- Be available on call to confer on any matter relating to the Corp's program.
- Give the Corp the benefit of my expertise and direction, as it related to their goal, and consulting assistance in other related areas.

In my association with the Corp, I worked also with city hall, community groups, individuals, and with various government agencies. The Corp and I met at least once a week and, at times, for four hours a day or over a weekend. During the weekend sessions, I conducted training seminars for the staff or for community groups on the topics of community organization, involvement of youth, and counseling, as well as on other technical matters, such as filling out credit application papers, and so on. The activities I performed included the following:

- Writing a summary paper on HUD, Manpower Progress; simplifying the writing for Corp members.
- Filling out the Corp's form for HUD: "Request for Preliminary Deter-

mination of Eligibility as Nonprofit Sponsor or Mortgagor (FHA-Form No. 3433, Rev. 1/68)."

- Completing the Corp's "Transmittal Notice No. 1. Counseling for Home-ownership for Low and Moderate Income Families (HM-7610.1)."
- Helping to complete the Corp's "Personal Financial and Credit Statement."
- Completing papers on requests for bonding.
- Conducting four training seminars for community people on the programs of housing for the poor.
- Conducting three "How to" seminars for the Corp, related to their particular program.
- Reviewing the personal and confidential records of all Corp members and of the Corp itself.
- Meeting several times with interested builders and other contractors.
- Preparing the Corp's application for a "Program Supplementary Funds Request" to the local government program center.
- Constructing a PERT chart for the entire projected program.
- Holding three private conferences with Bright City's representative from the mayor's office and two other conferences with local bankers.
- Completing many other forms, holding other high-level meetings alone, and meeting and talking with hundreds of other people in carrying out these activities.

It may appear that the consultant's role was clear-cut, but it was anything but that. Not only were there the practical questions of timing to be faced, but there were also unexpected conferences that the Corp was notified of at the last minute and which it was expected to attend, and unanticipated forms to be secured, filled out, and mailed which had direct bearing on the bigger issues of trust, confidence, and oppenness between me and the Corp. As things evolved, these issues were both raised and resolved explicitly and within a time frame conducive to full acceptance by both myself and the Corp, and obviously, unless this intergroup-relations process was taken care of first, there could be little, if any, mutually successful accomplishments or satisfaction on the part of either faction.

### My Personal Ethical Position

These activities were not the ones that constituted the core of any of the difficulties inherent in my role. Rather, my concern was with the issues and implications involved in the many questions listed below, which are concerned with ethical/moral and ethnic/ideological issues. A few are obviously only rhetorical; others were posed as guidelines for clarifying in my own mind the parameters and framework within which I should perform my tasks and interact with the different people involved in this program. To define my role, I asked myself these questions:

1. What should my role be: a resource for data only or a planning strategist?
2. Should I accept the job, even if I suspected that my values differed from the Corp's in relation to low-income housing or to perpetuating a black or racial ghetto?
3. Should I seek to subtlely influence the Corp into wanting to move out of this ghetto and not worrying about all of the long-standing city problems?
4. Should I tell them to fight city hall my way instead of their way?
5. How much should I share what I learned from them with the "downtown boys"?
6. How much of an advocate for their cause should I openly become?
7. And, knowing they might have money available for consultative services if they got their grant, how much and on what basis should I charge them?
8. What degree of mutual trust was or should be established in our relationship?

I do not wish to imply or pretend that my own clarification of my role took place in an orderly, sequential, and logical manner; it didn't. The answers to my questions came sometimes suddenly, sometimes slowly and stubbornly, and sometimes not at all. But in the main, answers came gradually while I was engaged in an activity related to a particular question. And then again, there were periods when I modified my own internal position on an issue, or simply held it in abeyance. At any rate, here are the answers, as I finally crystallized them:

1. My role was one of many faces: a resource for data, suggestions, ideas, and a planning strategist. I stayed open to the playing of many roles.
2. My values, as related to low-income housing, paralleled those of the Corp: there should and must be provision for this kind of housing market, and it must be spearheaded by a group sufficiently committed to the idea to see it through. The second part of this question was not quite as easy for me to handled. I resolved, however, that the possibility existed that, within a decade, these units would be part of the city's black ghetto, and then I reasoned that they already were. (My deepest personal commitment is to creating new patterns and arrangements of housing units that preclude such a possibility or at least the probability.)
3. *No.* Our democratic society can work best by having its citizenry worry about and work on these kinds of problems. Besides, my life for the last twenty years has been spent in just this kind of effort: worrying about all kinds of ghetto and city problems.
4. They should do it their way. I would help them avoid pitfalls or other harmful and ineffective methods through suggestions and ideas, if appropriate.
5. I resolved this issue by letting the Corp know in advance that I would share with the "downtown boys" only that knowledge which I, in my

best judgment, deemed necessary at the time to achieve the particular objective, and nothing more. I also helped them define for me and for themselves those areas they considered secret and confidential and those not closed.

6.  This issue is closely linked to question 5. I knew from experience that once I was perceived by the establishment as an ardent advocate for "a cause" my effectiveness in dealing with them would decrease accordingly. My stance and posture had to be one of objectivity, of a professional approach, of fairness and sound judgment. It could not be a biased position in the sense of having missionary zeal. And anyway, my relationship with the Corp meant that I was in their corner, working for them. At times I became their spokesman. At all times I was working in their behalf. At other times, I was in fact their advocate, depending upon all the circumstances of time, people, and issues. But I resolved that I would avoid becoming their chief advocate, because such a position would tend to blind me to some of the things that at times needed a fresh, questioning approach.

7.  On this issue, I drew up a schedule of fees that would hold true whether or not the Corp received a big grant. I also wrote a proposal for the Corp, which was accepted, that included consulting fees for my services and other categories of assistance.

8.  From my side of the street, I knew that, despite all we mutually agreed to on paper, the extent to which we mutually respected each other, enjoyed doing "our thing" together, and ironed out any differences that might arise all depended on a high degree of mutual trust. This extended even to their not having enough money to pay me at times while I continued to work even harder. Mutual trust kept us moving, for at times that was all we had going for us.

Once I felt I had these ethical issues resolved, doing my job was easy. But I was poignantly aware of the fact that the Corp was engaged in a "real war" (as they called it) with "whitey." They saw themselves as being treated as slaves—black slaves—and were out to wage this war accordingly.

### The Subjective World of the Corp

To fully understand the issues addressed below, it is necessary to describe this context of "waging a war" and the experiences of the Corp more completely. First, this was a self-initiated and self-directed project started by involved citizens. It was designed and perceived by them as an opportunity, perhaps never to be equalled, to exercise a calculated degree of direct control over a small facet of their lives, and to control it in a real, concrete sense, not in an abstract way. During their waking hours, all of these Corps members were faced with the nagging problem of physical survival for themselves and their families.

But along with agonies involved with mere physical survival—of keeping a job versus unemployment, of paying the rent, feeding the children, and the like—go the doubly energy-sapping strategies required to maintain the psychological-emotional equilibrium needed to keep going and to feel that "we can change things" for the better. This kind of total mobilization of energies from all internal systems is essential if one is to function effectively as a group member in bringing about these changes, though they may be small by other people's standards. It was this complex array of interacting dynamics that surrounded my performing effectively in relation to the phase of my work that I will now discuss, and which brought into play another whole set of considerations for me.

The Corp was a small ethnic/racial minority operating within the bounds of racism and, to them, imperial colonialism within Bright City's urban setting. To isolate these dynamics for my own resolutions, I called this category of questions, "survival and strategy ideology," in contrast to questions of ethics and philosophy, as such. The central concept here is one that postulates the Corp members as perceiving themselves as "subject citizens" in semienslavement. I accepted this definition as valid and as the basis for my direction and orientation. This concept is crucial in understanding the role definitions and functional decisions as they relate to the intervention process involving these subject citizens. These subject citizens in Bright City perceived their situations differentially, based on race and poverty, defined their problems differentially, and, thus, sought solutions based on this differential perception of themselves and all the others involved.

This is indeed a valid perception, as far as these subject citizens are concerned. But the Corp was also deeply aware that their perception of themselves was in actuality a reflection of the perceptions of themselves by others. The history of this country's treatment of its racial/ethnic groups attests to the fact that these groups are defined and perceived by the oppressors as subject citizens and are accordingly treated by the oppressors on a differential scale based on color (race) and poverty.

The significance of this historical fact of life in the United States with reference to my role is that I was required either to share this differential perception and operate from that stance, or to accept as valid their differential perception and operate as if I shared it, or, at worst, to operate without taking a position contradictory to that of these subject citizens. What this means in actual practice is highlighted by the questions I posed to help me clarify my own role and that of the Corp with respect to how the Corp would interact with me in crucial times when this concept was of major importance:

1.    Should I accept this position of "being at war" as being my own or as mine simply because I was working with my own people in this instance?

2.  Should the Corp be guided by my own racial/ethnic identification or by my competence, independent of my racial identity?

3.  Should the Corp compromise? If so, in what ways and on what points or positions?

4.  Should I help them organize to pressure the oppressor (city hall) as a function of my role?

5.  Should I be neutral and play it cool and be perceived as not one of them (in this instance, meaning "a black man") by the power institutions, that is, FHA, VA, and so on?

6.  How should the strong feelings of racism be handled, and by whom (by me, by the Corp, or by both)?

7.  What role should I play in helping the group decide when and how to define and accept relative sociological and psychological gains within a context of relative gains, if they were made in the context of general oppression within this or any society, independent of racism?

### My Own Inner Struggle for Resolution and the Answers

1.  I recognized from the beginning that my personal position on the issue of actual war was similar to, but not the same as, that of the Corp. I had always accepted as a working principle that the racial/ethnic minorities were at war with the institutions of the establishment, based on the same historical and social realities assumed by the Corp. For me also, life is a continuous personal battle between myself and the oppressors, who, because of my color, prevented me from functioning effectively—the same position as that of the Corp. Yet, I have always been able to separate social reality from the strategy necessary to deal with the reality. For me, this means that there are times when different strategy positions are taken in order to achieve specific objectives, independent of my philosophical or ideological position about racism and poverty. The situation and its peculiar dynamics, to me, should dictate what specific public stance is appropriate or inappropriate. But for the Corp members, understanding or accepting this kind of separation of social reality from strategies to cope with it was at times a strain for them because of their life experiences. I took this position in all matters and eventually convinced the Corp that survival was indeed the first priority for all of us, and that this meant playing it cool at times as far as racism was concerned, without compromising personal convictions and principles in any way. It means that, in the area of methodology, compromise was both legitimate and acceptable, as well as expected by all others involved.

2.  *No.* The Corp at all times had to be guided by their own ethnic-related convictions, independent of anybody else's racial identity.

3.  *Yes.* As mentioned in the answer to question 1, the Corp learned to

compromise on issues that related to methodology, techniques, or timing, but not on issues of fundamental principles. This distinction is crucial.

*Example 1:* At one meeting, I was called upon to react to a question regarding the eventual makeup of the board of directors of the Corp, once it was operating as a funded agency providing low-cost housing. The essence of the issue was whether the Corp would allow this new board to include representatives of all economic levels and ethnic/racial groups, in the vein of the poverty program projects, which by law had to have at last one-third representation of the groups being served with the remainder coming from the community at large. The answever had to be "no." The Corp would continue to decide who, and in what numbers, would be on its board, unless there were stipulations by a funding source that made such a board composition a condition for receiving the funds. To me and the Corp, this was a fundamental issue, not to be compromised. Since the Corp was formed by a group living in a restricted area of Bright City, since it was not under the poverty program guidelines, and since the Corp was following HUD's regulations. which did not mandate such a formula for board composition, there was no rational basis for the question especially as it was asked by a city representative.

Still, the bigger question was: if the reply were a categorical "no," and if the city had in mind plans to assist the Corp in securing poverty program funds, would this adamant reply preclude any further negotiations with the city for possible funds from that agency? After a brief in-house discussion, we decided together that the reply was still an absolute "no." But—and this is significant—if a funding agency made a concrete offer conditional on that kind of board composition, we would want to talk to them directly, in person, at that time. As it turned out, the city had no plans in mind for such funding and was willing to go along with the Corp's position on the matter of board composition, even had it found a source.

*Example 2:* When the issue of how the Corp was going to handle its accounting matters—by a firm chosen by the Corp or by one chosen by the federal government or by the city (which had offered the Corp these services)—came up, it turned out not to be a basic issue, but rather one of method and timing. The Corp trusted no one connected with the "feds" or the city. My position—which the Corp accepted, after an analysis of relevant conditions—was that the city's offer should be accepted. It was.

4. *Yes,* under appropriate conditions. At one point, I did draw up a plan to have a group of high-ranking black and white citizens put pressure on city hall to force them to take a public position on one aspect of public housing.
5. *Yes,* at times I should allow my blackness to speak for itself, since by any visual observation, I would be physically perceived as a black man. In the context of the dynamics of the Corp's working to improve and change the conditions of fellow blacks and others suffering similar injustices and

hardships, I was "one of them." At times, however, my *role*, not my color, was primary. In these instances, in addition to being both "black and one of them" I was also one of the technical experts sitting around the table with several non-black specialists, drawing upon one another's expertise in a given area. The point is that to have my blackness—however defined—always out front is both a hindrance to effective human interaction and unnatural role-playing. There are times when, even to me, blackness outwardly displayed or promoted is out of context and is of a patronizing and artificial nature. This leads naturally to the next question.

6. Feelings should be handled delicately at times, forcefully at times, always honestly and openly; the timing must be a matter of personal sensitivity and judgment. But such feelings should be handled and resolved within the person or groups experiencing them and by those most affected by them, or by a design of mutual agreement. At times, I was asked to handle some very sensitive matters of racism and, at other times, individual persons handled them; styles varied, as did the intensity of the emotions involved.

7. This question, as a peripheral issue, cropped up constantly in many disguises:

"What do they think we are—a bunch of fools?"

"Sounds good and that's not too bad a deal, but for so long the white man has handed us a bone and never come back to give us any more, except another bone."

"Yes, but if we're going for the whole hog, then let's go for the whole thing and not let him think we're satisfied with just a little piece of the hog—although I don't think this offer is that bad. But you know how The Man plays us for a fool."

"If we were white and were offered that much, it wouldn't be no big deal cause it would be white and white. But we ain't white, period."

I simply played this one by ear, because all of us soon realized implicitly that each day was different, that each event was unique and had its own configurations, and that all of us were in flux and changing our own positions on the issues subsumed in this question as the concrete instances crystallized. I handled this one by whatever mode seemed right for me at the moment: sometimes by silence, sometimes by a written analysis, other times by informal discussions with the Corp or, privately, with individual members.

I might note here that the subjects of racism and poverty were often discussed as agenda items. But the question of how to program strategies for dealing with the emotional and psychological effects of the establishment's systems that perpetuated racism and poverty bore the most fruit in concrete terms, as the

Corp worked with their own feelings and those of others in influential positions. This viewpoint is based not only on my own perspective but also on the informal comments of the Corp members themselves. While I wrestled with these issues from my perspective, the Corp was also involved with them from theirs, to which we now turn our attention.

## THE CORP: ITS ROLE, ITS ETHICS, ITS IDEOLOGY

The Corp did not define itself as an intervenor per se, nor did it interpret the range of activities in which it was engaged as that of social intervention. Defining the group in these terms is my choice. The members were aware, however, that their involvement was designed to redirect the resources and energies of several large government agencies with reference to those agencies' allocations in Bright City. If necessary, they had set out to force the city to redefine black people in Bright City by altering the structures through which the city dealt with them and perceived them.

For the purpose of this chapter, the term "social intervention" is used to refer to those particular activities, of whatever nature engaged in by the Corp, that were directed toward achieving the objective of acquiring the housing units and the funds to operate as the controlling agency of those units. Whether the behavior of the Corp was calculated, overt, or covert, as long as it was directed toward achieving the objective and utilizing other skills, my role was to give them specified input to help them achieve their goal more effectively.

### Ethical Considerations

From the beginning, there were certain questions of ethics/morality that faced the Corp. Some of these related to me as their paid consultant; others were centered more around their own rights and their status in the immediate community of the housing units, as reflected by their peers' behavior toward them. Those that related to me directly were relatively easy for them to handle among themselves and with me.

Questions of ethics arose only secondarily as openly discussed issues between the Corp and me; these were usually around particular situations. For example, the Corp was quite explicit in letting me know that the program was theirs, lock, stock, and barrel; that I was there because of my specialized knowledge and skill; that whether or not I shared their values relative to decent, low-cost housing for the poor was irrelevant to them and to my performance, as long as I did not allow my values, of whatever nature, to get in the way of my performing effectively.

This kind of objective performance was not quite so easy to bring about, however, between the Corp and other resource people. There was an electrical contractor, for instance, who was discharged by the Corp, despite his competence, because he didn't believe "in giving those poor people" top-grade wiring materials in their houses for "them to destroy and not appreciate." Then there was a minor dilemma created when the City Planning Department refused to demand detailed specifications from the landscaping contractor. The Corp was eventually able to persuade the department to issue such an order. The department's reason was that "that part of town could do with less elaborate lawns because too much landscaping would be out of context with the other surrounding neighborhoods."

Following is a summary of the ethical questions of the group, which relate to these instances and others:

1.  What should be the role of the selected consultant? What do we really want of him?
2.  Should he be hired to tell us what we ought to do or to whom we should sell these housing units and the price we should set?
3.  Will he sell us out to the VA or FHA? What can we know?
4.  How can we know that he shares our values relating to decent housing for the poor?
5.  Whose program will this turn out to be—his or ours?

### The Corp's Answers

1.  To them, initially, my role was easy to define: I was to help them do whatever they were not doing but ought to be doing to facilitate their getting the funds and the units. After our first meeting, the list of my activities, already discussed, was agreed upon as a framework and departure point.
2.  *No.* He may give ideas and help us determine how best to go about accomplishing a task, but he may not tell us what to do. As for the prices of the units, these were set within specified range limits by the government. The Corp insisted that they would select who should or should not buy the units—again, within the guidelines of the government program.

3 and 4.   These two questions were closely related in the Corp's view: "He may sell us out if he does not share our values. But we can learn what his values really are only as we work with him, despite what his references tell us." But the Corp was equally convinced that even if I didn't share their values on low-cost housing, it was entirely possible that I could and would be able to work effectively with them as their consultant. They were aware of how my personal behavior would eventually reflect my own values: they were willing to test me later, as we interacted.

5.  This question becomes crucial when we remember that I was originally hired because I was supposed to know how to plow through the red tape, get things done, and meet with the "big boys" and for my ability to persuade many affluent and influential people to join with and support the Corp's program. What, then, would prevent my using them and their contacts as an

opportunity to "push my own thing" in the name of the Corp? They were not naïve. They reckoned that the primary ingredients against this probability had to be my own integrity and commitment to the same objectives and goals they had. They were willing to take the risk because of my reputation and references.

With the Corp, it was not these questions that caused the most concern, although, logically, the considerations of top priority may at first appear to be those of an ethical nature. The Corp was primarily concerned, however, with ethnic/ideological issues, the counterpart to those listed earlier as survival-strategy ideology: they are one and the same, as perceived from our two different perspectives.

### Blackness and Whiteness

The Corp was made up of twelve black residents who had lived in the ghetto for an average of nineteen years. Seven of them had lived previously in these same project houses and had witnessed their deterioration and the typical tug-of-war over these units between the citizens, on the one hand, and the federal government and the builders, on the other. This experience was internalized as a personal insult by these residents. Moreover, this experience was further concrete proof to the Corp that "the white men" could and would do anything to black people, because they have money and power and the black people don't.

To the Corp, it was simply irrational that they should think of their project as benefitting all the residents of Bright City. This was nonsense to them. In their opinion these units could have been rehabilitated many, many years earlier. It was racism to them—plain exploitation of a powerless black minority—and they had to act because no one else cared enough to do anything about the situation. The money was available: there were many EOC and Model Cities programs operating in and around Bright City. The few sophisticated black people who did have the knowledge and know-how didn't care or didn't wish to initiate any action on their behalf, either because they were part of the establishment and could rent or buy large suburban houses or live in expensive apartments or townhouses or perhaps because they had despaired of fighting racial battles with city hall and always coming up the losers. But to the "little black people" of the Corp, owning a house was very crucial. In a concrete sense, they defined and perceived housing as:

- A value-object
- A symbol of stability
- An exercise of local and individual control
- An investment in the future
- A product of individual initiative and industry

- A symbol of upward mobility, or locked-in immobility and visibility of caste and powerlessness
- A right

As perceived by the Corp, white people generally could live as they choose; nonwhite people, specifically blacks, could only live in places and under conditions that were determined in one way or another by white people and the few nonwhites who were part of the elite "who run this country." As alluded to earlier, their on-going battle with city hall to effect their project was seen as a real war though, of course, without guns, violence, or other unnecessary equipment. Wars were fought on the formal battlefield with physical weapons and off the battlefield with other kinds of weapons. By virtue of the dynamics of this contextual thinking and perceiving, the Corp had implicitly created a set of criteria with which to evaluate the performance or input from me and all others. Thsese criteria were never written out and discussed as such; they were simply always there. They flowed naturally from this basic premise: that the ideology of blackness was a necessary tool for survival in Bright City (and in the whole United States, for that matter). More precisely, there were a few questions inherent in the stance on blackness:

- Are we black first and residents or citizens second?
- Shall we hire as a consultant anyone who does not share this ordering of priorities?
- Shall we compromise? On what? How?

In practice, this stance on blackness had first to be translated into specific actions. It meant, for example, that all general plans to achieve objectives or the overall goal were mapped out from the perspective of black people first and last. It also meant that I was acceptable to them to the degree that they felt I was comfortable with their position and to the degree to which my position—whatever it might be—forced them not to question their own blackness. It was irrelevant to them whether my postion on this issue was ever made known publicly or privately, since my behavior would soon tell them exactly "where I was coming from." They had already hired me and were alledgedly satisfied that my technical competence was not in question. They had checked me out and concluded that over a period of time I had what they were looking for: a demonstrated ability to effectively assist groups of all colors with various philosophies and ethnic ideologies achieve their own defined goals.

But it was not only competence that the Corp was evaluating. I had to be both competent and black, for my blackness was an ingredient of my competency. It really didn't matter what particular black ideology I espoused—Black Nationalism, Pan-Africanism or whatever. The point here was this: the Corp was agreed that whatever shade of blackness I embraced was a personal matter that we didn't even have to talk about. If at some point later on, our ideologies led us to place different priorities on the role of blackness as a first consideration in general planning, then, at that time, we'd face it.

The question of the Corp's compromising became a tool or strategy to be utilized deliberately and wisely to accomplish winning this battle of gaining power from the establishment; then, it was acceptable. Not to compromise and to lose when otherwise the Corp could, and would, have gained was unacceptable. The goal was to win each little battle, if possible. Exactly when and on what points to compromise and how much was essentially a decision made on a situational and contingency basis, as each movement progressed and revealed the next movement. Yet there were some very well-understood conditions and points that were outside the question of compromise. For example:

- The Corp must be the sole owner of the units—no questions asked.
- The Corp must control all funds generated from sales or rentals of the units.
- The Corp must be free to make final selections or to give final approval of contractors or others hired to perform work on the units.
- The Corp must control the process by which potential tenants or buyers would acquire occupancy of the units.
- The Corp must at all times choose its own members and appoint its own officers.

In matters with city and other officials, it was always a matter of the level of compromise, whether of principle based on their blackness or of strategy. For example, the Corp itself did in fact organize a group of respectable and creditable black, white, and other citizens to pressure financial and city officials on behalf of the Corp. These efforts were successful. This was perceived by the Corp as a pressure-power move and as a legitimate tool to help achieve their stated objectives. These were primary and secondary objectives, but only involved decisions of strategy: how should a black corporation secure title to these white, government-controlled units? How can this Corp retain control of internal matters and over all the processes attendant thereto? These incremental objectives should not be confused with their ultimate goal, which was clearly to secure government-owned units with government-grant funds and to sell them, according to government regulations, to buyers whose mortgages would be government-insured through the FHA, and to administer the whole enterprise with minimum government interference, all within the official policy of these same overnment-authorized programs.

## The Corp Resolves the Issue of My Blackness

In concluding this discussion on the Corp, it seems appropriate to end on a note relative to the central issue for the Corp: blackness. Two examples will be highlighted.

Two experiences were cited earlier involving an electrical contractor and the City Planning Department's landscaping contractor. In both of these instances, I played a rather direct and decisive role. In essence, in both cases I laid out the strategies for conferring with city hall and met with the dismissed contractor to ensure that neither party was in violation of any agreements; I also wrote the final draft reports on both instances.

As I have stated, the Corp evaluated me on the basis of my blackness, as functionally defined by them. In the two instances just cited, the Corp accepted my performance as positive proof of my blackness. After all, I had responded effectively to their requests and to their subjective, but unexpressed, fears and apprehensions. To them, this kind of intangible but effective communication between them and myself was perhaps the most important component of being black. But it was not just the physical color of skin, obviously, that they were concerned about; it was something else, a union in commitment to a value of human involvement in shaping their own destiny to the highest degree possible within their own possibilities. This was equally true with the Corp as they evaluated others, for some of their closest friends, three of their volunteers, and two of their hired resource and technical assistants were white. Yet, in the subjective realities of oppression as experienced by the Corp, these white people were part of the group and, thus, one of them. It may be more accurate to say, from a technical perspective, that these white people had been chosen because they had the rare ability to accept others as whole people first and had the capacity to identify with the conditions and the Corp without being phony or condescending or missionarylike. To them, color was irrelevant. They were accepted as genuine, and they had been personal friends of two Corp members over the last ten years or so.

Thus, blackness per se meant far more than color of skin or espousal of a certain ideology. It was also a feeling communicated through human interaction. And in spite of waging a war against the establishment, as often alluded to earlier, on an individual basis, the war had nothing to do with the Corp's ability to judge and to accept all people on an individual basis; it was not a war against individual people.

## CONCLUSIONS: PRESENT STATUS OF THE CORP PROJECT

The foregoing discussion naturally leads to the obvious questions. What happened? Was the Corp funded? And what is the current status of the Corp program? Before answering these specific questions, I shall briefly review the last meeting I had with the Corp.

The setting was one of analyzing and reviewing our progress to date. The meeting was called and chaired by the Corp president to explore the whole matter of the funds, trust between us, and just what was going on. At this time, all the details and mechanics for implementing the program had been completed. The only unfinished tasks related to receiving final approval from HUD and the

FHA and the subsequent awarding of contracts to selected bidders. There were legal as well as nonlegal issues to be covered.

One important legal matter was the question of the Corp's bringing charges against HUD, the FHA, and the original private developers; the attorney explained the legal implications involved in such a move and the position he felt should be taken by the Corp. The attorney's position, in brief, was that, maybe in this instance, there was evidence that the director of the regional FHA office was himself a partner in some of the private investor's businesses brought about through their mutual friendship and interests over many years. Further, that this particular office had already been questioned in the recent HUD-FHA housing scandals publicized nationally. He explained that there may have been a question of conflict of interest, of corruption, of using his office as FHA director to obtain favors for a friend, and abuse and misuse of his power and authority. This kind of misuse of office, however defined, is in violation of public trust inherent in such positions and, of course, must not be tolerated. Abuses of power and corruption of power may be illegal, but they are outside of the realm of the Corp's program per se and should be considered as separate issues from that of the Corp's seeking of funds. True, these issues, according to the Corp's evidence, are directly related to the Corp's *not* securing the HUD grant; and they must eventually be legally addressed. The Corp, if it wished, could file suit. But the Corp should know that if it did file suit without funds or means to see it through, any other alternatives—if they were discovered—to secure these units later would naturally be closed to the Corp, according to the attorney. No decision about filing suit was made at this meeting.

However, another disclosure was made at this meeting. I reviewed the letter that, in essence, stated the following: "In this housing program, decisions not to finance the Corp were made by the regional FHA office." It was also apparent, however, that there were governmental entities in favor of financing the Corp. These included:

- The regional HUD office
- The Washington, D.C., HUD office
- The city officials
- Most of the city government and nongovernment agencies and groups

So, the answer was "no." The Corp did not receive approval to purchase the units from the FHA regional office. This meant that the VA, which actually owned the units (that is, held mortgages on them), had also refused the offer made by the Corp.

Much has happened since that last meeting, as a direct result of the Corp's intervention, despite its not having been funded in August, 1973, to purchase and rehabilitate the units:

1. The Corp brought this whole matter to the attention of the NAACP and two other national organizations designed to protect citizens caught in this

kind of a situation. These groups have filed a class action suit on behalf of several community groups; among them is the Corp of Bright City. (I, as the consultant, do not know the status of this action.)

2.  The Corp continued its efforts to obtain governmental and private funds to administer a counseling program for low- and moderate-income families; they received enough funds to conduct such a program on a small scale for one year.

3.  The national FHA office has contacted the Corp and advised them of what course to follow and that the Corps complaints are being considered in conjunction with many others filed against these and other FHA officials and other governmental agency personnel.

4.  The Corp has been assigned one person by a government agency (agency deliberately unnamed) to provide technical assistance to the Corp and to aid it in preparing applications for funds to continue its present programs on an extended scale next year.

5.  I have been requested by one government agency to submit to it any evidence that might bear on the legal issues involved and have been informed that I may be subpoenaed, if deemed appropriate, should the matter go to trial.

It will soon be four years since I last worked for and with the Corp as a consultant, but they are still very active. The Corp is now considering other areas of community activities, as an indirect effect of their involvement in this housing program. Their tenacity and sincerity has brought them added respect and new status in Bright City. They are now the experts in housing and are widely sought as speakers, consultants, resource people, and so forth. They didn't get the housing units, but they did get added units of respect and status among themselves and among their peers and colleagues at all levels.

## REFERENCES

Communication Channels, Inc. Housing for the other America. Reprinted from *National Real Estate Investor.* New York: Author, 1970 (January).

National Committee Against Discrimination in Housing. *Housing and the poverty cycle: Program guidelines for local community action agencies.* New York:

U.S. Commission on Civil Rights. *Understanding fair housing,* Clearinghouse Publication 42. Washington, D.C.: U.S. Commission on Civil Rights Clearinghouse, 1973 (February).

# 15
# ON "UNETHICAL" AID
# TO A (STATISTICAL)
# OTHER

## PETER G. BROWN
### University of Maryland

Your life is threatened. The life of your child is threatened. The life of a person unknown to you is threatened. Your third pair of socks is stolen. Your child's third pair of socks is stolen. The third pair of socks of a person unknown to you is stolen.

How do these circumstances differ morally in terms of the appropriateness of responses? There are at least two elements relevant in formulating the answer: the person on whom the harm is inflicted and the degree of the harm. Is one entitled to make the same response on behalf of others as on behalf of oneself? Should the response vary with the degree of actual or potential threat? These are some of the questions that Chapter 14 by Carrol W. Waymon helps to focus.

Waymon describes the situation in which he served as a consultant as follows:

> The Corp was a small ethnic/racial minority operating within the
> bounds of racism and, to them, imperial colonialism within Bright

At the time this chapter was written, the author was a Visiting Fellow at Battelle Seattle Research Center. The opinions expressed in this chapter do not necessarily represent those of the Battelle Research Center, The Center of Philosophy and Public Policy, or their sponsors.

**327**

City's urban setting. To isolate these dynamics for my own resolutions, I called this category of questions, "survival and strategy ideology," in contrast to questions of ethics and philosophy, as such. The central concept here is one that postulates the Corp members as perceiving themselves as "subject-citizens" in semienslavement. I accepted this definition as valid and as the basis for my direction and orientation (p. 314).

What is of particular note in this passage is that, as a result of the state of war between blacks and the establishment, we are confronted with questions of survival and strategy ideology, in contrast to questions of ethics and philosophy.

One of Waymon's arguments seems to be that, in war, ethics is irrelevant because survival is primary. There is a sense in which this statement is, of course, true. Insofar as the term "ethics" is taken to refer to the niceties of civilized behavior, it is not relevant when issues of survival are at stake. But the scope of ethics need not be limited in this way, and Waymon's contrast is misleading. Under many circumstances, actions on behalf of self-preservation and survival are ethical both on behalf of ourselves and on behalf of others. Under these circumstances, behavior that would be unethical under other conditions—such as lying and the use of force—not only are permissible, but can become obligations. For example, a person could be obligated to lie if in so doing an innocent person whose life is threatened by an unjustified force could be saved. Similarly, self-preservation permits acts for oneself that suggest what may be undertaken and what may not. Moreover, it is worth noting that in the conduct of war between nations, moral rules are thought to apply, and those who do not adhere to them are subject to censure and to punishment if circumstances demand and permit.[1] Perhaps Waymon's point could be restated as contrasting the moral rules that govern normal and peaceful situations (where most individuals are complying with the rules for the most part) with situations where significant noncompliance by some individuals will lead to abridgement of normal rules and the adoption of other rules that justify tactics to restore compliance.

However the distinction is best drawn, Waymon is not as explicit as one would like concerning what actions are justified by the survival and strategy ideology. Apparently, he has in mind not revealing one's true feelings and thoughts in certain circumstances (p. 315), placing duties to one's race before those of citizenship (p. 321), and pressuring the establishment when possible (p. 315).

I want to concentrate on a particular aspect of the problem presented by Waymon: When and in what way may a person intervene so as to benefit another? Note that this is not the same as the question of when one is

---

[1] I am indebted to Dr. Preston Williams for help on this point.

obligated to help another. Nor will I concentrate directly on what one may do to protect oneself. Waymon supports the actions of the Corp, in part because they are aiding others in securing housing. I will focus on this latter kind of argument.

But Waymon concentrates on a subset of the issues of aiding another. In sum, the issue is this: When and how may one abrogate normal moral rules and adopt another set of moral rules to aid an individual or group of individuals whom one does not know?[2] In addressing this question I propose to defend the following proposition: One person may defend another against a third party and may do harm to that third party proportionate to that threatened when all three of the following conditions are satisifed:

1. No less harmful alternatives are available.
2. The third party's actions are unjustifiable.
3. The person is so authorized to act.[3]

The phrase concerning the unjustifiableness of the action contains a necessary caveat, for without it we would be justifying strong or even violent responses to fairly imposed burdens.[4] Authorization to act on behalf of others is also required if individuals are to be protected from unwanted interventions.

Authorizations may be of several kinds: those explicitly or tacitly granted by individuals or groups, those deriving from social customs or laws, and those couched in broad moral terms, such as appeals to principles of natural law. I

---

[2] A very difficult issue that I pass over—since it is not raised by Waymon—is when is one justified in making violent responses. "Their on-going battle with city hall to effect their project was seen as a real war, though, of course, without guns, violence, or other unnecessary equipment. Wars were fought on the formal battlefield with physical weapons and off the battlefield with other kinds of weapons." (p. 321). I assume, however, at a minimum, that the use of violence is a question with a very high threshold. In cases where it is justified at all, it is to be used only when all other means have been exhausted, unless those other means would be even more damaging and unpredictable than resorting to violence.

[3] Regrettably this raises another crucial issue that must also be left unaddressed. What is the relationship between duties to oneself and duties to others? Do my rights to act on behalf of others lead to obligations to act on their behalf? Do I have obligations to protect others when this means I must forego protecting myself? When am I obligated to forego pursuing my own objectives and developing my own talents? This issue can be raised in a particularly difficult form in the context of Waymon's chapter since here the other individuals whose interests are at stake are unknown to the actors.

[4] In evaluating the applicability of this statement and its conditions to the situation described by Waymon, I can only indicate the kinds of factors that would influence its application. Waymon's chapter is lacking in many of the details necessary for deciding whether the application would, in fact, be justified. For example: Did officials at HUD misrepresent the situation? Did members of the Corp? Was there conflict of interest on either side? Were there unnecessary bureaucratic delays? Did both sides have appropriate authorizations for their actions?

confine my comments to the first kind because, as will become clear, the sort of interest involved makes it relatively easy to develop an authorization in this case.

To decide whether and how the above rule (and its conditions) about defending another is applicable, we have to consider three factors:

1. The kind of interest being threatened or harmed.
2. Securing or deriving authorization for the protective action.
3. The rules that guide the kind of response that is justified.

In considering these factors, I will show that Waymon, at a minimum, does not supply the necessary facts and arguments to justify suspending ordinary moral rules, though I am not as clear as I would like to be about what suspensions Waymon thinks are justified. Moreover, particularly with respect to points (2) and (3), what evidence he does present seems to call into question the appropriateness of suspending certain moral rules. In the following discussion it should be borne in mind that I do not accept Waymon's statement that because of survival and strategy ideology, ethics is irrelevant. On the contrary, the main issue is one of establishing which moral rules are relevant.

## WHAT KINDS OF INTERESTS ARE AT STAKE?

I take it as generally expressive of reflectively guided intuition on these matters that one may take actions of sufficient strength to protect one's or another's interests. Unjustified force may be met with force and unjustified violent force with violent force. Unfortunately, the situations involving the use of force are misleading in their simplicity, because the character of the appropriate response (force) is frequently clear. In other circumstances, it is not so clear that the response should or could be of the same kind as the threat. To determine what sorts of actions could properly be taken by Waymon and the Corp, we have to look at the sort of actual or potential harm involved to the others Waymon wishes to aid.

What sort of interest is housing? Housing has not been accorded the constitutional status of a fundamental interest (*Lindsey v. Normet*, 405 U.S. 56, 74, 1972). A "fundamental interest" for constitutional purposes is an interest that is either constitutionally protected, such as free speech, or is instrumental in the exercise of an interest so protected. Clearly, the right to housing is not explicitly granted in the Constitution. It might be argued that housing is instrumental in rights so protected, such as voting, or in others that are themselves instrumental to protected rights, such as freedom within the marriage contract. However, since the Supreme Court has not accepted these arguments in respect to education (*San Antonio Independent School District v. Rodriquez*, 411 U.S. 1, 1973; *reh. den.* 411 U.S. 959, 1973), it is doubtful that it would accord such status to housing, which in at least some ways is less instrumental in achieving rights explicitly protected.

Be this as it may, the moral issue still remains open, and the moral arguments concerning rights to housing are certainly easier to make than the legal ones. Many of these arguments are cogently presented by Waymon. At the root of Waymon's and others' arguments is the notion that housing is primary, that adequate housing suitably located is essential to many other human endeavors.

This seems to me to be correct. At bottom, what is being said is that housing is what John Rawls has called a "primary good." Rawls (1971) defines primary goods as: "Things that every rational man is presumed to want. These goods normally have a use whatever a person's rational plan of life" (p. 62). Waymon is appropriately asserting that housing is such a good. We don't need to know if people are cellists or bankers, bricklayers or plumbers to know that they will want housing of at least a minimal standard and will want that housing to be located in such a way that they (and their families, if applicable) will have access to associated services like education, fire, and police services of adequate quality. Certain levels of services of these sorts are essential for a minimal life in an urbanized society, and they therefore serve as preconditions to the pursuit of any other objectives.

Waymon's argument is correct in pointing to the basic nature of housing in an urban society. To threaten a person's opportunities to secure housing is to pose a serious threat to that person's survival in our society. As such, it is an interest that, when unjustly threatened, warrants an appropriate protective response.

## SECURING AUTHORITY

When may one party act to benefit or prevent harm to another? A general, but not very informative, answer to this question is: When authority to do so has been secured. But where does authority come from?

One answer to this question of authorization has been developed around the notion of free and informed consent (cf. Brown, 1975, pp. 79–100). Authority to act for another may be established when the other voluntarily and with sufficient knowledge gives his or her permission to do so.[5] Consent is required to prevent individuals from taking actions on the part of others that the others do not believe to be in their interest. We often assume that consent is implied or may be presumed when time is short and the hazard is great. In cases such as potential drownings, severe accident, and so forth, we

---

[5] Other lines of argument for authority to act on behalf of another such as those developed around the "free rider problem" are not applicable here since a public good is not involved. (The "free rider problem" refers to the difficulty of excluding individuals from benefits to which they have not contributed.)

assume that people would give their consent to our intervention if they were asked. Under these circumstances it is simply not possible to obtain their consent. We assume that if the time were available, consent would be granted.

Is the situation described by Waymon analogous to that of the drowning individual where authority to act may be presumed? This is a very complex question. Its complexity derives in part from the fact that others here are individuals more or less unknown to the Corp. The Corp is not trying to find housing for specific individuals, but to increase the number of housing units available in a given section of the city. Those to be aided by this effort are not present in the way a drowning individual is.

The situation described by Waymon differs from that of the drowning person because the knowledge involved is more tenuous. If we have seen a man struggling in the water and going under, and then lying unconscious on the beach, we may be reasonably sure that he is in difficulty, and that he would desire appropriate aid. But, in the case of people we don't know or can't even see, is the knowledge of a different sort? To understand the plight of potential residents in the housing units requires knowledge of the housing market in the city in question, both on the demand and supply sides. This is more complex, but I see no reason to suppose that it is different in principle.

Insofar as a fundamental interest or, more accurately a primary good is involved, a case may be made along the lines of presumed consent. If a primary good is defined as something people may be presumed to want no matter what else they want, the circumstances may be similar to that of the drowning individual. We presume in this case that people will want their lives preserved, and we make this presumption without knowing the individual in most senses of that word. Under certain assumptions it would appear that the availability of housing was similar in that, as Waymon has persuasively argued, housing in all its facets is essential to achieving a multiplicity of other legitimate goals that we expect any reasonable person to desire.

But for this line of argument to work where Waymon is concerned, at least the following two conditions would have to be demonstrated:

1.  The individuals who would use the housing would not be able to obtain suitable housing elsewhere; that is, there would have to be a short supply at appropriate prices. (Defining "appropriate prices" would be tricky).
2.  The individuals must not have indicated that the Corp did not have the authority to represent their interests.[6]

Waymon does not demonstrate that the first condition is the case, though perhaps he could. In respect to the second condition, his argument may be in some difficulty. On page 295, he notes that "the Corp could legitimately claim

---

[6] This principle will hold for all adults with adequate information who are not coerced, unsuitably enticed, and so on.

that it had tried to broaden its base in the community: It was the latter that had decided not to become involved." This statement is hard to interpret. To the extent that members of the community felt that the Corp was not representative of their interests, and the community individuals were of the sort they wished to sell the housing to, the argument for presumptive behavior in their interest is not applicable. It may be the case that representative individuals for whom the housing was being sought were expressly denying the Corp authority to act on their behalf. If this is so, then one of Waymon's main justifications for intervening on their behalf falls down. Unfortunately, he has not supplied the information needed to fully evaluate this question.

## ON CHOOSING MORAL RULES

Fundamental to Waymon's position is the notion that a state of war exists between himself and the Corp on the one hand and the Department of Housing and Urban Development on the other. Unfortunately many of the details that one would need to know to decide which set of moral rules to apply are not included in his chapter (see footnote 4). This makes a direct and complete evaluation of his position impossible here. Consequently, I will suggest a kind of method to be used in deciding what moral rules to apply to novel situations[7] and make a necessarily limited application of this method to a hypothetical situation of a sort Waymon might believe was justified as a result of the state of war.

Much, if not all of human behavior is, or should be, governed by moral rules. But for the most part we do not pay explicit attention to them because conformity is automatic or because it is clear which rule should be followed. A fascinating aspect of Waymon's account is that it raises ethical questions not ordinarily addressed. How do we decide what rules to apply in novel situations?

I suggest the following method: Choose a moral rule or situation that is clear (and as similar as possible to the one in question) and then determine how and to what extent the novel situation is analogous to it. This can be done by beginning on one of two interrelated levels. Start with a situation that is morally clear and compare the problematic one to it, or take a rule with clear applications and examine whether the novel situation seems to fall under it. The former method is the one I followed in deciding whether consent of unknown others could ever be presumed. In this section I examine how the situation described by Waymon (with certain hypothetical additions) corresponds to one that is morally clear, try to abstract the rules that govern that case, and determine whether the hypothetical situation that might appear justified to Waymon falls under those rules.

---

[7] The novelty here is that Waymon asks us to examine what we may do on behalf of unknown others.

As noted earlier, it is difficult to know what Waymon believes is justified by survival and strategy ideology as opposed to ethics. However, to crystallize the issues, let us imagine a hypothetical situation. Suppose one were to argue that the situation justified misrepresentation, that because of the importance of the issues involved, the ordinary moral rules about truth telling could be suspended.

For illustrative purposes, take the issue of telling the truth on an official form to be submitted to the state where the matters of concern on the form bear on matters of substantial public and personal interest. Under what circumstances may one lie in a situation like this? Suppose you are an Ayran resident of Germany during the mid-1930s and that the Gestapo is passing out forms on which you must list whether you have individuals of Jewish descent living in your house. You are required to fill out this form and, in doing so, you assert that you are not providing such protection, in spite of the fact that you are hiding several Jews in your attic. I think few would contend that your action was immoral.

Two major elements would enter into your judgment on this dilemma. First, the Gestapo represents a repressive government with publicly announced sanctions of irrational policies to prosecute members of a certain ethnic/ religious group. Moreover, the Gestapo is known to be brutal in its treatment of individuals in that group. The classification of persons as Jews, who are thought of as inimical to the state's interests, is irrational both on its face and in substance. In short, the action on the part of the state is morally illegitimate. Second, if the Jews are discovered, they will be subject to extreme and irreversable damage, that is, to years of imprisonment and abuse or to death.

Would Waymon be justified in urging misrepresentation on a form to HUD? (I do not claim that he does urge it.) If he wants to justify such a tactic, he would have to simultaneously offer two sorts of arguments; that the institution and or its actions were illegitimate, and that severe and irreversible harm would result from telling the truth.

The root intuition that lies behind the permissibility of lying in this case is that, where the survival of an innocent party is threatened by an illegitimate force, the relevant moral rule has to do with the saving of innocent life, rather than the rules about truth telling. Why? Two factors about the situation justify reliance on principles for saving life rather than truth telling. One is the factor of relative harm. Far less harm is done by lying than would be done if the truth were told. More important, the illegitimacy of the Gestapo both as an institution and in its behavior justifies lying. This latter principle is governing.

The principle of relative harm—taken by itself—would not be sufficient to justify misrepresentation. In cases of morally and legally legitimate arrest, lying would not be justified, even though the harm might be great. Arguments justifying hiding suspects from the legitimate exercise of the law couched in terms of avoiding harm to the suspects would not be regarded as compelling. Cases where the harm is legitimately inflicted require promise keeping.

Even if we assume that the "do less harm" rule is operative, the situation by no means unambiguously supports our hypothetical misrepresentation. To justify this behavior under this rule, one would have to show that at a minimum there are reasonable grounds for supposing that the group Waymon wishes to aid will be aided more by lying than by truth telling. This is obviously a complicated empirical judgment. This activity could undercut confidence in the Corp and similar groups in the future, with results counterproductive to their interests.

Hence, to justify such misrepresentation one would have to show that the Department of Housing and Urban Development had exercised its authority illegitimately. Note further that Waymon and the Corp are in a position to appeal an adverse ruling. In fact, when Waymon's chapter was drafted, they were in the process of doing so. They have means to redress illegitimate behavior. Unless it can be shown that the process of appeal itself is unsuited to protection of the interests involved, it would appear that this avenue must be followed.[8] For instance, if the review process is so long and expensive that the interest at stake is vitiated, where the interest is fundamental, or where a primary good is involved, the action on the part of the state may be classified as illegitimate.

## REFERENCES

Brown, P. G. Informed consent in social experiments. In A. M. Rivlin & P. M. Timpane (Eds.), *Ethical and legal issues of social experimentation*. Washington, D.C.: Brookings Institution, 1975.

Rawls, J. *A theory of justice*. Cambridge, Mass.: Harvard University Press, 1971.

[8] Where one believes one is being mistreated by a public official, when does one have the right to suspend ordinary moral rules in order to achieve one's objective? The law on this point is rather clear. Take the issue of whether one may resist an unlawful arrest. A model penal code states that the use of force is not justifiable to "resist an arrest which the actor knows is being made by a peace officer although the arrest is unlawful" (American Law Institute Model Penal Code: July 30, 1972; Section 3.042(i) ). In the commentary on this provision it is noted "it should be possible to provide adequate remedies against illegal arrest, without permitting the arrested person to resort to force—a course of action highly likely to result in greater injury even to himself than detention" (American Law Institute Model Penal Code. Tentative Draft No. 8 May 9, 1958, p. 19). Since, the actions on the part of HUD are subject to review and are reversible, the situation described by Waymon appears to fall under this kind of rule.

# VIII
## FAMILY PLANNING
## PROGRAMS

# 16
# SOME ETHICAL CONSIDERATIONS IN FAMILY PLANNING PROGRAMS

### ROBERT J. LAPHAM
National Academy of Sciences

The study of ethics and population has received broad and considerable attention in recent years, with particular focus on the more emotionally explosive issues such as abortion versus the right to life and the use of effective contraception versus medical side effects. Another issue is voluntarism and the concern for freedom versus a perceived possible need for coercive or at least constraining measures to reduce population growth rates, and particularly on the international scene there is the issue of population programs viewed as assisting development efforts versus their being viewed as imperialistic and/or genocidal efforts that run counter to the best interests of developing societies or minority groups. More recently, the ethical issues involved in aging and dying are receiving attention. The recent U.S. Commission on Population and Growth and the American Future (1972) dealt with some of these and other related questions, as have Callahan (1971, 1973b), Warwick and Kelman (1972), and Dyck (1971, 1973). Much of the work of the Institute of Society, Ethics, and the Life

Appreciation is expressed to the participants in the conference and to the editors, especially Don Warwick, for their helpful suggestions, discussion, and comments. Particular thanks are due to Ms. Ellen Brandt for editorial review and ideas, and to Ms. Mary Geissman for editorial and typing assistance. Mr. Jeremiah Sullivan and Mr. W. Parker Mauldin also provided useful comments on the first draft of this chapter.

Sciences (an independent, nonprofit research and educational organization established in 1969 to examine the ethical, legal, and social implications in the life sciences and based at Hastings-on-Hudson, New York) has concentrated on ethical questions relating to population through the *Hastings Center Report* and the *Hastings Center Studies*. For the past 10 years, a continuing debate with ethical overtones has been carried out primarily in *Science* magazine.

It does not seem useful here to attempt another general overview, and the following discussion concentrates on ethical questions that exist in the context of three specific areas related to efforts to reduce fertility rates:

1. Large-scale family planning programs, particularly in developing nations—ethical issues that arise in the implementation of a series of programmatic procedures and actions that seem effective for increasing initial acceptance of family planning, for increasing continued use of contraception, and for reducing fertility levels.
2. Funding levels and sources—ethical issues related to the substantial increase of funds available in recent years for large-scale population programs, especially in developing societies.
3. A family planning–delivery system linking family planning to maternal and child health activities—ethical issues arising in the search for new family planning–delivery systems, and in the context of a major research project involving substantial populations to answer questions on the feasibility of and benefits derived from integrated maternal and child health–family planning programs.

In the discussion of these three areas, three major questions will serve as guides. In setting the goals for any social intervention, who speaks for the person, group, or community that is the target of the change effort? In selecting the means of intervention, how does one assure genuine participation in the change process to the people who are its targets? In assessing the consequences of social intervention, how does one take account of higher-order or unintended effects?

In this chapter, there is considerable mention of population policy, and it may be useful to define that term. For purposes here, I will use a definition by Berelson, for whom population policy is the "more or less deliberate effort by governments to affect the rates of population growth in their countries—not the incidental demographic effect but the intended one" (1974, p. 2). Berelson also limits his definition to governmental actions and to population growth; for the definition of population policy, he leaves aside nongovernmental efforts at population control. This definition of population policy is only one among several that might be utilized, but it may help focus the discussion.

There are values and ethical assumptions implicit in this definition of population policy, and these should be recognized. This definition derives in part from a particular conception of the "population problem." Some might argue that population growth is not a problem, and hence there is neither a need for nor any utility in this definition, and others might favor a definition that implicitly recognizes a population problem, but puts the emphasis on something other than population growth. One effect of Berelson's definition, both in the field of population and in this chapter, is to direct attention to one particular subset of germane population issues.

Since the focus of this paper is on ethical issues arising in the context of major family planning efforts in developing countries, one important ethical issue will not receive the specific attention it would if the focus were on developed societies. This concerns unmarried cohabiting adolescents and the ethical issues involved in the provision of contraceptives, abortion, and sterilization services to this group. A few remarks will touch on these issues, but in many of the Third World societies the age at marriage is low, and moral standards and local customs are such that the proportions of unmarried adolescents who engage in sexual relations are lower than in some developed countries. (The definition of "married" used in this chapter is broad and includes people in consensual as well as in legal unions.)

## NATIONAL FAMILY PLANNING PROGRAMS

In a review and evaluation of twenty national family planning programs (Lapham & Mauldin, 1972a, 1972b), a framework is presented that attempts to serve as a guide for answering these questions: how well are national family planning programs doing, what criteria seem important for distinguishing between more successful and less successful programs? Four sets of criteria are offered: (a) statistical, (b) programmatic, (c) fertility reduction, and (d) social, economic and health. Table 1 reproduces the application of the criteria in categories a, b, and c to seven of the twenty national programs, including the four countries with the highest 1970 rates of new family planning acceptors among married women of reproductive age (MWRA) and three of the four countries with the lowest family planning acceptance rates among MWRA. Our focus here is on the programmatic criteria, which are methods, procedures, and actions countries have adopted or might adopt in their attempts to achieve family planning acceptance and fertility reduction goals. A general finding of this review and evaluation is that national family planning programs with more "yes" answers to the questions dealt with in Part B of the table have higher acceptance levels. In the discussion below, these questions are explained, and particular attention is given to those programmatic criteria that pose difficult ethical questions.

*Does the government have a population policy that includes fertility reduction?* (Item B.1. in Table I)

Most countries with family planning programs have policies calling for fertility reduction with varying degrees of specificity. This is considered important as a

TABLE 1. A Family Planning Program Evaluation Framework Applied to Seven Countries with National Family Planning Programs

| Criteria and year program started | Korea 1961 | Singapore 1966 | Taiwan 1963 | Mauritius 1964 | Nepal 1965 | Turkey 1967 | Morocco 1966 |
|---|---|---|---|---|---|---|---|
| A. Statistical measurements | | | | | | | |
| 1. Total number of acceptors—1970 | 431,000[b] | 28,515[a] (1969) | 141,200[c] | 9,794 | 30,210[d] | (56,000)[d] | 23,814[d] |
| 2. Acceptors as percent of MWRA (15-44)—1970 | (10.1) | 8.3 | 7.8 | 6.5 | 1.3 | (1.0) | 0.9 |
| 3. Ratio of acceptors to net one-year gain in numbers of MWRA (15-44) | (3.7) | 5.8 | 3.4 | 2.5 | (0.6) | (0.4) | 0.3 |
| 4. Continuation rates | | | | | | | |
| a. 2-year first-method continuation rate, all acceptors | | | | | | | |
| IUD | 38 | * | 53 | * | n.a. | n.a. | n.a. |
| Pills | *[a] | * | n.a. | * | n.a. | n.a. | n.a. |
| b. Average 2-year continuation rate, all acceptors, all methods | n.a. | n.a. | n.a. | n.a. | n.a. | n.a. | n.a. |
| c. Percentage of acceptors who have avoided childbearing in the 3 years following acceptance | 77[e] | n.a. | 80[e] | n.a. | n.a. | n.a. | n.a. |
| 5. Percent of MWRA using contraception, 1970 | (33) | n.a. | 44 | 19+ | n.a. | 9.3 (1968) | (3.1) |
| a. Directly from the program | (28) | 25 | 24 | 18.5 | n.a. | n.a. | (1.1) |
| b. From the private sector | (5) | n.a. | 20 | <1 | n.a. | n.a. | 2 |
| 6. Percent of 1970 acceptor target obtained | 81 | 79 (1969) | 106 | n.t. | n.a. | 24 | 20 |
| 1970 target—number of acceptors per 1,000 MWRA | 125 | 105 | 74 | n.t. (1969) | n.a. | 42 | 45 |
| 7. Cost per acceptor (US$)[f]—1970 | 6.70 | 3.61 (1963) | 4.00 | 20.47 (1969) | 23.16 | 23.00 | n.a. |
| B. Procedures and supportive measures | | | | | | | |
| 1. Fertility reduction included in official planning policy | Y | Y | Y | Y | Q | N | Y |
| 2. Favorable public statements by political leaders | Y | Y | Y | Q | P | N | P |
| 3. Contraception readily and easily available, publicly and commercially throughout the world | Y | Y | Y | Q | P | P | P |
| 4. Customs and legal regulations allow importation of contraceptives not manufactured locally | Q | Y | Y | Q | Q | P | P |

| Item | 1 | 2 | 3 | 4 | 5 | 6 |
|---|---|---|---|---|---|---|
| 5. Vigorous effort to provide family planning services to all MWRA | Y | Y | Y | Y | P | P |
| 6. Adequate family planning administration structure | Y | Y | Q | Q | Q | Q |
| 7. Training facilities available and utilized | Y | Q | Y | Q | Q | Q |
| 8. Full-time home-visiting field workers | Y | Y | Y | Y | N | N |
| 9. Postpartum information, education, and service program | N | Y | P | Q | P | N |
| 10. Abortion services openly and legally available to all | P | Q | P | N | N | N |
| 11. Voluntary sterilization services (male and female) openly and legally available to all | Q | Q | N | N | P | N |
| 12. Use of mass media on a substantial basis | Y | Y | Y | Y | P | P |
| 13. Government provides substantial part of family planning budget from its own resources | Y | Y | Y | N | Y | P |
| 14. Record keeping systems for clients at clinic level and for program service statistics | Y | Y | Y | Y | Y | P |
| 15. Serious and continuous evaluation effort | Y | Q | Y | Q | P | P |
| **C. Fertility reduction** | | | | | | |
| 1. Evidence of decline attributable to program | | | | | | |
|   a. In age-specific fertility rates | Y | Q | Y | Q | N | N |
|   b. In marital age-specific fertility rates | Q | Q | Q | Q | N | N |
|   c. In crude birth rates | Y | Y | Y | Y | N | N |

Source: Adapted and reprinted with the permission of the Population Council from Lapham and Mauldin (1972a), Table 2, pages 36–38.

Note. Figures in ( ) indicate estimates based on partial data: MWRA = married women of reproductive age (ages 15–44); n.a. = not available; n.t. = no target; Y = yes; Q = qualified yes; P = partially; N = no.

a Asterisk indicates that two-year continuation rates are not available. The 12-month continuation rates are as follows: Korea, pill—26; Singapore, IUD—69; Singapore, pill—56; Mauritius, IUD—68; Mauritius, pill—53.

b With 20 percent estimated for duplication among methods. In Singapore in 1967 and 1968, 25 percent and 17 percent, respectively, of "acceptors" were acceptors of temporary methods. They were re-counted when they later accepted a clinical method such as the pill (Third Annual Report, Family Planning and Population Board, Singapore, September 12, 1969).

c Individual allowances made for reinsertions, repeat pill acceptors, and duplication of methods.

d With 5 percent estimated for duplication of methods.

e IUD acceptors only.

f These costs are based on local figures in most cases, with all acceptors counted and no allowance made for overlap among methods as has been done in Item A.1. above.

general guideline for policy makers at all levels who have responsibility for achievement of fertility reduction goals and also because openly supportive policies may
enable private medical practitioners to feel more secure that they are not
opposing the government when providing family planning services to clients.

One ethical question here concerns who determines the policy. Although in
some countries information from KAP (knowledge, attitudes, and practices
related to family planning) sample surveys has been used by national leaders in
determining policies on the initiation of family planning programs, quite clearly
in other cases, the general population, whose fertility hopefully will decline as a
result of the policy and specific service program organized on the basis of that
policy, is neither consulted nor involved in the policy determination. This is true
with many efforts aimed at improvement of the standard of living or the quality
of life, for example, new agricultural techniques or immunization programs to
control specific diseases. A subsequent and more difficult question is whether it is
always wise or in the best interests of those people to be provided with family
planning services to be involved in the determination of the policy. Do they
always have adequate information to make reasoned judgments? If not, and if
they are to be involved in making the policy, is the resultant time lag, which may
be considerable, a strong negative factor for the development of programs said to
be designed to improve the quality of family life and individual health and
well-being? Another issue concerns individual desires and perceived needs—for
example, lots of children may be advantageous or seem to be so to the individual
family—versus the so-called collective good, with the presumption that policy
makers are able to discern long-term societal needs more clearly than the
population at large.

However, one must not carry this trend of reasoning too far. In whose
benefit are existing policy makers primarily interested? Is a population policy
really an insincere ploy designed as a smokescreen to divert public attention
away from other social problems or lack of economic development? The latter is
not an uncommon accusation (Pradervand, 1970; Raulet, 1970; Remili, 1972).
How much influence is there from other countries, especially those who are
major powers in the population field, on the formulation and development of
population policies aimed at providing family planning services to high-fertility
groups? By what ethical criteria can attempts at the promulgation of population
policies in other countries or for other groups be judged? On the one hand, there
may be sincere concern for improving the quality of human life; on the other,
there may be self-interest ("larger numbers of people may affect the world we
live in," "famines may have international implications," and so on). All of these
are difficult issues.

*Does the leader of the country speak publicly and favorably about family
planning once or twice a year?* (Item B.2. in Table I)

There is a feeling among some family planning proponents that government
policy is all the more clear when occasionally (but not too frequently for

fear of overemphasis leading to a backlash) stated openly and positively by the political leaders of the country. Along with encouragement of segments of the general public, such statements may serve to encourage and motivate middle-level administrators. In one sense, this allows for some participation in the change process by those who are the intended targets; these and other statements by political leaders are not always accepted at face value and often lead to debate and discussion among the intended participants. If, however, the information provided through such statements is only partially complete, for example, failure to mention undesirable side effects when exhorting people to use certain methods of contraception, as occurred in Tunisia some years ago (Thorn & Montague, 1972), then a moral and ethical question must be raised. It will be difficult to find defensible grounds for failure to provide the most complete information available on side effects. This leads to other problems concerning the next programmatic criterion.

*Are the major contraceptive methods (pill, IUD, and condom) readily and easily available throughout the country in both public (free or subsidized) and private (commercial) sectors?* (Item B.3. in Table I)

The stress is on methods and making them widely available. Does the program really offer all clients a choice, together with information concerning relative advantages and disadvantages among methods? If program personnel subtlely or directly encourage one method over another, the client may not have free choice. To be sure, program personnel may have valid reasons for encouraging a woman who lives some distance from a supply point or a clinic to have an IUD inserted rather than to take pills, but the line may be rather fine between encouragement and an "either this or nothing" position. We will come back to this again when discussing the abortion and sterilization progammatic criteria. A basic question is who decides—the one delivering the services or the recipient—and that is not always easy to ascertain, nor is it always clear who should have the most say in that decision. Another point regarding choice of methods is whether recipients in one social group, say, a poor illiterate group, are more likely to be given one method, while another social group may be offered a different method. A key question is the availability of full information about each method.

An example of availability of methods comes from the Indian experience. The utilization of contraceptive pills is almost nonexistent in the Indian family planning program. IUDs, sterilization (for males and females), and condoms are the major available methods, with a small handful of pills being offered. The Indian government's reasoning is that the total side effects of contraceptive pills are unknown, and hence pills must be considered still experimental and are thus not made widely available. Also, Indian researchers are trying to develop their own pill, one that will have fewer side effects. One result of this policy is that millions of Indian women cannot use or even try a contraceptive method available to and used by some 65 million women in other countries. Yet the degree to which non-Indians should speak on this question is probably limited. My own value judgment is that no attempts should be made to tie other assistance to India to acceptance of pill availability on a large scale; that is, no attempts should be made to tell the Indian government that other assistance will be curtailed unless they promote pill distribution on a large scale. We will return to this issue later.

*Is there a vigorous effort to provide family planning services to all married women of child-bearing age in the country? Is there a group of workers whose primary task is to visit women in their homes (at least in rural areas) to talk about family planning and child care?* (Items B.5., B.8., and B.12. in Table I)

As noted earlier, the term "married" refers to persons in consensual as well as legal unions, and for some countries a more appropriate wording might be "any cohabiting person desiring such services," including husbands and unmarried persons of all ages. Such definitions raise an interesting question: why allow or even vigorously encourage one group such as married women, but not another, for example, husbands (for vasectomies) or unmarried cohabiting adolescents? The vigorous efforts in large-scale programs are usually aimed at high-fertility groups and especially those groups for whom provision of services is least likely to create ethical dilemmas or political embarrassment for decision makers. Providing contraceptive services to married couples who already have children and who want the government to provide such services is an easier policy to adopt (though not necessarily easy to implement) because adopting a policy that specifies provision of services to people in other categories might leave the decision makers open to attack for abetting promiscuity or for diminishing national moral standards.

With the focus here on large-scale family planning programs we should consider questions related to "a vigorous effort." The most successful family planning programs, defined as those with the highest contraceptive acceptor and utilization rates, are those that have undertaken vigorous efforts, often involving extensive use of home-visiting field workers. Vigor has many facets, however. It may mean a carefully administered program with serious attempts to keep workers well-trained and capably supervised, with adequate supplies ordered and available where and when needed, and so forth. It may also include some extent of omitting unfavorable knowledge, pressures that may be brought upon individuals by field workers anxious to reach monthly quotas of acceptors in order to retain their jobs or obtain promotions, and perhaps performance of operations such as vasectomies under conditions of questionable safety standards. Population control proponents might answer the latter by saying that birth rates are so great and pressing that these are minor problems in comparison to the need for vigorous efforts. This is not clear; vigorous family planning efforts, while undoubtedly necessary for substantial program success, probably should include some care not to ease across that fine line dividing provision of effective family planning education and services and coercive endeavors justified on the grounds of some greater good.

A side issue here is the falsification of records by workers at all levels in order to demonstrate that a vigorous effort has been carried out and has achieved good numbers of acceptors. In some programs a lack of careful supervision combined with a big push to achieve targets or produce large numbers of acceptors has led workers at lower and middle levels to be overzealous in their reports on local achievements.

Two other topics can be raised under the vigorous effort question— incentives, and the use of mass media.

## Incentives

Incentives either for recipients or for medical and other workers in family planning programs are often part of a vigorous national effort to reduce fertility rates. In Egypt, for example, an incentive of 1 Egyptian pound (about U.S.$2, depending on the exchange rate) was paid to doctors for each IUD inserted, with the proviso that the woman must return for a follow-up visit one month later and must retain the IUD. Recipient incentives involve cash payments or social security or educational bond-type payments at some future date for those who limit the number of children or who have no addition children. Several ethical questions can be raised about incentives. Who should get the incentive payment—the worker, the recipient, or both? How does the incentive affect free choice? Does an incentive system lead to abuses regarding full disclosure of information, for example, side effects or difficulties of reversibility of vasectomy or tubal ligation?

A cogent "Case Study in Bioethics" prepared by the Institute of Society, Ethics, and Life Sciences concerns the topic "Food Incentives for Sterilization: Can They Be Just?" (Veatch, 1973). The setting of the hypothetical case is a very poor country with a population that doubles every 21 years. The Family Planning Council has recommended drastic action: "every citizen who voluntarily agrees to accept sterilization will be given coupons redeemable for 100 kadis [the fictitious local currency assumed to be the equivalent of U.S.$20] worth of food. An individual who voluntarily requests sterilization after no more than two children would get another 100-kadi coupon. And to increase recruiting, a similar coupon would be provided for persons bringing to a government clinic anyone who subsequently accepts sterilization. In defense of this proposal, the council argues: 'No one will be penalized for having children; no one will suffer' " (Veatch, 1973, p. 10).

Edward Pohlman argues that the case is ethically justifiable.

The father of two children can either get sterilized and get 200 kadis, or not; under the status quo, he does not have these options. Not to offer the scheme might restrict freedom. Rapid increases in population result in many restrictions on true freedom. Freedom may be like seed: giving up a little for a population limitation scheme may produce a harvest of freedoms later—and avoid decreasing regimentation (1973, p.11).

He feels this proposal is a way for the government to organize ("manipulate" is the word he uses) individual behavior for group goals, noting that governments already do so by discouraging lawlessness, requiring certain sanitation procedures, and the like. Pohlman believes society "has a right to manipulate family size if (and only if) anticipated rates of population growth are judged to be severely harmful to the well-being of present and future members of the society as a whole." He concedes, though, that knowing when this latter point has been reached is difficult.

Daniel Callahan, on the other hand, argues against this proposal on ethical grounds. "The assumption behind any incentive program is that it is possible to induce, bribe or otherwise manipulate people into doing that which someone else wants them to do. Incentives would not be necessary if people were prepared, on the basis of their own motivations, to take the steps desired (by someone else). When they are not so prepared, then bait must be put before them." Callahan makes a major point that the government is asking for and obtaining a permanent benefit in return for taking a temporary step, a balance he finds unjust. "Had the proposal called for a food bonus in return for the use of contraceptives—a temporary benefit for a temporary avoidance of children—the transaction would be more just" (1973a, p. 11). He is not against incentive plans as such, but to the conditions of the incentives in this case. However, he puts forth arguments against incentive plans in general, for example, the need for poor people for food now: "the very nature of incentive programs in poor countries is to trade upon the needs of the poor, pushing them to make choices they would not otherwise make" (1973a, p. 12).

Lest we think of this case as a purely hypothetical situation, a review of the scope of benefits and incentives offered in the Ernakulum, India, vasectomy camps is indicative of the extent of incentives offered in major efforts. Two vasectomy camps held seven months apart in Ernakulum obtained 78,423 sterilization acceptors. The benefits included regular incentive payments, extra cash payments, food rations, a saree and a dhoti (local garments for a man and woman, respectively), and other items, all totaling 101 rupees (about U.S.$14) for male aceptors and 109 for female acceptors, plus free transport services and medicines (Krishnakumar, 1971, 1972).

### Mass Media

The use of mass media—newspapers, magazines, posters, pamphlets, radio, and television—on a major scale is often part of the vigorous effort adopted by a national family planning program. These mass media techniques can disseminate knowledge about methods and availability of services and about relationships between family health and family size, as well as provide the mechanism for exhortation and encouragement to use available family planning methods. Mass media contacts may also play an important role in educating young people about population by conveying to them the idea that to plan and control family size is possible, ethically correct from the government's standpoint, and a normal part of the marriage and family formation process. The ethical questions here might center on making information more widely available, and thereby expanding the range of choices available to citizens, versus the use of mass media in a manipulative manner designed to have people believe and act as the government wishes, for whatever reasons the latter may have. Does the one-way flow of mass media assist the process of participation in the change process by those who are the targets of the desired change? In one sense, yes, if the information provided is complete and reasonably accurate, since this may lead to informed discussion and the debate among groups within the target population, for example, housewives, co-workers, husbands and wives, and so on. On the other hand, we do not have to look far, spatially or temporally, for examples of the use of mass media in the form of TV and press releases in which there is clear attempt to mislead people and have them believe and act in ways designed to be of most benefit to certain selected individuals.

*Is a family planning information and education service provided by trained female workers to all women who deliver their babies in hospitals or maternity centers?* (Item B.9. in Table I)

This is the postpartum approach to family planning; the idea is that an appropriate, useful time to discuss family planning with the woman is when she has just been delivered of her baby (or had an abortion), and that those women who deliver in a hospital or maternity center can be contacted and either offered services immediately or referred to a clinic for services at a subsequent date, perhaps when the newborn infant is brought in for a check-up. An inherent element in the postpartum concept is the linking of maternal and child health care and family planning services: the latter can contribute to improved family health for the existing children, and this is a basic concept in the family planning–delivery system research project discussed later on in this chapter. Some persons associated with this approach argue that an ethical practice, from a medical point of view, is to prescribe contraception for several months after delivery, as a means of protecting the health of the mother.

The general focus and intent of this programmatic criterion is genuine service and concern for the welfare of both mother and child. One must be careful, however, that the situation is not used for coercive or semicoercive tactics. If the intent is to offer services and encourage the women to use effective contraception so that the chances of another quickly ensuing pregnancy are reduced, many observers would agree that the postpartum approach is ethically acceptable, especially in countries with family planning programs. Spacing of children has many advantages for the individual family, and contraception can be discontinued easily (in most cases—I know of one doctor in a developing society who cut the strings off the IUDs he inserted, so that women could not pull out the IUD themselves or with the assistance of a local midwife). However, if the situation is used to encourage sterilization—

"you're here at the maternity hospital anyway," "it's a good time to do it without others knowing," and so on—then questions of propriety should be raised; unfair advantage is being taken of a situation in which the woman is weak and just completing a difficult and perhaps painful experience. A difficult question may arise for the physician in cases of women who say they really want to be sterilized at this time. If the woman asking for sterilization has three children, is that different from the case of the woman who has just delivered her first?

*Are medically adequate, induced abortion services legally and openly available to all women?* (Item B.10. in Table I)

Induced abortion is one of the most frequently used methods of birth limitation in the world. In many nations, induced abortion is not legal or else is restricted to cases involving narrowly defined medical reasons or juridical reasons such as rape and incest. Elective abortion and abortion for social reasons are legal in most of the socialist countries, in Japan, Tunisia, China, North Vietnam, Singapore, Hong Kong, India, the United States, and several other Western nations, and under special circumstances in some other countries such as Zambia, Korea, and Cuba (Tietze & Dawson, 1973, 1975). Wherever there are adequate medical services and abortion has been legalized and is openly available, substantial numbers of women have sought induced abortion, and this has led to reductions in fertility. Thus, officials of national family planning programs often try to include abortion services to whatever degree is possible within the existing legal and cultural settings. For women who experience contraceptive failure, for women who conceive an unwanted pregnancy prior to knowledge of or acceptance of family planning services, and for women who become program drop-outs and subsequently have unwanted pregnancies, the availability of good abortion services provides a viable alternative and helps achieve family health and fertility goals.

This is not the place to discuss the ethics of abortion per se, but there are ethical questions to consider when abortion is part of a national family planning program. Equal availability of medically adequate services for all women desiring abortions is one problem. Legal abortion services should be equally available to rich and poor, to the unmarried as well as the married, and to people in urban and rural areas, since those who perform illegal abortions tend to provide much better services to persons who can afford to pay more. Another problem is the extent to which the occasion of a woman's seeking an abortion should be used to encourage or coerce her into accepting contraception or sterilization. The following examples may help focus this discussion.

For several years one hospital in Tunis performed substantial numbers of abortions and female sterilizations—substantial in the Tunisian context, that is. (For example, in 1972 the total number of social abortions in Tunisia was 4,621, and the total number of tubal ligations 2,459. In Tunisia, prior to September 1973, a woman was legally entitled to what has been called a social abortion if she had five living children. In September, 1973, the law was considerably liberalized, with first-trimester abortions allowed in an appropriate medical setting for any woman regardless of the number of existing children or her marital status; second-trimester abortions were allowed under somewhat more restricted medical guidelines. Before September 1973, other therapeutic abortions were also performed, with this definition sometimes applied to women with fewer than five living children. Prior to the liberalization of the law, most abortions of both categories were done in only a handful of hospitals in Tunisia.) The doctor in charge of obstetrics and gynecology in the above-mentioned hospital is a renowned Tunisian gynecologist, and for some time had a policy of refusing abortion services to many women returning for a second abortion unless that woman agreed to have a tubal ligation at the same time, a "complet" as it is called by this doctor. The reasons given included: the woman already has a substantial number of living children, she has twice demonstrated a desire not to have an additional child, and she has indicated inefficient use of contraception (with the exception of such cases as pregnancy with IUD *in situ*, and the like). Also, as this doctor said to me, there is a shortage of maternity beds in this hospital, so why should they be used for women who keep coming back for additional abortions? Yet, here is one case in which a client legally entitled to a service was being denied that service, unless the client agreed to accept sterilization. Dr. X faced the decision to apply or not apply this self-imposed policy many times each month and in so doing forced clients to make choices they might not have made otherwise.

A second example comes from India. The new abortion law in India was signed in August, 1971, and in a 1973 conversation with two prominent Indian physicians (one in charge of a no-birth-bonus pilot project, and the other a professor of obstetrics and gynecology) a question on how the new abortion law was working out in practice elicited the reply that abortions are done only if the woman accepts sterilization also, and that abortions are done only if there are two or more living children, with a few exceptions for unmarried girls. This policy was said to be overall and not just in the areas known directly by these two informants. The policy holds true, said Dr. Y, even for a woman who has two children and who desires a third, but who has gotten pregnant sooner than she wishes; that is, the spacing of children would not be consistent with that woman's desires. In such cases, the woman must accept sterilization in order to receive the abortion. In India, 85 percent of the abortions then being done were said to also involve a sterilization (tubal ligation). This raises some very interesting questions regarding coercion as well as the limiting programmatic effect this type of policy could lead to. The latter may be one unintended consequence of the actual application of the abortion law, if the above information is correct for major portions of India. Negative feelings about abortion and family planning might develop, with the result that a policy designed to accelerate fertility decline in India could have little effect on fertility and perhaps even have a downward effect on the level of acceptance of family planning. The implementation and effects of the abortion law in India merit very careful study.

An important aspect of the abortion question is that family planning, in some instances, is a substitute for illegal, often dangerous, abortion. This is a major motive for family planning in Latin America, and one can make a case that, wherever there are illegal abortions, appropriate alternatives should be provided and one of the easier alternatives might be family planning.

*Are medically adequate voluntary sterilization services (for males and females) legally and openly available?* (Item B.11. in Table I)

The inclusion of sterilization services in family planning programs is based on the belief that sterilization offers major advantages for the family health and welfare of couples desiring permanent protection against pregnancy. As with abortion, we will leave aside here the general ethical issues concerning sterilization—whether it is right or wrong in and of itself as a method of preventing pregnancy. Some of the major programmatic issues regarding sterilization have come out in the earlier discussions—full disclosure concerning reversibility difficulties, various pressures to accept this method, the difficulties for some clients to really have free choice in the matter, and the insistence in some cases that clients accept sterilization in addition to some other desired service.

*Does the government provide money it its own national budget, that is, from nonexternal sources, for a substantial part (about one-half or more) of the population and family planning program both for family planning services provided through regular health channels and for special population activities?* (Item B. 13. in Table I)

Internal funding, that is, funds to operate a program being provided by the government or major private groups within the country in which the program operates, is considered important for several reasons. First, for commitment to the achievement of population policies, governments should provide some substantial portions of their family planning budgets. This leads to questions concerning appropriate amounts and proportions to be provided by internal sources and external sources for a particular program. Donor agencies providing the major external funding want a say in how their funds are to be spent, a say in program emphasis, and usually some sort of review or audit of how their donated funds have been utilized, even if they are providing only one-third or one-half of the family planning budget. An ethical question here is the balance of influence, control, and decision making between the recipient country or organization and the donor agency. The degree of freedom of the recipient is probably compromised in direct proportion to the extent a program is financed by external donors. However, an ethical implication of this is that the poor countries in greatest need of external assistance are likely to have the least amount of freedom in choosing the type of program emphasis for their countries.[1]

Second, planning departments can never be sure that funds from external sources will continue for long periods of time. Thus, to ensure continuation of a program, it is advisable for the local government to assume much, and perhaps eventually all, of the budget support necessary for population activities. Third, the policy makers of each country can have greater control over the direction, type, and efficiency of the population program they desire and deem necessary when the money they are spending comes from their own coffers. It should be recognized, however, that there may be instances of countries strongly desiring programs but unable to finance them except from external sources. This third point relates very closely to the "who decides" question. This topic will be discussed further in the following section.

Running throughout the discussion of ethical questions related to these programmatic criteria are two sometimes divergent ideas. For program success and achievement of general or specific fertility reduction goals, these measures are useful guidelines for program administrators. "Do this" and "success" is more likely! On the other hand, the application of some of these programmatic measures raises questions about the degree of involvement of the intended recipients in the change process, who decides how to run the programs and inform the intended recipients about the offered services, including benefits and drawbacks, and also questions about unintended effects that may arise. Policy makers, sometimes with assistance from donor agencies, often decide that the severity of population growth rate problems warrants the efforts undertaken. Note that even the use of the phrase "severity of population growth rate problems" involves both empirical and ethical/value components. A set of factors (for example, population size, growth rate, and distribution) may be perceived at a given point in time as of little consequence, but at another point in time or when measured against some normative yardstick, a similar or identical set of factors may be perceived as creating difficulties or reducing actual or potential benefits and, hence, is a "severe problem" in need of urgent attention. Interestingly, foreign advisors or nationals who frequently attend international meetings may help set the intellectual framework within which certain trends are perceived as "problematic" and others defined with the label "severe."

An ethical issue raised in this discussion is implicit in the phrase "adequate information to make reasoned judgments." This presents one of the most difficult ethical issues regarding population policy and programs that may flow

---

[1] An opposite and important point of view has been advanced by a colleague: it is remarkable how little influence the donors have had. In spite of their best efforts, programs are still poorly managed, do not provide a full range of services, and so on. Donors have to live within the local framework and, at least at the present time, are not able to assist with the provision of a more ethical program in which family planning is more readily available to people who might wish to use it.

from policy implementation. Two ethical questions are: who can and who should determine the capacity of certain individuals or groups to make informed choices about matters affecting their destiny?

The 1973 case of two adolescent black girls in Alabama being sterilized is a rather dramatic example, including questions of coercion as well as provision of adequate information to permit rational decisions. In this case those involved include adolescent, parent, doctor, and later the courts, legislative bodies, and outside groups, the last three trying to set ethical and legal standards for determining acceptable actions and decision making in future cases (*New York Times*, September 21, 1973). An important element here is the set of conditions under which people can make informed choices. For the example of the sterilized adolescents, one can suggest that parental and adolescent consent are necessary, on the basis of full disclosure of all consequences including the possibility of failure associated with attempts to reverse sterilization operations. Also in cases such as this—involving girls whose knowledge and experience are limited by reason of age as well as social background—one might suggest the need for an *amicus curiae* to offer adequate information in addition to that provided by the parent and the doctor, because the process of sterilization is generally irreversible and is likely to have major long-term effects on the marriage and family-formation process for the individual involved. That is, the more determinative a given action is on future choices, the more care should be exercised by all involved parties to ensure adequate information before the fact.

A related aspect of this issue concerns the degree to which authoritarian dependence is an accepted part of the local social fabric. In some contexts an individual may find greater psychological freedom when others in authority are making decisions, but as noted in the earlier discussion concerning the so-called collective good, that reasoning should not be carried too far. As the Task Force on Ethics and Population has noted, freedom can be viewed also as "the capacity, the opportunity, and the incentive to make reflective choices and to act on these choices," and two qualities that increase the individual's capacity are knowledge and a sense of efficacy (1972, p. 10). In sum, it is fair to suggest that people concerned with ethical issues in population policy should recognize, but not overemphasize, limits on freedom and rationality in the population field.

## FUNDING LEVELS AND SOURCES

The past few years have witnessed a substantial increase in funds made available by major donor agencies for national family planning programs and population and fertility control efforts. Most of this increase is due to larger government contributions, particularly the United States government through the U.S. Agency for International Development (USAID), although private donations for population activities have also increased. The International Bank for Reconstruction and Development has joined the population donor agency group, and the United Nations has established the United Nations Fund for

Population Activities (UNFPA) which committed about $50 million in 1973 to the field of international population assistance (UNFPA, 1974). With attempts to account for duplication—that is, counting only once those funds provided by USAID to the UNFPA, by the Ford Foundation to the Population Council, and so on, the approximate donor funding levels for international population activities in the developing world, and excluding, for example, U.S. expenditures on U.S. family planning programs—funds are estimated as follows for the four years 1969–1972 (OECD, 1974, pp. 1–4), and the estimated amount for 1973 is something over $200 million.

| | |
|---|---|
| 1969 | $ 86 million |
| 1970 | $125 million |
| 1971 | $147 million |
| 1972 | $183 million |

There are a number of questions to review in this context, especially since there are indications that funding levels may continue to increase in the next years. One trend is the emergence of multilateral agencies in this field, with bilateral agencies such as the Swedish International Development Authority and USAID channeling substantial proportions of the population funds through the UNFPA. The increase in available funds brings additional problems, including several of importance in a discussion of ethics.

### How Is the Money Spent?

Are the funds made available for population program assistance utilized in the intended countries with programs, or is a substantial proportion spent in the donor countries themselves, for a variety of purposes that may have tangential or long-term utility, but which are not of immediate concern to a program administrator in a high-fertility country trying to develop and improve a national family planning program? Research is a major category of assistance by donor agencies, and much of the population research is carried out in the developed world. There is probably an ideal balance between long-term research for new and better contraceptives and the immediate needs of current programs to deliver services, but that balance is not easily discerned. Hankinson (1973) reports that a significant percentage of aid for research in the field of population is given to institutions and universities in the developed world. According to him, this has three drawbacks: (a) the lack of attention to assisting the development of research capacity in the developing countries, (b) "the aid benefits the donors more than the recipient country," and (c) "differences in interests, aims, and objectives can arise between the recipient country and the university or institution, which may have to meet other obligations, such as publications of research studies and staff development, as well as the practical needs of the recipient" (1973, p. 18).

Another category for which a substantial portion of donor agency funding is expended is technical assistance and administration. Most donor governments and agencies are reluctant to simply write checks; they want administrators and technicians who guide and monitor the utilization of the funds in the donor countries. Also there are shortages of appropriately trained personnel in many of the countries with national family planning programs. In some countries, problems arise with the total number and the quality of advisors and technicians provided. A family planning program with limited national personnel may have difficulty effectively utilizing a half-dozen or more foreign advisors in the population program. Of greater concern sometimes are the quality and basic interests of the advisors. A group of family planning officials from developing countries noted recently that their experience

> with foreign advisors in the population field had been almost always an unhappy one, and the general impression of the recipient group was that the first priority of the advisors that they had had was to follow their own interests rather than that of the host country, either by concentrating on work related to their own field of research or Ph. D. thesis, or by acting more as a "tourist" than as a working member of the country's program (OECD Development Centre, 1973, p. 33).

What is the correct approach to the provision of technical assistance and advisors, and what ethical criteria should govern the decisions in this realm? These questions are associated with the "who decides" issue, although here they apply more to the donor and recipient governments and agencies involved, rather than directly to the target population.

For those funds available for direct family planning program activities in the recipient country, sometimes there are questions and differences as to how to utilize them most effectively to achieve program goals. The givers of aid tend to want a say in the operation of the program, which leads to the next question.

### Who Determines How to Run a National Family Planning Program?

The recipient countries naturally desire a rather wide range of freedom in the operation of programs in their countries. The interest of donor agencies is to be responsive to government legislatures, boards of trustees, and other bodies that authorize the funds, in part to generate continuing funding and, in part, to report that a reasonable job has been done with funds already supplied. These interests are not always mutual. For example, recipient countries feel that funds should be used to support population policies and plans they have developed, through general program support or assistance for particular aspects of the plan already developed. Donor agencies, however, may come along with other ideas and urge that the funds be used for projects they deem most useful. The resolution of these differences is difficult and time consuming.

Another problem concerns the occasional willingness of donor agencies to supply contraceptives that may not meet the strict safety requirements in force in some developed countries. Likewise, donor agencies sometimes urge the distribution of contraceptive pills by paramedical or nonmedical personnel (using various checklists for screening doubtful cases), while in the donor countries these contraceptives are legally available only on medical prescription. Thus different standards are applied, on various grounds (such as, in the case of pill distribution by paramedical personnel, the relative risks of complications or death from childbirth versus the risks of side effects from pill usage, and the unlikelihood of better doctor/population ratios—especially in rural areas— in the near future). There is, in many cases, a different quality of service available in developed and developing countries, and some people suggest that it may be unethical to apply the standards of developed countries because this would prohibit availability to many of the poorer people in the developing countries. Also an argument is advanced that the standards are largely artificial, meaningless, and reflect the conservatism of the medical profession.

Similar ethical questions arise if a donor agency pushes for particular methods of fertility control such as abortion and sterilization in countries where such practices are not acceptable in the context of the local legal, cultural, and social settings.

## Time Lags and Related Problems

The time is often considerable from initial discussion concerning major donor assistance for general program support or specific project support to actual implementation of projects, with periods up to three years not uncommon. Even the last stages between agreement and the actual flow of funds can last a year or more. While primarily a procedural concern, one unintended consequence is a general feeling of discouragement and disillusionment on the part of the recipients. Not all of the blame for delays should be put on the donors' shoulders; administrative delays and bottlenecks are partly the responsibility of the governments of the recipient countries. This time-lag problem raises the additional question of the overall financial absorptive capacity of countries with national family planning programs. Is a level of $200-plus million in international assistance for population work the right amount? Would more in the near future be detrimental or helpful in reducing population growth rates? Who is to decide, and using what criteria? Does the population field know yet the best delivery systems for providing individual couples with the means to have the number of children they desire? These questions are more than theoretical. For example, in May, 1973, General William H. Draper of the Population Crisis Committee called for an annual expenditure of $2 billion to assist population programs in "the world's poor countries," excluding China (*New York Times*, May 7, 1973). The ethical dilemmas here include determination of levels and uses of external funding and problems of unintended consequences.

Reporting procedures suggested or required by donor agencies may improve program administrative procedures and point to problems that need to be solved. They may also cause the attention of skilled personnel (who may be scarce) to be diverted from regular tasks (as defined by the recipient countries) to other tasks that must be complied with in order to satisfy a particular donor. The resultant tensions may have the unintended effect of slowing down the whole process of developing a viable national family planning program, which is exactly opposite to the stated goal to be achieved by providing large-scale funding for population activities in developing societies.

Another aspect of required reporting procedures is based on the tenet that the funds are intended to provide specific services to particular groups of individuals, with only minimum amounts absorbed by bureaucratic procedures and personnel. Persons in local bureaucracies, however, may wish to use the funds in ways that enhance their own standing as individuals or in relationship to other departments, and such "enhancement" may have less to do with providing given sets of services than the donors find acceptable to their own established sets of values and procedural criteria.

In the larger context, solving perceived population growth rate problems is not easy, and the total time frame in the minds of donors and recipients, especially the former, may be much shorter than necessary. Population growth rates do not decline rapidly in most settings, and the expectations of "more money leading to quick results" are likely to go unmet. One effect of this may be cutting off or decreasing the levels of funds in a country before success has been given a reasonable chance to materialize. But then, who is to determine whether and when population funds are no longer having an effect? This is not only an empirical question. For example, whose standards will be used? A donor agency may decide that in a given country a point off the crude birth rate (CBR) per year for a given level of expenditures is effective, but a one-half point annual decline in the CBR is unacceptable and the use of funds ineffective. However, the recipient country might view a CBR decline of two points every five years as quite effective in their perceived and actual state of social and economic development.

### Proportion of External Assistance

A difficult question, raised earlier, concerns the maximum proportion of program support that should be supplied by external funding sources. Are there cases, especially in the early development of programs, in Bangladesh, for example, where almost total external support for a family planning program is justified? If so (and personally I have difficulties with a "yes" answer to this question), at what point should a recipient country pick up the tab itself? Can the recipient country, to say nothing of the intended target population, control its program—that is to say, its procedures, goals, contraceptive or fertility control methods, and so forth—while major external financial support is utilized? Asking the question this way implies that the country cannot; yet, one might sincerely argue that if a developing country is left to its own ways and resources, fertility decline is probably going to occur a few years later than would be the case with external assistance for population activities. How important are those few years or decade or two if that is the situation? The ethical questions relate to the "who decides" issue and under what circumstances countries can determine their own courses of action.

### Other Assistance Tied to Acceptance of Population Program Assistance

Tying food assistance or development programs to acceptance of population programs is apparently less of a problem now than it was a few years ago (OECD, 1973). Yet, it has not been eliminated completely, and since population funds are available in larger amounts now, the potential leverage exerted on governments of developing nations to adopt and implement national family planning programs in order to obtain development funds for other purposes might be considerable. Furthermore, the question of "tied aid" takes on new forms, such as the pressures to include the most advanced and efficient means of fertility control, for example, provide abortion using the vacuum aspiration technique, in order to obtain funds for a population program.

## A MATERNAL AND CHILD HEALTH–FAMILY PLANNING DELIVERY SYSTEM APPROACH

There is growing interest in programs that functionally integrate maternal and child health services with family planning. This interest arises in part from efforts to develop new systems for delivering effective family planning services, and in part because the improvement of maternal and child health is an important goal in itself in many societies. Also, this approach is an outgrowth of the relative success of hospital-based postpartum family planning programs in obtaining family planning acceptors (Zatuchni, 1970; Forrest, 1971; Sivin, 1972). One MCH/FP program being developed is a set of major research and demonstration projects in four or five countries, in largely rural areas with populations averaging 450,000, under a program that grew out of an earlier feasibility study (Taylor & Berelson, 1971). Three basic questions being studied in this program can be summarized as follows:

1. Are integrated MCH/FP programs feasible in rural areas?
2. Can substantial benefits in terms of improved maternal and child health and reduced fertility from these programs at replicable costs be obtained?
3. Is this an effective delivery system for family planning education and services?

This research demonstration program designed for a five-year period involves several million dollars from both donor agencies and recipient country governments, and covers approximately 1.6 million people. In one sense, it is an enriched program approach in difficult settings. There are several ethical questions we might review:

1. Is it fair to have an enriched program on a demonstration basis in one province of a country? This can probably be justified on several grounds, such as the desirability of testing an idea in one area and working out problems before expanding the coverage to larger groups of people, but it does mean that better services are being provided in one part of a country.

2. Assuming that a program of this sort can be implemented in one area, for example, covering a half million people, what are the possibilities for replication in terms of funding, trained personnel, and general administration and supervision in the rest of the country in the reasonably near future, say, the next few years? One of the key questions asks if this program is replicable in cost and manpower and administrative terms, and this concern led to careful attention in the design of each project. If a project becomes a nonreplicable showpiece, the expenditure of effort and money is probably not justifiable and may raise false hopes. The cost/replicability issue is difficult.

3. Is the MCH approach an indirect way of getting a family planning or population control program started in countries or regions where the direct approach is not possible? This does not seem to be the case in three of the projects funded in the program under discussion (Indonesia, the Philippines, Turkey), but as a general principle questions might be raised about indirect approaches to the provision of family planning services, and a sub-Saharan African country, where the direct approach to family planning is probably not possible on a large scale, has been included in this program (Nigeria). On the other hand, a strong point might be made that this type of program is offering services that are generally helpful and healthful for both mothers and existing children, and the intended recipients perhaps will be better able to accept those services they desire (health care?) and refuse those services they do not want (family planning?).

4. How does a country or group really decide what is the best way to deliver family planning services, and more generally, who is to decide what is the best use of available funds and personnel in the delivery of health care? If substantial funds go to an MCH/FP program that is basically preventive in nature, does this mean less funding is available for curative services? What do the recipients, that is, the target population, really desire? Probably curative services receive higher priority in their view than do preventive services, but is this really in their best long-term interest? In other words, how should long-term and short-term intersts be balanced?

5. How should a recipient country handle the potential problem of a major donor group's saying it will provide funds for this type of project, but only on the condition that certain procedures and methods be incorporated in the project? This is similar to issues raised earlier. The pressures upon a poor recipient government may be considerable.

6. Are there ethical issues regarding the overall idea of research projects involving nonnationals (groups and individuals) in developing societies? What precautions should be taken to ensure the rights of individual citizens in the project countries? The research aspects of these projects require the involvement and support for as much analysis as possible within each project country.

## SUMMARY

The focus of these remarks has been on ethical questions that arise in the organization and implementation of national family planning programs, with some attention to questions arising from the increased population program funding levels and from a major research effort. According to Berelson, there are only five things governments can do to implement population policies (as defined earlier).

They can (1) communicate with people in order to influence their demographic behavior in the desired manner, (2) provide services to effect the desired behavior, (3) manipulate the balance of incentives and disincentives to achieve the desired regulation, (4) shift the weight of social institutions and opportunities in the desired direction, and (5) coerce the desired behavior through the power of the state (1974, p. 2).

From an ethics viewpoint, there is a progressive difficulty of ethical issues as one moves from number 1 through number 5 on this list. Not all of these actions relate directly to national family planning programs, but they can serve as guides for asking about the kinds of actions that are best included in or best excluded from such programs, recognizing the need for variations from country to country because of differential priorities and goals.

This chapter was prepared while the author was a staff member of the Population Council. The views expressed here are those of the author; they do not necessarily reflect the views of the National Academy of Sciences.

## REFERENCES

Berelson, B. An evaluation of the effects of population control programs. *Studies in Family Planning,* 1974, *5*(1), 2–12.

Callahan, D. (Ed.). *The American population debate.* Garden City, N.Y.: Doubleday, 1971.

Callahan, D. Response: Food incentives for sterilization: Can they be just? *Hastings Center Report,* 1973a, *3*(1), 11–12.

Callahan, D. Bioethics as a discipline. *Hastings Center Studies,* 1973b, *11,* 66–73.

Commission on Population Growth and the American Future. *Population and the American future.* New York: Signet, 1972.

Dyck, A. J. Population policies and ethical acceptibility. In D. Callahan (Ed.), *The American population debate.* Garden City, N.Y.: Doubleday, 1971. Pp. 351–377.

Dyck, A. J. Procreative rights and population policy. *Hastings Center Studies,* 1973, *1*(1), 74–82.

Forrest, J. Postpartum services in family planning: Findings to date. *Reports on Population/Family Planning,* 1972, *8.*

Hankinson, R. Problems related to population assistance. In OECD Development Centre, *The constraints on population activities and the problem of absorptive capacity.* Proceedings on an Expert Group Meeting. Paris, December, 6–8, 1972.

Krishnakumar, S. *The story of the Ernakulam experiment in family planning.* Kerala, India: Government of Kerala, 1971.

Krishnakumar, S. Kerala's pioneering experiment in massive vasectomy camps. *Studies in Family Planning,* 1972, *3*(8), 177–185.

Lapham, R. J., & Mauldin, W. P. National family planning programs: Review and evaluation. *Studies in Family Planning,* 1972a, *3*(3), 29–52.

Lapham, R. J., & Mauldin, W. P. An assessment of national family planning programmes. In OECD Development Centre, *An assessment of family programmes.* Paris, 1972b.

OECD Development Centre. *The constraints on population activities and the problem of absorptive capacity.* Proceedings on an Expert Group Meeting. Paris, December 6–8, 1972a.

OECD Development Centre. *Basic figures on aid to population programmes.* Paris, 1972b.

Pohlman, E. Response: Food incentives for sterilization: Can they be just? *Hastings Center Report,* 1973, *3*(1), 10–11.

Pradervand, P. Les pays nantis et la limitation des naissances dans le Tiers Monde. *Développement et Civilisations,* 1970, *39–40,* 4–40.

Raulet, H. M. Family planning and population control in developing countries. *Demography,* 1970, *7*(2), 211–234.

Remili, A. Planification économique et planification démographique: Une équation complex. *Développement et Civilisations,* 1972, *47–48,* 34–48.

Sivin, I. Fertility decline and contraceptive use in the international postpartum family planning program. *Studies in Family Planning,* 1971, *2*(12), 248, 256.

Task Force on Ethics and Population. Ethics, population and the American tradition. In R. Parke, Jr., and C. F. Westoff (Eds.), U.S. Commission on Population Growth and the American Future, *Aspects of population growth policy.* Washington, D.C.: Government Printing Office, 1972.

Taylor, H. C., & Berelson, B. Comprehensive family planning based on maternal/child health services: A feasibility study for a world program. *Studies in Family Planning,* 1971, *2*(2), 21–54.

Thorne, M. C., & Montague, J. Family planning and the problem of development in Tunisia. Paper presented at the annual meeting of the Middle East Studies Association, Binghamton, New York, November, 1972.

Tietze, C., & Dawson, D. A. Induced abortion: A factbook. Reports on Population/Family Planning, Number 14, and Second edition, 1975.

UNFPA. *United Nations Fund for Population Activities, Report, 1973.* New York, 1974.

Veatch, R. M. Case studies in bioethics—Case no. 139. *Hastings Center Report,* 1973, *3*(1), 10.

Warwick, D. P., & Kelman, H. C. Ethical issues in social intervention. In G. Zaltman (Ed.), *Perspectives on social change.* New York: Wiley, 1973, 377–417.

Zatuchni, G. I. (Ed.). *Postpartum family planning.* New York: McGraw-Hill, 1970.

# 17
# A FEMINIST PERSPECTIVE ON SOME ETHICAL ISSUES IN POPULATION PROGRAMS

## SANDRA SCHWARTZ TANGRI

U. S. Commission on Civil Rights

## INTRODUCTION

Population programs are particularly vulnerable to ethical problems because of their size in funding and numbers of persons affected; because of the national level at which they originate; because of the frequently multinational inter-dependencies they represent; because the size, quality, and distribution of populations have always had political importance; and because the intervention aims at behavior that is central to several value systems and the subject of highly sensitive attitudes. The ethical issues deriving from these circumstances have been dealt with very competently by Robert Lapham (Chapter 16). Rather than elaborate on those, I shall concern myself with others that derive from my feminist perspective.

The basic premises of this perspective are that in the area of fertility, women's interests are primary; that women, therefore, should have primary

This chapter is a revised and expanded version of comments presented at the conference on The Ethics of Social Intervention at the Battelle Seattle Research Center, May 9–11, 1973. I wish to thank Nancy Russo, Lorna Marsden, Emily Moore, Gerald Dworkin, Donald Warwick, and Gregg Jackson for their comments on that earlier version of this chapter. The views expressed in this chapter are solely the views of the author and should not be attributed to the U. S. Commission on Civil Rights.

control over population programs; that the most important goal of population programs should be to give women control over their own bodies and reproduction, with fertility reduction a secondary goal; and that any program that will lead to reduction in fertility must also encourage liberating social changes that will provide women with opportunities for alternative means of satisfaction and status.

These premises are related to the basic values of freedom, justice, and security/survival (Callahan, 1971). Freedom is defined as "the capacity, the opportunity, and the incentive to make reflective choices and to act on these choices" (Warwick, n.d., p. E-14). Justice is defined as fairness in the distribution of good and harm. Security/survival, which is often considered the most basic value (Golding, n.d.), is defined as physical and psychological well-being.

## INTEREST GROUPS VIEWED FROM THIS PERSPECTIVE

### The Rights of Women as Mothers

Any consideration of ethical issues in fertility control must recognize that we begin with a biological fact: only one of the sexes can have babies. The advantages and disadvantages, as well as risks and benefits, associated with reproduction and its prevention do not accrue equally to both sexes. If they did—if there were no differences between the sexes in their reproductive functions—the same ethical considerations would apply to both sexes. However, such is not the case. Furthermore, of the various differences between the sexes, this one has the most social significance. In no culture that we know is a woman's fertility a matter of indifference. Because of its social and biological importance, women's ability to have babies, in contrast to men's inability, is a potential source of power that under modern conditions is unmatched by any physical advantages men may have.

Civilized society, in dealing with other significant disabilities, has in varying degrees created compensations for the deprived: artificial limbs, training, special care, special status, and so on. But in the case of fertility, instead of repairing the deprived (so that the good and harms associated with fertility and its prevention are fairly distributed), society has turned women's reproductive function into a net disadvantage by social customs that give power over a woman's body and her fertility to men.

Because security/survival is often considered the most fundamental value (Golding, n.d.; Smith, 1971), we do not violate the bodily integrity of one person to secure the survival of another without the donor's consent (Frances, 1972). In fact, a willing donor whose own welfare or survival would be threatened by the donation may be prevented from making it. We would not consider it ethical to require a person to give or lend his or her body or parts thereof for another's use. We would not think of doing this for organ transplants, experimental therapies, or blood donations. Yet, in the case of fertility, because continuation of the species requires that some women be fertile some of the time, all women are made subject to the social, legal, and political regulation of their own reproductive capacity by others, mostly male.

Bearing children requires women to bear all or some of the following costs: occupation of her body by the fetus; nine months of pregnancy and often a period of restricted freedom while caring for the infant; the physical and psychological risks of death, pain, disfigurement, major surgery (Caesarian), and permanent or temporary disability and disease; as well as many social costs[1] and benefits.[2] Since none of these costs is borne by men—either in general or by those donating their sperm—and since these should never be imposed unwillingly on anyone but only freely chosen, therefore the highest ethical priority in any intervention dealing with fertility is to give women control over their own bodies and reproduction. The issue here is that women should have the freedom to choose which costs and benefits to undertake: those associated with child bearing or those associated with its prevention.

Although the rights of women in the sphere of reproduction are primary, others also have some rights. If no person is an island, to some degree everyone has some interest in another's reproduction. Most discussions of these issues (Callahan, 1971; Smith, 1971) recognize that there are conflicts of interests and of rights between families and agencies or between minority populations and the society as a whole. Very few deal with conflicts of interest between husband and wife or between women and the society as a whole (Marsden, 1973). Most assume that a woman's interests are identical with those of her husband, her family, or her community. This is not necessarily the case. In the area of reproduction and with the broader ramifications of changes in reproduction, women are a distinct interest group. This is not to say that their interests are always in opposition to their husbands' or communities', but that they sometimes are.

There seem to be three quite different sets of relationships between women and others who are most important in these matters: would-be fathers, the medical and paramedical personnel who deliver services relevant to reproductivity, and the public interest (normally represented poorly, at best, by government). In each situation, the rights of one may be in conflict with the rights of the other.

### Would-Be Fathers

What rights do would-be fathers have? It has been said, in response to a strong feminist position, that "it takes two to tango." This is supposed to

---

[1] Discrimination, loss of status, and humiliation if the child is illegitimate. Even legitimate pregnancies often occasion discrimination and humiliation in role settings unrelated to maternity, for example, at work and in school.

[2] Enhancement of status if legitimate; limited rights to economic support.

refer to the fact that women cannot have babies without men. That is true—more or less. What is much more to the point is that men cannot have children without women.[3] If men cannot have children without the use of women's bodies, does this create extraordinary rights of men over women's reproduction and extraordinary obligations of women to men? No, because one person's desire does not obligate another person nor give the desirous one the right to take what he wants.[4]

In the relationship between the sexes, this issue arises in three different circumstances. (1) Does a man have the right to impose on a woman a pregnancy that she does not want? The answer is clearly "no," because it would contravene both her freedom and security of person. (2) Does a man have the right to withhold his contribution to a pregnancy? Yes, although what is done with the body's other waste products after they leave the body is not completely a matter of free choice. In this case, it seems clear to me that a man has a right to try not to become a father. (3) Does a man have the right, once a woman is pregnant by him, to prevent her from aborting if she wants to or to make her abort if she doesn't want to? The fact of asymmetrical reproductive functioning determines the answer. Again, because it is the woman who carries the pregnancy and who, therefore, carries the risks of either carrying to term or aborting, her freedom to choose which risks to take has precedence over his right to choose or reject parenthood. To deny her an abortion that she wants is to impose upon her a pregnancy she does not want—it is the same issue as in the first circumstance. To force on her an abortion that she does not want is to contravene both her freedom and her security of person. A man certainly does not have the right to use a woman's fertility to prove his masculinity, to satisfy his desire for heirs or immortality, or to control her movements or aspirations, though all of these may be satisfied if she wants to have a child by him. Ideally, neither partner could force parenthood on the other; either could refuse to become a parent.

This last discussion leads to the answer to a fourth circumstance: (4) Does a man have the right to make his will prevail over a pregnancy that he did not cause? As in circumstance 3, and for the same reasons, the answer must be "no." But if the context now is shifted from that of man as husband or lover, to man or woman as physician, do any new considerations arise?

## Medical Personnel

The doctor's role entails certain obligations different from the others. Unlike the would-be father or representatives of the public interest, the

[3] The artificial womb is a less immediate prospect than artificial insemination or biological fathers who do not know that they are fathers.

[4] None of the foregoing, nor what follows, constitutes strictures against persons in any relationship who undertake reasonable, that is, noncoercive and nondeceptive efforts to persuade another to a particular course of action. If so persuaded, the issue of conflict becomes moot.

physician's first responsibility is to the well-being of the patient. If a doctor's judgment about the best medical course to follow coincides with a woman's own preference, there is no conflict between doctor and patient though they may both be in conflict with others, including the would-be father, representatives of the public interest, or even the doctor's own personal beliefs.

But when there is a conflict, and it can occur on the whole range of issues from contraception to abortion, from treatment for subfecundity to determination of sex, what principles ought to adjudicate between the woman's right to freedom of choice and the doctor's professional opinion? Such conflicts occur routinely, and in areas other than reproduction. They are typically resolved through persuasion of one party by the other or by changing one's doctor. Whether this results in ethical outcomes depends on several things: first and most important, that there not be too great a power differential between the parties so that the persuasion does not become coercion; second, that there be full disclosure of information so that the persuasion is not deceptive; and finally, that the patient has real options to choose another doctor. For poor women especially, these conditions are often not met. Much of this dilemma would be resolved by eliminating the monopoly that doctors have on the delivery of fertility-related services. Much of the necessary skill and knowledge to practice effective birth control could become part of the general educational curriculum. This education should include disclosure of the risks and benefits of both child bearing and its various alternatives. Self-help clinics are another alternative to this monopoly.

### The Public Interest

In the third relationship, when there is conflict between the rights of the individual and the welfare of the group, I adopt Warwick and Kelman's (1973) criterion that the concrete needs of individuals should take precedence over some abstract notion of what is good for society. This principle applies in any conflict between a woman and representatives of the public interest. It also applies to personnel who deliver services relevant to reproductivity. Lapham has dealt very effectively with the ethical issues that arise when family planning programs that are supposed to represent the public interest infringe on the rights of individuals who are their targets (see Chapter 16).

In sum, it is my position that women's having control over their bodies is a fundamental value in and of itself and includes control over their own reproduction, that it is consistent with and required by other basic values held by most societies—security/survival of the individual and freedom of choice—and that population programs that do not increase the realization of this fundamental value are unethical.

## THE ETHICALLY IDEAL POPULATION PROGRAM

The remainder of this chapter describes what I would consider the major characteristics of an ethically ideal population program from this perspective, taking into account four aspects of the program (Warwick & Kelman, 1973): (a) *the choice of goals,* in which the major ethical considerations are the extent to which those who are affected by the program participate in the choice of the goal, who speaks for them, and who will benefit from the program; (b) *defining the target population whose behavior is to affected,* which depends on the definition of the problem to be addressed by the program; (c) *the choice of means used to implement the program* and the extent to which members of the target population genuinely participate in the program; and (d) *assessment of the consequences of the program,* both intended and unintended, in terms of who benefits and who suffers and which values are strengthened and which are weakened.

### Choice of Goals

The ethically ideal population program is, first of all, one that is designed by and in the best interests of those whose fertility is to affected. This, of course, means women. Men are not fertile; they are either sterile or nonsterile. They either do or do not produce viable sperm; they never produce babies.

Some role for men in population programs can be justified on the following grounds: first, under present social arrangements many men do live with and/or provide economic support for their children and are therefore affected by the number of their children. Second, men are a part of the general public whose welfare is affected by population dynamics. Third, there are men who are capable of acting in women's best interests (I would call them feminists). However, these do not provide justification for equal representation in such programs, since, as I have previously argued, third-party effects as experienced by men are not equal in ethical imperative to women's experiences as child bearers and rearers. Finally, if men are to be involved in population programs, it would be more appropriate for them to address themselves to the contraceptive needs of men.

The goal, then, of population programs as defined by the interests of women is to provide women with control over their reproduction, so that they have real freedom whether and when they do or do not choose maternity. There are very few women, I believe, for whom lack of reproductive control would be a desirable goal (Buckhout et al., 1972). Women will, of course, differ in what ends they wish to attain with that control. If women are enabled to control their own fertility, they are clearly benefitting from such a program. To achieve such control, the program would have to include treatment for the subfecund as well as contraception and abortion for the fecund.

### Who Speaks for the Target Group?

The question of representation arises at three levels. At the highest, or policy-making, level, the participation of women will be impossible without great improvement in the general status of women, including educational, economic, and political status. Nafis Sadik (1974), a Pakistani doctor, has argued this point most cogently:

> One positive step which is necessary is to involve women in the process of discussion and decision making on the means and the methods of family planning programs. That this even has to be said illustrates the anomalous situation in which decisions affecting the lives of women in the most direct and personal way are made without their direct participation. Even without taking into account the demands of natural justice, it would seem obvious that women themselves know best what their needs are and how they should be served (p. 53).

That effective participation in family planning programs is connected to the status of women was pointed out by the Western Hemisphere Regional Seminar on the Status of Women and Family Planning held in Santo Domingo in June, 1973. According to Sadik, the right of couples to determine freely and responsibly the number and spacing of their children was shown to be "closely related . . . to the extent to which they [women] are integrated into the social, economic, cultural and political life of the societies in which they live," and that this integration will require "basic economic, social, political and cultural reforms" (p. 35).

The same considerations apply at the lowest or receiver end of the program.

> Effective use of contraceptives is greatest among couples when the wife has influence in family decisions. And equality in decision making is positively related to both the wife's education and her participation in the labor force (p. 35).

At the middle or implementation level, where research and delivery are designed, women can participate only if they have the necessary training and experience. That their participation would make a difference in what research is done, in how much care is taken over safety precautions, and the degree of coerciveness applied has been argued by many writers (Buckhout, 1972; Jaffe, 1972; Marsden, 1973).

## Who Will Benefit?

If control over their bodies is to become a reality for women, they must be in a position to use that control. That means both psychological and environmental freedom to use that control. If freedom is the capacity, the opportunity, and the incentive to make reflective choices and to act on these choices, then making freedom of choice available to women implies much broader concerns than are found in most population programs. To give women the capacity, opportunity, and incentive to choose freely between motherhood and other role options ultimately requires the elimination of sex roles and socialization for these roles that arbitrarily foreclose alternatives,[5] the elimination of sex discrimination in all arenas, demystification of female sexuality, and deromanticization of heterosexual relationships. All these forms of programming thwart freedom of choice. They also contribute heavily to the pronatalist bias of most cultures. These larger goals are necessary concomitants of family planning, not only because without them women are not really free to choose activities other than maternity, but also because without these alternative avenues to status, a reduction in fertility would actually worsen women's position in some societies rather than improve it (Marsden, 1973).[6]

Thus, the second characteristic of the ethically ideal population is that it contributes to social changes that give women real freedom of choice regarding pregnancy, fertility, and all other alternatives or parallel activities.

### Defining the Target

These considerations, then, also put a new perspective on our consideration of the second aspect of population programs, which is the definition of the target of change. Unlike most population programs now extant, whose targets are married women in their role as reproducers almost exclusively (Lapham & Mauldin, 1972) and men as reproducers somewhat, the feminist perspective reveals that such programs ought to be equally concerned with changing the social institutions that perpetuate sex inequalities. In his article on "The Relevance of Social Research to Social Issues: Promises and Pitfalls," Kelman (1970) writes that:

> By focusing on the carriers of deviant behavior, social research has reinforced the widespread tendency to explain such behavior more often in terms of the pathology of the deviant individuals, families and communities, than in terms of such properties of the larger social system as the distribution of power, resources, and opportunities (p. 83).

An exact parallel exists in the focus of population planners on women's "excessive fertility" rather than on the entire pronatalist and sexist social system within which they live (Tangri, 1972).

---

[5] This does not mean the elimination of biological functions, which would be difficult or impossible to alter in any case, but only that these would be undertaken on a truly voluntary basis.

[6] It should be pointed out that the changes indicated here are not the same as modernization (Wilensky, 1967–1968). In fact, Western-induced modernization has often contributed to a *decline* in the status of women in developing areas. African women, for example, were not included in agricultural extension schemes because it was not understood that their part in farming was at least as important as that of men (Boserup, 1970; Sadik, 1974). The status of women in Thailand also suffered as industrialization and its attendant

By focusing on married women, population planners also fall into the trap of reinforcing the double standard of sexual behavior whereby unmarried women are penalized with illegitimate pregnancy while the man involved suffers no comparable penalty. From a feminist perspective, there is no ethical justification for depriving any category of women control over their fertility. Counterarguments to this position generally, in one form or another, posit that society has the right to deny certain options to unmarried women, either for their own moral benefit or in the interest of maintaining certain social institutions or because of socioreligious conceptions of retribution for sin. This kind of discrimination has to be judged as inconsistent with the value that social institutions must be judged in terms of their consistency with human needs (Warwick & Kelman, 1973). This is as true for programs that deny birth control to unmarried women as it is for those that coerce women into using such methods. It is as applicable to programs that discriminate on the basis of parity (number of children born) as it is to discrimination on the basis of marital status.

Age might be considered an ethical basis for discrimination in the providing of sterilization because of its relation to self-knowledge, knowledge of options, and time perspective, but it is my personal judgment that we generally set the so-called age of discretion considerably higher than warranted.

### Choice of Means

The third aspect to be dealt with is the choice of means used to implement the program. Under conditions of complete freedom of choice, as described earlier, we would expect women to want fewer babies than they do now (Tangri, 1972). Without 100 percent contraception, this would increase the number of unwanted conceptions, which is already considerable. Therefore, the third characteristic of the ethically ideal program is that the contraceptive agents be 100 percent effective, with abortion provided on demand.

Women who prefer less effective methods, that is, those who are uncomfortable with total control over this aspect of their lives, should also have the less effective alternatives available to them (such as the pill, diaphragm, foam, instruction for the rhythm method, and so on).

In this same vein, the fourth characteristic of the ethically ideal program is that the contraceptive agent should be completely safe and without physical or psychological side effects or long-term effects on fecundity or on subsequent offspring. Fifth, it should be easily available to everyone.

The problem of assuring genuine participation in the program by those who are its targets will remain commensurate with the degree of power or status

---

changes in residential patterns increased sex-role differentiation over what it had been (Hanks & Richardson, 1963). In certain respects, women are accorded more status in India than in the United States (Berreman, 1969).

differential between the target population and the program's personnel. We have already discussed the relation between program participation and the status of women at three levels of the program operation. There is the further consideration that, to the extent that men do not take women seriously or respect their rights as individuals, greater participation by women would be effected by replacing male personnel with women—who hopefully would not have such attitudes or who would not have them to as great a degree. Men's attitudes toward women can also be changed and should be.

Furthermore, if it is generally true that women prefer methods requiring the least intervention and males show greater preference for methods involving more outside intervention, as one study found (Buckhout, 1972), then female personnel would perhaps be less likely to advocate and adopt the more coercive methods.

Warwick and Kelman (1973) have suggested that, to the extent that manipulation is almost inevitably a feature of any social intervention, it would seem more acceptable that:

> the people affected participate in the process, their entry and exit remain voluntary, and their range of choices is broadened rather than narrowed; and to the extent that the manipulators are not also the primary beneficiaries of the manipulation, are reciprocally vulnerable in the situation, and are accountable to public agencies (p. 50).

All of the measures advocated here would be consistent with these desiderata. In particular, the point that the manipulators be reciprocally vulnerable in the situation suggests that female personnel should be in charge of programs directed at women and male personnel in charge of programs directed at men. In some parts of the world, this is indeed the practice because of customs that severely circumscribe heterosexual contacts.

This may contravene freedom both on the part of receptors and prospective program personnel. Furthermore, it may be argued that such practices further reinforce customs that keep each sex in its place. Yet, it seems only reasonable to maintain such practices, at least as long as the status differential between the sexes exists.

### Assessment of Consequences

Finally, we consider that aspect of the program that involves the assessment of its consequences. The first question is, if women exercise this control for their own benefit, that is, to achieve their personal fertility goals, what will be the net outcome in terms of population growth or decline? I have already suggested, as have many others, that under conditions of free choice the net impact would be a substantial decline in birth rate. In addition to the reasons given before, we must remember that women have historically been sensitive to the welfare of their community and may be expected to continue to be so. But suppose the community interprets its interests to be best served by augmenting its numbers? There are several situations where minority groups have interpreted their political interests in this way. There is, first of all, no clear ethical imperative against such a position (Smith, 1971). There is, however, a clear ethical imperative against the exploitation of women's fertility for others' political purposes. Giving women control over their own bodies is the first step in preventing such exploitation (Haden et al., 1968; National Black Feminist Organization, 1974).

One respect in which complete availability of contraception and abortion may diminish psychological freedom is that it may deprive women (particularly young women) of the legitimate reason (as defined perhaps by the peer group) for refusing to engage in sexual relations, since it reduces the risk of pregnancy or it removes a social support for refusing to have an abortion. These dangers can be diminished by increasing women's power to resist such pressures from men. The will to resist is strengthened by strengthening the woman's sense of her right to self-determination. When all women and men are feminists, every person will have this sense.

Among the possible unintended consequences of population programs not informed by the feminist perspective would be the reduction in status of women in cultures where maternity is their major source of satisfaction and exclusive claim to consideration. The measures advocated here would reduce that risk. How and at what rate such measures are to be introduced must, of course, be determined independently by the population at risk.

Would men suffer proportionately as women benefit from such a program? In the short run, men would be giving up certain powers and prerogatives that they now exercise over women and certain benefits that they derive from economic discrimination against women (Bergman, 1971). Ultimately, however, men should come to appreciate their own liberation from the heavy economic responsibilities they must now shoulder and from the restrictions on their own freedoms entailed by current definitions of the male sex role and to recognize that they too will have more rather than fewer options (though certain oppressive options would be closed). Furthermore, as the institutions of marriage and the family survive the stripping away of their coercive and chauvinistic props, family men will share in the improved fortunes of their mothers, wives, and daughters.

## REFERENCES

Bergman, B. R. *The economics of women's liberation.* Paper presented at the annual meeting of the American Psychological Association, Washington, D.C., September, 1971.

Berreman, G. D. Women's roles and politics: India and the United States. In C. C. Schrag and W. T. Martin (Eds.), *Readings in general sociology,* 4th ed. Boston, Houghton Mifflin, 1969. Pp. 68–71.

Black Women's Liberation Group, Mount Vernon, N. Y. Statement on birth control. In R. Morgan (Ed.), *Black sisterhood is powerful*. New York: Random, 1970, Pp. 360–361.

Boserup, E. *Women's role in economic development.* New York: St. Martin's Press, 1970.

Buckhout, R. Kaplan, E., Allen, D., Brick, B., Costello, K., Cox, J., Klemens, R., Mazur, J., Moxon, D., Ostermiller, C., Roller, M., Soares, R., Tapia, O., & Willits, S. *Population: Some minority views.* An extended version of an address to the Symposium on Population Control, Family Size, and Family Planning at the annual meeting of the Americal Psychological Association, Honolulu, 1972.

Callahan, D. *Ethics and population limitation.* New York: Population Council, 1971.

Frances, M. Abortion: A philosophical analysis. *Feminist Studies*, 1972, *1*(2), 49–63.

Golding, M. P. Security/survival: A brief analysis. *Hastings Center Report,* no date, E1–E11.

Haden, P., Rudolph, S., Hoyt, J., Lew, R., Hoyt, C., & Robinson, R. The sisters reply. In *Poor black women.* Boston: New England Free Press, 1968.

Hanks, L. M., Jr., & Richardson, J. Thailand: Equity between the sexes. In B. E. Ward (Ed.), *Women in the new Asia.* Paris: UNESCO, 1963. Pp. 424–451.

Jaffe, F. Access to abortion and family planning. *Women's role in contemporary society.* The report of the New York City Commission on Human Rights, September 21–25, 1970. New York: Avon, 1972.

Kelman, H. C. The relevance of social research to social issues: Promises and pitfalls. In P. Halmos (Ed.), *The sociology of sociology (The Sociological Review:* Monograph No. 16). Keele, England: University of Keele, 1970. Pp. 77–99.

Lapham, R. J., & Mauldin, W. P. National family planning programs: Review and evaluation. *Studies in Family Planning.* March 1972, *3*(3), 29–52.

Marsden, L. R. Human rights and population growth—A feminist perspective. *International Journal of Health Services,* March 1973.

National Black Feminist Organization. Statement of purpose. New York, 1974.

Sadik, N. A stronger voice for women. *Equilibrium,* April 1974, *11*(11), 34–35.

Smith, M. B. *Ethical implications of population policies.* Paper presented at the Symposium on Policy Implications of Population Problems at the annual meeting of the American Psychological Association, Washington, D. C., September 4, 1971.

Tangri, S. S. Policies that affect the status of women and fertility. *JSAS Catalog of Selected Documents in Psychology*, 1972, *2*, 107.

The Hastings Center Institute of Society, Ethics, and Life Sciences. *Population and four American values.* New York, no date.

Warwick, D. P. Freedom and population policy. *The Hastings Center Report,* no date, E1–E33.

Warwick, D. P., & Kelman, H. C. Ethical issues in social intervention. In G. Zaltman (Ed.), *Process and phenomena of social change.* New York: John Wiley & Sons, 1973. Pp. 377–417.

Wilensky, H. Women's work: Economic growth, ideology, structure. *Industrial Relations,* 1967–1968, *7*, 235–248.

# CONCLUSION

# 18
# THE ETHICS OF SOCIAL INTERVENTION: POWER, FREEDOM, AND ACCOUNTABILITY

**GORDON BERMANT**

The Federal Judicial Center

**DONALD P. WARWICK**

Harvard University

The cases reviewed in this book demonstrate the extraordinary ethical complexity of deliberate interventions in human affairs. Most of the issues raised in the previous chapters are not covered by available codes of professional responsibility. The authors have not concentrated on examples of frank deception or obvious coercion, as, for example, when "successful" participation in encounter groups or organization development exercises becomes a condition of continued employment, or good housekeeping is maintained in mental hospitals under the guise of "behavior therapy." Even these cases present difficulties for ethical judgment, especially when different groups hold different views of what is moral and when standards of legitimate intervention change over time. But still more complicated issues arise when individuals and institutions of good will engage the services of a professional intervenor to bring about seemingly positive changes in individuals, organizations, communities, or nations.

The examples cited in the previous chapters are largely of this sort: Business organizations hire consultants to improve morale and organizational effectiveness; a minority group seeks aid from a research and development organization to design and implement a community-controlled educational system; communities faced with rancorous crises bring in mediators to help resolve underlying conflicts; the government devises and tests a program to raise levels of income for the poor; the governments of developing countries work with international agencies to develop programs to promote reproductive freedom and limit the birth rate. The intentions and ambitions of the intervenors and their clients are usually beyond reproach. They are neither corrupt nor venal nor beset by unresolvable conflicts of interest. But they intend to change the behavior of other people in socially significant ways, and, most important, they have the resources to act on their intentions. The intention to produce a social change combined with the resources to act on it become the exercise of power.

The central ethical issue raised by this volume concerns the professional intervenor as an agent of power. Professional intervenors hold power deriving from their specialized knowledge, their privileged personal position, and connections with their clients. Often their clients are among the most influential in the society: corporate managers, government agencies, and international assistance organizations. Almost inevitably, the combination of a potent client and a skillful intervenor produces more leverage than is held by the population that is the target of the intervention. Regardless of anyone's intentions, ethical issues arise simply from the fact that a sizeable power differential exists between the intervenors and those intervened upon. Additional problems arise when the exercise of power is veiled or obscured by the white coat of the physician, the open collar of the encounter group leader, or the bland smile of the presumably neutral mediator.

Clients of the professional intervenor are not always powerful. Sometimes they are a relatively weak interest group who approaches the intervenor as an avenue toward increased power or at least practical help. Other ethical issues arise in this context, particularly intentional or unintentional misrepresentations of the intervenor's skills and influence.

Thus *power*, both within and behind professional interventions, is the first theme that emerges from the eight species of intervention described in this book.

The second theme is *freedom*, particularly the freedom of citizens to choose the degree of their participation in programs of intervention. Traditionally, discussion has centered on the freedom to refuse to become a subject of intervention. The issue of informed consent, first explored in biological research and medicine, is now also of central importance in social experimentation. But there is another relevant facet of freedom here, namely, freedom of access to the mechanisms of social intervention and change. How should the power or professional intervenors be distributed within and between societies? What are the relations between the forms of intervention discussed in this book and more traditional forms of professional activity that fall within our definition of intervention, for example, legal advocacy? Should the availability of newer forms of professional intervention follow a marketplace model, a public service model, both, or neither?

The third theme of our discussion is *accountability*, which emerges out of concern for protecting freedom against abuses of power by professional intervenors. Practitioners of the newer forms of social intervention have not yet come to grips with the problems of determining the legitimate extent of their accountability as professionals. During the last several years physicians, attorneys, accountants, and engineers have been forced by a surge of professional malpractice litigation to reconsider their obligations. There is greater awareness that citizens can successfuly press their complaints against incompetent or negligent professionals by filing suit. In part reactively, and in part through self-generated concern for the maintenance of high professional standards, various professional associations are reconsidering their codes of professional conduct. Practitioners of newer forms of social intervention can benefit from these experiences and perhaps avoid some mistakes already made by more established professions.

## POWER

Three separable but interacting power relationships arise in social interventions. They are the relationships between client and intervenor, the intervenor and the target of intervention, and the client and the target of intervention.

By "client," we mean the individual or institution who contracts and/or pays for the intervention. Sometimes the distinction between client and target disappears. For example an individual who chooses to obtain therapy from a mental health professional is the professionals's client and target as well. The distinction between client and intervenor can also become blurred, for example, when a government agency conducts a social experiment using its own research staff instead of an outside contractor. But usually the role of the client is distinguishable from that of the intervenor.

Interventions aimed primarily at individual change show characteristic sets of power relationships. Thus, behavior therapy, encounter groups, and organization development exercises involve either of two sets of relationships. In one case, which is the more relevant to our concerns, the client is in a position of power relative to the target. In this variety of behavior therapy, the client is typically an arm or agent of the state, such as a judge who assigns therapy as a condition of probation. The therapist, also often an employee or agent of the state, shares a position of power with the client relative to the target.

To the extent that encounter groups are used as part of institutional therapies, they follow the pattern of behavior therapy. In organization development, senior management is usually the client, and subordinates are the targets of intervention. Hence the power relationships are the same as in the other two interventions.

The second set of power relationships arises when a client arranges to be the target of intervention. For example, an individual enters private therapy or an encounter group, or senior management hires an organization development specialist to work on its own problems and potential. The ethical problems facing the intervenor in this situation are simpler than in the former case, because the element of explicit or implicit coercion of the target's participation is absent. The major obligation for the intervenor is the fair representation of the risks, benefits, and costs associated with the intervenor's efforts. Because behavior therapists are more closely allied with the traditional model of health services delivery, the extent of their obligation is clearer than the responsibilities of the encounter group agent or organization development specialist. The problem appears to be particularly sticky for the encounter group agent, at least as Glidewell expresses it, because of the importance, for the encounter process, of leaving the goals and anticipated results of the process relatively undefined. Nevertheless, the purely power-based ethical issues in this setting are minor relative to those that arise when the interventions are institutionally mandated.

Power relations among client, target, and intervenor become particularly complex at the level of community interventions. In the situation described by Huey et al., there was an unusual financial arrangement in which the intervening agency paid for the intervention not only as a public service for the clients, but also in order to develop its skills in a new area of research and development. Several key problems in the case, as delineated by Guskin, arose from the intervenor's uncertainty about its own role in the intervention and the extent of its legitimate commitment to the client. While the first steps of the intervention were marked by strong initiatives, the intervenor soon found itself in a reactive posture and out of its technical and political depth. The channels of communication and decision within the intervenor's organization were not always as open and quick as they should have been in such a delicate and volatile situation. As the project progressed, the scope of the intervenor's role and responsibilities underwent changes not fully understood by either intervenor or clients. Some problems might have been avoided if the client had been in a traditional fee-for-service arrangement with the intervenor. As it was, senior management of the intervening organization did not have the same obligation to the client as it would have had under a normal contractual arrangement. Initially, intervention was offered almost as a form of charity. However well intended, this power relation between intervenor and client weakened the client's position when the intervenor decided unilaterally to terminate involvement. The obvious lesson for the intervenor was the importance of establishing in advance, as clearly as possible, the limits on quality and quantity of services to be offered.

The chapter by Laue and Cormick offers an explicit prescription for the intervenor in community disputes when there are power differences between the parties involved. Laue and Cormick's theory of proportional empowerment almost inevitably puts the intervenor in an advocate's position, but this position does not cope with the problem of financing the intervention. Laue and Cormick assume that a neutral client (source of funding) will be available to finance the mediator's pursuit of proportional empowerment. In some instances such funding will be available. But when it is not, and the bill-paying client happens to be the most powerful party to the dispute, what principles should guide the intervenor's conduct? Should the intervenor refuse to accept employment from a powerful client when that client is willing to make important concessions? The "half loaf" of a material concession may sometimes be better than the "whole loaf" of proportional empowerment. And, as Williams points out, the nature of power differences between disputing parties can be subtle, ambiguous, and shifting. Hence, basing the formula for intervention on proportional empowerment may lead to mistakes in intervention. Some of these might be avoided by placing more emphasis on the merits of the cases presented by the parties than on the degrees of political power they have brought to the dispute.

Power relations in interventions at a national level are often clearer than those at the community level. The intervenor's client is either the federal government, as in the case of the Income Maintenance Experiment, or a party trying to influence government action, as with Waymon's intervention on behalf of the Corp. When the client is government, the target of the intervention is, typically, relatively powerless, so that the intervenor faces the same problems arising in interventions aimed at individuals. The particular additional interest of the chapter by Rossi, Boeckmann, and Berk comes from the status of the New Jersey–Pennsylvania intervention as a true experiment. There are, of course, many detailed issues of appropriate client and intervenor conduct that require ethical analysis in such large-scale social experiments. Without going over ground already covered by the earlier discussions, we want to emphasize a point so basic that it is sometimes overlooked in detailed discussions of such experiments, namely, the fundamental fairness of implementing social policy in incremental, reversible steps. Whatever the moral risks of competently conducted social experiments, they surely are smaller than the risks of implementing large changes in social policy without pretesting for adverse effects.

The relationship between Waymon and the Corp presents the clearest example of a fee-for-service intervention on behalf of a private client. Waymon's loyalties were sharply defined by the nature of his contract with the Corp. The Corp had a well-defined goal. Intervenor and the client were both relatively powerless vis-à-vis the agencies they had to deal with. Waymon's power in relation to the client was his knowledge about the relevant bureaucracies. The role Waymon played in the Corp's affairs was similar to the role taken by lawyers on behalf of clients negotiating with private parties or government agencies. Indeed, there is an issue to be considered when intervenors who are not lawyers intervene in situations involving litigation or other legal actions. However valuable Waymon's services were, they might have been enhanced by the use or threat of legal action in the face of bureaucratic obstructionism. Social intervenors have an obligation to understand the legal circumstances surrounding their intervention. Litigation and threat of litigation are powerful tools of social intervention. Although there may be reasons to choose alternative courses, intervenors insensitive to avenues of power through legal action may not be offering their clients the most effective service.

The chapter by Lapham illustrates power relationships in international interventions. Population control programs often rest on a very large power differential between the client and the target. The intervenor, in this case a U.S. or international organization, exports the idea of the intervention as well as its methods. Although nominally in service to the foreign government, the intervenor may hold power over it in its role as an agent of U.S. foreign policy. All the dangers of paternalistic coercion and manipulation are present—and all have taken flesh in one or another population program. Tangri emphasizes the moral traps most apparent from a feminist perspective. This is only one vantage point from which to evaluate programs aimed at getting people to do what they might not want to do. But, regardless of one's starting position in the analysis, the power differentials between client and intervenor, on the one hand, and the targets of the intervention, on the other, place the intervenor in a position of particular responsibility to ensure that the intervention benefits not only the client, but the targets as well.

## The Power of Definition

If a modern Machiavelli were to compose a handbook called *The Intervenor*, she or he might begin with the axiom that the intervenor's most important task is defining the problem to be solved in a way that minimizes impediments to solution. In particular, the intervenor should define the problem so as to forestall the need to justify the intervention. If one does not have to explain why intervention is necessary, one can move quickly to consider how to accomplish it.

Several chapters suggest that the most effective way to legitimate intervention is to portray it as promoting health or eliminating illness. "Health" and "illness" evoke such reflexive responses of acquiescence that the targets are likely to consider it precarious, if not sacrilegious, to challenge diagnoses made in those terms.

If the target cannot plausibly be defined as sick or as in need of treatment, the next best legitimation, especially in the United States, is the realization of human potential or the expresssion of the self. Kurt Back asserts that this language is especially appealing to upper-middle-class Americans who are bored or lack a sense of fulfillment. If the avenues suggested are blocked, a weaker but still adequate aura might be created by speaking simply of a "problem" or, with a more sophisticated audience, a "systems problem." Finally, of course, there is an upbeat rhetoric that moves away from "problems" to "opportunities" and "challenges."

The authors in this book describe the vagaries of fundamental justification for social interventions. Stephanie Stolz suggests that the goals of behavior modification are "to alleviate human suffering and enhance human functioning." Nowhere in the chapter, however, does she define what is meant by enhanced human functioning, nor does she specify the criteria by which reduced suffering is to be assessed. The problem with such ambiguity is that it is all too easy to accept the prevailing definitions on these matters and thereby justify the existing order. Thus, a client who comes to a therapist for treatment to stop homosexual behavior may show "enhanced functioning" and be "suffering" less when, after a series of aversion treatments, he becomes so nauseated at the thought of homosexual conduct that he does not engage in it. This example dramatically illustrates the power implications of social interventions. The deviants, who are usually weak vis-à-vis the combined forces of intervenors and clients, undergo behavior modification to bring them in line with the dominant norms of conduct in the society. The question of whether they are being cured for a disease or punished for their deviance never arises, for it is finessed by the very language used to justify the intervention. Stolz, of course, is aware of the power of ambiguity. A good part of her essay is devoted to spelling out the moral and practical difficulties produced by vagueness about who, precisely, is to benefit from behavior modification—the target of treatment, others in the target's immediate circle, a hospital or other institution, or the larger society.

Glidewell and Back emphasize that the theory and practice of encounter groups are filled with generally vague, even quasi-mystical legitimations. Glidewell speaks of "developmental benefits" and returning the group participant to society with "enhanced resources." But, as he readily concedes in his discussion of the problems of verification, it is virtually impossible to specify when a participant's resources, joy, self-awareness, authenticity, or empathy have been enhanced through group experience. The difficulty is due in large measure to the fuzziness of these terms and the ideas they stand for. Back takes the movement to task for failing to support the assertions that justify the encounter group intervention.

Organization development practitioners tend to be less cosmic in their justificatory rhetoric but not markedly more precise about their goals. Indeed, encounter methods are sometimes a feature of OD practices. Ambiguity is introduced by the vagueness of the term "organization development." As noted in the introductory chapter, "development" connotes an orderly unfolding toward some desirable terminal state. Unlike "change," which can be either for better or worse, "development" shares with "progresss" a positive, uplifting sense. Thus, an employee who objects to participating in an OD exercise has to fight an uphill ideological battle created by the self-justifying label associated with the intervenor's efforts. Adding to the positive charge on OD is the common tendency, as noted in Walton's chapter, to define OD as the promotion of organizational health and the quality of work life. As Warwick points out in his critique of these definitions, what is health for the manager may be disease for the worker. Further, mystifying labels such as "team building," "problem-solving sessions," and "growth sessions" can throw potential opponents to the intervention off-guard. Unions or other employee organizations prepared to deal with organizational change in direct negotiations may be perplexed when potential conflicts are submerged in the rhetoric of team building. And finally, if management is paying for the intervention, the intervenors may be compromised by a conflict between the seeming impartiality of their methods and the obvious partiality of their paymasters.

Similar ambiguities arise in the rhetoric of population programs, where the "population problem" is taken as self-evident and the solutions apparent to anyone with common sense. In the early 1970s, it was widely assumed and regularly preached to Third World leaders that population growth hampered economic development. It was also assumed, without adequate research, that poor people were eagerly awaiting the delivery of family planning services, and that their acceptance of these services would reduce the overall population problem. Recent events, especially the World Population Conference of 1974, have shown the ideological and empirical biases of these two assumptions, and hence the limitations of conventional wisdom about world population growth (cf. Conroy & Folbre, 1976).

Conceptual ambiguities such as those described benefit intervenors and their clients at the expense of the targets of intervention. Stolz shows clearly how the "sick" label is used to the advantage of prison and hospital authorities and, more generally, the society. Laue and Cormick also underscore the politics of defining the disadvantaged as victims of social illness and, therefore, as in need of therapy by qualified professionals. However well-intentioned interventions based on this definition may be, they have the effect of keeping weaker groups in a passive, dependent role and of convincing them that they are unable to shape their own destinies.

If our latter-day Machiavelli were to give the targets of social intervention one bit of advice, it might be this:

> Get completely clear on what problem is to be solved and who has defined that problem. Insist that the intervenor do the same. Set forth the objectives to be achieved and the criteria by which they are to be measured. And finally, let no mystique surrounding an institution or a profession replace or suppress discussion about the precise reasons for change.

## Neutrality, Advocacy, and Forensic Social Science

Perhaps the most tangled knot of issues raised in earlier chapters concerns the possibility or desirability of intervenor neutrality and, conversely, the limits of legitimate advocacy. Laue and Cormick assail the notion of intervenor neutrality as inherently hypocritical and misleading. A posture of impartiality, they argue, serves only to strengthen the position of the disputant already in power. Other chapters demonstrate implicitly what Laue and Cormick make explicit: The most effective stance in the quest for power is the one that appears least political.

The significance of apparent neutrality for intervenor power surfaces most clearly in the choice of language used to label the intervenor and the intervention. There is tension, for example, between the descriptions of encounter groups given by Glidewell and by Back. Back, who is critical of the movement, speaks of the intervenor as the group's "leader." Glidewell, on the other hand, goes to some lengths to explain why he, and presumably other practitioners, prefer the more neutral term "agent." Back insists that there is more to this difference than a semantic quibble. What is at stake, he believes, is the intervenor's honesty with the targets of the intervention as well as the acceptance of professional responsibility. The advantage of a bland image is that it eases the pressures on the intervenor to explain the hidden agenda present in most encounter groups. The more one is identified as a leader, the greater the likelihood of challenges to that position, and the more visible the manipulations made by the person in question will be. While both Glidewell and Back would agree that the maintenance of a low-power profile is a key technique in the intervenor's repertoire, they disagree about the extent to which the intervenor should own up to being a personally responsible cause of group activity. By denying or concealing such responsibility, the intervenor becomes free to organize the intervention around his or her preferred notions of health, growth, or fulfillment. What Glidewell portrays as wholesome facilitation Back paints as irresponsible, covert manipulation.

It would be inaccurate and unfair to claim that all attempts at intervenor neutrality are feigned or hypocritical. On some occasions, an intervenor may enter an arena of change with insufficient appreciation of the political forces at work, but with an expectation that good will and fair dealing will accomplish more than frank advocacy. But the results of a naïve intervention may satisfy no one. Thus Guskin criticizes the Seattle Urban Academy program, and especially its sponsors, for ignoring the political aspects of the situation in their quest for radical improvements in predominately black, central area schools. Guskin also criticizes the sponsors for hiding behind neutrality in order to protect their institutional interests instead of the interests of the community they had agreed to serve. While the charge is made with the benefit of hindsight, the tension of conflicting loyalties and goals is made apparent by Huey et al.'s presentation as well as Guskin's critique. The setting and circumstances of the Urban Academy intervention provide a rich case study of the practical and ethical difficulties of maintaining intervenor neutrality.

The several authors who directly address the question of intervenor neutrality agree that it is difficult if not impossible to achieve in fact, and some argue that it is undesirable in principle. However, there is no unanimity or conclusiveness among the authors about defensible alternatives. Laue and Cormick stand alone in asserting that intervenors should work toward proportional empowerment. Adding to the critique offered by Williams, we also note that the force of their dictum is weakened by the subsequent qualification that empowerment should be provided only to those groups whose values are in line with those of the intervenor. Without this stipulation, an intervenor following the Laue-Cormick scheme would be obligated to empower the National Socialist Party in the days of the Weimar Republic. Hence something like that proviso is required to avoid forcing the intervenor into an ethically untenable position. But it is so difficult to interpret in concrete cases (who, after all, will *not* claim to hold the values of freedom and justice?) that its usefulness as an ethical guideline is limited.

At the same time, a distinct virtue of the Laue-Cormick position is its explicitness. Others addressing the issue, including Stolz, Glidewell, and Walton, are less concrete in affirming alternatives to predetermined advocacy. There have also been important discussions of this issue by authors not represented here. One particularly interesting example is Alice Rivlin's concept of forensic social science, or social research as an intervention in the formation of social policy:

> Scholars or teams of scholars take on the task of writing briefs for or against particular policy positions. They state what the position is and bring together all the evidence that supports their side of the argument, leaving to the brief writers on the other side the job of picking apart the case that had been presented and detailing the counter evidence (Rivlin, 1973, p. 61).

Rivlin coined the term in a critique of *Inequality*, by Jencks et al. (1973), claiming it represented inadequate forensic social science. Although critical of the book, Rivlin applauded the forensic approach as "an extremely healthy development":

> It reduces the hypocrisy of pseudo-objectivity and hidden biases. If well used it can sharpen public issues and make social scientific research more relevant to real policy questions than it has ever been in the past (p. 62).

Forensic social science is thus offered as the latest broom to sweep away traditional ideas about the impartiality of the social scientist. Because attempted objectivity often degenerates into "pseudo-objectivity," and because exposed biases are less dangerous than hidden preconceptions, policy-oriented social scientists should state their preferences at the outset of their research and then work openly to achieve the ends chosen. It is not an oversimplification to say that in forensic social science all research and publications are intended as social interventions.

While Rivlin's label is new and provocative, the debate about knowledge for whom and for what is as old as the social sciences. From August Comte through the New Left, with an important stop at Max Weber, social scientists and their critics have hotly disputed the possibility and desirability of value neutrality and political commitment. Though this is not the place to review the complex issues raised by that debate, we note two that bear immediately on the present topic.

The first is the proposition that social scientists sometimes hide their policy biases behind masks of impartiality. The chapters in this book and the history of the social sciences leave little doubt about the accuracy of this proposition. While social scientists all disavow rigged research and misrepresentation of auspices and intentions, they agree less about the ethics and wisdom of conscious partiality.

The second and more controversial question is thus whether policy-related social science should be conducted in adversary form. Should the social scientist act more as a lawyer advocating the interests of a client, or as a scientist whose primary commitment is to the truth of a situation? If the choice is for the advocacy role, is it ethical to capitalize on the aura of objectivity that accrues to the social scientist willy-nilly because of the scientific stance of others in the field? When, for example, the social science advocate presents survey data on the effects of discrimination, should this be presented as objective information or as biased data designed to make a case for one side of a dispute? Can one have one's scientific cake while demolishing it with criticisms of its very existence?

In the debate over forensic or committed social science, much can be learned from the Anglo-American legal system. Litigation under this system is widely regarded as stylized combat, with lawyers behaving as adversaries whose adherence to prearranged rules of conduct is monitored by an impartial judge (Frankel, 1976). Unlike the situation in the social sciences, there is no debate about the legitimacy of the lawyer's role as a servant of the client's interests. Lawyers are expected to work for the client's goals even when they do not agree with those goals. *The Code of Professional Responsibility* of the American Bar Association reads in part as follows:

> The obligation of loyalty to his client applies only to a lawyer in the discharge of his professional duties and implies no obligation to adopt a personal viewpoint favorable to the interests or desires of his client (Ethical Consideration 7-17).

> The professional judgment of a lawyer should be exercised, within the bounds of the law, solely for the benefit of his client and free of compromising influences and loyalties. Neither his personal interest, the interests of other clients, nor the desires of third persons should

be permitted to dilute his loyalty to his client (Ethical Considerations 5-1).

The separation of personal opinion from professional obligation is clearest for the criminal defense lawyer, who is expected to work for the acquittal of defendants even when their guilt is certain. There is also a tradition in civil law of vigorous representation for losing or loathsome causes on First Amendment grounds of free speech. The lawyers of the American Civil Liberties Union often provide legal aid to individuals or organizations, such as the American Nazi Party, whose interests they may personally detest. Further, the American system of litigation assumes and requires for its success competent and vigorous advocacy on both sides of an issue. If lawyers could not defend clients or causes with which they personally disagreed, the adversary process of dispute settlement would collapse.

Even this brief review points up the limitations of social science conceived as a form of advocacy. Perhaps most fundamentally, neither the law nor society at large views social scientists primarily in an adversary role. There are no institutional mechanisms for ensuring that all worthy clients, especially those who are unpopular or despised, would have access to their services. There are no prearranged rules of conduct for the operation of an adversary system, no binding ethical standards for the protection of clients (such as the obligation to remain silent about information presented in confidence), no system of enforcement, and no judge to monitor the proceedings.

Moreover, public trust in the social scientist, as distinct from the adversary advocate, depends on the assumption that the social science professional will behave as a scientist. By some definitions, the term "forensic social science" would be a contradiction of terms, for it would imply professional behavior at variance with the commonly understood norms of science. These norms include three essential features.

First, the primary loyalty of the scientist qua scientist is to the faithful presentation of information obtained by generally accepted methods of data collection. The scientist may, of course, have a point of view about the issue under consideration, particularly when the research deals with policy questions. In this case, the opinion should be freely admitted, but not used to slant the collection and interpretation of data in favor of a predetermined policy option. It is precisely the point of good scientific practice to provide data insulated from the scientist's preconceptions about what the right answer should be. The scientific method is, after all, a series of devices for producing a social consensus about reality (Ziman, 1968). Social science obviously falls short of the ideals established in the physical sciences for the establishment of consensus. But the principle remains that the role of the scientist demands adherence to the best methods available for obtaining reliable and relevant information. This allegiance should transcend loyalties to employers, favored causes, or preferred theories. Researchers who place the interests of their clients above their loyalty to sound methods will do as much mischief to social policy and public trust as the hypocritical scientists scored by Rivlin. Those who feel that the models and methods of natural science are inappropriate to intricate human beings and complex social realities should make their own positions clear and disavow not only the methods but the label of science. It is the height of hypocrisy to chastise social science for its imitation of natural science while simultaneously accepting benefits from the aura conferred by association with the latter.

Second, scientists, as distinct from adversary advocates, have a positive obligation to publish the results of their work. Again, the obligation follows from the nature of science, which is not only knowledge but *public knowledge* (Ziman, 1968). It simply will not do, as forensic social science would have it, for scientists to leave detailing the counter evidence to their opponents. One reason, as Warwick points out in his discussion of social experiments, is that the opponents may not have access to the necessary information. If the advocates of a particular policy about income are the only ones with access to evaluation data on a related social experiment, the possibility of fair advocacy for all sides breaks down. The scientist has a positive obligation to present conclusions based on all relevant evidence, and to open the data to others who could further this objective. To behave otherwise may be good advocacy, but it is bad science.

Third, scientists should resist attempts by clients or other interested parties to influence the scope and content of publication. There are legitimate exceptions to this principle, such as state secrets about nuclear energy or proprietary interests in data collected under a contract. Nevertheless there is no place in science for the equivalent of a general privilege of confidentiality, such as that seen between lawyer and client, about data. Nor should we be forced to assume that all data are presented to portray the client or the cause in the most favorable light possible. The great irony of an advocacy approach for social science is that it would be effective only so long as its audience did not know that it was in operation. If the public came to assume that social scientists, like defense lawyers, were being as selective as possible in their presentation of a case, public confidence in social science would crumble—and properly so.

In sum, social scientists and lawyers operate out of different traditions, with different public understandings about their roles, different protections for their clients, and different ethical codes. Any attempt to cast the social scientist in an adversary role without changing the institutional structure to accommodate that role seems foolhardy and ultimately destructive of the very notion of social science.

## The Power of Professionalism

What differences, if any, should distinguish the ethics of social science from the ethics of intervention conducted by social scientists? A skeptic, observing that all the interventions discussed in earlier chapters were performed by intervenors with at least one foot in academic or research institutions, might suggest that we are constructing moral mountains on molehills of power. What reason have we to believe that these interventions represent a collection of professional skills sufficiently potent to warrant serious concern for the ethics governing their use? The substantive presentations have not included interventions by better-known and organized groups of intervenors: lawyers, social workers, union organizers, and lobbyists, among others. Given our emphasis on interventions coming more-or-less directly out of applied social science, how are we to describe the sources of the intervenors' power?

In general, the intervenors represented in this volume draw their professional power from three sources: image, specific knowledge, and skill. We have already discussed the power of definitions in the creation of a professional image conducive to effective intervention. While additional examples could easily be provided, it is sufficient to note that the success of an intervention in reaching predetermined goals may depend greatly on the targets' perceptions of the intervenor's legitimacy and effectiveness. With the possible exception of some forms of behavior modification, none of the intervention techniques described here is effective without substantial target cooperation. In fact, many of the techniques are aimed at winning cooperation from an initially suspicious or hostile group, and manipulations of public image are important in this effort.

The manipulations of image are a legitimate tool of social intervention if they do not involve misrepresentations of the intervenor's status or skill. For example, it is legitimate for professors at a leading university to identify themselves as such to the targets of an organization development exercise for which they have been hired by management as consultants. This is a manipulation equivalent to physicians' displaying their diplomas on the walls of their offices. It is similarly legitimate for an appropriately trained and certified clinical psychologist to be identified as "Doctor" in a hospital setting, even with an understanding that some recipients of the psychologist's behavior therapy may not know the difference between physicians and psychologists. An encounter group agent with appropriate credentials is similarly entitled.

We are not arguing that these intervenors should hide behind their titles, or the mystifying effects the titles sometimes create, when their skill or authority is challenged. But neither should intervenors be obligated to minimize their professional effectiveness by eschewing all symbols of special knowledge or skills that they in fact possess. To the extent that titles, uniforms, office settings, and so on, are symbols of earned rank and professional accomplishment, we find no compelling reason why these accouterments should not be legitimate parts of the intervenor's professional toolbox.

The knowledge and skills required for the various forms of intervention are more easily specified in some cases than in others. The primary skill at the command of behavior modification specialists is the ability to manipulate rewards and punishment in response to specific kinds of behaviors. In implementing this technique it is helpful, and sometimes essential, to have control over the environment of the person whose behavior is to be changed, but this control is usually provided by others, for example, the directors of a prison or hospital. The unique skills of encounter group leaders are difficult to specify, but they seem to include the capacity to structure group discussions to elicit or occasion a wide range of emotional responses. The intervenors commonly set the norms governing dress and behavior (informal dress, limitation of discussions to the "here and now"), make decisions about the size of rooms and their furnishings, set limits on certain topics and approaches, and apply knowledge about how to channel group discussions in certain directions and away from others. The skills seen among organization development practitioners are not unlike those of encounter group leaders, but often extend as well to relationships and issues unique to work organizations. Thus, while the encounter group leader would normally pay more attention to the relationship between the immediate group and its participants, the OD specialist would also develop specialized knowledge about relationships between and among work groups. The skills possessed by intervenors in education programs will, of course, depend on the precise nature of the intervention. In the case of the Seattle Urban Academy, the consultants brought with them general abilities in engineering and systems analysis, rather than tools uniquely applicable to educational change. Waymon's intervention in federally funded housing programs also drew on general consulting skills, including the ability to help the community group clarify its own objectives, to increase their capacity to work as an organization, to move sluggish bureaucracies, and to be aware of the political implications of any aspect of the intervention.

Laue and Cormick are explicit about the competence required of effective intervenors in community disputes. This includes not only the ability to negotiate but also the ability to teach others to negotiate. The authors further imply that the unique and perhaps most valued capacities of the crisis intervenor are a comprehensive view of the many interests at stake in the intervention and an ability to negotiate with these interests in mind. Rossi and his associates do not identify a single set of intervenor skills, though they emphasize the central role of economic theory and policy analyasis. They also give implicit recognition to the capacity for conducting a fair evaluation of an intervention's impact. In their discussions of population programs, Lapham and Tangri likewise focus more on policies and programs than on intervenors. It is clear, nevertheless, that such professionals as demographers, physicians, nurses, and clinic administrators play a vital part in the formulation and implementation of population policies. The chapters suggest, finally, that as one moves from the one-on-one intervention of behavior therapy to complex interventions such as population control programs, the salience of single groups of professional intervenors becomes smaller and the efficacy of a particular set of skills correspondingly weakened.

## A Typology of Effects

Given the power flowing from the intervenor's image and expertise, what are the predominant political effects of social interventions?[1] Taken with the Introduction, the 16 chapters suggest a useful typology of effects that divide fairly well into categories of system maintenance and system change.

### System Maintenance

Social intervention may help to maintain or strengthen a system in the following ways.

*Moral Legitimation.* The presence of highly visible, credentialed intervenors often reinforces the sense that the sponsoring body is upright, responsible, and entitled to its power and position. For example, organization psychologists or management consultants brought in for OD sessions lend the weight of their credentials and image to the firm that hires them. One has the sense that in settings ranging from prisons to population programs, social science professsionals now play the role once performed by priests who conferred their benedictions on secular events. Kurt Back is more explicit about the religious overtones of the encounter group movement, but others, especially Stolz, Warwick, and Guskin, also point to the legitimating function of the intervenor.

*Targeting.* Intervenors play a key political role in defining the problem to be solved through intervention and the specific targets for action. This targeting or channeling function is especially significant when the intervenors accept without question the definitions of problems or deviance held by the populace or established by a society's legal code. Stolz provides a sound analysis of the moral difficulties raised when behavior modification specialists not only accept societal definitions of deviance but in effect wreak vengeance by applying their most painful techniques to those who are considered the greatest offenders. By embracing and acting on a society's or an organization's definitions of problems and of deviants, intervenors work to maintain the status quo.

*Victimizing.* Carried to extremes, the process of targeting becomes victimizing. Social and political systems are often unified through the catharsis produced by scapegoating. As a way of achieving greater internal cohesion, nearly every society selects an enemy or demon on which it can project its guilt, frustrations, or discontents. In *The Crime of Punishment,* Karl Menninger

---

[1] The term "political" is used to cover any change in the distribution of power, influence, or authority in any of the units covered by the papers. These include the individual, the small group, the work organization, the community, the nation-state, and the international political system.

(1968) argued, for example, that the American public needs both crime and punishment as a means of ritual purification. Whether in total societies or encounter groups, professional intervenors may play a significant political role by defining the enemy and by providing moral sanction and impetus for retribution. A clear example is seen in the field of population policy. Historically, the strongest support for the practice of sterilizing the mentally retarded came from specialists in eugenics. Their clinching argument, one that captured the attention of no less a figure than Oliver Wendell Holmes, was that the "feebleminded," knowing no restraint, would breed furiously and thus adulterate the society's gene pool. Subsequent research showed that the empirical assumptions of this argument were flawed, that its exponents were largely of upper-class origins, and that the entire exercise could well be considered a case of scapegoating. Who, after all, is likely to rally less support than the retarded, especially after they have been portrayed for several generations as not only incompetent but lascivious? Microcosmic versions of this phenomenon arise in encounter groups and in organization development exercises when some participants, particularly those who hold out against group norms, become subjects for special opprobrium. The point to be underscored is that such scapegoating helps to maintain the system by channeling aggressions against the weak rather than against the powerful.

*Retreatism.* Social interventions may further promote system maintenance by encouraging or aiding those who experience frustrations with the system to retreat into the self or into groups embracing emotional but not political expression. The clearest case is the encounter group movement, which, according to Back, has strong elements of sociopolitical withdrawal. Robert Merton, who first used the term "retreatism" in sociological analysis, also noted its political consequences:

> The competitive order is maintained but the frustrated and handicapped individual who cannot cope with this order drops out. Defeatism, quietism and resignation are manifested in escape mechanisms which ultimately lead him to "escape" from the requirements of the society (Merton, 1957, p. 153).

*Adjustment.* Several of the chapters suggest ways in which interventions may encourage individuals and groups to adjust to a system by thinking, feeling, and acting within its prescribed limits. The most blatant example, cited by Stolz, is the application of behavior modification techniques to promote discipline and order in classrooms. Walton and Warwick also discuss the ethics of using organization development techniques to cool out opposition or otherwise to keep organizational tensions within manageable boundaries. At a broader level, Laue and Cormick are highly critical of intervenors who use their skills at crisis management to manipulate weak but intransigent parties into docile submission. Moreover, intervenors may in general promote adjustment by imparting or endorsing an ethic of feasibility. In this ethic, political, organizational, or other action is seen as acceptable only within the range of options approved by established authorities. The emphasis is on the possible and the practical, the down-to-earth and the nitty-gritty, rather than on schemes more disruptive to the underlying authority structures.

*Intelligence Gathering.* Professional intervenors may further strengthen the hand of established authorities by gathering information on dissent or dissatisfaction. Increasing attention has recently been focused on the role of the professional as a double agent. Physicians, psychiatrists, psychologists, management consultants, OD practitioners, encounter group leaders, crisis intervenors, and others are often in a position to gather privileged information on the discontents and strategies of opponents to the system. Walton notes the ethical dilemmas faced by OD practitioners who are asked to provide appraisals of employees encountered in their work. These professionals are in a better position than line managers to detect or observe employee dissidence. Crisis intervenors and consultants operating in the interstices of conflicting interests face similar dilemmas.

*Undermining Opposition.* The political advantage conferred by privileged information is that it gives managers and other authorities a better base for dealing with opposition. Professional intervenors may also wittingly or unwittingly work to undercut dissident forces. An unambiguous example arises when an encounter group leader or OD practitioner transposes what would otherwise be a labor-management issue into one of openness and trust in the here and now. Union leaders who may be perfectly able to protect their interests through conventional negotiating techniques may find themselves completely off-guard when confronted with a staged setting, an arcane language, and an elusive opponent. At a more subtle level, potential opposition may also be defused by group discussions relying on affective expression and group camaraderie to neutralize simmering conflicts over substantive issues like working conditions and pay rates. Union spokesmen have long been critical of the human relations movement for its implicit but nonetheless powerful support of management through the promotion of worker satisfaction. Whether their criticisms have an ethical or merely a political basis is open to question, but at the very least they point up the internal political implications of management consulting and OD. Back, Walton, and Warwick are explicit about this set of issues for encounter groups and OD, as are Laue and Cormick for crisis management.

### System Change

Whatever their boundary-maintaining effects, social interventions are, by definition, actions that produce or are designed to produce change. Many forms of deliberate intervention do not, of course, accomplish their stated objectives of change, but they may directly or indirectly bring about other significant modifications of individuals and social systems. The chapters in this book suggest four mechanisms by which systemic change can be effected.

*Consciousness Raising.* One of the potentially profound effects of social intervention is the heightened consciousness that something is wrong with one's life and the associated conviction that the situation could be improved. The impetus given the feminist movement by women's "rap groups" in the late 1960s and early 1970s is an important recent example.

Beyond a generalized sense of a problem or a hope for positive change, the intervention may also help individuals to step back from the structures that surround them and understand, however dimly, the forces shaping their lives. Sartre (1956) described the process by which European workers came to awareness of the possibility of revolt against their suffering. According to Sartre, the key psychological ingredient was the *contemplation* of suffering as a state in itself. Without that explicit consciousness,

> Suffering cannot be in itself a *motive* for [the worker's] acts. Quite the contrary, it is after he has formed the project of changing the situation that it will appear intolerable to him. This means that he will have had to give himself room, to withdraw in relation to it, and will have to have effected a double nihilation: on the one hand, he must posit an ideal state of affairs as a pure *present* nothingness; on the other hand, he must posit the actual situation as nothingness in relation to this state of affairs. He will have to conceive of a happiness attached to his class as a pure possible—that is, presently as a certain nothingness—and on the other hand, he will return to the present situation in order to illuminate it in the light of this nothingness and in order to nihilate it in turn by declaring: "*I am not happy*" (p. 435).

The Brazilian educator Paulo Freire (1971) also described the entire process of the development of consciousness. He pointed out that the awareness of oppressed individuals is often limited by virtue of the effort required to meet life's immediate needs as well as by a socialization process favoring resignation and fatalism. As a result, such people will usually attribute their condition either to supernatural forces above them or to their own inherent worthlessness. Both explanations involve strong elements of retreatism and resignation. Under these conditions, Freire contended, the potential for change will emerge only when these individuals begin to perceive that their condition is shaped by objective conditions in their environment.

Several chapters point up the consciousness-raising effects of social interventions. According to Glidewell, one of the explicit objectives of encounter groups is the promotion of self-awareness and insights into group processes. Back counters that the fences built around such experiences together with the dynamics of the group itself channel the attention of participants in certain approved and essentially nonpolitical directions. While the ideology of the encounter group movement as well as the predilections of its practitioners do seem to incline away from consideration of larger political forces, it is quite possible that once an individual's awareness of self and environment has been raised, the lessons might be applied to broader issues of power and authority.

*Delegitimation.* Social interventions may also foster change by challenging the legitimacy of a given system or its rulers. Because legitimacy arises from shared beliefs that authority is rightfully exercised by certain individuals or groups, interventions can challenge legitimacy by persuasively challenging the foundations of those beliefs. In the field of population studies, Mahmood Mamdami (1972) performed this function in a controversial study titled *The Myth of Population Control.* The reason that the book generated such controversy was that Mamdami took exception to the commonly held assumption that smaller families were in the interest of poor villagers. His data from field research in India apparently show that there are many reasons, including compelling economic considerations, for villagers to have large families. Since 1972 this work has been regularly cited by critics of the international population control movement as evidence of the movement's misdirected efforts.

An intervention may also aim to weaken the power bases of established leaders. Sometimes the mere fact that a leader is challenged at all will undercut the perception that he or she is all-powerful and immune to criticism. Success in small-scale sorties may encourage larger assaults. Laue and Cormick imply that constant challenges are needed to keep entrenched powers off-guard. Williams, in turn, criticizes them for advocating a level of confrontation that may erode the underlying political consensus and respect for authority. Williams suggests, by implication, that too much delegitimation may ultimately work against justice by replacing the notion of agreed-upon fairness with the principle of push-and-shove. Finally, the conflicts and tensions produced by the intervention may place more strain on the system than it can accommodate. Laue and Cormick appear to endorse crises as a legitimate vehicle for promoting minority interests. But carried to an extreme, constant crises can completely debilitate a social or political system. Argentina, known among Latin American scholars as "the conflict society," provides a national example of the limits of political delegitimation.

*Destabilization.* This term refers to deliberate efforts to kindle opposition, dissension, discord, and strife in a social or political system. Had we organized this volume before the overthrow of the Allende regime, we almost certainly would have added a set of papers on political interventions among nations, with special emphasis on Chile. We now have vivid documentation showing how the CIA, with the encouragement and assistance of multinational corporations, deliberately set out to foment dissension against the Allende regime in Chile. The methods used by the CIA included covert payments to opposition groups, harassment through international organizations, and encouragement of criticism through diplomatic channels. Unfortunately, none of the papers in this volume deals even indirectly with the phenomenon of destabilization.

*Enablement.* Interventions may further induce change by supplying opponents, minority groups, or other contending forces with the capacity, opportunity, means, or incentive to act. Laue and Cormick organize their paper around one form of enablement, the development of power for the powerless. Their discussion of empowerment is clear and cogent, but it does not exhaust the possibilities of enablement. Waymon notes how his intervention, which failed to meet its primary objective, seems to have led to an increased capacity on the part of the black corporation to deal with "City Hall" and the federal bureaucracy. As he puts it, "they are now the experts in housing and are widely sought as speakers, consultants, resource people, and so forth. They didn't get the housing units, but they did get added units of respect and status among themselves and among their peers and colleagues at all levels" (p. 325).

Interventions can also promote enablement by convincing people that they can be sources of social action. In some cases, this means contradicting the view that human actions are shaped by powerful external forces or insuperable biological drives. If people are convinced that their lives are shaped by forces beyond their control, they tend to act accordingly. Interventions can counter this tendency by teaching individuals and groups to see themselves as originators of action, capable of initiative, foresight, control, and above all, significant influence on others. Needless to say, this is not a matter simply of changing self-images, for objective power obviously counts, but increased efficacy has psychological as well as social and financial underpinnings. Glidewell, for example, makes explicit reference to increased competence and efficacy as the goals of encounter group participation.

Social interventions may promote system maintenance and system change in other ways, most notably through the actual contents of the intervention. Our list includes only the most common and general mechanisms.

### Evaluation Criteria

Finally, questions of power arise in the choice of criteria for assessing the processes and outcomes of social interventions. Contending interests will affect, first of all, the performance criteria established for the evaluation. A growing literature in evaluation research (Gurel, 1975; Sjoberg, 1975; Weiss, 1975) documents the influence of political considerations on the choice of yardsticks for judging programmatic success. The chapter on the New Jersey-Pennsylvania Income Maintenance Experiment shows that the selection of evaluation standards is not a matter of political indifference. The experiment's designers made a political judgment in deciding to have the evaluation focus heavily on the work-leisure trade-off—whether people would stop working and enjoy leisure above a certain income floor. This decision reflected the interests of academic economists hoping to devise new tests for static equilibrium theory and of OEO officials seeking a novel but politically feasible income policy. As Warwick notes, the evaluation criteria might have been different had the program designers consulted the poor, employers, congressmen, and other interested parties.

The politics of evaluation also surfaces in the assessment of family planning programs. Although neither Lapham nor Tangri discusses the point, there is evidence that the primary data collected on these programs, and the ways in which they are interpreted, reflect pressures from donors, advocates, and other interest groups (Marino, 1971). Given that the same organizations that advocate and fund international family planning programs also are the major sources of support for evaluations, it is not surprising that there has been a bias in favor of results showing that the programs lead to decline in fertility rates. In a review of the literature, Hilton and Lumsdaine (1976) show the gaps between the data presented and the conclusions drawn about the impacts of family planning programs.

Considerations of power and vested interests are no less salient in the choice of ethical criteria for the evaluation of social interventions. In this book, the most striking case of politically resonant ethical judgment is Tangri's advocacy of women's interests in population programs. While other groups, particularly men, have some claims in this area, Tangri contends that they are distinctly secondary to the interests of women. She is also quite explicit about the premises for her ethical judgment:

> Any consideration of ethical issues in fertility control must recognize that we begin with a biological fact: only one of the sexes can have babies. The advantages and disadvantages, as well as risks and benefits associated with reproduction and its prevention do not accrue equally to both sexes. If they did—if there were no differences between the sexes in their reproductive functions—the same ethical considerations would apply to both sexes (p. 364).

Women's rights are primary, therefore, because women have a greater stake in reproduction and thus a greater moral claim to control over any social intervention having to do with reproduction. As a result,

> . . . the most important goal of population programs should be to give women control over their own bodies and reproduction, with fertility reduction a secondary goal; and . . . any program that will lead to reduction in fertility must also encourage liberating social changes that will provide women with opportunities for alternative means of satisfaction and status (p. 364).

Because Tangri's paper is so frankly political in its endorsement of one set of group interests, it provides a useful foil for debate on the broader issue of whose needs and concerns should enter into judgments about the ethics of intervention. Several specific questions are raised by her arguments.

First, what are the moral groups for asserting that one social group should have primary control or disproportionate influence over a given kind of intervention? Tangri rests her claim on a biological fact—only women can have babies. She does not spell out in any detail why this particular biological fact should confer special rights, nor does she indicate whether other biological facts, such as racial characteristics, size, and genetic deformities, call for similar entitlements. Do those born with Down's syndrome, for example, have the right to primary control over programs on mental retardation, since their stakes in such programs are larger than those of the nonretarded?

Second, even allowing the validity of the biological view, are there not parallel rights that might be accorded to men in population programs? Tangri focuses primarily on the risks and benefits of pregnancy, where women's interests are obviously stronger. But what standards should apply to population programs that are aimed at men, such as the massive vasectomy camps organized in India? Should women, because of their biology, determine the organization and implementation of these programs, which are directed exclusively at the reproductive apparatus of men? The argument developed by Tangri seems to suggest that where the stakes are greater for men than for women, men have stronger moral claims for control over policy.

Third, if a judgment is made that the interests of one group have ethical primacy, questions remain about how those interests should be defined, and by whom, within the entitled group. In the case of women and population programs there are many ambiguities. Does the ethical position outlined by Tangri represent the views of all women concerned with family planning programs? Quite clearly it does not. Even in the United States, the women's movement is divided, for example, on the question of abortion. When one moves to the international scene, the picture is even more complicated. In Latin America, women's groups that support some objectives of North American feminism object strongly to the tone and moral reasoning of the movement. Even stronger criticisms would be forthcoming if U.S. feminists, intending to speak for the women of the world, placed their own principles at the foundation of policies governing international family planning programs supported by U.S. funds. Third World critics, both men and women, would quickly denounce such influence as political and cultural imperialism.

Fourth, what ethical calculus should be applied to social interventions when more than one set of group interests is at stake? Perhaps to dramatize her argument, Tangri ducks the difficult moral and practical questions posed by trade-offs. Her treatment of family planning programs oversimplifies the ethical issues at stake by dealing mainly with male and female interests. Closer analysis of existing programs suggests that there are also other interests involved, including the donor agencies, social classes, ethnic groups, and competing programs with their clienteles. Using a broader evaluation framework than that presented in Tangri's paper, the policy analyst might come up with the following questions and dilemmas:

When support for family planning programs comes from public funds (as it usually does), what priority should the promotion of women's interests hold vis-à-vis other possible areas of expenditure? For example, if family planning programs seem to be serving mainly urban, middle-class women, while malaria control programs benefit poor men and women in rural areas, how should decisions be made about the allocation of limited funds for health care? It would be difficult to sustain the argument that, whatever their income position, women's needs for fertility control should take precedence over the health or welfare needs of the entire population.

An Asian country has two major ethnic groups—the Chinese, who are reasonably affluent, and the Malays, who are quite poor, especially in rural areas. Surveys show that the Chinese women are highly motivated to practice family planning and would welcome assistance with means. The Malay women, on the other hand, seem more concerned about having fewer of their babies die than about limiting births. Should the government spend its health/family planning money in helping the Chinese women control their fertility or in assisting the Malays to reduce infant mortality?

The government of an African country discovers a segment of its population in which roughly equal numbers of both males and females show high rates of involuntary sterility. While the exact causes are not known, the government is confident that medical attention can relieve the condition for a significant number of those affected. Should the government-sponsored infertility clinics give greater or exclusive attention to women because of the devastating effect of infertility on their self-images, or to women and men in equal proportions as facilities permit?

These examples, and many others that could be constructed, show that ethical dilemmas posed by fertility control will not be resolved by any single-factor moral assessment. There is no reason to believe that other complex social interventions would respond any better to a unidimensional ethical scheme.

## FREEDOM

The discussion thus far has suggested that the balance of power in social interventions is often stacked against the targets of change. Most of the chapters in this book recognize the disparity in power and express concern about its implications for human freedom. The commentaries on freedom revolve around three central issues: capacity, opportunity, and safeguards.

According to the definition proposed in the introductory chapter, freedom requires above all the capacity and the opportunity to choose. The same criteria apply to informed consent and voluntary participation in social intervention. If the individuals involved do not have the ability and information to perceive and weigh the consequences of their participation, or if they are coerced, constrained, or manipulated by environmental pressures to participate, then their freedom has been impaired. The difference between capacity and opportunity should not be overdrawn, for in many circumstances the ability to understand an intervention grows out of the opportunity for first-hand participation. Nevertheless, this distinction offers a convenient way of highlighting the issues of freedom posed in many interventions.

### Capacity

A prime obstacle to freedom lies in people's inability to understand the nature and consequences of their participation in interventions. Sometimes, as with retarded persons, the difficulty arises from mental disabilities. In other cases, the barrier is inadequate information about the intervention and its consequences. In still other cases, freedom is obstructed by a mixture of limited abilities and inadequate information. The chapters provide examples of all three possibilities.

At the most basic level, Stolz notes the problems involved in obtaining consent for behavior therapy from those with restricted intellectual competence. Even with the most elaborate explanations, some people are unable to develop enough understanding of the intervention to protect their own interests. The key question, then, is how to safeguard those interests.

Encounter groups are usually conducted with people whose abilities fall within the normal range. Glidewell is generally optimistic about the capacity of normal adults to grasp the essentials of an encounter group experience. Though he admits that "some competence in negotiation by participants and some knowledge of their particular broader interests in other domains of development" (p. 79) are necessary, he is confident that the obstacles to freedom can be overcome by providing full information about the forthcoming experience. Back, on the other hand, questions whether encounter group participants are in a position to take responsibility for the consequences of the intervention. The difficulty, he notes, is not only inexperience, but also the air of the occult that surrounds the entire encounter group movement. If, as Back claims, participants are responding to subliminal seductions as much as to open disclosures, the problem of informed consent becomes unusually tangled.

The issue of limitations in capacity is especially relevant in programs designed to assist the socially or educationally disadvantaged. A frequent concomitant of poverty and low status is a restricted frame of reference for evaluating the contents, costs, and benefits of interventions. The very poor often lack the education, the experience, and the social contacts needed to appreciate what is at stake for them in a complex social or medical program. Rossi, Boeckmann, and Berk suggest that limitations of this sort affected subjects in the New Jersey–Pennsylvania Income Maintenance Experiment. They point out that the executing organization went to considerable lengths to inform the participants about the conditions and implications of their participation. Nevertheless, a follow-up study indicated that the households involved had only an imperfect understanding of the plans. Although it was crucial, from the standpoint of the experiment, for participants to understand the tax rate applied to additional earnings, only a small proportion of the households had such an understanding. Both those authors and Warwick correctly note that such findings raise serious questions about the efficacy of current means of obtaining informed consent.

The same question arises in family planning programs. Lapham asks how much information should be given to recipients of pills and other contraceptive devices, particularly when disclosures of side-effects may frighten potential participants away from the program. Warwick (1975) has questioned whether poor and illiterate people in developing countries are able to understand and evaluate information on such risks and side-effects. Particularly when recipients have little understanding of their own bodies and medicines have strong magical or religious overtones, formal explanations may not have their intended effects unless accompanied by other, less formal communications. These examples and others in this book show the error of assuming that the targets of change need only full disclosure in order to enjoy informed consent to the intervention. The chapters also underscore the need for follow-up research to determine how well explanations designed to produce informed consent were understood by the recipients. The results mentioned by Warwick and by Rossi et al. are not encouraging.

A question raised but not adequately addressed in this book concerns the limits of disclosure. While most authors agree that informed consent as conventionally defined is ethically desirable in social interventions, they seem unsure about how far disclosure should be carried. For example, does the specialist on behavior modification have a moral obligation to reveal the precise techniques that will be used to reshape a person's behavior? Should the encounter group leader or agent set forth in clear terms not only the general nature of the experience but also the precise manipulations to be used? Is it desirable, for example, for the leader to explain why the furniture has been arranged in certain ways, why the group is to focus on the here and now, how the leader will operate to steer the group in particular directions, and so on? Should crisis intervenors lay all of their cards on the table, including full disclosure of the panoply of techniques at their disposal? Should administrators of family planning programs candidly admit that, despite the health rhetoric used by the clinic and the government, the true purpose of the program is a reduction in the birth rate? The chapters are, in general, silent on these questions, but they show little enthusiasm for full disclosure. Even Laue and Cormick, who go as far as any of the other authors in advocating openness, stop short of recommending complete revelation of techniques and intentions.

The most likely reason for this hesitation about total disclosure is that advance information about hidden agendas and backstage manipulations could easily undercut the intended effects of the intervention. Fully informed about how their agent operates, encounter group participants might focus too closely on the agent's actions or enter into the spirit of the game by trying to counteract the agent's influence through parallel tactics. Similar reactions might be seen in behavior modification, organization development, crisis interventions, and in any area of intervention where the intervenor relies on identifiable strategies and techniques. With housing, education, population, and income maintenance programs, on the other hand, the reactive effects of disclosure would probably be less striking. The reason is that this last set of programs relies less on covert manipulations and specific techniques than on skills and intentions that are closer to the surface. Even so, one could imagine some fallout from the income maintenance experiment if participants were told that the government wanted to see if they stopped working above a certain income level, or in family planning programs if clients were informed that the clinic had to meet certain targets of sterilizations in order to stay in operation the following year. Thus, the question of how much disclosure should be required in social interventions remains open in these chapters.

### Opportunity

Individual freedom is also constrained by obstacles and pressures found in the environment. The most obvious pressure, which arises in several spheres of intervention, is outright coercion. The chapters indicate that individuals have been forced to receive behavior modification, to join encounter groups, to take part in organization development exercises, to be sterilized, and to submit to other interventions against their will. The difference between coercion and lesser degrees of pressure depends in large part on the severity of the sanctions applied against people who refuse to participate. Where the penalties for noncompliance are large, such as with the loss of a job or the threat of physical harm, the term "coercion" properly applies. There is strong opposition to coercion in this book. Glidewell, Back, Lapham, and Tangri are specifically opposed to the use of force in the interventions that they review. Stolz is clearly in favor of informed consent and opposed to the use of aversive techniques as a form of retribution, but she leaves the door open to the coercive application of behavior modification techniques in certain limited circumstances.

In other cases, the constraint on freedom arises not from direct coercion but from group pressures or strong threats and inducements. In organization development, the management may clearly state that employees are free to participate or not, as they see fit. But this freedom may prove hollow if most members of a work group see fit to participate and the holdouts feel under pressure to close ranks. Both Walton and Warwick point out how the power imbalances commonly seen in OD exercises may deprive employees of genuine freedom of choice. The extent of group pressure may also affect freedom to depart from an ongoing intervention. In the case of encounter groups, Glidewell claims that one clear source of protection for participants is their right to leave at any time. He fails to note, however, that the potent forces of the here and now—forces he identifies as the prime source of influence in this intervention—may erect formidable psychological barriers to departure. Once the short-term group culture is created and individual positions are staked out, disaffected participants may think it an unconscionable loss of face to drop out at the height of their distress. Freedom may thus be compromised precisely because the encounter group has succeeded in convincing the participants to shed their normal identities and take up new roles in the constructed microculture. As Walton suggests in one of his examples, the same difficulty may arise in OD sessions. When one member elected to withdraw, the others set out in hot pursuit. These examples underscore the need to place freedom in the specific context of the intervention and the forces that it generates.

Finally and ironically, individual freedom may sometimes be seriously compromised by the offer of positive rewards and inducements. The most dramatic example in recent years, one mentioned by Lapham, is the use of financial and other material incentives to promote voluntary sterilization in India. In dozens of communities, family planning workers offered men and women money, food, clothing and other rewards for submitting to vasectomy or tubectomy. At first blush, the provision of such incentives might seem like the pure enchancement of freedom—the poor are helped and yet are not forced to accept anything that they do not want. But this is an overly rational assessment of the situation. At a deeper level, there is a serious ethical difficulty raised by the fact that these bonuses have the greatest appeal for those who have the fewest resources. To an Indian farmer earning 70 dollars per year, 20 dollars is a substantial amount of money. In a recent review of the ethics of population incentives, Veatch (1977) lays out the various moral problems raised by the use of incentives in population programs. Warwick's paper on social experiments also suggests that providing income supplements to the poor may carry liabilities as well as benefits for freedom. Once again the key question is whether the offer of incentives exploits the disadvantaged by playing on their economic need. A major difference between incentives for sterilization and income maintenance, however, is that in the former the rewards are used to induce individuals into actions that may lead to serious regret or harmful consequences, while with income maintenance the potential harms are relatively slight. Nevertheless, we must still ask if it is ethically justified to use material rewards to promote behavior change in social interventions. As a rule of thumb, we might suggest that the greater the difference in the attractiveness of the incentives across socioeconomic groups, and the greater the potential harms at stake in adopting the rewarded behaviors, the more serious the ethical issues posed by the inducements.

## Safeguards

Given the many limitations of capacity and opportunity, what steps might be taken to safeguard human freedom in social interventions? The authors offer numerous suggestions, ranging from fairly conventional steps for the protection of human rights to far-reaching changes in the condition of participants. The suggestions differ especially in their underlying assumptions about the capacity to understand an intervention. Some, taking this ability for granted, focus mainly on improving the volume and quality of information needed for rational decisions. Others are less optimistic in their views about capacity and, at the extreme, feel that it is completely lacking. The following typology of proposed safeguards is organized around differences in assumed capacity to grasp the nature and consequences of social interventions.

### Improved Information

Where it can be assumed that participants or target groups are in a position to understand the intervention and to protect their own interests if given adequate information, the challenge is to provide this information in the most intelligible manner possible. Glidewell insists that even a person undergoing psychotherapy is often in a position to decide about the costs and benefits of an encounter group experience. The key duty of the agent, therefore, is to supply the person with clear and complete descriptions of the likely costs and benefits of participation in the group and of the agent's professional qualifications. Glidewell also suggests that the agent request the potential participant to consider how useful the benefits of group participation will be. Glidewell thus assumes that most people need no development of their basic intellectual competence in order to be able to grasp the significance of an encounter group. What they lack is good information about the experience itself and about the background and experience of the leader/agent. Walton also presumes basic capacity in his recommendation that, as a protection for informed consent, OD services be more accurately labeled.

Stolz goes further in arguing that objective information about the intervention might best be presented by unbiased sources. She suggests that in some cases individuals are perfectly able to understand what is at stake in behavior modification, but that they may be misled by practitioners who have potential conflicts of interest. The intervenor may, for example, sincerely want to help a person overcome a phobia, but at the same time feel professional pressure to fill certain cells in a research design. Stolz suggests that under these conditions the most responsible course of action would be to have all explanations made by a sympathetic, informed party who is mainly concerned with the participants' interests. Moreover, in cases where the stakes for the individual are particularly high, he or she could be given arguments in favor of and against participation by advocates for each decision.

This proposal, although complex to administer, could be applied in many spheres of social intervention. In organization development, the sponsoring unit might be asked to hire a counterconsultant who would explain to potential participants the costs and disadvantages of their involvement. Family planning programs might also enlist the services of a social worker or some other qualified person to explain to clients the advantages and disadvantages, including the physical side-effects and psychological dangers, of the various methods of birth limitation. To be effective and to avoid the biases present with other workers in the clinical setting, this person should ideally be on a separate payroll, not be directly connected to the national or regional family planning programs, and be organizationally accountable to somebody (such as an ombudsman's office) primarily concerned with the recipients' welfare. The expense and administrative complexities of this safeguard should not prevent it from being considered when the trade-offs are large but difficult to apprehend.

### Participation

Several chapters cite joint participation and negotiation as effective means of aiding informed consent and otherwise protecting freedom. The assumption behind such proposals is that people have the basic capacity to protect their interests, but need more than information to do so. Specifically, they should have the chance to take part in decisions about whether there should be an intervention at all, when and where it should take place, and how it will be conducted. Walton emphasizes the importance of negotiations on the question of whether there should be an intervention. In addition to meeting an ethical desideratum, bringing the eventual targets of intervention into the early decision-making and planning stages alerts the intervenor and client to possible mistakes in the conception of the intervention. In particular, when the intervention is ill timed, strong objections during the planning stage can avoid the harms that would result if the original idea were implemented.

Stolz sees great merit in joint planning for behavior modification but notes the difficulties of carrying this out when the recipient is retarded, senile, incarcerated, or suffers other restraints on the freedom to participate. Glidewell regards negotiations about goals and limits as among the most significant protections for participant freedom in encounter groups. Huey and his associates also cite constant communication with community groups as a means of protecting the targets of change. An important and ironic flaw in the Seattle Urban Academy intervention was the lack of sufficient attention to communicating with groups in the establishment, particularly the school board. Warwick joins Rossi et al. in citing the lack of participation by policy makers and the heavy influence of academic economists as both ethical drawbacks and practical limitations on the New Jersey–Pennsylvania Income Maintenance Experiment. While the various chapters reveal many ambiguities about participation, such as who should participate in which decisions, with what knowledge, and to what limits, they generally endorse participation in threshold decisions and planning as an effective safeguard for freedom.

### Empowerment

Laue and Cormick contend that, left to their own devices, the disadvantaged are often not in a position to participate as equals in negotiations about conflict resolution. The most ethical solution, therefore, is neither to rely on the survival of the fittest nor to turn the matter over to outside bodies, but to enlarge the ability of the weak to represent their own interests.

> The intervenor should promote the ability of the weaker parties to make their own best decisions through helping them obtain the necessary information and skills to implement power. The intervenor should assess the relative level of information, negotiating skills, and analytical ability of the parties and, if there is a considerable differential, help even the odds through training or other forms of advocacy (p. 221).

The chapters suggest several other areas in which variations on empowerment could be applied with good effect. OD participants, for example, could be given a short course on the uses, processes, contents, and consequences of this set of techniques. Clients of family planning programs might also be given instruction, in appropriate language, on significant aspects of human anatomy and physiology. With basic information on the functioning of their own bodies, women would be in a much better position to comprehend the risks and benefits of the pill, the intrauterine device, and other methods of fertility regulation. Similarly, in an income maintenance program participants might be instructed about tax rates and other salient aspects of their own economic situation. Such information might not only enhance the candidate's ability to make an informed choice about participating in the intervention, but also improve his or her comprehension of the main experimental variables. While it is not without its own ethical difficulties, the suggestion that empowerment be used as a guarantor of freedom is one of the most significant proposals made in this entire volume.

*Pilot Testing*

In certain circumstances decision makers may wish to determine whether a given kind of intervention deserves to be introduced on a full scale. The assumption is that those who will ultimately be affected by the intervention, such as the population of potential users in a national family planning program, either will not know enough about the intervention to give an informed opinion in advance of its introduction, or cannot feasibly be reached for their views. A common solution in this case is to devise a pilot project to test the applicability of the intervention on a small scale. Walton recommends this approach as a means of promoting informed consent in organization development. A problem with this approach is that the model of decision making is essentially elitist: Management makes the final determination with no direct participation by employees. Pilot testing could be considered a form of participation when a serious effort is made to learn the reactions of those affected by an intervention and to take these into account in decision making. Paternalism could be further avoided by making the results of the pilot program known to the larger population for which the intervention is intended.

*External Safeguards*

In some forms of intervention the operating assumption is that the targets of change either have no capacity to look after their own interests or are at such a disadvantage vis-à-vis the intervenors that they need outside protection. Children, the senile, and the mentally retarded usually lack the capacity to understand the risks and benefits of behavior modification and other forms of intervention. Prisoners may be under enormous pressure to accede to any request from correctional authorities. Under these conditions, as Stolz points out, institutions often turn to advisory committees or use other means for obtaining proxy consent. Parents or guardians may be consulted, advocates may be appointed, and the clients themselves may be offered as much choice as possible given their limitations. But, as Stolz emphasizes, the safeguards offered by these proxy bodies may be illusory, in part because they are all too likely to represent the values and goals of the client rather than the target of the intervention. Class differences between the intervenors and the targets of change, excessive deference to professional expertise, vested interests on the part of parents, guardians, and institutions, and a host of other factors may make the protections more apparent than real.

## ACCOUNTABILITY

Should social intervenors be held accountable for their professional action or inaction? If so, to whom, for what, and with what methods of enforcement? Perhaps predictably, our authors favor professional accountability as a principle, but none is specific about details. Adding to the usual hesitations about recommending restrictive standards may be the amorphousness of social intervention as a profession. With the exception of behavior therapy, which is rooted completely in psychology, none of the interventions is closely linked to a single academic discipline or an established profession. From encounter group leadership to family planning programs, from organizational development to the implementation of income maintenance experiments, virtually all the theories and skills of the behavioral and social sciences are brought to bear at some point. Some areas of intervention, such as organization development and crisis intervention, seem to be developing as hybrid specialties in their own right, while others, such as family planning programs, are accomplished by teams of individual specialists. Still other interventions, such as those exemplified by Waymon's work for the Corp, represent the application of nonspecialized savvy to particular problems. This diversity makes it difficult to set down detailed principles of accountability that will hold with equal validity across all spheres of social intervention. But we can explore some of the major issues of accountability and seek analogues from other professions, especially law.

### Accountable to Whom?

Three interrelated meanings of accountability may be distinguished: personal, legal, and professional. First is the personal responsibility one takes for one's actions. There is a widespread presumption, recognized in such statements as the Nuremberg Code and the University Declaration of Human Rights, that individuals, no matter what their status or profession, are morally accountable for their behavior. Thus the social intervenor has no right to kill, maim, lie, cheat, steal, or otherwise violate accepted moral codes in carrying out an intervention. Just what those codes should be and how obligatory they are for any individual are matters of endless debate, but the resulting ambiguities do not negate the concept of personal accountability. At the same time, some of the most severe moral dilemmas for the intervenor arise from conflicts between personal moral standards and the perceived requirements for effective interventions. To cite one example, the organizer of a compulsory sterilization program in India may feel simultaneously that such activities are a violation of human rights, yet are necessary to deal with the pressing social problem of population growth.

A second, very different, form of accountability, is legal liability. The essential notion behind malpractice litigation is that professionals are liable to their clients or patients for damages done and perhaps for additional penalties as well. We must distinguish, however, between the legal and the ethical aspects of liability. We may all agree that patients of physicians, clients of lawyers, and clients or targets of social intervenors have the right to take these professionals to court if they believe that (a) the professional has practiced negligently or unethically, (b) the patient, client, or target has been damaged thereby, and (c) alternative approaches for compensating the damaged party have not produced a satisfactory result. It is just as clear that the legal outcome of the suit is morally open: it may or may not reflect a just resolution of the dispute. Patients or their lawyers, for example, may misrepresent a physician's verbal statements to make a more compelling case to the jury. In general, the move to accountability through litigation may be taken as a failure of other, less drastic means of bringing a dispute to resolution. To date, the concept of legal liability for social intervenors has been more theoretical than actual, except in the areas of behavior therapy and encounter group leadership. But if the rise in malpractice suits against lawyers and physicians is any indication of what might be expected in these fields, the threat may soon become reality.

Different from both personal responsibility and legal liability is professional accountability to some recognized body of people in a specific occupation. This form of accountability presumes an accepted set of standards governing professional conduct. The specificity, legal status, acceptance, and enforcement of these standards vary widely across professions. Medicine appears to have the clearest standards and is also more closely regulated than other professions. For physicians, the Hippocratic oath, with its broad principle of benefitting the sick, has been joined to much more explicit codes, such as the International Code of Medical Ethics and the Declaration of Helsinki (Veatch, 1975). Rules governing medical practice in the United States also arise from such sources as state licensing commissions and hospitals, which allow or withhold from physicans the privilege of practicing in them. Hospitals are, in turn, regulated by a national accrediting committee whose sanctions are very important, among other reasons, in the hospital's search for public funding. In general, then, the physician's professional conduct is regulated by groups both within and outside of the medical profession.

The mechanisms for promoting professional accountability among lawyers and accountants also include regulations from both public and private bodies, including state licensing agencies, courts, and bar associations. In one area of practice, securities registration and transfer, the appropriate accountablity of both professions to the federal Securities and Exchange Commission is a matter of intense concern and debate. The traditional principle of strict lawyer-client confidentiality, for instance, is being replaced by what some securities lawyers call "the resign and rat rule": If the client is not making a full disclosure of facts in issuing a stock prospectus, the lawyer must resign his or her service with the client and report the lack of disclosure to the Securities and Exchange Commission (*Meyerhofer v. Empire Fire and Marine Insurance Co.*, 1974; Comment, 1975). Failure to take this step may result in a malpractice suit against the lawyer initiated by the stockholders or the SEC (*SEC. v. National Student Marketing Corporation*, 1973). One SEC commissioner has gone so far as to recommend a fundamental change in the loyalties of the securities lawyer. To an increasing degree, he believes, this attorney will work more as a public auditor than as the traditional advocate who must keep the client's secrets (Comment, 1975, at 136). While this debate about the proper accountability of the securities lawyer has come to a head in recent years, as early as 1935 Justice William O. Douglas, then head of the SEC, remarked: "If the mores of our legal bishops were changed, we would have solved the major problems of finance" (Comment, 1975, at 141).

The experience of securities lawyers may hold important lessons in establishing norms of accountability for social intervenors. While the rhetoric of forensic social science holds the great appeal of permitting intervenors and researchers to choose sides with the "good guys," it dodges ethical issues far more subtle than that rhetoric would imply. The ideal of scientific objectivity may be only a myth in the social sciences. Our ideological biases and *a priori* policy preferences may be impossible to disentangle from our choices of problems, methods, and interpretations. Apparent intervenor neutrality may always be a hypocritical or self-deluding posture. But it is not at all clear that these lamentable conditions should be sanctified into virtues through baptism by advocacy. In our haste to don the robes of the advocate, we may trip over lawyers hurriedly divesting themselves of the same garb.

With the possible exception of behavior therapy, the social interventions described in this book are not covered by agencies of accountability as powerful as those regulating medicine, law, and public accounting. A threshold question is whether they should be. Will greater professional regulation of intervenors correct abuses of power and lead to a net increase in human freedom? Consider, for example, community interventions such as those described by Laue and Cormick. When intervenors adopt proportional empowerment as a goal and work to achieve it, they are engaging in behavior that is properly called political. As such, the behavior is protected by constitutional guarantees of free expression. Were the intervenor acting solely as a citizen, there would be few legitimate grounds for regulation. The more difficult question is whether there should be explicit standards of accountability because the intervenor is acting as a professional. The answer to this question will depend on one's assumptions about the value and appropriateness of regulation in general as well as about its urgency in the particular sphere of intervention (Coase, 1977; Kessel, 1977). Given current ambiguities and ambivalences about the appropriate loci of accountability for social intervenors, individual practitioners are thrown back on broad principles and ethical rules-of-thumb.

The earlier chapters point to several dilemmas concerning the locus of accountability in intervention. One is the question of relative accountability to the client and the target of the intervention. Stolz raises this issue very clearly for behavior therapy. Should the therapist be accountable mainly to the person receiving the therapy, the institution in which the person is confined, or the larger society? When there are conflicts of interest between the target and the client (the individual or agency employing the therapist), how should they be resolved? Sarason and Sarason suggest that the therapist's obligation is to reconcile these interests by acting simultaneously as an advocate for the patient's welfare and as a promoter of institutional well-being. In theory this is an ideal resolution of the dilemma, but it will break down in the hard cases where the interests are in sharp conflict. From the standpoint of professional accountability, moreover, it leaves practitioners in a most vulnerable position, for they must harmonize conflicting interests with no accepted guidelines or principles for doing so. Given the current surge of malpractice suits, therapists are unlikely to be satisfied with broad injunctions to be effective dual agents. The problem of divided loyalties is also raised in other chapters, including the discussions of organization development, the Seattle Urban Academy program, the income maintenance experiment, and the population control programs. The chapters provide no conclusive answers, but they do suggest several working principles.

First, they underscore the need for intervenors to be clear about their accountability to their clients. Only too often, it seems, well-intentioned professionals enter a complex situation without a real understanding of whom they are working for and the potential conflicts of interest that might arise. Sometimes it is difficult to know in advance what directions the intervention will take once it is launched, and which actors and interest groups will present moral claims. But in many interventions even a modicum of forethought could alert intervenors to major pitfalls. Conscious of the hazards ahead, they could seek outside advice on responsible ways of resolving possible ethical dilemmas or take steps to reduce these dilemmas by astute negotiation of the terms of reference of their own interventions. Organization development practitioners, for example, might set down as a specific condition of their employment that management refrain from asking for appraisals of specific individuals or work units.

Second, several of the chapters make a strong case for open disclosure of the intervenor's prior commitments and loyalties to the client. If, for instance, a behavior therapist is primarily in the service of a prison and only secondarily concerned with the personal welfare of inmates, that therapist should make this fact clear to all concerned, including the inmates chosen for therapy. Similarly, as Laue and Cormick recommend, if a crisis intervenor is brought in to serve as an advocate for one of the parties to a dispute, this person should not pretend to be a mediator. In general, the question of who is to be served by professional intervenors seems fundamental and deserving of much more careful analysis than it has received in this volume.

A related question concerns the ethical obligations of the professional intervenor in dealing with the familiar dilemma of value neutrality versus commitment to superordinate moral standards. While, as noted earlier, most of the authors regard value neutrality as self-deceptive and misleading to others, they hedge their bets about positive commitment. At one extreme Stolz mentions behavior modification specialists who see themselves as "super technicians" with no obligation to question the values of those using their services. The problem of the intervenor as hired gun arises in every area of intervention. Walton asks if OD practitioners should question the values and practices of the organizations that hire them, including their definition of the problem to be solved by OD. His case studies suggest that the practitioners themselves are divided on this point. At the opposite extreme, Laue and Cormick take the position that there can be no neutrality, and that advocacy for the powerless is the order of the day. They do not indicate, however, whether crisis intervenors should wear their principles on their sleeves for all to see, or whether they should bill themselves as mediators but work, in essence, as closet advocates. The dilemma is acute, for intervenors who openly identify themselves as advocates for one side will obviously stand little chance of being hired as impartial mediators.

One of the more vexing problems raised in these chapters is the issue of accountability to society. Glidewell and Stolz, in particular, speak of society as an entity with rights and obligations in social intervention, but neither gives any precise indication of how its values and interests are to be articulated. Who speaks for society, and how does the intervenor deal with variations across classes, minority and ethnic groups, and other social divisions? And, when programs cross national lines, which society's standards should apply, and what status should be accorded such cross-cultural instruments as the Universal Declaration of Human Rights? In her chapter, Stolz makes two points that deserve emphasis. First, the mere fact that a society holds certain values, preferences, or prejudices does not make its norms a valid basis for ethical judgments about social interventions. For example, widespread moral disapproval of pedophilia does not provide automatic entitlement for behavior therapists to use aversive conditioning to change pedophiliacs. Second, given the nebulous definitions of society and its standards, it is all too easy for intervenors to project their own biases onto this murky mass and then defend them as society's will. One unambiguous conclusion from this book is that interventions justified on the basis of society's interest should be subjected to careful scrutiny and strong moral challenge.

### Accountable for What?

The second broad question of accountability centers on the precise contents of professional responsibility. The chapters suggest four areas in which abuses have been seen and professional standards may be needed.

*Competence.* Given the ill-defined and "learn-as-you-go" quality of many interventions, together with the unconventional blends of skills required to bring them to completion, is it meaningful to speak of minimal standards of competence for intervenors? Or, to turn the question around, are there some forms of professional incompetence that appear often enough to warrant concern? Several authors answer in the affirmative, pointing to two kinds of abuses. The first is a sheer lack of qualifications for undertaking the intervention. Guskin criticizes the Battelle consultants for having an inadequate background to advise Seattle's black community about educational changes. As a result, according to Guskin, the intervenors had to fall back on generalized process skills too diffuse for the task at hand. Similarly, Walton speaks of a competence-confidence gap in organization development, while Warwick criticizes OD practitioners who enter a new setting without adequate information about its context and unique features. Second, questions of competence arise in choosing particular models of intervention. Walton and Warwick question the ethics of force-fitting OD interventions to situations where they might not be appropriate, as when solutions derived from industrial organizations are uncritically applied to government agencies. Laue and Cormick are emphatic on this point:

> Intervenors trained in one conceptual approach . . . should not transfer their intervention models uncritically to a different system setting (a racial/community dispute involving multiple parties, for example). To do so is to increase the probability that issues will be diverted and that the outcomes will not meet the most basic needs of the disputants (pp. 221–222).

These authors are especially critical of attempts to apply labor relations models to crisis situations. Along the same lines, Guskin questions whether the Battelle consultants should have relied on consensus strategies for educational change when contest strategies might have been more appropriate to the political nature of the intervention. The difficult questions raised by these criticisms are: Who is to judge what standards of competence should apply, especially in uncharted areas of intervention; and should intervenors be held accountable by the standards of foresight or hindsight? The chapters suggest that, while it is often difficult, if not impossible, to know what mixture of skills and strategies is in order, certain common mistakes, such as force-fitting, can be anticipated and avoided.

*Truth Telling.* To judge from these chapters, one of the more common ethical abuses in social interventions is false advertising or raising unwarranted expectations about the intervenor's abilities. Back takes encounter groups to task for creating a kind of sociotherapeutic seduction. Glidewell also recognizes the issue of truth in advertising, but seems more sanguine than Back about handling it through open disclosure at the point of the participant's entry. Similar questions of truth telling arise in national family planning programs, particularly with communication campaigns promising the poor a better life if they limit their family to two children.

*Honoring Guarantees of Confidentiality.* In many spheres of intervention, participants are told or assume that what they say and do will be held in confidence. Recipients of psychotherapy, participants in encounter groups and organization development, clients of family planning programs, and candidates for income maintenance may come to believe, rightly or wrongly, that their words, deeds, and misdeeds will not be held against them outside the intervention. The chapters point up several ethical difficulties with express or implied guarantees of confidentiality. The most obvious and the easiest to resolve is the broken promise. As Walton's chapter makes clear, intervenors have violated promises of confidentiality by discussing the performance of OD participants with management. Such violations would seem to be a flagrant and unquestioned breach of personal and professional ethnics. The ethical situation is more complicated when the intervenor, acting in good faith, promises confidentiality, but does not have the legal backing to honor the guarantee. Rossi and his associates show how this problem arose when a district attorney sought data on individual participants in the New Jersey–Pennsylvania Income Maintenance Experiment. While the sponsors of the experiment had every intention of honoring their promises, they found that their data enjoyed no legal protection or privilege and thus could be subpoenaed. Given these risks, the intervenor has two basic options: make the usual promises in the hope that the question of a subpoena will not arise; or tell the people involved that the intervenors will keep the information confidential, but that there is a slight chance that it could be subpoenaed by the government. As Warwick observes, the first choice suffers from inadequate disclosure of important information, while the second may so frighten respondents that they will not participate in the intervention. This dilemma is now being given serious consideration by the National Commission on the Protection of Human Subjects of Biomedical and Behavioral Research.

*Higher-order Effects.* Though the authors of the lead chapters were asked to analyze the ethics of higher-order or unintended effects in social interventions, the response was limited. Even those who did comment on this question seem to have had a difficult time placing it in perspective. The most obvious reason is that higher-order and especially unintended effects are, almost by definition, elusive and outside the paradigms of conventional ethical assessment. Further, since these effects are likely to appear in areas two or three steps removed from the scene of direct action and may surface months or even years later, there are formidable problems in attributing causality. The chapters suggest nonetheless that the question remains ethically salient, if intellectually hazy. Glidewell argues, for example, that the intervenor has a manifest responsibility to assess the indirect outcomes of encounter groups. The task may be daunting, but there are options available, including controlled experiments and a more limited follow-up of selected participants. This type of long-term assessment would also go some distance in generating the kinds of information needed to deal with Back's criticisms of encounter groups.

Other types of higher-order effects would be much more difficult to isolate and analyze through conventional social science research methods. Following Williams, for example, one might hypothesize that a latent and long-term consequence of Laue and Cormick's empowerment strategy is to undermine the political system. As more and more groups become empowered and use their new-found skills to demand increasing benefits from the society, the government's capacity to resolve crises and accommodate demands will break down. In Latin America or Africa, the result might be the collapse of civil government and its replacement by a repressive military regime. In the United States, the effect would probably be less drastic, perhaps public backlash leading eventually to a repressive, law-and-order administration. From an analytical point of view, it would be virtually impossible to trace the chain of causation from the advocacy of empowerment through the escalation of interest group demands to the breakdown of the existing order and the installation of a more reactionary government. From an ethical standpoint, one would also be hard put to argue that, even with this development, strategies of empowerment should be scaled down or avoided. But, whatever the conceptual and empirical complexities, higher-order or unintended consequences at this broad level must enter into any serious ethical assessment of social interventions. Warwick's chapter on social experiments suggests some steps that might be taken.

## Protection versus Paternalism:
## The Intervenor's Dilemma

The strongest undercurrent of ambivalence in these chapters courses around the issue of protecting those intervened upon against more powerful forces in the society, against the intervenors, and even against their own limitations and urges. In essence, the question boils down to the difference between responsible protection versus deleterious paternalism.

There seems to be little doubt that some groups of individuals, such as children, the retarded, and the institutionalized, do need protection against interventions designed by others. But what about normal adults, especially those who voluntarily seek out interventions such as encounter groups? Even here the authors reveal mixed feelings. Glidewell, for instance, generally leans toward treating adults, including those currently in psychotherapy, as rational decision makers who are able to act in their interest when given adequate information. Nevertheless, he holds that because agents have greater knowledge than the participants about the pitfalls of encounter groups, they are obligated to set limits on the experience. Among the common protections are a ban on violence and drugs, limits on scapegoating, and a clear norm that individuals are free to join or stay apart from the group. Moreover, "one powerful limit on danger to individual welfare is the right to interrupt any activity in order to analyze its nature, its antecedents, and its consequences" (p. 90). Most of the other authors seem to agree with the principle implicit here: allow people to decide when they can exercise reasonably free choice, but institute protections when there is clear danger that inexperience would seriously impair judgment.

Laue and Cormick maintain that the most efficacious way of providing protection and avoiding paternalism is through empowerment. When the weak are strengthened to the point that they can challenge not only their opponents but also the intervenors, they are no longer in need of either external safeguards or professional tutelage. While at first sight, this seems an appealing solution to the problem of paternalism, closer examination suggests that it may simply displace the problem. It is, after all, the intervenors who decide who needs to be empowered, and how, and it is they who determine when the proper types and levels of empowerment have been attained. If the method operates as straightforwardly as Laue and Cormick imply, the intervenors only move to a position of higher-order paternalism. They seem to sit above the fray, pulling levers to draw some individuals and groups to a higher level of competence and leaving others where they are. Accountability is particularly difficult because none of the groups to be empowered is likely to ask why the intervenors have chosen them and not their opponents, or why they are being given some negotiating skills and not others. An impartial observer perched above both the intervenors and those with whom they work might further ask if those being empowered are being given the most effective skills and tools for challenging the position of the intervenors. Even with the best of intentions, and by Laue and Cormick's own persuasive logic, intervenors are interested in the intervention and, therefore, will be tempted to avoid forms of empowerment that may complicate their interventions. Thus, while there are many ethical merits to the strategy of empowerment, one would be naïve to treat it as a panacea for resolving complex questions of power. Taken as a whole, these chapters suggest that the dilemma of protection versus paternalism will remain alive as long as there are power differentials in social intervention. We further suggest that even the attempt to reduce these differentials will involve significant questions of professional power and accountability.

## REFERENCES

Coase, R. H. Advertising and free speech. *The Journal of Legal Issues*, 1977, *6*, 1–34.
Comment. The duties and obligations of the securities lawyer: The beginning of a new standard for the legal profession? *Duke Law Journal*, 1975, *1975*, 121–147.
Conroy, M., & Folbre, N. *Population growth as a deterrent to economic growth: A reappraisal of the evidence.* Hastings-on-Hudson, N.Y.: Institute of Society, Ethics, and the Life Sciences, 1976.
Frankel, M. E. The adversary judge. *Texas Law Review*, 1976, *54*, 465–487.
Freire, P. *The pedagogy of the oppressed.* New York: Herder and Herder, 1970.
Gurel, L. The human side of evaluating human services programs: Problems and

prospects. In E. L. Struening & M. Guttentag (Eds.), *Handbook of evaluation research*, Vol. II. Beverly Hills, Calif. Sage, 1975.

Hilton, E. T., & Lumsdaine, A. A. Field trial designs in gauging the impact of fertility planning programs. In C. A. Bennett & A. A. Lumsdaine (Eds.), *Evaluation and experiment*. New York: Academic Press, 1975.

Jencks, C., et al. *Inequality*. New York: Basic Books, 1972.

Kessel, R. A. Ethical and economic aspects of governmental intervention in the medical care market. In G. Dworkin, G. Bermant, & P. Brown (Eds.), *Markets and morals*. Washington, D.C.: Hemisphere, 1977.

Mamdami, M. *The myth of population control: Family, caste and class in an Indian village*. New York: Monthly Review Press, 1972.

Marino, A. KAP surveys and the politics of family planning. *Concerned Demography*, 1971, *3*, 36-75.

Merton, R. *Social theory and social structure*. New York: Free Press, 1957.

Meyerhofer v. Empire Fire & Marine Insurance Co., 497 F.2d 1190 (2d Cir. 1974), *cert. denied*, 419 U.S. 998, Nov. 11, 1974.

Rivlin, A. M. Forensic social science. *Harvard Educational Review*, 1973, *43*, 61-75.

Sartre, J. P. *Being and nothingness*. Trans. H. E. Barnes. New York: Philosophical Library, 1956.

Securities and Exchange Commission v. National Student Marketing Corporation, 360 F.supp 284 (District of D.C. 1973).

Sjoberg, G. Politics, ethics and evaluation research. In E. L. Struening & M. Guttentag (Eds.), *Handbook of evaluation research*, Vol. I. Beverly Hills, Calif.: Sage, 1975.

Veatch, R. M. Ethical principles in medical experimentation. In A. M. Rivlin & P. M. Timpane (Eds.), *Ethical and legal issues of social experimentation*. Washington, D.C.: Brookings Institution, 1975.

Veatch, R. M. Governmental incentives: Ethical issues at stake. *Studies in Family Planning*, 1977, *8*, 100-108.

Warwick, D. P. Contraceptives in the third world. *Hastings Center Report*, 1975, *5*, 9-12.

Weiss, C. H. Evaluation research in the political context. In E. L. Struening & M. Guttentag (Eds.), *Handbook of evaluation research*, Vol. I. Beverly Hills, Calif.: Sage, 1975.

Ziman, J. *Public knowledge: The social dimension of science*. Cambridge: Cambridge University Press, 1968.

# AUTHOR INDEX

# SUBJECT INDEX